Northern New Spain

la tierra descubierta

JOHN L. KESSELL

SUNSTONE PRESS

SANTA FE

Northern New Spain

la tierra descubierta

JOHN L. KESSELL

SUNSTONE PRESS

SANTA FE

Book Design by Tim Blevins. Title, volume, season and year, and page range of New
Mexico Historical Review articles by John L. Kessell anthologized in this volume
follow in chronological order of appearance in the journal.

Sunstone books may be purchased for educational, business, or sales promotional use.
For information please write: Special Markets Department, Sunstone Press,
P.O. Box 2321, Santa Fe, New Mexico 87504-2321.
Printed on acid-free paper

LIBRARY OF CONGRESS CATALOGING IN PUBLICATION DATA

(ON FILE)

WWW.SUNSTONEPRESS.COM
SUNSTONE PRESS / POST OFFICE BOX 2321 / SANTA FE, NM 87504-2321 /USA
(505) 988-4418

Contents

Acknowledgments

The idea for the book you hold came from consummate bookman David Schneider, not from John. David rallied a knowledgeable team that included skilled bookmaker Tim Blevins, Editor Durwood Ball of the *New Mexico Historical Review* (2000–2023), and Rick Hendricks, New Mexico State Records Administrator, who collaborated with John over half a lifetime.

Preface

John Kessell is an editor's dream. Every manuscript submitted by him for review and publication by the *New Mexico Historical Review* is a gem of historical research and writing. He clearly conceives the topic, knows its position in the historiography, asks penetrating questions of his sources, uses the most valuable original documents, and interprets the historical episodes with the sharpest conceptual tools, often his own experience of the human condition. The scholarly product from John's pen, whether a book, an article, or a review, becomes a significant item in the relevant historiography: Spanish and Mexican borderlands; the American Southwest; western exploration; public memory of the Spanish past; and others.

John is a writerly historian. He narrates a powerful human story in a compelling, distinct, and unique voice. His books and articles—real labors of love—breathe with human vignettes and sparkle with fascinating details. All pieces submitted to the *Review* are immaculately prepared. In all honesty, the editorial values in a Kessell piece of any length are unequalled in my three decades in book and journal publishing. The prose is clear, pithy, and poetic. No period, semicolon, or comma is out of place. His notes are properly styled and formatted. Even a fussy, cranky editorial curmudgeon like me has almost no labor to burn on a Kessell manuscript beyond coding the text and notes for the typesetter. My staff and I should enshrine John in the *Review*'s editorial offices and chant to his image at the start of each day.

The *New Mexico Historical Review* has published twenty articles, plus numerous review essays and book reviews, by John Kessell during his five-and-half-decade association with the journal. (Only one other southwestern historian surpasses his productivity in the journal.) John published his first article, "The Puzzling Presidio: San Phelipe De Guevavi, Alias Terrenate," in the *Review* under the editorial helm of the legendary Eleanor B. Adams, one of his historical and editorial mentors at the University of New Mexico in Albuquerque. John's final entry, "Not So Fast, Mr. Jefferson: How a Mexican Priest and the Ghost of Bernardo de Miera Saved Texas and New Mexico for Spain," appeared in the summer 2020 issue under my editorial office. Although John says no other unpublished pieces lie dormant in his files, I would review and publish any overlooked Kessell manuscript—article, essay, or review—that he dropped on my desk. What journal editor wouldn't?

John Kessell is a gift to the discipline of history and field of Spanish and Southwest borderlands. I hope all readers enjoy these jewels of historical research, writing, and interpretation. I love every one; I'm sure his readers will enjoy them too.

Durwood Ball, Editor
New Mexico Historical Review

Introduction

Readers of this volume of the collected articles of John L. Kessell in the *New Mexico Historical Review* who are familiar with his work will be reminded of a truly unique voice among historians of the Southwest. Those who are new to John's writing will be informed and enriched by the encounter. By looking at the twenty articles in chronological order, one can see a good bit about the trajectory of John´s career, how his interest developed over a career spanning more than forty years. There are five articles that derive from his research on Spanish colonial Sonora, which includes present-day southern Arizona, four that are drawn from his work on the Vargas Project, and one that deals with both Sonora and New Mexico. Ever the Hispanofile, but with a marked sensitivity to the plights of the conquered, there are two articles that explore the anti-Spanish Black Legend. There are two memorial pieces to dear friends and colleagues. Three articles relate to his most recent work on Bernardo de Miera y Pacheco. Finally, there are three more articles that do not fit neatly into any category other than that they were topics that John found interesting and worthy of an article.

What was obvious from the very beginning was the quality of the research and the engaging narrative style of the writer; moreover, it was clear that his colleagues in academe were taking notice. The first article, "The Puzzling Presidio: San Phelipe de Guevavi, Alias Terrenate," published in 1966 when John was not yet "Dr." Kessell, received the annual award for the best article in the *Review*. Interestingly, the following year, ever the servant of historical accuracy, John published a note pointing out that two individuals had corrected his placement of the presidio.[1]

This first article grew out of John's years of research on Spanish colonial and Mexican Sonora, including present-day southern Arizona, as did the first five articles he published in the *Review*, although the fourth article, "Campaigning on the Upper Gila, 1756," straddled the modern borders of Arizona and New Mexico. It was in the article, "Friars, Bureaucrats, and the Seris of Sonora," that John's ability to portray the human condition stamped itself as something quite different. Historical writing about the desert Southwest would never be quite the same.

John began his narrative in his inimitable way with this cogent observation: "The old friar's hemorrhoids were killing him." What a way to capture a moment and set a scene! More to the point, this passage illuminates John's ability to convey the very human aspect of the actors in the historical drama he was portraying. In addition, there is something of a historical truth here, whether the friar's suffering was recorded in the documentary record or not, John told it like it had to have been—colorfully, humorously, to be sure—no less honestly for that. Already in these first few articles, John was demonstrating the ability to research and write about the region, moving seamlessly from the seventeenth through to the eighteenth century. Of this first group of articles, two came out in the sixties, and the remaining three in the seventies.

John's next article in the *Review*, published in 1979, was something of a departure from his earlier publications. Rather than the narrative history one had come to expect, this is a straightforward essay on sources for the history of Abiquiu, New Mexico, which someone associated with the community asked John to write. Although very thorough for its time and still a useful place to start, much of the information is dated, and what is more important, much new source material has come available in recent years, such as the microfilm collection of the Archivo Histórico del Arzobispado de Durango at New Mexico State University and a considerable trove of sacramental records from Abiquiu that was thought lost but has resurfaced.

Two articles on Diego de Vargas followed in the 1980s; eventually there would be four articles related to the late seventeenth and early eighteenth centuries—the Vargas Era. The first was a reappraisal of his life and contribution to New Mexico history, and the second, an inquiry into the famous painting of Vargas, the original of which is in Madrid. "Diego de Vargas: Another Look" announces the Vargas Project at UNM, an endeavor that occupied John in some fashion for more than twenty years, from 1980 until 2002 when the sixth and final volume was published. As for the painting, it is certainly not the work of a great master and, as John points out, may not have been painted from life. Curious that, because there is a rather diminutive statue of Vargas, reminiscent of a garden gnome, that is clearly modeled directly after the painting. A copy of the painting, which at one time hung in the home of the then Marqués de la Nava de Bracinas in Madrid, was referred to by family members as "El Hombre Feo" (The Ugly Man).

Otherwise occupied with teaching at UNM, working on the Vargas Project, and doing a stint as interim editor of the *Review*, John did not contribute an *NMHR* article in the decade of the nineties. He did, however, publish a review essay, which is not part of this collection, "A Bolton for the Nineties—The Spanish Frontier in North America: A Review Essay" in 1993. The subject of the essay is David J. Weber's *The Spanish Frontier in North America*. John summed up Weber's contribution to the historiography of Spain in North America this way:

> The *Spanish Frontier in North America* is this generation's masterwork on the subject. At an imaginary unveiling, I should like to think that Herbert E. Bolton and Father Jack Bannon, once they regained the power of speech, would be first to congratulate the artist.[2]

John retired from UNM in 1996 and was granted emeritus status. He served as interim editor of the *Review* from July 1999 through July 2000 before making way for current editor Durwood Ball.[3] It fell to John, as the person who knew her best, to pen a tribute to Eleanor Adams. "Eleanor Burnham Adams: Woman of Letters, 1910–1996," is a brief biography and heartfelt goodbye to a person who was very influential in John's career and a dear friend. Adams, as was sadly typical for women scholars of her generation, never got the recognition for her scholarly accomplishments she was owed. Nevertheless, as John points out in the article:

> Numerous authors, colleagues, and students sought her coun- sel and friendship. With patience and good humor, she taught us to scrutinize historical documentation, to appre- ciate the editor's role, and to write and think more clearly.

In 2002 John contributed a retrospective on the Vargas Project that he called "Reinstalling the Spanish Component." This essay was the afterword for the sixth and final volume of the Vargas journals, *A Settling of Accounts*, which also appeared in 2002.

Richard W. Etulain, one of John's former colleagues from the His- tory Department at UNM, published an anthology entitled *Western Lives: A Biographical History of the American West* in 2004. Draw- ing on his extensive knowledge of Sonora and New Mexico, John con- tributed a lively narrative history of Juan Bautista de Anza, father and son, which is included in this collection. Once again, on display was

John's ability to evoke a historical moment, painting a vivid picture in just a few words. Writing of the senior Anza he said:

> The news stung. Shouted from horseback, blurted in cantinas, whispered at mass, it fell on disbelieving ears. For as long as most could remember, Juan Bautista de Anza, captain for life of the garrison at Fronteras, had been their protector. Yet on 9 May 1740, Anza lay dead, victim of an Apache ambush.

In 2006 John published an article on Spanish efforts to intercept Lewis and Clark. This was an annotated version of the article that had first appeared in *The Quarterly Journal of Military History*. In later years John would come to put his curiosity about and familiarity with the explorations of Lewis and Clark, as well as Zebulon Pike (who also puts in an appearance in this article), to use as he explored mapping of the western US in other writings.

In 1991 Ramón Gutiérrez related the story of a murder perpetrated by two Pueblo women.[4] His account was rather sensational, and, as it turned out, erroneous in several particulars, including the name of the victim, the details of the murder, the motive of the murderers, and the punishment they received. In his meticulous 2008 retelling of the events, John set the record straight. A delicious detail is the inclusion of an image of an original document presented at trial depicting the murder weapon—a knife—in the margin.

John contributed three articles to the *Review* in 2011. The first of these was one he was doubtless honored to write but one he would have rather not have had to pen because it was a brief memorial to David J. Weber, whom John called a friend for four decades.

During its several decades' duration, the Vargas Project came to look upon and speak about the conflicts between Pueblos and Spaniards in the seventeenth and early eighteenth centuries as one long, intermittent war fought in three phases. This is the topic of the second article published in 2011. As John presents it here the first phase of the Pueblo-Spanish war began with the arrival of Oñate's colonists, the second with the 1680 Pueblo Revolt, and the third with the beginning of Vargas's reconquest 1692. The third of three articles John published in the *Review* in 2011 lays out the case for this way of looking at Pueblo-Spanish relations.

The third article of 2011 is, as its subtitle suggests, a reflection on Juan de Oñate and the Black Legend. John has never been one to court controversy for the sake of it as is the wont of many scholars. In this instance, however, he does. The article is a revision of an address given to a now-defunct organization that called itself the New Mexico Hispanic Culture Preservation League. In this article John challenges the idea that Oñate enforced the sentence that Acoma men aged twenty-five and older were to have one foot cut off and render twenty years of personal servitude for their actions in the 1599 Battle of Acoma. John found unconvincing the documentary evidence that the punishment was carried out and marshaled other arguments for doubting that all the feet were cut off all the Acomas who were sentenced.

Two years later John published an article on Miera y Pacheco and announced the publication of his long-awaited biography, scheduled to appear on 4 August 2013, the three hundredth anniversary of Miera's birth. Almost four decades after he "met" Miera as alcalde of Pecos, subject of his classic book *Kiva, Cross, and Crown* (1979), John had finally completed his study of the remarkable Spaniard.[5] For many readers, this article was an introduction to an individual John had come to know almost as well as he had known Diego de Vargas and for just as long.

John returned to Miera again in 2016 in a brief article about a curious stained-glass image of Miera and Fathers Vélez de Escalante and Domínguez in the Colorado State Capitol in Denver. John visited with the artist, Carlota D. Espinoza, who explained the symbolism of the elements in her artwork. The stained glass was a project to commemorate the Centennial of Colorado statehood and the Bicentennial of US Independence in 1976.

John's penultimate article in this collection appeared in the *Review* in 2019. In it he revisits a topic about which he had written in 2011. On this occasion, after quickly narrating the events of the Pueblo-Spanish War of 1680–1696, revising the periodization slightly, John invites the reader to consider those events in the context of value judgements deriving from the Black Legend of Spaniards as conquerors and the White Legend of Spaniards as bringers of civilization.

In 2020 John contributed the twentieth article in this collection to the *Review*. This piece draws on the research for two of John's latest books, *Whither the Waters* and *Miera*. It recounts how Miera's 1778 map played a role in delaying the US annexation of Texas and New Mexico.

Biographical Sketch[6]

John Lottridge Kessell was born on 2 April 1936 in East Orange, New Jersey, to John S. Kessell and Dorothy Lottridge Kessell. John's father grew up in his native South Australia. He graduated from medical school in Adelaide and went to Scotland to become a fellow of the Royal College of Surgeons at Edinburgh. Although it took two tries to pass the exam, John senior was obviously proud of his accomplishment. He always went by John S. Kessell, MD FRCS (Ed). Dr. Kessell married Dorothy Lottridge in London, and six years later became a US citizen. As soon as the Second World War broke out, Dr. Kessell enlisted in the United States Army Air Forces.

Although his specialty was urology, in the military Dr. Kessell's practice was more general. He served for the duration of the war stateside, one of his duty stations being Tonopah Army Air Field, Nevada. John's father was transferred to Hammer Field in Fresno, California, which turned out to be so similar in climate to South Australia, where he grew up, that he moved the family from New Jersey when John was seven years old.

John fondly recalls a family story about his maternal grandfather Silas Lottridge. Grandfather Lottridge was a high school chemistry teacher. Thomas Edison had a laboratory in East Orange, and the story goes that the great inventor said he would not think of having any of his children take chemistry from anybody but Silas Lottridge. John's mother, Dorothy, was also a physician. She attended Swarthmore, Cornell, and Womens' Medical College in Philadelphia (class of 28). She had first considered nursing, but a sage counselor at Swarthmore told her, "Dorothy, I think thee would do better giving orders than following them!"

Dorothy worked for the State of California running healthy baby clinics in the San Joaquin Valley for the immigrant workers, most of whom were from Mexico. John presumes she must have had a translator and may have known some Spanish, but he was too young or too uninterested at that time to talk to her about it, which is ironic given how important the language was to become to his life's work. For several years after that, his mother was employed by Fresno State as a physician.

Had you told seven- or seventeen-year-old John that he would grow up to be a revered professor and not just a historian but the dean of Southwest historians, he would have been fairly certain you had lost your grip on reality. He would have rather gone running or fishing than contemplate such a future.

John's parents, both being physicians, might well have agreed. Quite logically they envisioned him following their example and becoming a doctor. Not satisfied with his academic progress and judging that he was misspending his youth with best friend Carl Schwarz, John's folks packed him off to the exclusive and expensive Menlo School in Atherton, California, a private, college preparatory boarding school for a year of finishing. Figuring—correctly as it turns out—that the school had cost his folks a lot, John decided that since Fresno State had one of the best averages in the country of getting students into the medical school, he would initiate his college career there. In addition, he attended several of his father's surgeries and took some biology classes in college. He reckoned, however, that although he would have been a fine physician, he did not want to pursue medicine as a career.

Instead, John found that he enjoyed the history classes he took with a diminutive professor, Francis Wiley, whose wife had taught John three years of Latin at Fresno High School. At Fresno State John recalls taking his first Spanish class, learning the rudiments of the language. After earning his undergraduate degree in the History Department in 1958, John took ship for Australia certain that as a young American, the Australians would all want to hire him, but nobody did. Still, John found that his money was no good as his many relatives and Australians in general graciously picked up the tab for whatever he wanted to do.

Rather than return to the US as originally planned, John continued his travels, which would eventually take him all around the world. On the way back to the States, he visited Spain for the first of many times, remaining there for a month. He chanced to be there toward the end of Francisco Franco's long dictatorship and recalls that he did not know much about what was going on, why the trains were running on time, or why everywhere you walked on a beach there were members of the Guardia Civil carrying their weapons and wearing distinctive, shiny tricorns. One thing he realized, though, was that he loved being in Spain and its people. A lifetime of romantic attachment to and frustration with the language of Cervantes in pursuit of ever-elusive fluency had also begun.

Once again in California, John enrolled at the University of California determined to join the diplomatic corps, having had a taste of world travel and liking it a great deal. With that in mind, he sought out the International Relations Department, but he was not prepared for that course of study. To hear him tell it, he was not really into any sort of studying, but from his apartment in the Berkeley Hills, John looked out on a rather spectacular view. He could see all three bridges in the Bay Area. He could peer out through the Golden Gate on a clear day, and when it was foggy, he could see just the orange tops of the Golden Gate Bridge. Also within view were the Bay Bridge and the San Rafael Bridge. John could time a ship from when it came up through the Golden Gate until it arrived in the Oakland estuary.

Because he had never even taken a class in political science, he felt very much like "a fish in deep water." He earned two C pluses, and since successful graduate students do not get C pluses, John managed to talk his way into the History Department. There he earned A minuses and got out of Berkeley with a terminal Master's in 1961. Nobody said, "Go on ahead." There was no encouragement to get his Ph.D.

While in graduate school, John heard a lecture by Horace Albright, the second director of the National Park Service.[7] Albright spoke about the role of a historian in the national parks. John knew the Park Service hired historians, and he found the idea intriguing. In the bowels of the Bancroft Library, they began to call him "Ranger John," because he was considering the Park Service as a career.

John's effort to become a diplomat had not gone anywhere, but he took the federal civil service exam and landed a job as a junior historian at Saratoga National Historical Park in upstate New York. John married Marianne Ricks in July 1961,[8] and they immediately took off for the East, driving a Chevy Impala, which they called "Clemmie." John served in Saratoga for a year and a half. Immediately after taking up his post in New York, he began to try to get into the Southwest because he had a great interest in the region. The Kessells drove coast to coast on four separate occasions, and each time they went out of their way to pass through the Southwest. Before his extended visit to Spain, John had never had a particular interest in Spanish language or the Mexicans who lived on the other side of Fresno and attended different schools. He did not specialize in Latin America in college, although he recalls a beginning Spanish class. Still, he was drawn to the Southwest and knew he wanted to make it his home. To John's delight, Robert Utley, who was the Park Service regional historian in Santa Fe, managed to get him transferred from Saratoga to Tumacácori National Monument in southern Arizona. The move did not come off without a hitch. Beacon Van Lines initially delivered the Kessell's belongings to Tucumcari, New Mexico, before redirecting them to southern Arizona, where they arrived on Christmas Eve.

Once established in Tumacácori, John soon realized that, like so many other sites in the Southwest, it had really only been considered an archeological site. People were concerned why the tower had not been finished and why the west wall was always wet. Those were the questions, it seemed, to ask rather than who built it, why, for whom, and what was going on here. From the beginning, John was more interested in the people who lived in a place than in historic structures.

John visited the University of Arizona where Professor Bernard "Bunny" Fontana and Father Kieran McCarty, OFM, directed him to documentation on the Tumacácori mission. He was fascinated by the baptism, marriage, and burial records that survived for that mission. And he began working on that material. John was largely an autodidact paleographer; experience and necessity were his only instructors. Sacramental records are very pro forma, but there were so many different priests and different handwriting systems that the exercise of learning to decipher them was like working with a paleography manual.

John was fortunate that his parents had friends in Berkeley who went away during the summer. So, he was able to stay in their home in the Berkeley Hills for two summers in a row in 1964 and 1965, and the Park Service paid him to conduct research at the Bancroft Library. That was his first opportunity to just wallow in so many documents, and he became an expert in reading and interpreting original Spanish material. His summers at the Bancroft enabled John to put together the information—photocopies and microfilm of hundreds of documents bearing on the history of the Jesuit and Franciscan periods—he needed for the two volumes on the Jesuits and the Franciscans in Arizona: *Mission of Sorrows: Jesuit Guevavi and the Pimas, 1691–1767* (1970), and *Friars, Soldiers, and Reformers: Hispanic Arizona and the Sonora Mission Frontier, 1767–1856* (1976).[9] That experience was pivotal because it got John deep into the history of the Spanish Southwest, something he had never intended to do.

John had developed within the Park Service something of a reputation as someone who was interested in research. Robert Utley had moved to Washington and had become the chief historian of the Park Service, and he was bringing research people into Washington. Considering that the nation's capital was not a place to raise their daughter, Kristie, John and his wife decided that he would, with new interest and motivation, try the doctoral program at UNM. Donald Cutter recruited him to UNM, and with a renewed interest, John had no problem with his studies.

In 1968 John and the family spent six months in Seville, living in an apartment in the picturesque Barrio Santa Cruz and doing research in the Archivo General de Indias, just around the corner. His love of the Spanish language and Spain deepened during that magical half-year. To this day John loves it when he encounters someone, say, a Mexican in the post office with whom he can exchange a few words in their native language. It thrills him that he can do that. But he readily confesses, "Where that came from, I really, really don't know."

John may well have been the first Ph.D. to graduate with distinction at the university, receiving his doctorate from UNM in 1969. In any event, he sailed through and then decided that because of his previous experience and contacts with the National Park Service, he need not pursue a job in academia. John then embarked on ten years as a historical freelancer. At that time, he linked up with Eleanor Adams and began to do the research for his history of Pecos Pueblo, *Kiva, Cross, and Crown*. She helped by directing John to sources. They had met in Albuquerque back in 1965 when John stopped by her office to drop off an article for her to consider publishing in the *Review*. John subsequently served as her assistant editor on the *Review* between 1970 and 1972. John became something of a surrogate son to Miss Adams, who never married, and they remained close until the end of her life.

During his decade of freelancing, John also worked on a book project funded by the State of New Mexico through the Cultural Properties Review Committee that became the *Missions of New Mexico since 1776* (1980), as a kind of companion volume to the Eleanor Adams and Fray Angelico Chavez volume, *Missions of New Mexico, 1776*.[10]

Kiva, Cross, and Crown came out 1979. Father Charlie Polzer, SJ, had by that time begun the Documentary Relations of the Southwest at the University of Arizona. He wanted John to move to Tucson to join his team of scholars working with Spanish documents about the history of the Southwest. John thought, "Well, why can't I stay in New Mexico and do something in New Mexico?" Casting about for possibilities, they identified the rich trove of documents from the late seventeenth century to the early years of the eighteenth century as a unique resource for New Mexico. Out of that evolved the Vargas Project.

Successfully pitching the idea of a "Southwestern Adams Papers," a Hispanic founding father to take a seat at the table with George Washington and Thomas Jefferson, John received a Guggenheim Fellowship, along with the first year of what would become more than a decade's worth of funding from the National Historical Publications and Records

Commission. The grants needed an institutional home, and as it happened, in 1979 Don Cutter went, as he often did, to Spain for a year. John took over his classes at UNM, thus establishing the necessary connection with the History Department and the university.

Although his classes were popular, John was very much of two minds about teaching. Before heading off to class, John drank a witches' brew of a concoction he referred to as "pep up," a thoroughly disgusting milkshake to steel him for teaching, to get him to and through class. He professes to have loved small seminars where everyone could get into the meat of a topic, but big classroom teaching never really held any appeal. The days when he had really been "on" and delivered a good lecture were satisfying; other days, not so much. He preferred research and the work of the Vargas Project.

In 2000 he married his current wife, Vi Matthews. In 2002 the sixth and final volume of the Vargas Project was published. Upon retirement in 1996, John had entered his most prolific period, continuing to write, publish, and lecture on the history of Spain in the Southwest. Among his publications after retiring are five books. First were two major interpretative works: a volume covering the whole of the Spanish Southwest, *Spain in the Southwest: A Narrative History of Colonial New Mexico, Arizona, Texas, and California* (2002), and *Pueblos, Spaniards, and the Kingdom of New Mexico* (2008), which presented John's interpretation of Spanish colonial New Mexico.[11] These were followed by a labor of love, a collection of letters his father wrote to his mother during World War II, entitled *East Orange by Christmas: My Father's Love Letters from London, 1933* (2010).[12] In 1975, when he was conducting research for his book on Pecos, John encountered Diego de Vargas and Bernardo de Miera y Pacheco. Over the course of two decades, he more than did justice to the former. When he met Miera, he determined that one day he would write the Spaniard's biography. In 2011 John traveled to Spain, spending a month researching Miera. He went to the Archivo General de Indias in Seville with the thought that somehow, he might find something new. He did not, but from that time on his research and writing was focused solely on Miera. So it was that in 2013, some forty years after John first made Bernardo's acquaintance, *Miera y Pacheco: A Renaissance Spaniard in Eighteenth-Century New Mexico* was published.[13] At a book signing someone asked John if Miera's 1778 map was so notable, what effect did it have on subsequent cartography of the region. The answer came in 2017 when UNM Press published *Whither the Waters: Mapping the Great Basin from Bernardo de Miera to John C. Frémont*.[14]

A revised edition of *Miera* in Spanish has recently come out in Spain: *Forjado en la frontera: Vida y obra del explorador, cartógrafo y artista don Bernardo de Miera y Pacheco en el Gran Norte de México* (2022).[15] It is in every way fitting that John's work has appeared in Spain and in a Spanish edition, given his love for the country and the language.

Rick Hendricks
State Records Administrator

Notes

1. John L. Kessell, "To be Noted," *New Mexico Historical Review* 42, no. 3 (July 1967): 210.

2. John L. Kessell, "A Bolton for the Nineties—The Spanish Frontier in North America: A Review Essay," *New Mexico Historical Review* 68, no. 4 (October 1993): 40.

3. John L. Kessell, "Editor's Introduction, *New Mexico Historical Review* 74, no. 4 (October 1999): 349–51; Jennifer Norden, Javier Marion, Jeffrey C. Sanders, Anthony J. Goodrich, Evelyn A. Schlatter, Kyle E. Van Horn, James M. Scholz, and Patrick J. F. Killinger, "Acknowledgment to Editor John L. Kessell," *New Mexico Historical Review* 75, no. 4 (October 2000): 453–54.

4. Ramón A. Gutiérrez, *When Jesus Came, the Corn Mothers Went Away: Marriage, Sexuality, and Power in New Mexico, 1500–1846* (Stanford, Calif.: Stanford University Press, 1991).

5. John L. Kessell, *Kiva, Cross, and Crown: The Pecos Indians and New Mexico, 1540–1840* (Washington, D.C.: National Park Service, 1979).

6. This brief biography is based on a series of remembrances, including his obituary, that John wrote and shared with me, as well as two interviews I conducted with him in Durango, Colorado, in September 2022.

7. Horace Albright served as the first assistant director of the National Park Service under Stephen Mather. Albright filled in as acting director while Mather was ill during the early years of the National Park Service. He also served as superintendent of Yellowstone National

Park from 1919 to 1929, before officially taking over as the second director of the National Park Service from 1929 to 1933. "Horace Albright (1890–1987)," The National Parks: America's Best Idea, accessed 22 September 2022, https://www.pbs.org/kenburns/the-national-parks/horace-albright.

8. John and Marianne's daughter, Kristin "Kristie" Anne, was born in Tucson late in 1965. John and Marianne divorced in 1989.

9. John's doctoral dissertation, completed in 1969, at UNM, was published as *Mission of Sorrows: Jesuit Guevavi and the Pimas, 1691–1767* (Tucson: University of Arizona Press, 1970). John completed the second volume, *Friars, Soldiers, and Reformers: Hispanic Arizona and the Spanish Mission Frontier, 1767–1856* (Tucson: University of Arizona Press, 1976) on contract with the Park Service.

10. John L. Kessell, *The Missions of New Mexico since 1776* (Albuquerque: University of New Mexico Press, 1980); *The Missions of New Mexico, 1776: A Description by Fray Francisco Atanasio Domínguez, with Other Contemporary Documents*, translated and annotated by Eleanor B. Adams and Fray Angelico Chavez (Albuquerque: University of New Mexico Press, 1975.)

11. John L. Kessell, *Spain in the Southwest: A Narrative History of Colonial New Mexico, Arizona, Texas, and California* (Norman: University of Oklahoma Press, 2002), and John L. Kessell, *Pueblos, Spaniards, and the Kingdom of New Mexico* (Norman: University of Oklahoma Press, 2008).

12. John L. Kessell, *East Orange by Christmas: My Father's Love Letters from London, 1933* (Santa Fe: Sunstone Press, 2010).

13. John L. Kessell, *Miera y Pacheco: A Renaissance Spaniard in Eighteenth-Century New Mexico* (Norman: University of Oklahoma Press, 2013).

14. John L. Kessell, *Whither the Waters: Mapping the Great Basin from Bernardo de Miera to John C. Frémont* (Albuquerque: University of New Mexico Press, 2017).

15. John L. Kessell and Javier Torres Aguado, *Forjado en la frontera: Vida y obra del explorador, cartógrafo y artista don Bernardo de Miera y Pacheco en el Gran Norte de México* (Madrid: Desperta Ferro, 2022).

THE PUZZLING PRESIDIO
SAN PHELIPE DE GUEVAVI, ALIAS TERRENATE

JOHN L. KESSELL

HE BENT OVER HIS MAP and far up in the right-hand corner, almost beyond the Spanish realm of knowledge, the Jesuit map maker printed clearly the names of two still heathen villages: one was "Guebavi" and the other "Ternate."[1] Even in 1692 they were quite distinct; perhaps fifteen or twenty leagues[2]—forty or fifty miles—apart, and on different rivers. Yet, half a century later, when Pimería Alta was far better known, the names of both, Guevavi *and* Terrenate, were seemingly bestowed at the same time upon a single presidio. If the missionaries at Guevavi and the soldiers who garrisoned the new presidio were not confused by this nominal ambiguity, their superiors certainly were. And historians, removed not only by leagues but by years as well, have fared no better. Just where was the puzzling presidio—especially during its initial decade, 1742 to 1752—at Guevavi, or Terrenate, at both, or somewhere else?

Guevavi, on the Santa Cruz River in Arizona less than ten miles northeast of Nogales, was a Piman Indian village introduced to Christianity in 1691 by no less a pair than the famed Jesuit Fathers Kino and Salvatierra. On what became a main route to and from discovery its inhabitants were treated to the spectacle of expeditions coming and going, and for a short while in 1701 they even had a resident Padre of their own. Though Guevavi's missionary potential was fully recognized, not until the year 1732 did conditions permit another Black Robe to come and to live with the people of the village. Then, and for the next thirty-five years, Guevavi, bearing alternately the names of all three principal

1

archangels, was one of the six or eight precarious Jesuit missions of Pimería Alta.

Terrenate, on the San Pedro River in Sonora some forty miles east of Nogales and just south of the Border, became in the Spanish design a stock ranch. Of Apache raiding in the early 1690's, Don Juan Mateo Manje recalled: "Already these enemies had devastated and consumed the ranches (*estancias*) of Terrenate, Batepito, Janos, and San Bernardino, where there had been more than one hundred thousand head of cattle and horses."[8] To the surrounding mountains and plains and to the river that drained them through the valley of the Sobaípuris to the north, Terrenate gave its name. It lay at the valley's gateway not far from where the road from the presidio of Fronteras crossed the river. It was strategically important.

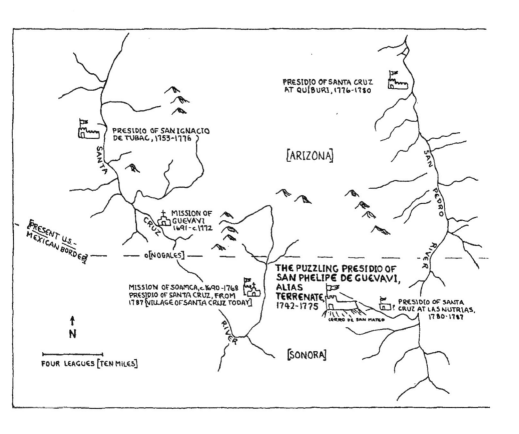

PRESIDIO OF SANTA CRUZ
AT QUÍBURI, 1776-1780

PRESIDIO OF SAN IGNACIO
DE TUBAC, 1753-1776

[ARIZONA]

SAN PEDRO RIVER

+ MISSION OF
GUEVAVI
1691-c.1772

PRESENT U.S.-
MEXICAN BORDER

o[NOGALES]

MISSION OF SOAMCA, c.1690-1768
PRESIDIO OF SANTA CRUZ, FROM
1787 [VILLAGE OF SANTA CRUZ TODAY]

THE PUZZLING PRESIDIO OF
SAN PHELIPE DE GUEVAVI,
ALIAS
TERRENATE,
1742-1775

CERRO DE SAN MATEO

PRESIDIO OF SANTA
CRUZ AT LAS NUTRIAS,
1780-1787

N

FOUR LEAGUES [TEN MILES]

[SONORA]

2

THE CREATION of a new presidio for Pimería Alta was a thirty-five year old brain child before it grew into being. As early as 1706 Manje had suggested it to the viceroy in a report which for other reasons brought the wrath of the Jesuits down upon his head.[4] He felt that "it would be advisable to erect another presidio of forty or more soldiers for the defense of this frontier . . . in the place most appropriate," without which, he emphasized, all Sonora faced certain ruin.[5] The viceroy may well have been impressed, but he failed to act upon the request and Manje turned his energies toward his own defense. Fronteras on its eastern fringe remained Pimería Alta's lone presidial check against the gathering fury of the Apache.

During the early years of the eighteenth century sporadic military inspections were made in and about Pimería Alta. Captain Antonio Bezerra Nieto, commandant of the presidio of Janos east of Fronteras, did not, however, see the need for a new presidio. He urged instead, Jesuit expansion north toward the Hopi country.[6] In 1718 Bezerra did prod the casual captain of Fronteras, Don Gregorio Alvarez Tuñón y Quirós, into making regular patrols against the Apache, although this officer was accused of doing everything but fighting Indians.[7] By the mid-1720's the Jesuits themselves had begun in earnest a long and unsuccessful bid for a settlement and a presidio of one hundred men—double the usual strength—on the distant Gila.[8] Manje meanwhile bided his time.

On a remarkable general inspection of New Spain's entire northern frontier, lasting from 1724 to 1728, Don Pedro de Rivera aimed at reform and economy, at getting the most out of the existing system, for the king's men and monies were short.[9] November 1726 found Don Pedro shaping up the garrison at Fronteras. Although no new presidio was forthcoming, Pimería Alta did profit. Tuñón y Quirós got the sack, and capable Juan Bautista de Anza, the elder, replaced him. Presidial administration was regularized and scheduled patrols were ordered to subdue enemies and cultivate friends.[10] During his extended tour Rivera also observed the missionary at work, and even while the military frontier in Pimería Alta stood still, the inspector's high praise of the Jesuits

3

gave new impetus to missionary expansion. To Guevavi, to Bac, and to Soamca—mission fields fallow for thirty years—Captain Anza escorted three tyro missionaries in the spring of 1732. All too soon their inconstant charges the Pimas would demonstrate the need for continued military surveillance, but that did not automatically mean a presidio at the mission of Guevavi.

Soon another opportunity came to Manje, now dean of Sonora's veterans. Don Manuel Bernal de Huidobro had become governor of a newly created political entity called Sinaloa, or Nueva Andalucía, which included Sonora and Pimería Alta. Obeying his viceroy's wishes, Huidobro set out to inspect the new province. Here was a chance for the citizens of a harassed frontier to present their case directly to the governor. As their spokesman they chose Manje, and on July 8, 1735, he signed his *representación* in their behalf to Governor Huidobro. In part it read:

> I am obliged to repeat for Your Lordship (even though it may seem incidental) several clauses from a declaration which was requested of me and which I dedicated in 1706 to the Most Excellent Señor Duque de Alburquerque, viceroy of Mexico, along with a book describing discoveries of the Pima tribe and the adjacent heathendoms to the northwest of this province. While His Excellency granted other things, he denied the founding of a new presidio of forty soldiers for this advanced frontier, to be situated at the ranch and landmark (*herma*) commonly called Terrenate, thirty leagues distant to the west of the presidio of Santa Rosa de Corodéquachi [alias Fronteras] . . . .[11]

Closely following his earlier report, Manje told of the advantages Sinaloa could expect if the new presidio were erected and the disasters the province faced if it were not. Governor Huidobro was impressed. But before he sent Manje's recommendation to the viceroy, he submitted it, as standard procedure dictated, to the criticism of other knowledgeable and experienced men of frontier affairs. Don Augustín de Vildósola, Don Gabriel Prudhom Heyder Butrón y Muxica, and Don Juan Bautista de Anza read it and commented.[12] Fathers Cañas, Toral, and Echagoyan added their opinions.[13] All agreed: Manje's proposal was sound. The new presidio had gained strong backing. It was to be located at Terrenate. So far no one had suggested a presidio at Guevavi.

Once again the Manje plan was sidetracked. Violent events in other quarters overshadowed the need for a presidio at Terrenate. Major revolts of the natives in Baja California and of the mainland Mayo and Yaqui kept Huidobro defensively engaged. In their suppression the governor's fortune began to fall and that of sargento mayor Vildósola began to rise. When next a proposal for a new presidio came from Sinaloa, it would be Vildósola's and it would get action.

IN HIS CAPITAL the Duque de la Conquista, recently arrived viceroy of New Spain, had called for high-level talks. The new interim governor of Sinaloa, Don Augustín de Vildósola, in a report of March 17, 1741, had suggested that an all-purpose one hundred man presidio be erected at a place called Pitic, today Hermosillo. (He had mentioned neither Guevavi nor Terrenate.)[14] On April 12, 1741, a preliminary junta de guerra was convened. Present in addition to the king's ministers were "other intelligent and experienced persons having intuitive knowledge of that province."[15] The former frontier promoter and ex-alcalde mayor of Sonora, Captain Prudhom, was there, and it may have been he who brought Guevavi and Terrenate into the discussions. On April 27 a full-fledged junta de guerra y hacienda agreed unanimously upon a course of action.[16] And on June 12, Viceroy Pedro de Castro Figueroa y Salazar, Duque de la Conquista, Marqués de Gracia Real, etc., decreed it.

For the peace and prosperity of the entire province of Sinaloa two new presidios were to be founded and two existing presidios relocated. As Vildósola had suggested, a new presidio was designated for Pitic among the troublesome Seri. Its strength was set at fifty men, not the one hundred requested, and it was to be known, in honor of the viceroy, as San Pedro de la Conquista.

The already established garrison of Sinaloa was to be moved to Buenavista, there to watch over the Yaqui and Mayo. Its new name, San Bernardo de Gracia Real, also reflected one of the viceroy's titles. Turning next to the Apache frontier in the north, the Duque de la Conquista decreed:

> That between the missions of Guevavi and Santa María Soamca, at the place on the river [presumably the Santa Cruz] which the governor may deem most appropriate on the advice of knowledge-able and experienced persons, the other of the new presidios be placed with a like number of fifty men including officers. From this place ready communication must be possible with the previously mentioned presidio of Pitic. The new garrison will contain the numerous tribes of Upper Pimas, Sobaípuris, Pápagos, and Coco-maricopas, and in the event of an emergency it will, like the other presidios, protect the interior of the province (*centruará la Provincia*).
>
> Above all, it will be able to defend the province from the frequent attacks of the Apaches and from their extortions and hostilities.
>
> The new presidio will join for this purpose in action and commu-nication with the presidio at Terrenate, to which point the existing presidio of Santa Rosa de Corodéguachi [alias Fronteras] shall be transferred with the fifty men of its garrison including the officers of the company. This place is the most appropriate for its coopera-tion with the presidio of Guevavi by means of forays to impede the invasion of the Apaches on that front and to communicate on the other with the presidio of Janos . . .
>
> The presidio to be erected in the place known as Guevavi shall be called San Phelipe, and the presidio of Corodéguachi, which is to be transferred with its Captain Don Francisco Antonio Bustamante y Tagle to the place named Terrenate, shall be entitled in the future San Fernando. As captain of the new presidio of San Phelipe, which is to be situated at Guevavi with fifty men including lieutenant, en-sign, and sergeant at Royal expense, henceforth Captain Don Joseph Gómez [de Silva] is assigned in appreciation of his great merit and the extensive services he has performed for His Majesty in that province . . .[17]

He could not have been more explicit. A new presidio, named in honor of the king of Spain, was to be founded between the missions of Guevavi and Soamca, presumably taking Guevavi as its place name. The presidio of Fronteras, relocated and renamed for the heir apparent, was to begin operations at Terrenate. Both Guevavi and Terrenate figured now in the viceregal plan, each as a separate place, each with its presidio. But the viceroy did not stop there. His decree continued: "And if . . . the governor believes that some variation is necessary as to the sites where the presidios are to be positioned, not only with regard to suitability of places but for maximum success in guarding the province and for greatest ease of cooperation between the garrisons, I leave to him the means and concede to him the authority to alter the arrangement . . . ." And alter it the governor most certainly did.

To augment the presidial garrisons, the viceroy went on, settlers were to be congregated "voluntarily or by persuasion" nearby. As an inducement they were to be given land. Construction of soldiers' quarters and fortifications was to begin immediately, and the two new garrisons were to be promptly and properly equipped. For these purposes funds would be made available. In conclusion, the viceroy cautioned the governor to be diligent in keeping down costs to the royal treasury, but not, he added wisely, at the expense of settlers or Indians. Then, to all that he had decreed, the viceroy put his name and rubric and turned his attention to other pressing matters at hand. On paper, on June 12, 1741, he had created a presidio of San Phelipe de Guevavi; he had moved another to Terrenate and called it San Fernando: the next move was Vildósola's.

WHEN HE OPENED the packet of official mail containing the viceroy's decree of June 12, 1741, Vildósola found enclosed a transmittal letter of the same date. From it, and from the decree itself, the governor learned of the freedom he was to be allowed in implementing the decree. So that the king be best served and current conditions on the frontier best met, wrote the viceroy, you need not follow the provisions of the decree to the letter, but "you will reach agreement with the captains and other officers together with experienced persons to serve as a basis for the changes . . . and, as soon as it is practical in your opinion, you will prepare documentation with which at your own time you will report to me, not failing to mention what was done to arrange the best and most fitting course of action."[18]

Though the documentation must still lie bundled together on a dusty shelf somewhere, it is safe to suppose that Vildósola submitted copies of the viceroy's decree and related documents to men of provincial affairs, both military and church.[19] To what degree he was guided by their counsel is not so safe a supposition. But no matter, he did alter the viceregal plan. First, the governor decided against the transfer of his two existing presidios: the garrisons of Sinaloa and Fronteras would remain where they were. Choosing locations for two new presidios was far more important business. One of them he would place at Pitic in accordance with the Viceroy's decree: he, after all, had suggested that site himself. The place for the other new presidio he would change; and it would become, in the minds of others, the puzzling presidio of Guevavi, alias Terrenate. What he had decided upon, Vildósola outlined in his dispatch of October 8, 1741, to Mexico City.[20] Two months later his decisions were warmly approved.[21]

For maximum protection of Pimería Alta the governor had exercised fully the freedom granted him by the viceroy. Rather than place the new northern presidio at or near the mission of Guevavi and move the garrison of Fronteras to Terrenate, he chose instead to build the *new* presidio at Terrenate and leave that of Fronteras where it had proven at least somewhat effective. This was just what Manje had advocated six years earlier. Not only had Vildósola endorsed Manje's recommendation at that time, but he had since stationed a temporary detachment of troops at Terrenate.[22] Thus, three factors favored the Terrenate location—its obvious strategic importance at the head of the San Pedro River Valley, its strong backing, and the precedent of troops already there. A new presidio to check the increasing incursions of the Apaches was a natural for Terrenate, not for the mission of Guevavi.

It was a too-inclusive name for the proposed presidio that caused much of the later confusion. Since the viceroy had authorized a presidio named San Phelipe de Guevavi, and since funds had been allocated for construction and maintenance of a presidio named San Phelipe de Guevavi, it seemed wise for administrative purposes to retain that name, even though the location was changed by more than forty miles. A deferential nod to the Duque de la Conquista, Marqués de Gracia Real, also seemed sensible at the time. Since the Sinaloa garrison was not to be relocated and rechristened San Bernardo de Gracia Real, the words Gracia Real were transferred to the new Terrenate presidio. The full name of the latter then became San Phelipe de Gracia Real de Guevavi, reflecting at once king, viceroy, and a site it might have occupied but never did. "Alias Terrenate," indicative of the presidio's actual location, was an afterthought.

BEFORE RETURNING to the frontier to join Captain Gómez de Silva and his men as they set about founding a presidio at Terrenate, it is both revealing and disconcerting to watch the confusion develop in Mexico City. In the case of the puzzling presidio, what was decreed and what was reported accomplished bore little resemblance to what actually went on five or six hundred leagues away. To add to the muddle, no fewer than six different names were applied to the new northern presidio in its first six years. No sooner was it created than it fell prey to proposals from every quarter: abolish it, decreed a new viceroy; retain it, countered the governor; move it west toward the Gulf of California; move it, but somewhere else. And then, of course, there was the misleading association with a mission called Guevavi which alone had borne that name until 1741. No wonder higher officials lost track and historians erred.

Hardly had the viceroy's proclamation been acted upon when this misleading account appeared. Its author, concerned only with the two new presidios, disposed of the first and moved on to the second:

Another presidio, bearing the title San Bernardo Gracia Real, was ordered placed between the new missions of Guevavi (*Guevac*) and Santa María Soamca which are the most northerly of Sonora.[23] For these two presidios, in a junta de guerra which the viceroy Duque de la Conquista called (while he was in the port of Veracruz preparing to resist the Englishman who was attempting to invade it),[24] 51,000 pesos were appropriated, 10,000 to begin the fortifications of these presidios and the remainder for advance payment of the soldiers. All this is gathered from a letter of the said governor [Vildósola], written to the viceroy and dated October 8 of this year 1741.[25]

The reader could hardly be blamed who envisioned faraway in the north between two Indian missions called Guevac and Soamca a new royal presidio named San Bernardo. After all, the statement was documented. Following innocently many years later, the renowned historian Bancroft bestowed the name San Bernardo Gracia Real upon Terrenate.[26] The puzzle was begun.

An anonymous report, probably by a Jesuit who knew what he was writing about, found its way to Mexico City and was dubbed "Noticias de la Pimería del año de 1740."[27] Its author claimed for the mission village of Guevavi a substantial two hundred families, but not one presidio. To the east of the mission of Soamca, however, at a distance of five leagues, or about twelve miles, was "the new presidio named San Felipe Grazia Real, also called by another name Terrenate." The variety of place names and patrons was growing. Was the presidio between Guevavi and Soamca or five leagues east of the latter at Terrenate? Was its patron San Bernardo or San Phelipe? Perhaps two patrons were better than one.

The viceroy Duque de la Conquista died ten weeks after authorizing the new presidios. Vildósola's letter of October 8, 1741, telling of his compliance with the June 12 decree, arrived too late. The president of the Audiencia, as interim chief of state, thanked the governor in the behalf of God and king for pacifying the province and for taking steps to place the new presidios, which he wisely refrained from naming.[28] The next viceroy, Pedro Cebrián y Agustín, Conde de Fuenclara, was intent upon thrift. Among the many matters brought to his attention and scrutinized with economy in mind was a report that recently "two new presidios were constructed, one at the place called Guevavi, named San Phelipe, and the other at that called Pitic, entitled San Pedro de la Conquista."[29] The annual cost of each was 20,665 pesos, much too much in the opinion of a viceroy who sat in judgment fifteen hundred miles from Apache arrows and Seri spears.

The Conde de Fuenclara's decree to Governor Vildósola began: "In order to relieve in every way possible the Royal Treasury from the straits to which the present war has reduced it, I have resolved the extinction and dismissal of the two presidios which the Duque de la Conquista erected in the jurisdiction of that government [Sinaloa] . . ."[30] Just like that! Vildósola was beside himself: he would suspend the order until the viceroy came to his senses. Surely some evil person had got the viceroy's ear. Abolishing the presidios was tantamount to abolishing the province. If it was not the impassioned plea of the governor[31] that changed the viceroy's mind, it was a royal cedula of November 13, 1744.

The king now favored expansion. Baja California and Pimería Alta must be secured and the frontier advanced to the Gila and the Colorado and beyond. Perhaps, reasoned the king, "for maximum security the garrison of Pitic could be transferred to Terrenate and that of the latter place to the missions of the Upper Pimas. . . ."[32] Here was expansion without added expense. Such royal reasoning prompted a response from the Jesuit Provincial of New Spain. Father Cristóbal Escobar y Llamas proposed that "the presidio of San Matheo de Terrenate, which has no determined place," be moved closer to the mission of Soamca and that detachments be stationed at the missions of Guevavi and Bac.[33] The viceroy in the meantime had sent a dispatch to the captain of "the presidio of San Phelipe Gracia Real, Terrenate or Guevavi," asking about the possibilities of moving the presidio westward.[34]

Where the puzzling presidio was and where it was going two kings failed to clarify when each named a new captain for it. On June 15, 1746, Philip V commissioned Don Pedro Vicente de Tagle Bustamante captain of "the presidio of San Pedro de Gracia Real, or Guevavi,"[35] apparently here combining the names of both new presidios in one. On July 2, 1747, Ferdinand VI, because Tagle Bustamante had died, proclaimed Don Santiago Ruiz de Ael captain of "the presidio of San Phelipe de Jesús de Guevavi."[36] Wherever it was and whatever they chose to call it, at least it was being supplied with captains.

Other contemporary published accounts are understandably misguided. The author of a semi-official description of New Spain, entitled *Theatro Americano*, devoted a chapter to "the presidio of San Phelipe de Jesús de Guevavi."[37] He gave a latitude and longitude fix on the presidio,[38] and stated that it was in a gully five hundred and sixty leagues northwest of Mexico City and four leagues east of Mission Santa María Soamca. Though several pages later he doubled the distance to Soamca, consistently he called the presidio San Phelipe de Jesús de Guevavi.[39] A Jesuit history, which appeared a decade later, read: "The mobile presidio of *Terrenate* was fixed at *San Phelipe de Jesús Guevavi*, or so it seems from *Theatro Americano* which treated it under this name. One may suppose that it was already erected there by 1748 in which year that work was published in Mexico. Guevavi is located among the Sobaípuris on a plain . . . a few leagues from the mission of Soamca where Father Escobar [y Llamas] proposed that it might be established."[40] On the map to accompany the latter account the presidio of "San Felipe de JHS" was spotted northwest of Soamca and either at or near the mission of Guevavi.[41]

The Marqués de Altamira may have tacitly admitted that he did not know where the puzzling presidio was when he called it in 1747 "the presidio of Guevavi, alias Terrenate."[42] Even among officials who did know, or who should have known, this ambiguous title caught on and was used for nearly thirty years. San Phelipe remained the presidio's most frequent patron, though he was sometimes San Phelipe de Gracia Real and sometimes San Phelipe de Jesús. Most often the presidio was called simply Terrenate. Bancroft made another valiant effort to solve the puzzle, but again he missed the mark when he wrote: "In 1741 the presidio of Terrenate was founded, but the site was changed more than once, and for a time before 1750 the garrison was apparently sta-

The Presidio at Terrenate, December 1766. Courtesy British Museum. (Note compass rose; the bottom of the map is north.)

Camino de Fronteras

Pequeño Rio de Terrenate

Camino del Tubac

PLANO

13

Aerial view of the presidial vicinity by John Kessell, 1964.

tioned at or near Guevavi."[43] After a closer look at the frontier he might have revised his statement to read: "In 1741 the presidio of Terrenate was authorized, but it was not founded until the following year. For more than three decades it occupied the same site. In spite of its association with the name Guevavi, at no time was the garrison stationed at or near that mission."

CAPTAIN Joseph Gómez de Silva's commission as first commandant of the new garrison of San Phelipe was effective on the date of the presidio's authorization, June 12, 1741. When his company of fifty men was activated is not certain, though both January 1 and June 1, 1742, have claims. The Marqués de Rubí, reviewing the Terrenate garrison in 1766, recorded the declaration of one Tadeo Figueroa "soldier and corporal in the said garrison since the first of January, seventeen forty-two."[44] Yet, when compiling the results of his inspection, Rubí reported "that although the date of the formation of this company is not evident from a single document, it seems from lists and from the reports of the oldest soldiers to have been created on June 1, 1742."[45]

The formal founding of a presidio at Terrenate may also have taken place on June 1, 1742. In a defamatory letter written June 13 to Captain Bustamante of Fronteras, Governor Vildósola chided: "It is probably evident to you that Captain Don Joseph Gómez de Silva is now in the area of his command working with the new company. You will thus be free of this care [maintaining twenty-five troops at Terrenate] and that presidio [Fronteras] will find itself with seventy-five men." With only fifty men, Vildósola continued, Bustamante's predecessors had been far more successful than he at containing the rampaging Apache.[46] Whatever the reaction of Bustamante, Captain Gómez de Silva and his men were in the area of Terrenate by June of 1742 and they had a presidio to found. For the recruits there were adobes to make, timbers to cut, and corrals to build. On September 26 a wedding celebration provided an excuse for respite. Father Ignacio Xavier Keller, tall, fair, blue-eyed Moravian Jesuit from the neighboring mission of Soamca, performed the ceremony.[47] One of the two prescribed witnesses was none other than the post commander himself. Life and duty at the presidio of San Phelipe had begun.

As the nearest priest, the missionary at Soamca became interim chaplain to the new garrison.[48] Until a permanent chaplain could be induced to brave the uncertainties of the frontier, it was he who baptized their children, married their lovers, and buried their dead.[49] These services he recorded in the books of his mission. From mid-1742 the Spanish names he entered increased as Terrenate grew. Captain Gómez de Silva was joined by members of his family. Don Pedro Gómez de Silva, presumably a son, and Lorenza de la Peña, perhaps a daughter-in-law, were frequent godparents to the presidio's newborn. On November 4, 1743, Padre Keller baptized an addition to the Gómez clan, a granddaughter of the captain it would seem, born to Don Manuel Joseph de Sosa and Doña María Nicolasa Gómez de Silva. A muster roll of the new company could almost be compiled from the entries in the Soamca baptismal register—Lieutenant Francisco Xavier de Escalante, Sergeant Joseph Bejarano, Corporal Juan Manuel de Escalante. During the initial years, soldier and settler relied for their spiritual needs on the strong-willed Father Keller.

That the garrison of San Phelipe was never stationed at or near the mission of Guevavi can be convincingly demonstrated by comparing the Guevavi and Soamca books of baptisms, marriages, and burials for the ten years 1742 to 1752.[50] The comparison need not be carried further because it is obvious from the voluminous testimony poured forth during and after the Piman revolt of 1751-1752 that no presidio was then in the vicinity of Guevavi. Nor, for that matter, did anyone even hint that there ever had been one. Furthermore, by 1753 an additional presidio had been founded at Tubac, only seven leagues north of Guevavi, much too close if indeed there had been a Guevavi garrison.

Father Keller's counterparts at the mission of Guevavi were Fathers José de Torres Perea, from 1741 to 1744, and José Garrucho, from 1745 to 1751. They were responsible for the Spanish settlers within Guevavi's jurisdiction, particularly those of the San

Luis Valley extending south from the mission and bending with the river eastward toward Soamca. At no time during the 1740's did Fathers Torres Perea or Garrucho regularly minister to the new garrison of San Phelipe. Soldiers from the presidio whose duty it was to patrol Guevavi and escort its Padres on their rounds did indeed appear as witnesses or godparents in the Guevavi books.[51] And when once, on May 22, 1745, Father Garrucho for some unexplained reason baptized the child of a couple he labeled "residents at the presidio of San Phelipe," it was plainly an exception worth noting. Late in 1753 Father Francisco Pauer, Garrucho's successor at Guevavi, became interim chaplain of the newly founded presidio of Tubac. From that time on, but not before, Guevavi's Padres were responsible for a nearby garrison and Guevavi's books began to swell with the names of soldiers.

On the estancia of Terrenate there stood, some five leagues east of Soamca, a distinctive little mountain of light-colored rock. It commanded a sweeping view of the surrounding hills and plains. In its shadow was a smallish canyon through which coursed the headwaters of the Río de Terrenate or San Pedro. Nearby was sufficient pasture, and with some effort firewood could be scouted. Locally, this place was called San Mateo. If not an ideal place for a royal presidio, it was at least a suitable one. Father Keller, who knew the country well, first hinted that this was the site on which the captain and his men had built. On October 1, 1743, at what he called "the presidio of San Mateo," the Padre from Soamca baptized a baby boy for whom Captain Gómez de Silva and Lorenza de la Peña were godparents. It was no doubt from Keller that Father Provincial Escobar y Llamas got the name San Mateo de Terrenate, by rights the most accurate of all the names applied to the puzzling presidio. Governor Vildósola confirmed the garrison's location on May 26, 1746, when he described it to the viceroy: "Five leagues distant from Soamca to the east, in the place named San Mateo, is situated the presidio of San Phelipe de Guevavi, containing principally the Apache tribe."[52] So that the door remain shut to that enemy, Vildósola urged the viceroy not to move the presidio from San Mateo; and it was not moved.

When he submitted his lengthy report of May 26, 1746, Vildósola may have innocently added another name to Terrenate's growing list. He simply proposed that a presidio be erected at the Baja California port of San Phelipe de Jesús. But that was enough. It was an easy transition from San Phelipe de Gracia Real to San Phelipe de Jesús, at least among the uninformed. Those officers who actually served at Terrenate during its first decade, however, seemed to respect the presidio's correct formal name, though they frequently dropped the Gracia Real. On May 8, 1744, to evade an annoying summons, Captain Gómez de Silva pleaded illness "at the royal presidio of San Phelipe de Guevavi, Pimería Alta."[53] The following year Lieutenant Escalante, conducting a criminal investigation at the presidio, used the same name.[54] In the riotous correspondence to, from, and about the presidio during the Piman uprising, it was often labeled "San Phelipe Gracia Real, alias Terrenate."[55] Later, when the memory of the founding viceroy had faded, the name may indeed have been changed officially to San Phelipe de Jesús.[56] It was, regardless, as Teodoro de Croix admitted, the same presidio "known by the names of San Felipe de Gracia Real, San Felipe de Jesús de Guevavi, and Terrenate . . . founded in the year 1742."[57]

The physical appearance of the royal presidio of San Phelipe located at San Mateo de Terrenate cannot have been nearly as impressive as its string of names. It was far from a solidly constructed fortress set astride the Apache plunder trail. It was more a place to live in, and to leave from on campaigns. It must have looked more temporary than permanent, causing some to refer to it as having no fixed location. It was as one officer reported "a vagueness without any defense."[58] What buildings there were seemed characterized only by disarray.[59] At least there was a parade ground, for there the troops were reviewed on September 20, 1751, as they set out on a routinely ineffective Apache campaign.[60] The presidio's appearance had hardly been improved by the year 1774 when the Adjutant Inspector of Presidios, Captain Antonio Bonilla, described it in these words:

The presidio of Terrenate is established on a small hill of hard, whitish rock which they call San Mateo. Its scanty population is divided into two quarters (*barrios*). In the one they call the upper quarter are situated the captain's house, which although large is rather incommodious and in poor repair; the guard post (*cuerpo de guardia*); the extremely indecent church, which is no more than the porch of the captain's house; the presidio's parade ground; and some scattered large huts. In the quarter which they designate as below, because it is at the foot of the hill, are the rest of the houses or huts without the order of streets and in the greatest disarray. . . .[61]

That was Terrenate in 1774, a year before the oft-threatened transfer of the garrison actually began. For more than thirty years it had maintained an uncertain though continuous existence in one location. It had earned a claim to permanence. A generation had grown up in this place. Twenty soldiers reviewed by Inspector Bonilla in 1774 gave their birthplace as Terrenate.[62] More than one of them, sons of Terrenate's first soldiers, had been baptized by Father Keller back in the early forties.[63] Bonilla's census of Terrenate settlers included several ex-soldiers retired from the rigors of regular campaigning.[64] Tadeo Figueroa, already mentioned as one of the company's original recruits in 1742, had earned his pension by serving a lifetime in the garrison.[65] If in 1774 the royal presidio of San Phelipe de Guevavi, alias Terrenate, seemed permanent to anyone, it must have seemed so to Tadeo Figueroa. Yet a move was imminent.

Almost from the time Captain Gómez de Silva and his men committed themselves to build at Terrenate in 1742, their superiors had questioned the location. Typical was the proposal of the auditor of war, Marqués de Altamira, who suggested in 1751 "that the presidio of Terrenate could leave its incommodious terrain in the *cañada* of San Mateo and advance twenty leagues to the north, establishing itself in the valley of El Quíburi."[66] Back in 1698 Father Kino's ally Chief Coro had won an impressive victory over the Apache near Quíburi, thus demonstrating the success a garrison stationed there might expect.[67] While years passed and a variety of alternative locations were considered, the presidio remained at Terrenate, though support for a move to Quíburi gathered. In 1774, following the cautious lead of the Marqués de Rubí, Captain Bonilla chose instead a site on the Arroyo de las Nutrias, only a league and a half or two from Terrenate, and preliminary construction may have been begun at that place.[68] One year later, however, on a summer inspection tour, Colonel of Infantry Don Hugo Oconor suspended the construction at Las Nutrias and ordered the advance to Quíburi.[69] Thus, in 1775, the days of the presidio at Terrenate were numbered.

The garrison's ill-fated transfer north to Quíburi, near present Fairbank, Arizona, was accomplished late in 1775 or early in 1776. Taking the name of a nearby Indian village, it then became "the presidio of Santa Cruz, formerly of Terrenate."[70] Though the old fort began to crumble, it was not abandoned entirely. In 1779 a detachment of eight men still guarded "el antiguo presidio de Terrenate."[71] At Quíburi the main garrison met with a bloody reception, and "because of the continuous hostilities which the presidio suffered at the hands of the Chiricahua Apaches, and most particularly because they killed in very little time Captains Tovar and Trespalacios with all or the greater part of the company on both occasions, it was decided to abandon it."[72]

After only five years the survivors of a bold but unsound proposal limped back from Quíburi, bringing with them the name Santa Cruz. Their old quarters at Terrenate were in ruins,[73] so at Las Nutrias the troops built temporary barracks "to shelter themselves from sun and rain."[74] There they stayed from 1780 until at least the spring of 1787, too busy fighting or anticipating Apaches to build a permanent presidio. In the latter year, 1787, Captain Manuel de Echeagaray made a careful reconnaissance of the abandoned mission village of Soamca.[75] It was, he reported, an ideal site for a permanent presidio.[76] In less than a month he was ordered to begin gathering and preparing building materials.[77] Again the garrison moved and again it took with it the name Santa Cruz. At Soamca the presidio formerly of Terrenate, Quíburi, and Las Nutrias, found permanence. As the presidio of Santa Cruz it lasted well into the Mexican period.[78] And today, as the village of Santa Cruz south of Lochiel, it is a stop on the Ferrocarril del Pacifico.

As FENDER of Apache blows and policeman to the Pima the royal presidio of San Phelipe de Guevavi, alias Terrenate, existed from 1742 until 1775. It occupied the site known locally as San Mateo de Terrenate. It was not transferred to the mission of Guevavi, more than forty miles away, nor, before 1775, anywhere else. It was puzzling, particularly during its first ten years, only because at least six different names were applied to it, and because someone was continually advocating new locations for it. While pursuing a solution to the puzzle of the presidio's whereabouts, which like most puzzles in retrospect seems not very difficult, the temptation to do more has been great. Bolton called Terrenate a "place with a border-town history that would furnish a theme for a great novel."[79] Perhaps, with the path partially cleared, he who would write that history will be motivated. The raw material is there in abundance. And surely the story of that many-named presidio at Terrenate, the "vagueness without any defense" that held its ground for one third of the eighteenth century, is a story well worth the telling.

NOTES

1. The Jesuit cartographer was Father Adamo Gilg, missionary at Santa María del Pópulo. His illustrated map, dated February 1692, was certainly among the earliest to include place names in Pimería Alta. It has been published in Francisco Xavier Alegre, S.J., *Historia de la Provincia de la Compañía de Jesús de Nueva España*, ed. by Ernest J. Burrus, S.J., and Félix Zubillaga, S.J. (Rome, 1956-60), vol. 4, between pp. 144-45; and more recently in Charles C. DiPeso and Daniel S. Matson, "The Seri Indians in 1692 as Described by Adamo Gilg, S.J.," *Arizona and the West*, vol. 7 (1965), between pp. 40-41. According to Father Pfefferkorn, Guevavi meant "large river" and Terrenate "thornbush" in the Piman tongue. Theodore E. Treutlein, ed., *Sonora: A Description of the Province by Ignaz Pfefferkorn* (Albuquerque, 1949), pp. 237-38.

2. The league, a somewhat variable unit of measurement on the northwestern frontier, was generally equal to about two and a half miles.

3. Luz de Tierra Incógnita, Segunda Parte, Cap. 2. Archivo General de la Nación, Mexico (cited hereinafter as AGN), Historia, vol. 393.

4. For some of the details of Manje versus the Jesuits, see Herbert E. Bolton, *Rim of Christendom* (New York, 1936), pp. 557-65.

5. Conclusion de esta Obra y nota del estado presste. Espiritual, Y temporal que tienen estas Misiones de la Prova. de Sonora y lo mucho que combendra el fundar Un nuebo Presidio . . . , Bacanuchi, December 3, 1706, Biblioteca Nacional, Madrid.

6. John A. Donohue, S.J., *Jesuit Missions in Northwestern New Spain, 1711-1767*. Unpublished Ph.D. dissertation, University of California (Berkeley, 1957), p. 13.

7. Bezerra Nieto was at Mission San Ignacio on February 12, 1718, urging the natives of Pimería Alta to remain steady in their faith. Archivo de Hidalgo del Parral. A blistering inventory of the excesses and abuses of Captain Tuñón y Quirós is Father Luis Xavier Velarde to Father Joseph María Genovese, Nuestra Señora de los Dolores, March 8, 1722. AGN, Archivo Histórico de Hacienda, Temporalidades (cited hereinafter as AHH, Temp.), leg. 278.

8. Donohue, pp. 19-20.

9. Pedro de Rivera, *Diario y Derrotero de lo Caminado, Visto y Observado en la Visita que hiso a los Presidios de la Nueva España Septentrional*, ed. by Vito Alessio Robles (Mexico, 1946).

10. Donohue, pp. 89-91.

11. Representazion que hizo el Vecindario de esta Provincia a Manuel Bernal de Huidobro Primer Governador. . . . Real de Nuestra Señora de

Aranzasu y Tetuachi, July 8, 1735, Archivo General de Indias, Seville, Audiencia de Guadalajara (cited hereinafter as AGI, Guad.), leg. 135.

12. Vildósola, Aranzasu, July 26, 1735; Prudhom, Motepore, July 30, 1735; Anza, Ures, August 13, 1735, *ibid*. The *pareceres* of Vildósola and Anza are translated in Donald Rowland, "The Sonora Frontier of New Spain, 1735-1745," *New Spain and the Anglo American West* (Los Angeles, 1932), vol. 1, pp. 147-64.

13. Cañas, Arispe, August 23, 1735; Toral, Banámitzi, August 24, 1735; Echagoyan, Babiácora, August 26, 1735. AGI, Guad. 135.

14. Vildósola to the viceroy, Sinaloa, March 17, 1741, AGI, Guad. 188. This entire legajo is entitled Espediente sobre haber separado el Virrey de Nueva España, á D. Agustin de Vildósola del Govierno de Sinaloa: años de 1741, a 1750.

15. AGI, Guad. 135.

16. *Ibid*.

17. Viceroy Duque de la Conquista, Veracruz, June 12, 1741, *ibid*.

18. Viceroy Duque de la Conquista to Vildósola, Veracruz, June 12, 1741, AGI, Guad. 188.

19. The procedure was much the same in 1752 when Governor Ortiz Parrilla sought to position the presidio soon after founded at Tubac, Testimonio, Quaderno no. 11, AGI, Guad. 419.

20. Vildósola's dispatch of October 8, 1741, is almost certainly one item in that still missing bundle of documentation. It was alluded to by Villavicencio and by Mota Padilla. See notes 21, 25, 28, *infra*.

21. Pedro Malo de Villavicencio to Vildósola, Mexico, December 5, 1741, AGI, Guad. 188.

22. Vildósola to Captain Francisco Antonio Bustamante, Buenavista, June 13, 1742, *ibid*.

23. Mission San Xavier del Bac, near Tucson, was sixty miles farther north than either Guevavi or Soamca.

24. Admiral Vernon threatened Veracruz. The viceroy had hastened to that port to supervise defense measures. Hubert Howe Bancroft, *History of Mexico* (San Francisco, 1883-88), vol. 3, p. 354.

25. *Historia de la Conquista de la Provincia de la Nueva-Galicia, Escrita por el Lic. D. Matias de la Mota Padilla en 1742* (México, 1870), pp. 521-22. If only we knew what Vildósola did write on October 8, 1741, to the viceroy.

26. *History of the North Mexican States and Texas, 1531-1800* (San Francisco, 1886-89), vol. 1, p. 528.

27. AGN, Historia, vol. 16. Printed in *Documentos para la Historia de Mexico*, Tercera Serie (Mexico, 1856), pp. 837-40.

28. Villavicencio to Vildósola, December 5, 1741, AGI, Guad. 188.

29. Los Oficiales Reales Dan cuenta con 4 Testimonios, de averse erigido, dos nuevos Presidios . . . , Mexico, April 28, 1744, AGI, Guad. 135.

30. Viceroy Conde de Fuenclara, Mexico, June 15, 1744, AGI, Guad. 188.

31. Vildósola to the viceroy, Pitic, June 24, 1744, AGN, Historia 16; *Doc. Hist. Mex.*, 3 ser., pp. 675-82. The date must be a copyist's error. Vildósola could hardly have replied only nine days after the viceroy wrote the order: surface mail today is not much faster.

32. Royal cedula, Buen Retiro, November 13, 1744, AGI, Guad. 188.

33. Father Escobar to the King, 1745, copy certified November 30, 1745, AGN, Reales Cédulas, vol. 67.

34. Viceroy Conde de Fuenclara to Vildósola, Mexico, October 8, 1745, AGI, Guad. 188.

35. Patente de Capitán, Aranjuez, June 15, 1746, AGI, Guad. 506.

36. Patente de Capitán, Buen Retiro, July 2, 1747, *ibid*.

37. José Antonio de Villa-señor, *Theatro Americano, descripción general de los reynos, y provincias de la Nueva España, y sus jurisdicciones* (Mexico, 1746-48), vol. 2, pp. 374-77.

38. Contemporary latitudes and longitudes for the puzzling presidio were no less varied than its locations on contemporary maps. *Theatro Americano* placed it at 32° 20' north latitude, 254° 30' longitude east from the meridian of Tenerife in the Canary Islands. Father Juan Nentuig (Descripcion Geografica, natural, y curiosa de la Prova. de Sonora, IX, ii, AGN, Historia, 393) made it 32° 40' latitude, 264° 12' longitude. Engineer Nicolás LaFora put Terrenate at 31° 35' latitude, 253° 54' longitude. *Relación del viaje que hizo á los presidios internos* . . . ed. by Vito Alessio Robles (Mexico, 1939), p. 24.

39. Villa-señor, vol. 2, pp. 374, 394, 400.

40. Miguel Venegas, S.J., *Noticia de la California, y de su Conquista Temporal, y Espiritual* [ed. Andrés Marcos Burrièl] (Madrid, 1757), vol. 2, pp. 552-53.

41. This map has been republished recently in George P. Hammond, *Noticia de California* (San Francisco, 1958), p. 4.

42. Marqués de Altamira to the viceroy, Mexico, October 2, 1747. AHH, Temp. 278.

43. *History of Arizona and New Mexico, 1530-1888* (San Francisco, 1889), p. 362.

44. Figueroa's declaration, one of eight by soldiers of the garrison, was dated at Terrenate, December 9, 1766. Testimo. del Quaderno de declaraciones recividas a los soldados del presidio de Terrenate . . . , AGI, Guad. 274.

45. Extracto de la Revista de Ynspeccion . . . Presidio de Terrenate. Marqués de Rubí, Presidio de San Miguel, February 21, 1767, AGI, Guad. 511.

46. Vildósola to Bustamante, June 13, 1742, AGI, Guad. 188.

47. Mission Santa María Soamca, Libro de Casamientos y Entierros, 1735-1768, MS. in A. L. Pinart, Colección de Pimería Alta, Bancroft Library, University of California, Berkeley.

48. The mission of Soamca was most frequently said to be five leagues west of Terrenate. Father Keller had served there since 1732.

49. The first full-time Terrenate chaplain may have been Miguel de la Vega whose name appeared in the Soamca books of baptisms on March 18, 1749, and then reappeared from time to time through the fall of 1751. Soamca, Libro de Bautismos, 1732-1768, and Libro de Bautismos y Casamientos de los Pueblos de Visita, 1743-1754, in Pinart. "Padre Vega" was mentioned at Terrenate during the Piman rebellion, after which he may have quit the garrison. Lieutenant Ysidro Sánchez de Tagle to Diego Ortiz Parrilla, Terrenate, ca. December 17, 1751, Testimonio, Quad. 2, AGI, Guad. 419.

50. Most of the pages from the Guevavi books covering the period 1740 to 1767 are preserved in a bound manuscript volume labeled "Tubaca y Otros" in the Archive of the Bishop of Tucson, Arizona.

51. For example, four soldiers—Juan Manuel Escalante, Manuel Amesquita, Salvador Azedo, and Nicolás Soto—were witnesses at the weddings of eight native couples in the village of Supquituni December 18, 1743.

52. Vildósola to the viceroy, Pitic, May 26, 1746, AGI, Guad. 188. This is a long general description of Vildósola's entire jurisdiction. For that portion dealing with Pimería Alta he followed almost word for word the anonymous "Noticia de la Pimería" cited in note 27, supra. An Indian village called San Matheo had been listed as a visita of Santa María Soamca as early as 1732. Father Christóbal de Cañas, et al to Bishop Benito Crespo, Pimería Alta, July 31, 1732; certified copy, Durango, November 19, 1733, AGI, Guad. 135. Translated in George P. Hammond, "Pimería Alta After Kino's Time," NMHR, vol. 4 (1929), pp. 220-38. San Matheo was shown to be northeast of Santa María on an inaccurate, post-1732 version of one of Father Kino's celebrated 1701 maps. Reproduced in Bolton, Kino's Historical Memoir of Pimería Alta (Reprint: Berkeley and Los Angeles, 1948), vol. 1, p. 331.

53. A legal battle royal had grown out of Vildósola's degrading remarks about Captain Bustamante. Presentazon. del Despacho de su exa. al Cap. D. Joseph Gomez Silba para su cumplimto., Presidio de San Phelipe, May 8, 1744, AGI, Guad. 188.

54. One Don Pedro Jácome Ynduz had been accused of playing fast

and loose with some pearls belonging to the Indian captain general of the Pima, Testimonio de Autos, Quaderno no. 1, 1744-1746, AGI, Guad. 329.

55. Keller to Captain Santiago Ruiz de Ael, Terrenate, January 17, 1752, Testimonio, Quad. 3, AGI, Guad. 419. Captain Joseph Díaz del Carpio, Diario, February 24 to March 6, 1752. Quad. 4, ibid. Father Phelipe Segesser to Ortiz Parrilla, Ures, May 25, 1752. Quad. 11, ibid.

56. During the Rubí inspection of 1766, Engineer LaFora noted that the presidio of Terrenate was "called also San Felipe de Jesús Guebabi." Relacion, pp. 124-25. In carrying out his 1774 inspection, Captain Bonilla used that name several times, as did Colonel Oconor in 1775. AGI, Guad. 272 and 515.

57. Croix to Joseph de Gálvez, General Report, Arispe, October 30, 1781. Translated in Alfred B. Thomas, Teodoro de Croix and the Northern Frontier of New Spain, 1776-1783 (Norman, 1941). The quotation is from page 200.

58. Ensign Joseph Fontes to Ortiz Parrilla, Terrenate, ca. December 17, 1751, Testimonio, Quad. 2, AGI, Guad. 419.

59. Fontes to Ortiz Parrilla, Terrenate, December 17, 1751, ibid. The presidio's disarray is evident from the map of Joseph de Urrutia.

60. Ruiz de Ael, Diario, September 21 to October 11, 1751, Testimonio, Quad. 7, AGI, Guad. 419.

61. Estado General del Vecindario del Presidio de S. Felipe de Jesus de Guevavi, alias, Terrenate . . . 4 de Junio de 1774, signed by Bonilla in Chihuahua, July 16, 1774, AGI, Guad. 272.

62. In addition to the regular garrison at Terrenate Bonilla also reviewed the fifty men of a temporary flying company created in 1767 to serve in the Elizondo expedition against the Seri. Revistas, ibid.

63. For example, Antonio Escalante, son of Juan Manuel Escalante, baptized July 7, 1744; Lucas Grijalva, son of Manuel Grijalva, baptized November 9, 1744; and Vicente Valenzuela, baptized February 22, 1745, son of Miguel Valenzuela, "one of the first soldiers who entered the king's service when the presidio of Terrenate was founded, and in which company he served first as squad leader and later as sergeant." Soamca, Libro de Bautismos. Miguel de Valenzuela, Declaration, San Ignacio, February 4, 1752, in Testimonio, Quad. 8, AGI, Guad. 419.

64. Estado General del Vecindario, AGI, Guad. 272.

65. Not the least of Tadeo Figueroa's services he rendered as an interpreter during parleys that finally brought the rebel Piman leader Luis Oacpicagigua to terms in 1752. Declaration, San Ignacio, March 9, 1752, Testimonio, Quad. 4, AGI, Guad. 419.

66. Croix in Thomas, p. 203.

67. See Bolton, *Rim*, pp. 379-84.

68. Revista, AGI, Guad. 272.

69. Copias de todos los oficios pasados al Capitan del Presidio de S. Phelipe de Jesus de Terrenate y sus respuestas correspondientes a la revista . . . Julio de 1775, AGI, Guad. 515.

70. The site of the presidio of Santa Cruz and those of nearby Indian villages have been excavated by archeologists. Their detailed report is Charles C. DiPeso, *The Sobaipuri Indians of the Upper San Pedro River Valley, Southeastern Arizona* (Dragoon, Ariz., 1953).

71. Extracto de la revista, February 9 to 12, 1779, signed by Roque de Medina, Presidio of Santa Cruz, March 3, 1779, AGI, Guad. 272. On modern maps of Sonora there are often three Terrenates shown: one labeled "Terrenate Viejo" which corresponds to the site of the puzzling presidio; another a few miles northeast across the railroad tracks; and a third just south of Ímuris and west of the highway to Magdalena.

72. Simón Elías González, Informe, May 20, 1814, MS. in Pinart, Colección de manuscritos relativos a la región septentrional de Mexico, Serie 1, Bancroft Library.

73. Croix in Thomas, p. 205.

74. Jacobo Ugarte y Loyola to Marqués de Sonora, Arispe, May 14, 1787, AGI, Guad. 287. At least two inspections, both by Roque de Medina, were made of the Santa Cruz garrison while it was presumably at Las Nutrias, though little was said about the site. Extracto de la revista, December 8 to 10, 1782, signed by Medina at "Santa Cruz," December 10, 1782, AGI, Guad. 518. Extracto de la revista, February 3 to 5, 1784, signed by Medina, Santa Cruz, February 6, 1784, AGI, Guad. 285, and 519. Service sheets for the officers of the garrison are in AGI, Guad. 286.

75. The Apaches demolished Soamca in 1768 and Cocóspera became the mission *cabecera*. Fray Juan Santiestevan, missionary at Cocóspera in 1787, favored the garrison's move to Soamca.

76. Echeagaray to Ugarte y Loyola, Santa Cruz, April 20, 1787, AGI, Guad. 287.

77. Ugarte y Loyola to Marqués de Sonora, May 14, 1787, AGI, Guad. 287.

78. Even then the proposals to move the presidio did not cease. In 1828 Colonel Ignacio Arvizu wanted it transferred from Soamca to a place below "Tiburi," there to be joined by the Bacoachi company of Ópatas. José Agustín de Escudero, *Noticias Estadísticas de Sonora y Sinaloa* (Mexico, 1849), p. 73. A lieutenant of the United States Army who had the pleasure of several days in Santa Cruz in 1848 described it as "an old and compact ranche, inhabited I may say, by one company of Mexican

state troops, though none of them would be taken for soldiers, officers included. . . . The town is completely surrounded by a wall." Henry F. Dobyns, ed., *Hepah, California! The Journal of Cave Johnson Couts . . . 1848-1849* (Tucson, 1961), p. 54. Those forty-niners who chose the southern overland route to fame and fortune also passed through Santa Cruz.

79. Bolton, *Rim*, pp. 360-61, note 2.

FATHER RAMÓN AND THE BIG DEBT,

TUMACÁCORI, 1821-1823

JOHN L. KESSELL

THAT MR. GADSDEN's bargain lopped off for the United States the two northernmost remnants of a Spanish mission territory known as Pimería Alta no one much cared in 1853. A couple of crumbling mission churches, little more than curious relics of a primitive, ill-conceived imperialism. Yet today, romantic partisans who drive with their house guests eight miles from downtown Tucson to Mission San Xavier del Bac hail it the "White Dove of the Desert," finest example of Spanish colonial architecture in the entire Southwest. And though vastly outnumbered now by tourists in Bermuda shorts, local Pápago Indians still consider San Xavier their place of worship. The other church, sadly deteriorated and abandoned before United States occupation, has been patched up and for decades venerated as a secular shrine on U.S. 89, a National Monument visited by hundreds of thousands. Perhaps there would have been nothing substantial enough to commemorate at Tumacácori National Monument had the last resident missionary been less tenacious, less worldly, and less effective as a debt collector.

It all began in 1691 with the advent of Father Kino. At his behest the Pima of Tumacácori learned to cross themselves, to harvest wheat and tend livestock. After Kino, a succession of Jesuits followed. Smallpox and measles came too, and Spanish settlers. Then in 1767 the king of Spain summarily banished the Jesuits from his realms and sent the Franciscans into Pimería Alta. Now their Padre wore a grey robe instead of a black one, he began to live at Tumacácori instead of fifteen miles south, but otherwise, to the diminishing

29

number of Pima Indians, mission life changed little. Neither did Mexican independence greatly alter the routine, at least not for a while.

On January 2, 1821, the Padre of Tumacácori sold most of the mission's cattle to raise money for church construction. He left, however, before the proceeds were fully realized. So his successor, no less resolved to continue the building, entered into correspondence with the mission's debtor, a wily opportunist disinclined to settle up. Soon they were contending: on the one hand the missionary to whom no money meant no church; on the other, the potential cattle baron whose delaying tactics, in the context of such unsettled times, might have rid him of the obligation by default. Thanks to their letters—preserved in the Bancroft Library of the University of California—we know the outcome. But first to introduce Father Ramón.

IN HARSH, wind-swept northeastern Spain where the Ríos Jalón and Jiloca come together, the conquering Moors built Calatayud. Into this city, eleven centuries later, walked or rode Ramón Liberós, a small-town lad, barely fifteen. He sought the Franciscan convent. When he had convinced the friars of his good faith, he knelt and received on May 11, 1804, the habit of that venerable Order.[1] There, within the womb of a religious community, Ramón Liberós might have spent the rest of his life, protected from the death throes of the old regime. Instead, fortified by years of orthodox philosophy and theology, Father Ramón chose to take his place in the world of insurgents, constitutions, and the French disease: he would become a missionary.

Recruited by the touring *comisario colectador* for the Franciscan missionary college at Querétaro in New Spain, the young priest in the spring of 1813 began the longest journey of his life. From the port of Alicante he rode out a stormy passage down the south coast and through the Straits to the Puerto de Santa María across the bay from Cádiz. There, at the expense of the liberal Spanish government he was outfitted for the Atlantic crossing, acquiring various articles of clothing and bedding, a penknife and box for writing sand, some scissors, a comb, two pounds of chocolate, two quarter-pounds of tobacco, a set of Father Echarri's[2] works, a duffle bag, a trunk with padlock, two pounds of biscuits, a crucifix with chain and hook, a breviary, and a tin urinal. Thus provided with his spiritual and temporal necessities, Ramón Liberós "of slender build and light complexion, with blue eyes, black hair, and sparse beard" climbed aboard the frigate *San José*, alias *El Comercio*, and joined six fellow Franciscans in prayers for a safe voyage. On July 16, 1813, they sailed for Vera Cruz.[3] In New Spain meanwhile, Viceroy Calleja was setting up the insurgent Morelos for the kill.

The little band of Spanish friars reached Querétaro, a hundred and fifty miles north of Mexico City, early in January 1814. Perhaps because of the depressed and unsettled conditions then prevailing on the northern frontier, Father Ramón did not continue on to the missions. For years he prayed and studied and bided his time. Back home in Spain a restored King Ferdinand swore forcefully at the liberal Constitution of 1812 and then was forced to swear by it. Seizing the moment, Mexican conservatives and opportunists struck for independence, proclaiming in addition the sanctity of the Holy Mother Church and the equality of Creole and Spaniard. Because of the guarantee of religion, the Franciscan college at Querétaro and its missions were initially little affected by Mexican autonomy. Now, in fact, Father Ramón got his chance. As secretary to the Father Prefect he rode along early in 1822 on a routine visitation of the college's northernmost missions, those of Pimería Alta.

THE SHALLOW Río Santa Cruz flowed on north. Big cottonwoods, freshly leafed out in early April, marked its course through the dry country ahead. In contrast, bare, scrubby mesquites covering the rolling mesas encroached from both sides on the narrow and meandering green line. The two Padres, who had crossed the Atlantic together, now followed an acequia that struck off from the river's west bank through meager farm plots toward the base of a rugged and parched sierra. Likely it was getting warm.

Tumacácori lay there in the spring sun, an unprosperous-looking village, its barren plaza dominated by the hulking adobe walls of what was to be a new church, begun nineteen years before and still unfinished.[4] The mission's barefoot congregation—some one hundred and twenty Indians and seventy-five *españoles y castas*[5]—worshipped, those who still bothered, in a cramped and frequently patched chapel inherited from the Jesuits two generations before. Presumably, amid these poor surroundings the visitor and his secretary found resident missionary Juan Bautista Estelric, a native of Majorca possessed of an unfortunate penchant for trouble.[6]

The inspection lasted several days, and turned up some disquieting irregularities. Estelric had served at Tumacácori little over a year. Yet during that short tenure, word of his quarrel with the Creole commandant at Tubac had reached the Bishop of Sonora; Father Juan's illnesses and "his phlegmatic nature" had brought the Father President one hundred and fifty miles to investigate; and now, most serious of all, he was linked in scandal to *una mujer que le asistía.*[7] To his credit, Father Juan had tried to complete the church, though even this good intention had gone awry when a bad debt he contracted caused suspension of the work. Unworthy as he was to continue his ministry, Estelric stayed on at Tumacácori a few more weeks, while his superiors decided what to do with him. Then, sometime after he recorded the burial on May 2, 1822, of little Mariana de Jesús, a Pima, Juan Bautista Estelric rode out of the village in disgrace.[8]

As Tumacácori's new Padre, Ramón Liberós set about familiarizing himself with mission administration. While sorting through the archive he came upon a document that seemed to demand his immediate attention. It was a legal contract between the mission and a certain Lieutenant don Ignacio Pérez[9] entered into by Estelric on January 2, 1821, soon after the latter had arrived at Tumacácori. Having seen at once the need for a new church and at the same time thousands of rangy Mexican cattle grazing the mesas, Father Juan had made up his mind to sell beef and hire builders. Lieutenant Pérez, it seemed, needed cattle to stock a new hacienda. So the bargain was struck: four thousand Tumacácori cattle at three pesos a head.[10]

That Tumacácori had four thousand cattle to sell in 1821—of a total 5,500 head—was the result of more than a decade of generally good range conditions in the Santa Cruz Valley, a lessening of Apache raiding, and the stockman's touch of Father Narciso Gutiérrez, a tough Castilian who endured as missionary from 1794, when mission herds were reckoned in hundreds, until 1820, when they roamed by the thousands. So rapidly did the mission's livestock increase under the supervision of Father Narciso, that the people of Tumacácori petitioned in 1807 for deed to the range lands of a neighboring *pueblo despoblado*. By 1818 the count stood at five thousand cattle, twenty-five hundred sheep and goats, and six hundred horses. The cattle herds of Tumacácori and San Xavier del Bac together accounted for more than half the total run by all eight Pimería Alta missions.[11] When don Ignacio Pérez and his kind began buying on such a large scale, however, mission herds were rapidly diminished. One missionary advised Pérez in the spring of 1821 that anyone wishing to buy cattle in Sonora had better have with him a mold for coining spot cash. Speaking of cash, he continued, it had been rumored that Pérez could not pay for all the stock he was accumulating. "Where," inquired the Padre pointedly, "*are you going to get that much money?*"[12]

The terms of the Tumacácori sale called for four thousand pesos in cash upon receipt of the herd, another two thousand in six months, and the remaining six thousand within a year and a half. In mid-February Pérez' associate, don Rafael Elías,[13] paid the initial installment and his vaqueros headed up the herd and moved it south. When the second payment fell due, don Ignacio tarried.

Estelric, with a payroll to meet, boldly wrote a sight draft for a thousand pesos on the cattle buyer's account.[14] It had been honored, but as far as Liberós could tell, no further payment had been received. As a result, the new church stood far from complete as envisioned by his predecessors, but not really, in the opinion of Father Ramón, that far from utilization. In fact, if the debt owed Tumacácori were collected, the church might be put to the Lord's use in a matter of months.

He began courteously, writing from Tumacácori, May 29, 1822:

> My very dear brother[15] and Señor:
> I greet you most warmly, and inform you that I am now in charge of this mission. . . . While examining its papers I came across one from which it appears that . . . you are obligated to deliver to this mission the sum of one thousand pesos in cash, over and above the five thousand that it seems have already been paid. As for the remaining six thousand, it appears that the full amount is due in October of this year.[16]
> I beg that you be so kind as to deliver to this mission the said amount due, and the remainder just as soon as it is possible, for the mission needs the money to continue its building program. It was for this reason that the cattle were sold.
> I am your most affectionate brother, servant, and chaplain, who kisses your hand.
>
> Fray Ramón Liberós[17]

As the Padre of Tumacácori phrased his polite opening bid, don Ignacio Pérez was making good his claim to the sprawling San Bernardino grant. On May 21, 22, and 23 in Arizpe, the provincial capital, he purchased at public auction the legally-allowable four *sitios* of land—17,354 acres—for ninety pesos plus fees. At that rate, roughly two hundred acres a peso, each head of cattle bought from Tumacácori was equivalent in cash value to six hundred acres of land. Moreover, Pérez' San Bernardino bargain included control of so-called "overplus" lands that must have swelled the total grant to a hundred thousand acres. Don Ignacio plainly hoped to become a cattle baron, but in his original petition he had sought to impress the authorities by suggesting that the San Bernardino under his ownership might become a frontier buffer state where raiding Apache would trade lance for seed and plow.[18] The Apache would come all right, but hardly on don Ignacio's terms.

To the enterprising and ambitious Pérez, almost certainly a Creole if not a mestizo, Mexican independence offered exciting prospects. He admired the dashing opportunist Iturbide, and found it profitable, accepting humbly a captain's and then a lieutenant colonel's commission. Even though Iturbide's Three Guarantees ostensibly protected the Church and Spaniards, there had been talk to the contrary. What effect, Don Ignacio might have pondered, would the disenfranchisement of the Church and the expulsion of all *peninsulares* have on the debts he owed to Tumacácori and several other missions administered by Spanish Franciscans? Only a fool, or a poor businessman, would have failed to grasp the implications.

Pérez now hit upon what must have seemed to him a clever stratagem. From Arizpe on July 2, 1822, he wrote directly to Father Prefect Francisco Núñez. He described in detail the current pitiful state of his personal finances, and then proposed that he be allowed to provide toward his debts not cash, but "blankets from Encinillas, delivered at Tumacácori at two pesos each."[19] Not only would the Pérez household be saved from utter ruin, but the Padres, by reselling these marketable blankets, would reap a handsome profit. "And though it becomes nothing more than a matter of raising revenue, this is always preferable to contemplating a bad debt." He must have smiled at the thought of Franciscans-turned-blanket-salesmen —until he got the Father Prefect's reply: "As for the proposal you make me about the blankets, it is not within my authority to resolve, for the missions act separately, one from the other, in the management of their temporal affairs. . . . Accordingly, I suggest that you correspond with them separately."[20] It was, at least, a very good try.

In the City of Mexico and elsewhere throughout the realm, thoughtful and hungry Mexicans were reflecting upon the first hundred days of Agustín I, their emperor *hecho en México*. Not a few were disenchanted. At Tumacácori the insects were worse than ever. It had been sticky hot. Father Ramón ticked off the days. On September 6, 1822, precisely three weeks after the final payment should have arrived, he wrote again. When he had carefully reviewed for Pérez the terms of the contract, he reminded his adversary that a thousand pesos had been overdue for more than a year "despite the repeated letters that Father Estelric, my predecessor, informed me that he had written you." And what of the courteous letter Liberós himself had directed to Pérez at Arizpe? While construction of a church languished for lack of cash, Pérez, it seemed, had not the decency to reply. "In view of all this," reasoned Father Ramón, "I can do no less than insist, with heart-felt regret, that you arrange for delivery at this mission of the seven thousand pesos you owe without any more delay." If Pérez failed to act, Father Ramón was now prepared to take the offensive by whatever means "seem appropriate." "The lack of an answer to previous letters," he concluded, "is reason enough for sending this one to you certified. . . ."[21]

The firm line paid off. On September 24 from Chihuahua, don Ignacio deigned to answer. It was a letter calculated to melt the resolve of even the most hardened debt collector. Pérez' father had died. His mother and a flock of dependents had narrowly escaped "a thousand evils" at the hands of the creditors, thanks only to don Ignacio's timely scraping together of fourteen thousand pesos. There were unfortunate circumstances, all of them beyond his control, to explain why he had not answered the first letter. As for the "numerous letters" of Father Estelric, that was clearly a matter of exaggeration: he had received only one "so full of indignities" that he could hardly believe it.[22] Lastly, don Ignacio himself had been gravely ill with incapacitating chills and fevers. In view of all he had suffered, and with the alleged sympathy of his "great friend" Father Núñez, Pérez suggested that he send one thousand pesos in cash and one thousand in goods with his mother when she returned to Sonora in October. Surely Father Ramón would consent to an extension on the remainder.

You may be sure that I shall remit by my mother the one thousand pesos in cash and as much again in goods. And, if you wish, I shall send you one hundred serapes of fine colors at eight pesos each, these being the sort that are sold with much esteem in that province for ten to thirteen pesos. Concerning this, I await your decision.

I hope that the openheartedness of the Father Prefect, moved by an unfortunate family and its great financial burden, is, because of its merit, fully engraven upon the heart of your Reverence, and, taking it into consideration, that you will grant me the already facilitated extension. As for the need you have alluded to, rest assured that I shall cover the account I have pending at that mission.

Consider me, your Reverence, one of your most reliable brothers. Because of what I beg you, please impose upon me your orders as your attentive friend and loyal servant who kisses your hand.[23]

With partial payment seemingly assured, Father Ramón stepped up the construction. On October 1 he blessed an adjunct to the new church, a spacious, walled cemetery. Then ten weeks later he had the bones of Father Narciso Gutiérrez dug up from beneath the packed-earth floor of the old church. Solemnly he bore them the forty yards to a fresh grave in the sanctuary of the new church, and there on the second anniversary of Father Narciso's death he reburied them within the walls begun by that enduring missionary two decades before.[24] Perhaps the sanctuary with its impressive dome was now complete, but work on the body of the church went on. Father Ramón was counting on the pesos and goods promised in Don Ignacio's letter. By the end of January, however, his patience had expired. There seemed to be no alternative: he would have to carry the battle to the camp of his adversaries.

Doña Gregoria Pérez was startled indeed by the presence of Father Ramón in Arizpe. One thousand pesos in cash? as much again in goods? Why, no, Ignacio had said nothing to her. Well and good; he would ride over the mountains to Janos, another hundred and fifty miles, and meet the wily Pérez face to face. "This very day I would have undertaken the trip had not yesterday my friend Don Rafael Elías arrived in this city." Elías, acting for Pérez, had brought a token payment of three hundred and sixty pesos in cash and seven hundred and thirty-two in goods. Welcome as this gesture was, Father Ramón refused to relent. "As for the extension you proposed to me, I regret deeply that it cannot be granted." The plight of "a village without a church" was to Father Ramón's way of thinking far more serious than that of a careless speculator temporarily down on his luck. Nevertheless, that day, February 3, 1823, Father Ramón credited the account of Don Ignacio with one thousand thirty-two pesos two grains, holding out sixty pesos in goods, perhaps for travel expenses.[25]

A week later he was back at Tumacácori where an episcopal circular awaited him. It requested that public prayers be said to aid Emperor Agustín on his trip to Vera Cruz, a trip that had taken place during the past November. On February 9, Liberós signed the circular in compliance,[26] unaware of how desperately the Emperor now needed prayers. Anti-imperial sentiment had burst forth all around him and its forces were converging on the capital. In a matter of weeks the empire of Iturbide would fall. Anti-clerical, anti-Spanish republicans would inherit the government. And while Lieutenant Colonel don Ignacio Pérez would support the empire "until its final hour," he would make no hasty payments to missions that stood every chance of extinction under the new regime.

Despite the manifold uncertainties of these times, Ramón Liberós did not lose sight of his high calling. He was first and foremost a priest. As minister of the mission at Tumacácori and interim chaplain to the run-down Tubac garrison three miles north, he took seriously his role of spiritual shepherd. He baptized their newborn, married their lovers, and buried their dead; but even more, he worried about their souls. He took to heart their transgressions, and when the burden seemed too much to bear, he wrote to the Bishop. How, he craved to know, could he put the fear of God into his apathetic flock? "I have not ceased, insofar as it has been possible for me, to guide them along the path of salvation. Yet some individuals, forgetting the end for which God Our Lord created them, live as though they were not Christians and scorn the precepts of Our Holy Mother Church." Since Ash Wednesday, six weeks before, he had been exhorting them "from the pulpit and in private" to fulfill their annual spiritual obligations. Furthermore, he made clear the consequences they might expect if they did not. "And the result has been scorn, babbling, and a reluctance to confess. I tell your Most Illustrious Lordship (it is public knowledge and notorious) that some of them have not confessed for seven or eight years!"[27]

The Bishop had no sympathy for transgressors. He advised Father Ramón to use formal admonition, public excommunication, and even anathema to shape up his congregation.[28] But then the Bishop did not have to live with these people.

If only he could bring these weapons of the Church to bear on don Ignacio Pérez. By late spring, Father Ramón's dander was up. Writing to Pérez "wherever he is," Tumacácori's Padre told of the measure he had taken and why.

> Finding myself without a church and suffering certain indignities in order to borrow the little with which work has been done, I have resolved to dispatch with full authority don José María Sotelo, along with the foreman of this mission, don José Antonio Orosco. To them you will pay in cash, current coin, the entire amount you owe, and in addition, whatever they demand of you for the losses and expenses suffered by this mission because you have not fulfilled your part of the contract.
>
> If you do not turn over the entire amount immediately (*pronto pronto*), turn over to these men without delay the two thousand cattle that have not been paid for, with all of their increase for three years. One or the other, cash or cattle, must be delivered at this mission at your expense and risk: it being understood that if you do not, these men have my authority to take whatever steps they feel are warranted, for which they already have instructions.[29]

Sotelo and Orosco, both residents of Tubac and frequent godfathers to local babies, were no match for the slippery Pérez. Once they caught up with him at the Chihuahua presidio of Janos, he stalled them unmercifully. And not till mid-August did he offer an explanation to Father Ramón. His every effort, he then assured his creditor, had been directed toward raising money to pay the debt. Before leaving Chihuahua City he had arranged for an advance large enough to cover the whole thing; he had merely to return to that capital and pick up the cash. "But days passed, to my concern and to that of your envoys, to whom I have not ceased to manifest sufficient documentary proof of my good intentions." He had even suggested a plan to his general whereby the money might have been raised. "Now," he was forced to admit, "at a most inopportune time the General has left for Durango."

But Pérez had yet another scheme, one he now proposed directly to Liberós, because Sotelo, he claimed, did not have enough authority to decide the matter. It involved a herd of two thousand cattle belonging to don Ignacio "in that far province." Since the government had seen fit to leave him at Janos with his "arms folded," he suggested that Sotelo, Orosco, or one of his own trusted agents accompany the herd to market in his behalf and collect the money. Or perhaps Father Ramón preferred that a draft be issued against the drover of the herd. Either way, enough to pay Tumacácori could be raised. There was, however—and here don Ignacio pressed his point—an even better way. If Father Ramón would merely consent to wait a little longer, only till October, the value of the herd would go up, almost certainly to triple the amount due. "Therefore, my friend, have a little patience" and, he might have added, "join me in speculation."

So that Father Ramón would not think ill of him, don Ignacio explained why he had delayed this long. He might indeed have sold the herd earlier to the government, but that solution was risky at best because of the treasury's critical shortages. As for driving the herd overland to Tumacácori, that was out of the question. The drought of the past year had been so severe that not a single head would have survived such a drive. Furthermore, "rapid political changes" had rendered the transfer imprudent. It was, therefore, up to Father Ramón to choose from the alternatives offered. "Any other measure is unnecessary and excessive in view of the very substantial payment I am making [not to mention] embarrassing for me and dilatory for your Reverence."

Tumacacori in the 1820's. Painting by Cal N. Peters, 1965. Courtesy National Park Service.

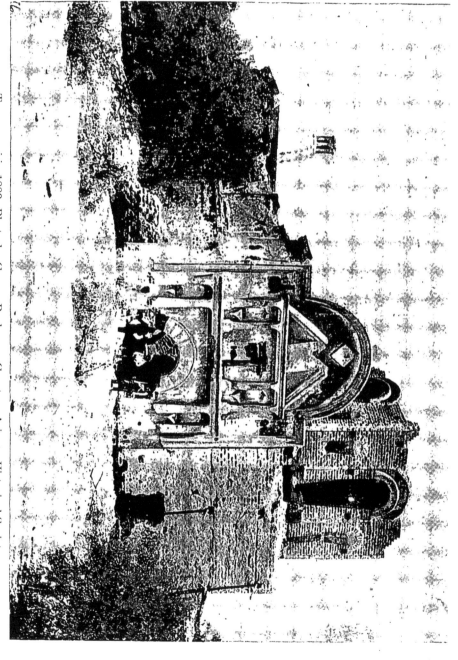

Tumacacori in 1889. Photo by George Roskruge. Courtesy Arizona Historical Society.

Understand, your Reverence, my just reasons and rest assured that I am wholly dedicated to closing our account at the earliest moment. Gratified by the kindness and consideration with which you have been so good as to favor me thus far, I hold your Reverence in the highest regard. I shall come to that mission in person just as soon as I am relieved of this garrison, for I am anxious to give you an *abrazo* and reiterate that I am, as always, your humble friend and servant who kisses your hand.[30]

Father Ramón tore open the long-awaited letter. He should have known. What was he to do now? Thanks to Pérez' duplicity, he himself was now a debtor, unable to repay the money he had borrowed. Worse, with his credit gone, he had been forced to take the step he dreaded—he suspended work on the church for lack of funds. The bitter disappointment only strengthened his resolve. He called for a horse and provisions. There was no other way. He rode south and west, paying little heed to the thunderheads building over the mountains. He had determined to lay the whole tedious matter before his superior and beg for permission to go find Pérez. Have a little patience. *Madre de Dios!*

Father President González was sympathetic. Don Ignacio owed the mission of Caborca money too. But perhaps another letter would suffice, an appeal to Pérez as a decent and sensitive human being and as a brother of the Third Order of Saint Francis. Surely he must not realize the anguish he was causing Father Ramón. "Now wearied of chasing hopes with no consolation, he arrives here asking for permission to come there and, by virtue of the right which the contract gives him, to collect the money or the two thousand head of cattle. He is determined," continued the Father President, "not to return until he has obtained complete satisfaction." Father Ramón did not enjoy the business of debt collecting. "This task saddens him. It is contrary to his compassionate nature, and to true and fraternal affection."

For Father Ramón's own good, the Father President denied his request. Instead he told Pérez to forward "two thousand pesos and the envoys' expenses" to Tumacácori immediately, and the balance within the year. "I hope you will take advantage of this moderate and fraternal compromise and of the fact that I did not deem necessary the Father's coming or the measures he might have resorted to . . . that the mission receive what it so justly deserves and needs so badly."[31]

Toward the end of his long ride home, a dejected but still determined Father Ramón reined up at the rancho of Calabasas, ten miles short of Tumacácori. He carried in his saddlebags the letter from Father President González to don Ignacio Pérez. Yet the trip had been a failure. His superior had not only denied him the satisfaction of a personal confrontation with Pérez, but he had compromised with the scoundrel. Perhaps while the courier waited, the Padre of Tumacácori sat down at Calabasas and wrote a letter of his own to accompany the Father President's. Time had run out. Don Ignacio must pay cash or take the consequences. Sotelo was empowered to do whatever was necessary to get results: "Either he has the authority already or I can grant it!" In addition to the two thousand pesos, Father Ramón demanded that Pérez pay the envoys' expenses:

That is, five pesos daily for the three, from the day they left Tumacácori. Otherwise, you may expect me at any moment, knowing that I shall not be earning two pesos or five, but whatever fits my mood and the discomfort I shall be forced to suffer on your account. . . .

These measures by me may seem irregular to you, but, my friend and brother, ever since I took charge of this mission and made clear to you the straits it was in, you have (speaking in Castilian as we were taught) entertained a pure fraud! What do you expect me to do? First you arranged with my Reverend Father Prefect to send immediately one thousand pesos, and nothing happened; afterward you promised to send with your good mother by October a thousand pesos in cash and a thousand in goods, and still I am waiting. You have declined to answer my letters and have paid no attention to the debt, and now you have cajoled my envoys four months with fond and always false hopes.

In view of all this, what can I expect? *You* can expect *me* soon, for I am now resolved not to give up the matter at hand. I shall come to Chihuahua, Durango, Mexico City, or wherever I must if you continue deaf and oblivious to my supplications. I wish you the best of health. Command this your wretched brother (which truly I am, seeing that on your account I cannot continue the church) and loyal servant who kisses your hand.[32]

That did it. Father Ramón had an answer in less than three weeks. Written by Pérez' business associate, Don Rafael Elías, it came from San Bernardino and was dated September 7. In tone it was almost contrite. "Things have come to such a pass that I consider it necessary to make the greatest sacrifices in order to pay in cash the remainder due that mission." The herd was on its way to market. Furthermore, don Rafael agreed to underwrite the entire debt just in case the cattle sale did not proceed as expected. "And as of now, I endorse this letter with the full validation necessary, or I shall give separately whatever proof of obligation your Reverence wishes."[33]

Quickly, before anyone had second thoughts, Father Ramón accepted. Don Rafael Elías, prominent rancher, businessman, and public servant was a far better risk than Pérez.

Be it recorded by this document which I am sending to don Ignacio Pérez that, in accordance with the letter which don Rafael Elías wrote me from San Bernardino dated September seventh, eighteen hundred and twenty-three, I recognize the transfer of the debt said don Ignacio Pérez owes this mission to the above-mentioned don Rafael Elías. Said debt consists of the five thousand eight hundred and forty-three pesos four reals remaining on the herd of four thousand cattle sold to him,[34] plus five hundred and twenty-three pesos for the expenses that the agent and envoys of the mission have incurred in the attempted collection of the expressed sum. This amount in full don Rafael Elías must pay, by virtue of the above-mentioned letter which I admit under obligation toward payment of the debt, within eight months from today's date. Tumacácori, September fourteenth, eighteen hundred and twenty-three.

Fray Ramón Liberós
Minister of Tumacácori[35]

If he did not go immediately into his unfinished church and say a prayer of thanksgiving, he should have. He had won.

PRESUMABLY Don Rafael Elías kept his promise to pay the 6,366 pesos four reals, for subsequent correspondence is silent regarding the matter of the big debt. Father Ramón continued to supervise construction of the church, and though it was never entirely finished, he put it to use.[36] Perhaps the new structure served to bring his wayward congregation closer to God. He himself was forced to leave them abruptly, not of his own choice, in the spring of 1828. Soldiers escorted him out of the village. In Sonora antimission interests had finally prevailed and the Spanish Franciscans were being banished. He may have looked back. The church stood over the village, mute and impressive, with scaffolding still clinging awkwardly to its facade.

Somewhat later, in Arizpe, the town council was involved in raising funds for a campaign against the Apache. It was having trouble with a debtor. One of its members had written "imploring him earnestly" to pay up "all or some part of the fifteen hundred pesos he owes for the hacienda of Santa Rosa." But the councilman was skeptical. "I doubt very much that he will help out this treasury, which, in my opinion, will have to sue Citizen Ignacio Pérez. . . ."[37]

But that, fortunately, was of no concern to Ramón Liberós, wherever he was.

1. Lista de los Religiosos de este Apostolico Colegio de la Santa Cruz de Queretaro . . . 1824, photocopy, Bancroft Library, University of California, Berkeley (cited below as BL), Bolton Research Papers, No. 380. Liberós was born in the Villa de Mazaleón, archbishopric of Zaragoza, on April 7, 1789.

2. Fray Francisco Echarri, author of *Directorio Moral* (Valencia, 1770, and later editions).

3. Documents concerning the "mission" to the college of Querétaro of 1811-1813 are in the Archivo General de Indias, Seville (AGI), Audiencia de México, leg. 2736. The group with which Liberós sailed constituted the sixth and final wave. Lista de la misión que colectó el P. Comisario Fr. Francisco Núñez que vino en trozas incompleta . . . , Archivo General de la Nación, México (AGN), Misiones, tomo 18.

4. As early as May 18, 1803, F. President Francisco Moyano had written that Tumacácori's church was being "erected anew." Noticia de las Misiones que ocupan los Religiosos del Colegio de la Santa Cruz de Querétaro . . . 1802 . . . , AGI, Audiencia de México, leg. 2736.

5. Estado de las Misiones de la Pimeria Alta . . ., 1820, F. President Faustino González, Caborca, January 4, 1821, Archivo del Gobierno de la Mitra de Sonora, Hermosillo (AGMS).

6. A brief notice of the visitation appears in Tumacácori's Libro de Bautismos dated April 6 (or possibly 8), 1822. From the surviving baptismal, marriage, and burial records, it appears that Estelric had served at Tumacácori since January 1821. These records, bound in one volume and labeled "De Calabasas Bautismos," are preserved in the Archive of the Bishop of Tucson. Also extant is the Tubac Libro de Entierros y Casamientos, 1814-1824, MS in the A. L. Pinart Colección de Pimería Alta, BL.

7. At first F. President González explained to the Bishop of Sonora that Estelric had been removed from Tumacácori because of his poor health. González to the Bishop, Caborca, October 4, 1822, AGMS. Later he was forced to lay the whole sordid affair before the prelate. González to the Bishop, Caborca, December 4, 1822, AGMS.

8. For several years scandal followed wherever Estelric went and "secret communiqués" kept the Bishop informed. But because the Sonora frontier was chronically short of priests, Father Juan survived. Not till late 1835, at the run-down mission of Guásavas did his career finally end. He died at the age of fifty-one, suddenly, *sin sacramentos*. Notice of his death appears on a fragment of the Guásavas Libro de Entierros preserved in the parish archive of Granados, Sonora.

9. For a short biographical sketch of Ignacio Pérez, see Francisco R. Almada, *Diccionario de Historia, Geografía y Biografía Sonorenses* (Chihuahua City, 1952), pp. 562-63.

10. Liberós to Pérez, Tumacácori, May 29, 1822, Sept. 6, 1822. A. L. Pinart, Colección de manuscritos relativos a la región septentrional de México, BL. In this collection, cited below as Pinart Col. mss., there is a whole series of documents concerning Pérez' cattle buying activities, for the most part original letters from missionaries demanding payment and unsigned, rough draft answers apparently used by Pérez as file copies. There is of course some chance that the clean, signed letters sent out by Pérez varied slightly from the drafts he retained. Hubert Howe Bancroft in his *History of Arizona and New Mexico, 1530-1888* (San Francisco, 1889; reprint, Albuquerque, 1962), p. 385n, wrote: "In 1822 a new church was in process of construction or extension, but work was for a time suspended on account of trouble about the pay for 4,000 cattle that P. Estelric had sold to obtain funds." Tubutama, Caborca, Sáric, and Bacadéguachi were among the other missions suffering because of Pérez' failure to pay off his debts. Presumably the pesos involved were *pesos de plata* of eight *reales,* or reals, each, then on a rough parity with the U.S. dollar.

11. At the end of 1820 Tumacácori stood second in estimated number of cattle to San Xavier del Bac which had 5,700 head, but first of all the missions in sheep and goats (1,080), horses (590), and mules (60). Estado de las Misiones de la Pimeria Alta . . . 1820. Ray H. Mattison, "The Tangled Web: The Controversy Over the Tumacácori and Baca Land Grants," *Journal of Arizona History,* vol. 8 (1967), p. 73. Estado Espiritual y Temporal de la Pimeria Alta . . . 1818, F. José Pérez, Oquitoa, December 31, 1818, AGN, Misiones, tomo 3.

12. F. José Gómez, Tubutama, March 23, 1821, Pinart "Col. mss."

13. Don Rafael Elías González, a member of one of Sonora's most illustrious families, later served as governor of his state. He was a great-grandfather of President Plutarco Elías Calles. Almada, *Diccionario,* pp. 241-42.

14. Estelric to Pérez, Tumacácori, September 10, 1821, Pinart "Col. mss." The attached sight draft was dated at Tumacácori the same day and later receipted by Félix Antonio Bustamante, who may have been master builder on the Tumacácori project.

15. Pérez was a member of the lay Third Order of Saint Francis.

16. Here Liberós erred. The final payment was due in mid-August, not October.

17. Liberós to Pérez, Tumacácori, May 29, 1822, Pinart "Col. mss."

18. Mattison, "Early Spanish and Mexican Settlements in Arizona," NMHR, vol. 21 (1946), p. 311. As part of the legal procedure attending the

grant, three witnesses testified that Pérez had a sufficient number of cattle, over four thousand one of them declared, with which to stock the San Bernardino.

19. Pérez seemed to have had some trouble deciding on the price. He first wrote the word *trece* and scratched it out, then the figure 14, apparently reals. Finally, over the 14 he wrote what appears to be 2 ps. Unsigned draft, Pérez to Núñez, Arizpe, July 2, 1822, Pinart "Col. mss." The Encinillas district in the state of Chihuahua lies some fifty or sixty miles north of the capital city. During the colonial period an *obraje*, or textile mill, was established at the hacienda of Encinillas and worked by prison labor. It continued to operate after Mexican independence. See Almada, *Resumen de Historia del Estado de Chihuahua* (México, 1955), p. 125.

20. Núñez to Pérez, Santa Magdalena, July 5, 1822, Pinart "Col. mss."

21. Liberós to Pérez, September 6, 1822.

22. Here Pérez was exaggerating. Estelric had been guilty of bluntness perhaps, but not indignities. "Because of the dire straits in which I find myself to continue the construction I have begun, I have felt obliged to issue a draft in the amount of one thousand pesos. . . . I urge you please to pay the amount on sight, in the knowledge that if you do not I shall be forced to take other measures to recover it and provide for my needs, steps which will be for me most painful but indispensable." Estelric to Pérez, September 10, 1821.

23. Unsigned draft, Pérez to Liberós, Chihuahua, September 24, 1822, Pinart "Col. mss."

24. De Calabasas Bautismos. In 1935 F. Narciso's remains were moved again, this time to the mortuary chapel at San Xavier where they rest today beneath an inscribed marble slab.

25. Liberós to Pérez, Arizpe, February 3, 1823, enclosing receipt of the same date, Pinart "Col. mss."

26. Circular of the Bishop of Sonora, Culiacán, December 6, 1822, signed by Liberós, Tumacácori, February 9, 1823, AGMS.

27. Liberós to the Bishop, Tumacácori, May 8, 1823, AGMS.

28. Unsigned letter book copy, the Bishop to Liberós, Culiacán, June 6, 1823, AGMS.

29. Liberós to Pérez, Tumacácori, May 21, 1823, Pinart "Col. mss."

30. Unsigned draft, Pérez to Liberós, Janos, August 15, 1823, *ibid.*

31. González to Pérez, Caborca, August 24, 1823, *ibid.*

32. Liberós to Pérez, Calabasas, August 27, 1823, *ibid.*

33. Unsigned draft, Elías to Liberós, San Bernardino, September 7, 1823, *ibid.*

34. Between February 3 and September 14, the date of this document, the principal seems to have been reduced by one hundred and twenty-five pesos.

35. Transfer of debt, Liberós, Tumacácori, September 14, 1823, Pinart "Col. mss."

36. The last letter written by Fr. Ramón from Tumacácori yet come to light was dated November 25, 1825. John L. Kessell, "A Personal Note from Tumacácori, 1825," *Journal of Arizona History*, vol. 6 (1965), pp. 147-51.

37. José María Mendoza to the Governor, Arizpe, June 22, 1833, Archivo Histórico del Gobierno de Sonora, Hermosillo.

THE MAKING OF A MARTYR:
THE YOUNG FRANCISCO GARCÉS

JOHN L. KESSELL

THE would-be chronicler, a Franciscan, his face flushed and taut, sat hunched forward with pen and paper before him. How could he convey the horror of that day? Then words came, in metaphors: all Nature stood still, aghast—the willows withered, the cottonwoods blanched, birds wept and fish knew not where to swim. Even the sun darkened ominously, and the river ran red. On that sweltering day, July 17, 1781, the Yuma ran wild. Yelling as they came, they swept over the two intrusive Spanish settlements, the bastard garrison-missions meant to hold the Yuma Crossing and simultaneously civilize a heathen people. In their wrath they killed, slashed, and burned: they ripped altar linens into loincloths and before they were done with it, they beat to death their missionaries, four Franciscans, one of whom they decapitated.[1]

Later, a ransomed woman captive told how two of the friars died. They had survived the initial onslaught and were leading some women and children away from the scene, when a dying man's plea for confession caused them to turn back. As they rested, the hostiles surprised them. In the woman's words, "The Fathers were just then taking a few swallows of chocolate. The rebels said to them, 'Come on quit drinking that, because we're going to kill you.' Said Father Garcés, 'Let us have a few more sips.' But their persecutors viciously and tyrannically snapped at him, 'No! Quit it.' The Father obeyed, leaving the chocolate, and followed them to his martyrdom."[2]

The death of Father Garcés was tragic, but it was not unexpected. For thirteen years, since his arrival at "heathen and isolated"

51

San Xavier del Bac near Tucson, he had displayed an almost total disregard for his personal safety. All the friars who accepted Pima missions in the wake of the Jesuits' expulsion had orders to acquaint themselves with the environment, with the rivers, mountains, and plains, and most especially with the scattered native peoples.[3] Yet none had complied so wholeheartedly, so recklessly, as Garcés.

With no more baggage than a little jerky and pinole, he had ranged from the Sonoran Desert to the Santa Barbara Channel, from the bottom of Havasupai Canyon to the mesa top at Oraibi.[4] It was he, the Franciscans say, who convinced Captain Juan Bautista de Anza to chance a trail overland from Sonora to California. In Mexico City and Madrid, at councils of state, viceroys and ministers of the king consulted his diaries and his suggestions for expanding and securing the northern frontier. The king himself had commended Father Garcés. But the friar hardly nodded; he really never cared for renown. He was happiest on the trail, anticipating the next crowd of curious heathens, who on most occasions made welcome this eminently down-to-earth, trusting stranger.

FORTY-THREE YEARS before the massacre on the Río Colorado, Antonia Maestro, wife to Juan Garcés, a farmer, was very pregnant. The baby, God willing, would arrive about Easter time that year of 1738, in the second reign of King Philip V. Juan and Antonia, like almost everyone else of their age in the village, were cousins, and had therefore to request a dispensation to wed. They had been married now nearly ten years. Their first son and heir, Juan Francisco Dionisio, was a lad of eight and a half. Josepha Casimira was two. Little Francisca Antonia, who died in infancy, would have been five.[5]

For generations the Garcés and Maestro families had lived in Morata del Conde in the Kingdom of Aragón. A good day's ride south from Zaragoza on the main post road to Madrid brought one to the base of a mountain pass. If here he took the dirt track leading west off through the foothills he soon looked down upon the narrow, cultivated valley of the Río Jalón and the uneven rooftops of Morata. The typical house was a two-story structure of rock or adobe with weathered red-brown tile roof. The animals were sheltered below, a family above. Some two hundred such homes, closely built, pressed in on the plaza and the palace of the Count of Morata. Because most of the villagers worked as tenants on the Count's estate, they owed him periodically a portion of their produce, which included hemp and flax, grain, fruits and vegetables, and sheep. They tended his olive trees and his vines, and pressed from the fruit oil and a hearty red claret.

Holy Week came and went and the midwife still waited on Antonia Maestro. Ten days later, on Wednesday, April 12—the birthdate of her now deceased daughter—she was delivered of her fourth child, a son. Next day, in the parish church of Santa Ana adjoining the Count's palace, the infant was baptized. Rector Pedro Gerónimo Villalba officiated. An uncle, Francisco Garcés, the personal chaplain of the Count and Countess, stood as godfather, as he had for the other children of Juan and Antonia. They called the boy Francisco Thomás for two of his uncles, and Hermenegildo in honor of the Saint whose day it was.[6]

Seventeen months later the Bishop of Tarazona and his retinue arrived in Morata on an official visitation. Among the studiously scrubbed children brought to the church that day for confirmation was Francisco Thomás Hermenegildo Garcés Maestro. On that occasion another uncle, Domingo Garcés, vicar of neighboring Chodes, acted as sponsor. So many men of the Garcés clan were clergymen in fact, that the priesthood had become a family tradition.[7] It was, therefore, not unusual that Domingo Garcés somewhat later arranged to bring up his nephew Francisco in the rectory at Chodes, no more than twenty minutes' walk from Morata.[8]

While the boy was still very young his mother gave birth to four more children, two who died and two who lived.[9] As Francisco grew he was able to help his uncle more and more in the daily business of administering a parish. In effect he was serving an apprenticeship, presumably with time out to join the other boys in fishing for *barbos* beneath the ancient one-span stone bridge or assaulting the castle ruin high on a rocky summit behind the village.

By the time he was fifteen, the religiously inclined second son of Juan and Antonia had resolved to become a friar. He asked that proof of his baptism and confirmation, his untainted Christian lineage, and his good character be remitted through the Bishop of Tarazona to the Franciscans, who, upon consideration of the evidence, deemed Francisco Garcés a likely candidate.

They told him to report to a convento only ten miles from home. Long before he reached it he could see its stone silhouette half way up a mountain side. San Cristóbal de Alpartir, harmonious and gothic, rested partly on the shoulder of the mountain, partly on a terrace of fill held back by massive, buttressed retaining walls. Church and cloister, life-sustaining spring deep in a cave, garden and orchards, all were then enclosed by a lesser wall which descended part way down the mountain. On a clear day the view was endless; you could see the Pyrenees. When a storm closed over the mountain the convento seemed to loose touch with the earth, to drift with the howling wind.

The friars lived there on their own terms, above the bustle of the world, where only the distant, hollow clang of a goat bell or the shout of a peasant in the valley far below disturbed their routine. They observed the stricter rule of the Franciscan reformers known as Recollects, but they were not hermits. They came down from their mountain often, and when the unprosperous village of Alpartir in the valley was without parish priest, the friars filled in.[10]

They instructed him summarily, heard his confession, and then in a moving service they invested Francisco Garcés with the habit of their venerable Order. Another friar who later served in the Sonoran desert at mission San Xavier del Bac recalled the solemn investiture as "a ceremony which would have caused a rock to melt. By the embrace of all the fathers, I became a brother of them all. Just think what that means, to be a brother of so many."[11]

During his years of preparation and study, the young friar demonstrated more tenacity than brilliance. Later a superior would apologize to the viceroy of New Spain for the crude, unpolished manner in which Garcés expressed himself.[12] Yet he survived

Morata del Conde (Jalón), Zaragoza, Spain
Birthplace of Fray Francisco Garcés

Fray Francisco Garcés and Fray Juan Barreneche
Martyrs of the Yuma Massacre, July 1781
Late 18th-century oil painting, artist unknown
Courtesy Museo Municipal, Querétaro, Mexico

classical studies and philosophy. For sacred theology they sent him off to the big convento in Calatayud, over the mountains toward Madrid.

There young scholastics studied long and hard, with customary time off for a hike in the country. To the unsophisticated Garcés, who all his life preferred physical to mental exertion, these breaks were a blessing. Once beyond the city's walls, he would wander off from his classmates. He liked to talk to people who worked the land like his parents. With them he could relax; he did not have to compete. He knew which end of a plow turned the furrow, and they responded to him.

One old peasant truly idolized the youthful Franciscan. When suddenly the old man sickened, he sent a friend into town to the convento with a message urging that Father Garcés come quickly to confess him. "Father Garcés?" repeated a puzzled friar, "we have no Father Garcés here." Soon the messenger was back, insisting. When finally he described the man he sought, the superior realized that he must be referring to Brother Francisco, the theology student, who of course could confess no one.

What was the superior to do? The sick man would have no one but young Garcés. There seemed no alternative but to summon the student and send him along with a qualified confessor. When Brother Francisco assured his ailing friend that he would remain with him after he confessed, the old laborer relented. Some while later he died in Garcés' arms. He had left his worldly goods to the Franciscans, with instructions that a beautiful picture of the Immaculate Conception be painted and hung in the convento as a token of his affection for his young friend, "Father" Garcés.[13]

IN his early twenties now, Francisco Garcés walked again along the highway north over the mountains, more convinced than ever that the scholar's life was not for him. He surely visited home. He was on his way to a Franciscan house hardly two hours beyond, on the outskirts of the bawdy little town of La Almunia de Doña Godina.[14] In the refectory of the convento there was talk of foreign missions.

Two friars from a missionary college in Mexico were at this very time traveling about Spain recruiting, visiting conventos, and writing letters.[15] They told of the brotherhood and the daily regimen in the college and of the critical shortage of missionaries to carry the light of the gospel among ignorant heathens in such strange provinces as Texas. Their words excited young Garcés.

His printed *patente*, or license to join the mission of friars bound for the College of Querétaro, reached him just about Christmas time, 1762. In a month he was on his way, twenty-four years old, eager, and apparently just ordained.[16] He and another friar, who had set out from a mountain-top Recollect house north of Zaragoza, strode south together. Neither man ever returned.

Garcés' traveling companion overshadowed him in every respect. Tall and thin, Juan Crisóstomo Gil de Bernabé was a dozen years older, learned, and extremely pious. A full black beard and curly hair framed his round face; his small eyes shone with zeal. As his junior, Fray Francisco was obliged to join Gil in spiritual exercises all across Spain—Calatayud, Madrid, Córdoba, Sevilla, on the way to the port city of Cádiz.[17] Later, in the missions, Garcés would discover that Gil was as tough as he was pious.

On the road they were expected to make eight leagues a day—something over twenty miles—for which the royal treasury reimbursed their Order, seven copper reales for each friar. To keep missionaries going out to the Indies, the Crown paid for their recruitment, outfitting, and transportation. Gil and Garcés were only two of the twenty-four priests and two lay brothers authorized late in 1761 for the Querétaro college, which since 1749 had received no increment from Spain. In Madrid they met the leader of the mission, slender, persistent Fray Joseph Antonio Bernad, Doctor of Sacred Theology and former professor in the University of Zaragoza. He was just leaving for the south to enlist another half dozen friars and to congregate his recruits. His assistant, Fray Miguel Ramón Pinilla, ruddy veteran of the Texas missions, remained in Madrid to present the final list to the Council of the Indies.[18]

By twos and threes they arrived in Cádiz. Their average age was just under twenty-eight. They came from all parts of Spain.[19]

While they got to know one another, Father Bernad busied himself with last-minute details: confirmation from the postal administrator of the official distance each friar had traveled to get to Cádiz,[20] an insurance policy to cover their baggage against the hazards of the sea,[21] a clearance from the local agent of the Inquisition for the books they were taking with them.[22]

Enough business was transacted in this animated, noisy, littered "Gateway to the Indies" to keep twenty-eight registered notaries and their staffs working long hours. Here the bishop designate of Yucatán, a Dominican, swore that his servants were baptized Christians;[23] there Don Hugo O'Conor, later Commandant Inspector on the northern frontier, signed a power of attorney in favor of Colonel Domingo O'Reilly.[24] They sat in crowded anterooms—Franciscans of rank returning to the Americas after their Order's general chapter in Italy; full-bearded Capuchins bound for New Spain to solicit alms for their missions in Tibet; and artisan Gonzalo Pomar contracting to carve a massive new retablo for the convento where Father Garcés and the others waited to sail.[25]

As they rode at anchor in the harbor of Cádiz His Majesty's twin frigates *Júpiter* and *Mercurio* looked discouragingly small. From stem to stern they measured no more than one hundred and ten feet, about the length of two Greyhound buses parked bumper to bumper. In rank cabins below decks, where upper and lower wooden planks served as berths, there was not room to stand up.[26] Yet port officials had ordered that the friars destined for Querétaro be taken aboard "with all the comfort and decency to which they are entitled." They would be apportioned between the two ships: Father Bernad and one contingent aboard the *Júpiter*, Father Pinilla and the other on the *Mercurio*.[27]

The ships' crews could be seen hoisting specially constructed watertight crates, each bearing the royal coat of arms, up over the side and into the hold. These contained quicksilver for the mines of New Spain. On private account both ships carried bars of iron, crated steel, and barrels of brandy. The friars' gear—ten trunks, eleven boxes, and various small containers of paper, chocolate, and liquor—was divided and stowed on July 23. Next day deck hands took aboard most of the food; on the twenty-sixth, and twenty-seventh, four hundred chickens each ship, sausages, dried codfish, lamb, and veal; and last the mail, royal and private.[28]

As they moved with the tide out of Cádiz harbor on August 1, 1763, the twin frigates looked like walnut shell toys alongside their escort, the seventy-four-gun man-of-war *Guerrero*. The big ship would shepherd them for a week through pirate-infested waters off North Africa, but only as far as the Canary Islands.[29] West of the Canaries lay the open sea, where wind screamed through the rigging, the swells grew mountainous, and the two little frigates lost visual contact.

Shown on the passenger list as "of average build, sparse beard, not overly swarthy, with black eyes and black hair,"[30] Father Garcés was aboard the *Júpiter*, with Father Bernad and eleven others.[31] Most of them lay cramped in their berths, limp and dizzy, raising up only to vomit again. Water and filth sloshed back and forth beneath them. Everything stank. For fear of fire, the ships ovens had been doused—all food was cold. Two friars originally enlisted in the Querétaro mission, who sailed instead for Buenos Aires, tried to explain to their brethren back home what it was like during a storm:

> The ship, as if it were momentarily on the highest part of Mount Lapido, would plunge suddenly to the deepest part of the river, and then as quickly rise to the same height. Each wave, or mountain of water, that broke against the side of the ship made every joint creak, so that with each blow we expected the end. Other waves, reaching as high as the main yards, washed over the ship soaking it from stem to stern. As a result such a quantity of water flooded the decks and hold that we had to operate the pumps without letup. Bunks swam. When one huge blow broke over us only a miracle saved the captain, three of our friars, and two Jesuits from being swept into the sea. All around there were gasps, sighs, and acts of contrition.[32]

The *Júpiter* pitched crazily. Her pumps fought a losing battle; she seemed on the point of foundering. To lighten her, the captain, a scrappy Basque career officer, yelled for the sailors to jettison eight cannon. Later, the Viceroy of New Spain would complain that Captain Calvo failed to report to him the loss of His Majesty's ordnance and therefore deserved censure. Calvo retorted almost insolently that he would file his report not with the Viceroy but with the navy. The case reached Spain, where the Secretary of State suggested to the Minister of the Navy that the captain be reprimanded for his *tono de independencia*.[33] Yet he had saved his ship. In mid-September, battered and sodden, the *Júpiter* raised Puerto Rico.[34]

Twenty-seven days she lay in a cove on the island's northwest coast for fear of sailing during the equinox, which, as any sailor knew, was folly. On November 8, one hundred days out of Cádiz, the *Júpiter* cast anchor in Veracruz harbor. The following day the friars disembarked praising God. Two of them, seriously ill, were sent inland immediately, while the rest cleared customs.[35] The royal mail sped ahead to Mexico City by fast rider. With a scowl the viceroy read the final text of the peace treaty with Great Britain; and he noted a royal order calling for the *Júpiter* and the *Mercurio,* once unloaded and reoutfitted, to sail without delay for Havana.[36] But where was the *Mercurio?*

About the time Garcés and his dozen companions reached Querétaro, a coastal trader put in at Veracruz with news of a shipwreck. The *Mercurio,* after repairs in Cuba, had sailed on, gambling against the jinx of the equinox. What was left of her still clung to a reef off the windward coast of Yucatán. Hastily officials at Veracruz got together a salvage team: every effort must be made to save His Majesty's quicksilver.[37] Later it was learned, incidentally, that the friars aboard had survived. One of them, Father Gil, was a hero.[38]

At the college Francisco Garcés was well enough liked though, as one of the older friars put it, "this Father is very simple and artless."[39] He neither smoked nor used snuff, and in the convento he never said much. Because he was not yet old enough to confess women, Fray Francisco took to confessing children, which some of his brethren thought foolish, though fitting enough for him. Soon word of this plain, warmhearted new friar spread through the plazas and streets of the city. Children flocked to the cloister. People who did not know his name, called him simply the Children's Padre.[40]

WHEN the summons came for Franciscans to replace the banished Jesuits in Sonora, Garcés was among the first to volunteer. He had come to America to serve among heathens. "I am glad," he wrote from the most distant mission, "that I have no Spaniards in my care. . . . There are plenty of Indians. I like them and they like me."[41] He saw them as human beings, underprivileged and earthy perhaps, but deserving—like the peasants of Spain and the children of Querétaro—and he approached them as such. They laughed as he struggled to learn their language, and he laughed too.

"I am very content in this wilderness," he reported to the Governor of Sonora, "even anticipating the sicknesses and other trials that may ruin me."[42] He was a born missionary. No one paid him greater tribute, unintentionally, than squat, balding Fray Pedro Font, his companion on the *Júpiter* and later on the trail, and as urbane as Garcés was rustic:

> Father Garcés is so well suited to get along with the Indians and go among them that he appears to be but an Indian himself. Like the Indians he is impassive in everything. He sits with them in the circle, or at night around the fire, with his legs crossed. There he will sit musing two or three hours or more, oblivious to all else, talking with much serenity and deliberation. And though the foods of the Indians are as nasty and dirty as those outlandish people themselves, the father eats them with great gusto, and says that they are good for the stomach, and delicious. In short, God has created him, as I see it, solely for the purpose of seeking out these unhappy, ignorant, and rustic people.[43]

That these same heathens would someday destroy him would not have dissuaded the friar from Aragón. He foresaw trouble with the Yuma, but he accepted the challenge. So long as they spared his life he would strive in manly imitation of Christ to redeem their souls. If they rose up and killed him, heaven would be his reward. How could he lose? As the chronicler said, "God chose him, and that is the sum of it."[44]

FR. JOSEPH ANTONIO BERNAD,

de la Regular Obſervancia de N.S.P.S.Fran-
ciſco , Predicador Apoſtolico , Doctor en
Sagrada Theologìa , Ex-Guardian del Colegio de Propaganda Fide de la S. Cruz de la
Ciudad de Santiago de Queretaro en las Indias Occidentales , y actual Comiſſario de la
Miſsion del miſmo, &c. Al *Rr. Fran. Garcia Theologo
de la Sᵗa. Prov. de Aragon* ſalud , y paz en N. S. Jeſu-
Chriſto.

POR quanto el Rey nueſtro Señor (que Dios guarde) movido de ſu
acoſtumbrada piedad , y catholico zelo de la Converſion de las Almas , ſe hà dignado conceder à dicho Colegio Apoſtolico una Miſ-
ſion de veinte y quatro Religioſos Sacerdotes; para cuya admiſsion,
y conduccion me tiene dicho Colegio conferidos ſus Poderes , y N. Rmo. P.
Fr. Mathias de Velaſco , Lector Jubilado , Theologo de ſu Mageſtad en la
Real Junta de la Immaculada Concepcion , Padre de las Santas Provincias de
Caſtilla , y de los Angeles , y Comiſſario General de todas las de las Indias,
ſu bendicion , y licencia , para elegir , juntar , y conducir dichos Religioſos
al referido Colegio , à fin de que ſe emplèen en la Converſion de los Infieles
à nueſtra Santa Fè Catholica , y reduccion de los pecadores à verdadera pe-
nitencia , baxo la diſpoſicion , y obediencia de los Prelados de dicho Colegio:
Por tanto , haviendoſe movido V.A. mediante eſta noticia, y pedidome, que
le reciba en dicha Miſsion , deſeoſo de ſacrificarſe en tan ſanto empleo , y
conſtandome , como me conſta , de la virtud , literatura , y demàs prendas
neceſſarias , que para ello ſe requieren , y concurren en V.A. deſde luego,
por eſta , le admito. Y para que V.A. conſiga el fin de ſus ſantos deſeos,
haviendo recibido eſta Patente, firmada de mi mano , la preſentarà al R. P.
Guardian de eſſe Convento , y tomada ſu ſanta bendicion , con teſtimonio,
que haga fè del dia en que partiere, (aviſando antes al M. R. P. Provincial de
eſſa Santa Provincia , ſin eſperar ſu reſpueſta) paſſarà V.A. al Puerto de Ca-
diz , donde eſtarà à la obediencia del M. R. P. Vice-Comiſſario de Indias; lo
qual ningun inferior à N. Rmo. podrà impedir à V.A. ſó pena de Excomu-
nion mayor *ipſo facto incurrenda* , y demàs que preſcriben las Bulas de
NN. SS. PP. Adriano VI. Innocencio XI. y ultimamente de N. SS. P. Clemente XIII. (que Dios proſpère) en ſu Bula , que empieza : *Paſtoralis officii*,
dada en Roma en 30. de Agoſto de 1760. Y para que V.A. no carezca de
merito en ſu viage, le impongo el de la ſanta obediencia; y ſuplico con el
mayor rendimiento à los RR. PP. Guardianes de los Conventos , por donde
V.A. tranſitare , que le reciban benigna , y caritativamente , como à hijo
de obediencia. Dada en *Queretaro en 15 de Dize. de 1762.*

Fr. Joseph Antᵒ Bernad
Comiss. de Miss.

*Parte el contenido en esta Comision de San Rosario de la villa
de los Almurios a Valore, y entes de Enero del 1763.*

Jh. Franco Dalbal Ex-Diff. y Secret.

Patente, December 15, 1762. Courtesy Archivo General de Indias, Sevilla, Spain.

NOTES

1. Fray Francisco Antonio Barbastro to Fray [Juan] Agustín [de] Morfi, Tubutama, September 25, 1781, Biblioteca Nacional, México, Archivo Franciscano, New Mexico documents, leg. 10, no. 63. Later, in his unpublished history of the Franciscan missions of Sonora, Barbastro included a less metaphorical but more detailed description of the Yuma Massacre. "Compendio, de lo mas notable, que han trabajado en Sonora los hijos del Colegio de la Santa Cruz . . . desde el año de 1768 hasta el de 1783," Babiácora, September 10, 1788, selected documents relating to Pimería Alta, mainly 1767-1800, from the Fr. Marcellino da Civezza Collection, Pontificio Ateneo Antoniano, Roma (Civ. Col.), 202.35, microfilm 305, University of Arizona Library. When describing the Sonora missions the resident chronicler of the College of Querétaro followed Barbastro's account closely. Juan Domingo Arricivita, *Crónica seráfica y apostólica del Colegio de Propaganda Fide de la Santa Cruz de Querétaro en la Nueva España*, segunda parte (México, 1792), pp. 504-509 *et passim*.

2. María Ana Montiel to Barbastro, Altar, December 21, 1785, Civ. Col., 202.32.

3. "Instrucciones del Venerable Discretorio a los Padres de Sonora, para govierno suio, y de las Missiones," Querétaro, August 4, 1767; K, no. 3, leg. 14, Archivo del Colegio de la Santa Cruz de Querétaro (SCQ), housed at present in the Convento Franciscano, Celaya, México; typescript, Mission San Xavier del Bac, Tucson.

4. Elliot Coues, ed. and trans., *On the Trail of A Spanish Pioneer, the Diary and Itinerary of Francisco Garcés (Missionary Priest) in His Travels through Sonora, Arizona, and California, 1775-1776*, 2 vols. (New York, 1900). Another copy of the 1775-1776 diary, edited by John Galvin, has appeared elegantly as *A Record of Travels in Arizona and California, 1775-1776* (San Francisco, 1967); and in Spanish more humbly as *Diario de exploraciones en Arizona y California en los años de 1775 y 1776* (México, 1968). For translations of Garcés' 1774-1775 diaries, see Herbert E. Bolton, *Anza's California Expeditions*, 5 vols. (Berkeley, 1930; reprint, New York, 1965), vol. 2, pp. 307-92.

5. "Quinque Libris de la Iglesia Parrochial de Morata de el Conde . . . comienza en el año de el Señor de 1732," Archivo Parroquial, Morata del Jalón (changed from Conde) (Zaragoza), Spain.

6. *Ibid.* The chronicler Arricivita saw prophetic aptness in Garcés' three given names: They represented the parts "he enacted in life and in death, for he was a son of Saint Francis professing his Rule; he emulated Saint

Thomas, going out to the Indies to proclaim the gospel; and he died like Saint Hermenegild, giving up his life for Jesus Christ." *Crónica seráfica*, p. 540.

7. Another uncle, Pedro Garcés, by 1740 had succeeded Villalba as rector of the parish of Morata. The confirmation took place on October 2, 1739. "Quinque Libris."

8. Arricivita says that the boy's parents, seeing his inclination toward things religious, entrusted his upbringing to an uncle, Mosén Domingo Garcés, parish priest of Morata. *Crónica seráfica*, p. 540. Domingo Garcés was vicar of Chodes, a smaller village with distinctive round plaza, across the river a kilometer distant. "Quinque Libris." Mosén was not a given name but a title commonly used by clergymen in Aragón.

9. They were: Isabel Antonia, b. July 2, 1740, d. May 4, 1742; Miguel Mariano, b. September 3, 1742, d. September 27, 1742; Miguel, b. July 21, 1743; Theresa Juaquina Thomasa, b. October 16, 1746. "Quinque Libris."

10. The convento of San Cristóbal de Alpartir is today a stately, abandoned ruin. In the village of Alpartir documents survive that tell of the relationship between village and convento. Archivo Parroquial, Alpartir (Zaragoza), Spain.

11. [Maynard Geiger, O.F.M.], "A Voice from San Xavier del Bac (1802-1805)," *Provincial Annals* (Franciscan Province of Santa Barbara), vol. 16 (1953), p. 7. The voice was that of Fray Ignacio José Ramírez.

12. Fray Romualdo Cartagena to Antonio María Bucareli, Colegio de la Santa Cruz de Querétaro, January 29, 1773, certified copy, México, April 26, 1773, Archivo General de Indias, Sevilla, Spain (AGI), Audiencia de Guadalajara, 513; translated in Bolton, *Anza's California Expeditions*, vol. 5, p. 55.

13. Arricivita, *Crónica seráfica*, pp. 540-41, following Barbastro, "Compendio."

14. The church of San Lorenzo de la Almunia still stands. Since its secularization it has been used as a fort, a factory, and a warehouse. In the parish church of La Almunia are preserved a number of beautifully illuminated choir books made by the friars of the convento during the 1760's.

15. Fray José Antonio Bernad to the Guardián del Colegio-Seminario de Herbón, Madrid, November 17, 1762, and Fray Miguel Ramón Pinilla to Fray Antonio Estévez, Madrid, February 15, 1763, *Archivo Ibero-Americano*, vol. 3 (1915), pp. 68-73.

16. Garcés' patente was dated December 15, 1762. At the bottom of the document, the superior of the convento, Fray Francisco del Leal, certified that the missionary-to-be left La Almunia on January 25, 1763. AGI, Contratación, 5545A.

17. Gil's physical description is based on the *despacho de embarcación,* Cádiz, July 18, 1763, *ibid.* Arricivita, *Crónica seráfica,* pp. 516, 541.

18. AGI, Contratación, 5545A.

19. Evidently Father Bernad planned to congregate some of them first in Sanlúcar de Barrameda. By summer, however, they were all in Cádiz where they appeared before the port authorities for clearance to embark. *Ibid.*

20. *Ibid.*

21. Riesgo, Registro 19, Mathias Rodríguez, 1763, Archivo de Protocolos Notariales, Cádiz, Spain (APNC).

22. Licencia, Cádiz, July 12, 1763, AGI, Contratación, 1566.

23. Licencia para embarcarse a favor de Fray Antonio Alcalde, Cádiz, January 31, 1763, AGI, Contratación, 5506.

24. Poder general, Registro 12, Francisco Hanecast, 1763, APNC.

25. AGI, Contratación, 5506. Contrato de obra, Registro 19, APNC.

26. The documents refer to the two ships as twin *fragatillas,* or small frigates. They mounted twenty guns each, and were sailed by a crew of about a hundred. The *Júpiter,* third of that name, was built in Cádiz by Mullón. Launched in 1753, it was decommissioned at the same port in 1770. "Lista alfabético de buques a. e.," Museo Naval, Madrid, Spain. The *Mercurio* does not appear on this list.

27. AGI, Contratación, 5545A.

28. Ramo de azogues, 1761-67, AGI, Audiencia de México, 2199, Contratación, 1565-66.

29. Julián de Arriaga to the Marqués del Real Tesoro, Madrid, August 9, 1763, *et al.,* AGI, Juzgado de Arribadas, 43.

30. Physically Garcés was a very average Joe. It does nothing for his story to make him "a well nigh perfect physical specimen, tall, well-formed, of iron frame, and absolutely fearless." Raymund F. Wood, "Francisco Garcés, Explorer of Southern California," *Southern California Quarterly,* vol. 51 (1969), p. 188.

31. Despacho de embarcación, Cádiz, July 18, 1763, AGI, Contratación, 5545A. Four of the original recruits did not sail with the mission.

32. Fray Andrés Antonio Martínez and Fray Juan José de Castro to the Guardián del Colegio de Herbón, Buenos Aires, July 31, 1764, in Ramón F. Blanco, O.F.M., *Apuntes históricos sobre el Colegio de Misioneros de Herbón de la Esclarecida Orden de S. Francisco* (Lugo, 1925), p. 247.

33. Marqués de Cruillas to Arriaga, México, November 24, 1763; Calvo to Cruillas, Vera Cruz, November 30, 1763, certified copy, México, April 8, 1764, *et al.,* AGI, Audiencia de México, 1507. Calvo, satisfacción a los cargos, October 19, 1764, Archivo General de Simancas, Spain, Marina, 25.

34. On September 17, 1763, officials in Puerto Rico signed a receipt

for mail put ashore from the *Júpiter* at La Aguada de San Francisco. AGI, Contratación, 1566.

35. Cruillas to Arriaga, México, November 11, 1763, no. 29, AGI, Audiencia de México, 1507. The two sick friars were Fathers Antonio Ramos and Henrique Echaso de Acedo. N, leg. 2, no. 8, SCQ; excerpts at the Academy of American Franciscan History, Washington, D.C.

36. [Arriaga] to Cruillas, Madrid, July 7, 1763, and Cruillas to Arriaga, México, November 11, 1763, no. 31, AGI, Audiencia de México, 1507.

37. Cruillas to Arriaga, México, January 2, 1764, *ibid.*

38. Arricivita, *Crónica seráfica*, p. 517.

39. Cartagena to Bucareli, January 29, 1773.

40. Arricivita, *Crónica seráfica*, pp. 541-42. Barbastro, "Compendio."

41. Garcés to Fray Sebastián Flores, San Xavier del Bac, August 13, 1768, Civ. Col., 201:24.

42. Garcés to Juan de Pineda, San Xavier del Bac, July 29, 1768, printed in *Documentos para la historia de México*, Cuarta Série, vol. 2 (México, 1856), pp. 367-70.

43. Diario que formó el P. Predicador Apostolico Fr. Pedro Font . . . en el viage que hizo a Monterey; translated in Bolton, *Anza's California Expeditions*, vol. 4, p. 121.

44. Barbastro, "Compendio."

CAMPAIGNING ON THE UPPER GILA, 1756

JOHN L. KESSELL

Just west of the Continental Divide, where the headwaters of the Río Gila break out of the imposing Sierra de Mogollón, the two commanders joined forces. Captain Bernardo Antonio de Bustamante y Tagle, trail-dusty after the long ride from Chihuahua, reined up with sixty presidial regulars and as many tough Tarahumara Indian archers. From Sonora, tracking hostiles en route, Captain Gabriel Antonio de Vildósola, fifty regulars, one hundred and forty Ópata Indian auxiliaries, a party of armed settlers, and a Jesuit chaplain had gauged their march to arrive at the rendezvous by the appointed day, November 24, 1756.

Over three hundred fighting men in all, they made their base camp on the shallow Gila near present-day Cliff, New Mexico, with feed, wood, and water close by. This site in the pleasant, unpeopled valley, with its meandering river and its cottonwoods now all but bare, they knew as Todos Santos. The assembled regulars, whose irregular uniforms bore the stamp of frontier cavalry, had been recruited for this joint campaign from Guajoquilla, Agua Nueva, and Janos in Nueva Vizcaya, and Fronteras and Terrenate in Sonora, so that no one garrison on the cordon was left severely undermanned. These were *soldados de cuera*, troops born in the saddle who took their name from the heavy, sleeveless, multi-layer leather coats they wore, the best of which were made in New Mexico of buckskin. For additional protection they carried oval bull-hide shields. When fully armed the frontier horse soldier wielded a steel-tipped lance, a short sword for close quarters, a brace of pistols, and a regulation, muzzle-loading musket, or *escopeta*, which he was reluctant to fire. So long as a soldier could brandish his loaded musket, even the bravest Apache had respect for him. Once he fired however, any of his adversaries who survived was capable of launching a deadly barrage of arrows while he reloaded. Hence the Indian auxiliaries, outnumbering the presidials almost two to one, Tarahumara and Ópata who could match the Apache arrow for arrow.[1]

The forty-eight-year-old Bustamante, ranking officer of the combined expedition, owed his position more to blood than merit. A peninsular Spaniard and relative of New Mexico Governor Juan Domingo Bustamante, he had served without apparent distinction as lieutenant of the Santa Fe garrison and as lieutenant governor of the province. He had supervised the reestablishment of Sandía pueblo, brought in a few trespassing Frenchmen, and tried vainly to keep the Navajo at Cebolleta and Encinal.[2] In 1750 when Comanche ambushed a large hunting party of Pecos Indians killing a hundred and fifty of them, then ambushed the Spaniards sent out in response killing ten of them, Bustamante at the head of seven hundred men had ridden forth to punish the barbarians. The following account of what happened to don Bernardo while camped on the Arkansas River is based upon a sarcastic report by two Franciscans, obviously no admirers of the lieutenant governor.

Early one morning as the commander lay in bed *como si estubiera a el lado de su muger* (as if he were at his wife's side) a Comanche war party descended on the sleeping camp and ran off 1,131 horses. On pain of death Bustamante forbade pursuit, and instead returned to Santa Fe bragging of a victory. Almost on his heels came the Comanche to barter. Brazenly these Indians poked fun at the Spaniards and told how a mere ten warriors and twenty women had done the deed![3]

Shortly thereafter don Bernardo left New Mexico to assume command at Cerro Gordo in Nueva Vizcaya.[4] When that presidio was deactivated he received orders to build a new one for a sixty-man mobile company at Guajoquilla, today's Ciudad Jiménez in southern Chihuahua.[5] As far south as his garrison was—nearly five hundred miles from Todos Santos—Captain Bustamante had to reckon with the Gila Apache. To halt their frequent incursions he urged construction of another presidio, to plug the gap between El Paso and Janos, thereby preventing "numerous outrages of robbery and killing."[6] The other alternative was to carry the message of Spanish steel to the very lairs of the enemy. For that purpose, don Bernardo had ridden to the Gila in 1756.

His second-in-command, Captain Gabriel de Vildósola of Fronteras, enjoyed all the advantages of blood and station that Bustamante did, but he had talent too. Son of a hot-headed ex-governor of Sonora, the thirty-four-year-old Basque had earned a considerable reputation as an Indian fighter. He was in fact soon to be hailed "scourge of the Apache, hero of the entire province, and shining ornament of the Spanish military."[7] He may have brought with him to the Gila his young protégé, a fatherless lad by the name of Juan Bautista de Anza.

Though Bancroft claimed for it "the first definitely recorded exploration of the region,"[8] the Bustamante-Vildósola expedition was not without precedent. Nine years earlier the Viceroy Conde de Revillagigedo had ordered a massive general campaign to crush once and for all the Gila Apache and their confederates, by which he meant all the hostiles—Western Apache, Yavapai, and others— who lived in and raided from the so-called Apachería, an immense crescent of territory stretching from the middle Río Grande west to the lower Colorado. Until the Spanish military cleared out this great rats' nest, the king was wasting his cédulas when he called for colonization on the Gila and the Colorado, for reconquest of the apostate Hopi pueblos, and for a highway of communications between New Mexico and Sonora. On raid after raid hostile bands descended to steal and burn, then vanished into the fastness of their wild country; only to come again the next season, as one contemporary put it, "like the waves of the sea."[9]

The 1747 campaign was meant to make the frontier safe for expansion. The viceroy's goal of perhaps a thousand men in the field required the cooperative effort of three provinces and five presidios—Santa Fe, El Paso, Janos, Fronteras, and Terrenate. So strongly did he feel about the campaign that he decreed a fine of six thousand pesos (about ten years' salary) as well as perpetual loss of rank for any presidial captain who defaulted; and for the governor of New Mexico an eight-thousand-peso fine and dismissal, or worse. As commander-in-chief he named the senior captain, Alonso Victores Rubí de Celis of El Paso, and as principal consultant, or *comisario*, for the campaign the prominent and controversial New Mexico friar Father Juan Miguel Menchero.

This was to be an all-out effort. Indicative were the viceroy's instructions to the captain at Terrenate: recruit as many Indian auxiliaries as you can, not only Upper Pima, but also Sobaípuri, Pápago, Cocomaricopa, Níxora, and all other tribes who hate Apache. The whole frontier was asked to contribute provisions. As usual the viceroy enjoined participants to offer the hostiles a chance to accept the Faith and settle down; if they refused—as he knew they would—then give them no quarter, have at them *a sangre y fuego*.[10]

At first the strategy called for a simultaneous invasion of the Apachería from all sides with the various contingents joining forces deep in enemy territory. But when the governor of New Mexico, Joaquín Codallos y Rabal, defaulted, the original plan of attack was scrapped. Codallos, who earlier had assured the viceroy "I shall do blindly all that is ordered of me,"[11] suddenly shifted priorities when Ute and "Chaguago" Indians savagely attacked Abiquiú. He simply did not have at his disposal the military resources to cope with the northern crisis and at the same time take part in the viceroy's pet project. Therefore, instead of dispatching thirty soldiers, forty settlers, and sixty Indians to rendezvous with Captain Rubí de Celis on the Mimbres River September 30, Governor Codallos girded against the northern raiders and set about gathering testimony to calm an angry viceroy.[12]

With the New Mexico contingent out of the picture, the remaining four commands combined for a march in force through the Apachería. In the grumbling, swearing, laughing expeditionary force of seven hundred rode a young militia captain from El Paso, later colonial New Mexico's foremost cartographer. As engineer, Bernardo de Miera y Pacheco was charged with mapping their route.[13] Though neither the map nor any of the campaign journals demanded by the viceroy has come to light, it is possible from other contemporary sources, sketchy though they are, to piece together the expedition's futile operations.

Provisioned for a four-month campaign, they advanced up the Río Grande to the Jornada del Muerto and from there struck west for the Río Mimbres. Herding well over a thousand remounts, and strung out as they skirted the mountains, they gave clamorous notice of their presence. From the Mimbres Valley the expedition crossed over to the Gila, probably passing by the future site of Silver City. Small detachments operating from the main body charged into canyons and assaulted rocky summits in an effort to trap hostile bands. Although no body counts are available, they evidently took some captives.[14]

Descending the Gila into present-day Arizona they came upon and named the Río San Francisco. Following its course upstream the Spaniards and their mixed Indian allies campaigned north across the Mogollón Plateau. Now in the very heart of hostile territory, the seven hundred found no one to punish. The Apache, no fools, had temporarily vacated their haunts and were raiding the frontier with impunity.[15]

The big expedition of 1747 had a secondary objective: to explore approaches to the provinces of Zuñi and Hopi. Ever since the Great Revolt of 1680 the Hopi had thumbed their noses at Spanish domination. Though most Spaniards took for granted their eventual reconquest, a question of religious jurisdiction had arisen. Who would actually lead these wayward souls back to the lap of the Holy Mother Church, the Jesuits of Sonora or the Franciscans of New Mexico? Father Menchero, representing the latter, meant to insure a victory for the friars. When the weary column wound down out of the mountains onto the North Plains in the vicinity of Zuñi Salt Lake, no one knew just where they were. Menchero urged them on. When they came to a trail the irrepressible Franciscan volunteered to reconnoiter it with the Captain of Fronteras and a small detachment. It led to Ácoma. Doubling back with Ácoma and Laguna auxiliaries to guide them, Menchero and company rejoined the others and all moved on to Zuñi.[16]

There they found a large delegation of Hopi *principales* waiting for them. Having got word that Spaniards were coming, perhaps to build presidios in Hopi territory, these representatives had hastened to Zuñi to prostrate themselves before Captain Rubí de Celis and the friars "promising to do whatever was desired of them, and giving assurance that already they were completely loyal, even as before their rebellion."[17] The Hopi performance was convincing, but the weather proved even more so. Fierce cold and heavy snows caused Rubí de Celis to cancel the proposed excursion to Hopi.[18] At Zuñi he mustered out his Pima auxiliaries who made a beeline south for their desert thereby demonstrating the feasibility of a direct route between New Mexico and Sonora.[19] He then ordered the rest of the expedition eastward toward the Río Grande. The Hopi went home smug.

The weather did not improve. Drifting snow impeded the progress of men and horses. By early December the half-frozen hundreds had reached the Río Grande near Albuquerque. Their only thoughts were of home. At this juncture Governor Codallos, having met the northern challenge, decided to join the general campaign. In a selfish effort to favorably impress the viceroy he sent his lieutenant governor, the trusty Bernardo de Bustamante, and a hundred and fifty-five men slogging through snow and ice to catch up with Rubí de Celis.[20] At Sevilleta, north of Socorro, they did. Rubí had absolutely no use for them then, and he told them so. Back in Santa Fe Bustamante reported that despite the foul weather he had, both going and coming, observed military regulations "with vanguard and rear guard and the remounts always close, night and day, with the necessary men for their protection and a change of pickets each of the four watches."[21]

The costly, little-known general offensive of 1747, "Father Menchero's campaign" as the people called it, had kept an estimated seven hundred men in the field for three months and a thousand miles. Evidently the first large-scale, concerted effort against the Western Apache—a quarter century before the Provincias Internas—the 1747 campaign has been virtually ignored, probably because it failed so miserably.

"They returned," wrote one high-ranking Jesuit bitterly, "without having gained a single advantage."[22] The harassed missionaries of Sonora, who had contributed Indian auxiliaries, horses, provisions, and money, complained that the Apache raiders were now bolder than ever. In 1754 the departing governor of Nueva Vizcaya warned his successor, "Today one cannot venture beyond the outskirts of Chihuahua without danger of enemy attack."[23] The bishop of Durango, whose immense diocese included the beleaguered northwest, reported his revenues from tithes down fifty per cent on account of Indian depredations.[24]

SOME OF THE MEN who camped at Todos Santos with Captains Bustamante and Vildósola late in November of 1756 were veterans of Father Menchero's campaign. They had no illusions about the enemy. This time there was no talk of crushing the Gila Apache at one blow. They would search out and destroy hostiles wherever they found them, from the Gila Wilderness west to the San Simón Valley, in the hope that, as the Jesuit chaplain put it, "through punishment, the enemy's boldness will be checked." In other words, an eye for an eye.

The reports Bustamante and Vildósola submitted to headquarters, that is to the governors of Nueva Vizcaya and Sonora, have been lost or buried in the archives.[25] We have only the chaplain's account. Not the routine daily log of a military man, the observations of Father Bartolomé Sáenz lack the continuity that would permit a precise camp-by-camp retracing of the expedition's exact route. Yet he included much that would not have concerned a soldier.

Addressing himself to a Jesuit superior in Mexico City, Father Sáenz tried to provide information that would prove useful "should the reduction of this bellicose Apache nation ever be achieved." Of more interest to him than tallying Apache Indians killed or captured was the countryside itself, the varied scene of cactus and piñon pine, of impassable gorge and saline flat. He stressed the region's potential, limited though it was, and told of likely mission sites, of mesquite beans and mescal, of the fish in the Gila and the beaver on its banks. He commented on the Apache way of life and on the visible remains of earlier occupation. He was fascinated by a doll found in the debris of an Apache camp and by stone ruins and painted potsherds. As his horse sweated and stumbled under him he pondered the origin of the ancients who had built along the Gila. And he, like so many travelers after him, was led to speculate. Finally, with tongue in cheek, he told how the Sierra de Mogollón got its name.

For the swarthy, pock-marked, forty-one-year-old Father Sáenz, a Spaniard by birth, life on the frontier had been a constant trial. Some eight years earlier he had arrived at the notorious mission of Caborca in the Sonoran Desert. Try as he might he could not win the confidence of the fickle natives. Day after day they opposed him, till finally he broke under the strain and begged to be recalled. His superiors considered the case, then entrusted him to the good-natured missionary at Guevavi near present-day Nogales, Arizona, for occupational therapy. A few months later, a new man, he accepted the mission of Cuquiárachi south of today's Douglas.[26] There, with the presidials at Fronteras as neighbors and with his Ópata charges seemingly content, Father Sáenz might have looked forward to an uneventful ministry—but for the Gila Apache.

Time and again they swept down to terrorize his mission. One San Juan's Day eve four of his Ópata were outside sawing boards for a new cart. Before they knew it, the Apache had them: three died, one got away.[27] On the trail to Todos Santos in 1756, Bartolomé Sáenz no longer needed therapy. By this time, he was a veteran.

For weeks they chased Apache on the upper Gila. Then in column they swung south to San Simón. Ahead in the distance loomed the dark and rocky Sierra de Chiricahua, traditional gathering place of Apache raiders. Looking over their fatigued

men and spent horses, the captains decided against an assault. Instead they declared the campaign at an end, parted company, and rode for their respective presidios with what captives and booty they had. The final tally as recorded by the governor of Sonora credited the campaign with thirty braves killed, two brought back alive, and thirty-seven women and children captured,[28] which totals, incidentally, do not square with those of Father Sáenz. Soon Apache spokesmen appeared to negotiate the usual exchanges. To ransom their dependents, the hostiles agreed to deliver up "their wretched Christian captives who wail in barbarous confinement under their crude mistreatment."[29]

The 1756 Bustamante-Vildósola expedition killed some Apache braves, giving the others something to think about and something to avenge; it brought back Apache women and children for use as slaves or for barter; it proved that Spaniards were men; but as a deterrent to future Apache raiding, it, like Father Menchero's campaign, failed notably. "During November and December . . . 1756," wrote Father Sáenz' superiors in their annual report to Rome,

> the Captain of Fronteras penetrated to the most remote places of these Apache, taking many prisoners and leaving not a few of the enemy dead . . . a demanding journey that covered nearly two hundred leagues [over five hundred miles]. With all this, who would have believed it? Hardly had he returned to his presidio when the Apache returned to their attacks on our missions. Although the same captain successfully drove them back again . . . they caused several deaths, committed depredations, stole whatever they found, and everywhere spread new though familiar terror and sudden dread.[30]

A year later Chaplain Sáenz rode again with Captain Vildósola and Lieutenant Anza on an arduous mid-summer campaign to and beyond the Gila. Again they took captives. When the Jesuit questioned these Apache about the dark-colored blankets and buffalo robes they had in their possession, he was made to understand that these trade items had come from a sheep-raising people seven days to the north. They must mean the Hopi, reasoned Sáenz, who proceeded in his report to outline a scheme whereby Jesuit chaplains operating from the south with military expeditions might peacefully penetrate and lure back to the Church the apostate Hopi pueblos.[31] That the king and the Jesuit hierarchy had already conceded the spiritual reconquest of the Hopi to the Franciscans of New Mexico had not apparently impressed Bartolomé Sáenz.

The Gila Apache kept coming. Father Sáenz grew increasingly critical of the inadequate protection afforded his mission by his neighbor Captain Vildósola.[32] The retaliatory expeditions seemed only to provoke the Apache further. A bolder solution was needed. Bishop Pedro Tamarón y Romeral of Durango, reviving the one-mighty-blow strategy of 1747, conceived of a great pincers movement that would encompass the entire Apachería. The crux of the bishop's proposal was an invasion of infantrymen—three to four thousand of them!—supported by presidial cavalry. Judged financially and militarily unfeasible, the plan did provide a theoretical precedent for later general campaigns.[33] New Mexico map maker Bernardo de Miera y Pacheco, who looked upon the hostile "Province of Gila" as Spain's one great obstacle to expansion north and northwest, offered an alternative. Instead of hit-or-miss expeditions from without, he called for the establishment of three heavily garrisoned settlements within—one in the valley of San Pedro de Alcántara,[34] apparently in the vicinity of Todos Santos; a second on the Río Mimbres; and a third on the Río Grande opposite the paraje of San Pascual some forty-five miles north of today's Truth or Consequences.[35] Miera's plan too was deemed impracticable.

By the late 1780's a partially effective solution had been put into effect. It involved three proven elements: 1) Indian diplomacy designed to break up key hostile alliances—Gila Apache and Navajo, for example—and set enemy against enemy; 2) a large-scale program of welfare and trade concessions to reward and render dependent those bands who chose to ally with the Spaniards or settle down; and 3) relentless military pursuit of unregenerates. The Western Apache were in a sense controlled,[36] and for a generation the frontier breathed easier. But it proved only a respite. In the welter of Independence, Mexico killed the dole and that killed the peace. When the U.S. Army marched in at mid-century, the region was as much a lair for Apache marauders as it had been a hundred years earlier.

It is not surprising that the soldiers in blue believed themselves the first campaigners on the Río Gila, or that they considered their occasional victories uniquely heroic.[37] Colonels Dixon S. Miles and W. W. Loring had never heard of Captains Bustamante and Vildósola.[38] They were as ignorant of their Spanish predecessors as was James Ohio Pattie, that footloose braggart who during the mid-1820's trapped beaver on the upper Gila, "a river," in his words, "never before explored by white people."[39]

That would have amused Bartolomé Sáenz, who observed the same animal on the same river a long time before.

FATHER SÁENZ' superiors filed his brief chronicle in the central archive of the Jesuit Province of New Spain in Mexico City. In 1767 with the summary expulsion of that Order, the Sáenz document and hundreds more bearing upon the northern missions passed to the Franciscans. Late in the century the chaplain's account was copied and included in the so-called "Memorias de Nueva España," a monumental collection sent to Spain as documentation for a proposed general history of the Indies. Today the triplicate set of the Memorias is preserved in Mexico City as the first thirty-two volumes of the Archivo General's Sección de Historia.

In the case of the Sáenz document the eighteenth-century copyist not only left out several lines and altered others, but he also mistranscribed the author's name—Father Sáenz became Father Sánchez. This copy later appeared in print in *Documentos para la historia de México*, Cuarta Série, tomo 1 (México, 1856), pp. 88-94, inaccuracies and all. Hubert Howe Bancroft, following the *Documentos* version, devoted a paragraph and a long footnote (*North Mexican States*, vol. 1, p. 557) to the Bustamante-Vildósola expedition, citing as his source Father Bartolomé Sánchez.

Meanwhile, the Mexican government had suppressed religious houses and confiscated their archives. Most of the material seized wound up in the newly created Biblioteca Nacional, where the original of Father Sáenz' report remains today, part of the immensely rich manuscript division.[40]

THE CHAPLAIN'S ACCOUNT

Important   The Peace of Christ, etc.

My very esteemed Father Procurator and Rector
Juan Antonio Baltasar:[41]

Now that Father Visitor Carlos de Rojas[42] has requested the annual financial statements and letters for Your Reverence, I am taking the opportunity of sending this with the desire that Your Reverence enjoys perfect health, and that the short account you have waited for suffices as best it can. Actually I still do not know if Your Reverence has done me the favor this year of sending all or part of what I requested last year for our dependents.

Having been designated by the Father Visitor, I set out on November 1 [1756] with Captain don Gabriel on an Apache campaign. We proceeded from this presidio of Fronteras[43] on a direct line northeastward some eighty-four leagues to the place called Todos Santos.[44] This is where the Río Gila issues forth from the great Sierra de Mogollón,[45] of whose interior, until now, nothing has been known, and consequently nothing of the source of this extremely large river. At this rendezvous we were joined by sixty regulars from the presidios of Janos, Agua Nueva and Guajoquilla[46] commanded by Captain don Bernardo de Bustamante, and sixty Tarahumara archers. Added to those who accompanied us they brought our total strength to one hundred and ten regulars and two hundred auxiliary archers, for we had brought with us one hundred and forty Ópatas and some fifty regulars, ten from the presidio of Terrenate,[47] and the rest from this presidio of Fronteras, as well as a number of citizens from the Oposura Valley.[48]

In getting to this place [Todos Santos] to join forces on November 24, we had time to spare. It was not wasted however. Instead, the following ranges were reconnoitered in search of the enemy: the Pitaicachi, Embudos, Espuelas, Enmedio, and Las Ánimas, these being southeast of this presidio in the direction of Janos.[49] Only in the Sierra de las Ánimas were traces of a *ranchería*[50] found, and although five braves were overtaken, because they were erroneously thought to be an advanced party of Ópata, they managed to get themselves out of the neat circle which our men were already forming.

From the Sierra de las Ánimas via the waterhole in the Playa de Santo Domingo[51] we traveled to the north, beyond that waterhole some thirty leagues through an area without water, until we reached the Río Gila. On this leg of the journey while searching for water in a canyon, enemy tracks were discovered accidentally. Following them, the soldiers succeeded in killing two and in capturing another two in the range they call the Peñol de los Janeros.[52]

From the Gila we proceeded, more to the east than to the north, some twelve leagues to the waterhole of Santa Lucía[53] through rough terrain, and from there six more leagues to the waterhole of Todos Santos. Here it was intended to reconnoiter the Sierra de Mogollón, though the reconnaissance was carried out only in so far as thirty Tarahumara climbed one of the summits near the outlet of the Gila to see if there were a route into the interior along the river bed. They went up at night, and they observed the following day that at a short distance from the outlet two forks of the stream united forming the Gila. The first, of greater volume, flowed from south to north; the second from north to south, and both, once joined, flowed west.[54] The way along the river bed revealed itself to all appearances impossible because the many boulders would have prevented passage of the horses, and even more so in the narrows that were descried up the forks.

At this point a detachment set out to the north for the Río de San Francisco[55] to find out if by following its bed or banks one could get through either to the northeast, the direction from which it flows, or to the west, toward which it runs. It was found impassable in either direction because of the narrow gorge between sheer crags of great height along its banks. During this journey from one river to the other, some twenty leagues, the soldiers came upon the tracks of two rancherías. At the first they were only able to capture a single brave and kill two; at the second, seven women and children (*piezas*) were seized. Both rancherías were in flight, having got word of the nearness of our troops.

From Todos Santos on, one begins to see ruins of ancient buildings with square patios, as well as other vestiges of earthenware jugs, ollas, and pots decorated with a variety of colors of paints.[56] On the ground I also saw clearly that they had brought an irrigation ditch which carried the water to their fields at that very extensive site. It is large enough for a fine town or mission should the reduction of this bellicose Apache nation ever be achieved. At the place called La Casita downriver to the west there is another similar site, perhaps ten leagues distant.[57] Here also I saw similar ruins. I am convinced that between here and the Pimería, toward which the currents of this river lead, the Seven Cities, of which there is some knowledge, must have been built.[58]

Ten leagues from this site of La Casita, also downriver, we came upon another similar and extensive one.[59] Because it was new to as many of us as gathered there, and because it was an excellent wanderers' rest, it was given the name of San Francisco Xavier. Six leagues from here in the same direction, Captain don Gabriel de Vildósola assured me, the levelness of the country along this river was much more apparent. It was not possible to go on down to the confluence of the Gila and the equally large San Francisco, as I wished to, because our main objective remained the same. Thus, the fact that traces of a ranchería had been found in the area between the two rivers caused the commanding captain, don Bernardo de Bustamante, to seek their punishment. This resulted in his capturing eleven women and children and leaving three of the enemy dead in the field.

No less good fortune accompanied Captain don Gabriel operating from Todos Santos on the bank of the Gila nearest the San Francisco along a stretch of some five leagues where the river flows through a gorge.[60] Pursuing another ranchería he surmounted the heights and by sheer determination stayed on its trail against a torrent of hardships caused by the rugged terrain, until he succeeded to the greatest degree in the greatest triumph. Indeed, that stronghold only provided the enemy, wishing to flee the assault, with a fatal precipice. There seventeen women and children were captured in addition to those of the enemy who died obstinate in their defense, who apparently were seven in number.

United at the place called La Casita, we continued on to San [Francisco] Xavier. Six leagues from here both a group of fifty Ópata who were accompanying don Gabriel and he himself came upon different tracks, which they followed in two detachments. These tracks led them to the Sierra de San Marcial[61] south of the Gila. Both rancherías, in different places, were assaulted, ten women and children were captured, and three of the enemy were left dead, if not more, because the number only wounded who fled was not calculated.

From San Xavier we swung back to the south to San Simón[62] where the troops separated because of the impossibility of operating in the Sierra Chiricahua (*Chiguicagui*), an extremely rugged range. We returned to this presidio [Fronteras] with the horses in bad shape on account of the diseased swelling of their feet (*gabarro*) they suffered at the outset of the campaign. Something at least had been done to see if, through punishment, the boldness of the enemy would be checked. Fifteen captive children came to my village of Cuquiárachi to see if any sort of work gang (*pueble*) could be made of them. Captain don Gabriel determined this, and the governor approved it.

Because the Apache had turned to robbery even during feigned peace and had stolen some cattle from the vicinity of the presidio, once again last February 21 the captain sent word that auxiliaries be recruited from these villages. Proceeding to the Sierra Chiricahua, more than thirty leagues distant, they succeeded in killing seven, counting men and women, and they brought back twenty-one captive children. They say that there were many Apache in this range, and it does not surprise me, because at this season already the rancherías are gathering in a certain rugged area nearby. The braves come together to plan their campaign, after which they divide up into bands to rob and kill throughout the whole province, just as we have experienced these past years.[63] I well know that don Gabriel wants to gather auxiliaries and set out next month on a campaign, though the rigors of winter leave the horses in such bad shape I do not know that they could last long on such a campaign.

The Apache country possesses sites for settlement only along the Río Gila. San Bernardino, fifteen leagues distant from this presidio, would support some population.[64] The place called San Simón in addition to being alkaline does not accumulate sufficient water for this purpose, although the land is extremely open. It is twenty-two leagues from San Bernardino. From San Simón north to San Xavier on the Gila must be just short of twenty leagues. The Cañada de Guadalupe,[65] San Luis,[66] and the Playa de Santo Domingo hardly have enough water to raise cattle alone. Only at the waterhole in the Cañada de Santa Lucía near Todos Santos is there some, as well as decent lands for a small settlement.

Of the various mountain ranges the largest, most massive, and roughest appears to be the Mogollón, although up until now it was thought to be the Chiricahua. The latter range, because it is not a source of water, being located in such a cold place, seems less commendable than the former. Moreover, from appearances, it is plainly just a great lofty spine some fifteen leagues long.[67]

The Apache plant plots of maize from Todos Santos along the entire Río Gila and in the Cañada de Santa Lucía. From the place called La Casita on up the Gila and around Santa Lucía there are already many piñon pines. Mescal[68] begins at about the half-way point between the Gila and San Simón coming this way. On the plains of the Playa de Santo Domingo and San Simón one finds an abundance of mesquite beans (*péchita*),[69] and in the rocky places close by the Indians have bored holes in the shape of mortars in which to grind them. In addition, even on the plains themselves they have stones bored in this fashion and metates.

As for game, there are deer, mule deer, pronghorn, rabbits, jack rabbits, and quail. The Gila abounds with two kinds of fish about three quarters of a vara and even a full vara [about thirty-three inches] long. Although the *matalote* is somewhat bony and also appears to be not very heavy there, the other kind is very easy on the digestion.[70] I did not see, nor did I learn that they had caught even a single catfish, which is all one finds here in Sonora in the rivers. The Gila also nurtures beaver which gnaw and fell the willows and cottonwoods.[71] Shrub willows also are found along its banks.

The Apache do not seem to have permanent homes; instead, wherever they stop to gather a bit of maize or grass seed,[72] they build a few little half-huts of no more than branches. In the ranchería that don Gabriel assaulted, a decorated doll of *jigüites*[73] and little deer hoofs was found; also many prepared deer skins and buffalo hides which they say are brought by the Comanche, whom the Apache call Natage,[74] in trade for horses and mules.

The distance from Todos Santos to New Mexico, don Bernardo de Bustamante maintained, he would cover without doubt in three days; and several more experienced persons who had already gone from there to Zuñi said the same thing.[75] The name Mogollón came to be applied to that range, Bustamante related, because a governor of New Mexico named Mogollón[76] was on the trail of some horse-stealing Apache who drove them into that range on the New Mexico side. Some citizens who were ahead of him entered the mountains but seeing their extreme ruggedness and that the horses were in there, turned around to get out. Just then the governor arrived. When asked, the citizens informed him that the horses were in a place from which it would be impossible to free them because of bad terrain and because the Apache were many. He scoffed at this reasoning and, attributing it to their cowardice, commanded his soldiers to enter. And with them he went directly to where the horses were. As he got near them, so many Apache sprang forth upon him that he had to depart with the greatest difficulty, fleeing, leaving behind him dead seven of his soldiers. He even lost his hat. This memorable event gave to the range the name of Mogollón.[77]

This is what can be noted. If indeed some of it is worthy of note, it is because of the diligence Your Reverence displays in the acquisition of information that may facilitate the conversion of these heathens whose invasions have ruined the inhabitants of these frontiers. Your Reverence will pardon the nuisance and overlook with your accustomed charity the defects of so prolix a narrative.

May God Our Lord guard the life of Your Reverence many years. I commend myself to your Masses. Village of San Xavier de Cuchuta,[78] March 6, 1757.

I serve Your Reverence from the heart,

Bartolomé Sáenz, S.J.

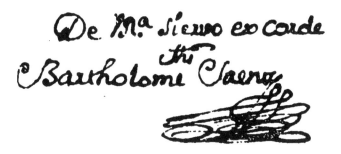

1. Max L. Moorhead, "The Soldado de Cuera: Stalwart of the Spanish Borderlands," *Journal of the West,* vol. 8 (1969), pp. 38-55. For an enlightening discussion of arrow-shooting Indian versus firearm-toting Spaniard, see also Luis Navarro García, *Don José de Gálvez y la Comandancia General de las Provincias Internas del Norte de Nueva España* (Sevilla, 1964), pp. 65-69. The key role of Indian auxiliaries on the northern frontier is spelled out in Oakah L. Jones, Jr., *Pueblo Warriors and Spanish Conquest* (Norman, 1966).

2. Fray Angélico Chávez, *Origins of New Mexico Families in the Spanish Colonial Period* (Santa Fe, 1954), p. 150. Henry W. Kelly, "Franciscan Missions of New Mexico 1740-1760," NMHR, vol. 16 (1941), pp. 47-48, 63-67, 266-69.

3. Fr. Juan Sanz de Lezaun and Fr. Manuel Bermejo to Fr. Juan Antonio Abasolo, Santa Ana, Oct. 29, 1750; Biblioteca Nacional, México, Archivo Franciscano, New Mexico documents (BNM), leg. 8, no. 82. Kelly, pp. 181-83.

4. Patente de capitán, Buen Retiro, April 4, 1752; Archivo General de Indias, Sevilla, Spain (AGI), Audiencia de Guadalajara (Guad.), leg. 506. By 1752 Bustamante had served twenty years in the frontier military. For another twenty years and more he would remain as captain of the Guajoquilla garrison, even after its move north to San Elzeario in the 1770's.

5. Viceroy Conde de Revillagigedo to the governor of Nueva Vizcaya, México, Oct. 26, 1753; Archivo General de la Nación, México (AGN), Provincias Internas, tomo 94. Navarro García, pp. 111-12. Francisco R. Almada, *Resumen de historia del estado de Chihuahua* (México, 1955), pp. 110-11.

6. Informe, Bustamante, San Felipe el Real de Chihuahua, Aug. 29, 1754; AGI, Guad., leg. 194.

7. Salvador Ignacio de la Peña, S.J., "Convite Evangélico . . . 1760," cap. 15; University of Arizona Library, Tucson, Film 71. The king confirmed Vildósola as captain of Fronteras in 1754. Patente de capitán, Buen Retiro, Nov. 20, 1754; AGI, Guad., leg. 506. In 1766 during his inspection of the northern presidios, the Marqués de Rubí, who had no praise for Bustamante, described Vildósola as "one of the most commendable officers of these provinces and worthy of being distinguished by some show of the Royal Gratitude." Extractos de revista, Guajoquilla, May 25, 1766, and Fronteras, Nov. 20, 1766; AGI, Guad., leg. 511. For a brief biographical

sketch of Vildósola, see Almada, *Diccionario de historia, geografía y biografía sonorenses* (Chihuahua, 1952), pp. 826-27.

8. Hubert Howe Bancroft, *History of the North Mexican States*, vol. 1 (San Francisco, 1884), p. 557, n. 12.

9. Informe, José de Berroterán, México, April 17, 1748; quoted in Navarro García, p. 108.

10. Revillagigedo to Gov. Joaquín Codallos y Rabal, México, June 22, 1747, transmitting campaign plan of the Marqués de Altamira, México, June 14, 1747; Spanish Archives of New Mexico, State of New Mexico Records Center, Santa Fe (SANM), no. 479.

11. Obedecimiento, Gov. Codallos, Santa Fe, July 30, 1747; *ibid*.

12. Diligencia, Gov. Codallos, Santa Fe, Dec. 6, 1747; SANM, no. 483. The raid took place in August; a girl and an old woman were killed and twenty-three women and children carried off. Years later Father Sanz de Lezaun recalled Codallos' ineffective measures to punish the enemy, alleging that Comanche, not "the poor heathen Yutas," had been to blame. Charles Wilson Hackett, ed., *Historical Documents relating to New Mexico, Nueva Vizcaya, and Approaches Thereto, to 1773*, vol. 3 (Washington, 1937), pp. 476-77. Kelly, p. 180. The name Chaguago, variously spelled, referred to a Ute subgroup.

13. Memorial, Miera y Pacheco, enclosed with his letter to the king, San Felipe el Real de Chihuahua, Oct. 26, 1777; BNM, leg. 10, no. 39. A 1758 Miera map, including the territory traversed by the 1747 expedition, is in AGN, Californias, tomo 39.

14. Eleanor B. Adams, ed., *Bishop Tamarón's Visitation of New Mexico, 1760* (Albuquerque, 1954), p. 89.

15. Juan Antonio Baltasar, S.J., in *Apostólicos afanes de la Compañia de Jesús* [1754] (México, 1944), pp. 431-32.

16. Adams, p. 89.

17. Fr. Silvestre Vélez de Escalante to Gov. Pedro Fermín de Mendinueta, Zuñi, Oct. 28, 1775; BNM, leg. 10, n. 28a; translated in Alfred B. Thomas, *Forgotten Frontiers: A Study of the Spanish Indian Policy of Don Juan Bautista de Anza, Governor of New Mexico, 1777-1787* (Norman, 1932), pp. 150-58.

18. Menchero to the Vice Comisario General, Santa Fe, Feb. 29, 1748; BNM, leg. 8, no. 52.

19. Vélez de Escalante to Mendinueta, Oct. 28, 1775. To further prove the feasibility of travel between New Mexico and Sonora, Vélez told the story of Manuel Tomás, a Christian mestizo servant of don Joaquín Rodríguez, chaplain of the Terrenate garrison in Sonora. While en route to hear a confession one day in 1754 don Joaquín and his party were set upon by

Gila Apache under the notorious chief Chafalote. The lone survivor, Manuel Tomás, was led blindfolded six days north to the hostiles' secluded ranchería near the Río San Francisco. There he was rescued by the lieutenant alcalde of Zuñi, don Marcial Barrera, and a hundred Zuñi warriors operating three days south of Zuñi. Brought to New Mexico, Manuel Tomás was living proof that the journey could be made from south to north.

20. Diligencia, Codallos, Dec. 6, 1747.

21. Derrotero, Bustamante, Santa Fe, Dec. 24, 1747; SANM, no. 483. Jones, pp. 118-20.

22. Baltasar, p. 432. Gerard Decorme, S.J., *La obra de los jesuítas mexicanos durante la época colonial, 1572-1767*, vol. 2 (México, 1941), p. 436.

23. Gov. Alonso de Gastezi quoted in Navarro García, pp. 112-13.

24. Navarro García, p. 113.

25. Not even in the 1770's, 1780's, and 1790's, when other expeditions were projected into the upper Gila country to punish Apache and open communications between Sonora and New Mexico, did anyone cite the precedent of the 1756 campaign. Thomas, pp. 30-56, *et passim*; and George P. Hammond, "The Zuñiga Journal, Tucson to Santa Fé: The Opening of a Spanish Trade Route, 1788-1795," NMHR, vol. 6 (1931), pp. 40-65.

26. AGI, Contratación, leg. 5550. John L. Kessell, *Mission of Sorrows: Jesuit Guevavi and the Pimas, 1691-1767* (Tucson, 1970), p. 97.

27. Bartolomé Sánchez [sic] to Father José Roldán, Cuquiárachi, July 24, 1758; printed in *Documentos para la historia de México*, Cuarta Série, tomo 1 (México, 1856), pp. 94-97.

28. Gov. Juan de Mendoza to Father Carlos de Rojas, San Miguel de Horcasitas, Feb. 15, 1757; *ibid.*, pp. 84-88. Navarro García, p. 87.

29. Mendoza to Rojas, Feb. 15, 1757.

30. Ernest J. Burrus, S.J., ed., *Misiones norteñas mexicanas de la Compañía de Jesús, 1751-1757* (México, 1963), pp. 38-39.

31. Sánchez [sic] to Roldán, July 24, 1758. Bancroft, p. 558.

32. Except for a brief assignment at the mission of Banámichi, Father Sáenz continued to serve at Cuquiárachi until the Jesuits' rude expulsion in 1767. He died in November 1768 on his way to exile, a victim of the cruel march across Mexico. Alberto F. Pradeau, *La expulsión de los jesuítas de las provincias de Sonora, Ostimuri y Sinaloa en 1767* (México, 1959), pp. 221-24.

33. Adams, pp. 87-94. Navarro García, pp. 122-24.

34. It is possible that the 1747 expedition, of which Miera was a member, reached the Gila Valley near Todos Santos on the feast day of the Spanish Franciscan San Pedro de Alcántara, October 19, and that Father Menchero named the place in honor of that saint.

35. Miera to the king, Oct. 26, 1777.

36. See Moorhead, *The Apache Frontier: Jacobo Ugarte and Spanish-Indian Relations in Northern New Spain, 1769-1791* (Norman, 1968), pp. 115-42, 170-99.

37. See Ralph Hedrick Ogle, *Federal Control of the Western Apaches, 1848-1886* (Albuquerque, 1970); and Dan L. Thrapp, *The Conquest of Apacheria* (Norman, 1967).

38. Cols. Miles and Loring commanded the southern and northern columns respectively of Col. B. L. Bonneville's 1857 offensive against the Western Apache. Miles' southern column "moved quickly into an unknown country along the upper Gila." Ogle, p. 38. For much of the way in fact Miles retraced the 1756 route of Bustamante and Vildósola. See "A Map of the scout of Lt. Col. Miles's southern column through the country of the Coyotero Apaches in June and July 1857, by B. L. E. Bonneville," Aug. 1857; National Archives, Record Group No. 77.

39. Timothy Flint, ed., *The Personal Narrative of James O. Pattie of Kentucky* (Chicago, 1930), p. 71.

40. Carpeta 197/875. Father Norman M. Whalen of Benson, Arizona, kindly loaned me his microfilm of the original Sáenz document.

41. The influential Father Baltasar, who had served from 1750 to 1753 as Father Provincial, highest-ranking Jesuit in New Spain, was now rector of the Colegio de San Andrés in Mexico City as well as procurator, or treasurer, of the missions. For a biographical sketch, see Peter M. Dunne, S.J., *Juan Antonio Balthasar, Padre Visitador to the Sonora Frontier, 1744-1745* (Tucson, 1957), pp. 33-44.

42. Father Rojas, missionary at Arizpe, had been named Father Visitor, or superior, of the Sonora missions in 1753. During much of his long career he held some elevated position, including that of Father Visitor General of all the Jesuit missions in northwestern New Spain. Pradeau, pp. 210-14.

43. Thirty miles south of present-day Douglas, the presidio of Fronteras had been erected in the early 1690's to protect the northeastern sector of the Sonora frontier.

44. Todos Santos, in the vicinity of today's Cliff, had been suggested a decade earlier by Vildósola's father as a possible site for a 100-man presidio. Navarro García, pp. 89-90. Though Miera y Pacheco failed to show it on his 1758 map, in the 1760's the name appeared on several maps whose makers seem to have relied on the Sáenz account for their renditions of the upper Gila region. See for example, "Sonorae Tabulam," *ibid.*, no. 65, following p. 112. On Gerónimo de la Rocha y Figueroa's 1784 map of the upper Gila and environs, Todos Santos was again omitted. Thomas, map following p. 252. For a thorough treatment of later U.S. forts and encamp-

ments in the area, see Lee Myers, "Military Establishments in Southwestern New Mexico: Stepping Stones to Settlement," NMHR, vol. 43 (1968), pp. 5-48. A league was equal to about two and a half miles in this case. Eighty-four leagues, or two hundred and ten miles, *on a direct line* would have put the Vildósola contingent well beyond Todos Santos. Counting their deviations, however, they might easily have covered that distance.

45. Father Sáenz included as part of the Sierra de Mogollón the mountains labeled on some present maps the Diablo Range. From his vantage point near Todos Santos he could see only the southern portion of the Mogollón Mountains.

46. The garrisons of Janos, Agua Nueva, and Guajoquilla guarded Nueva Vizcaya; all were located in the present Mexican state of Chihuahua. Janos, founded in 1690, lay some ninety miles south of the midway point between Lordsburg and Deming, New Mexico. It was the next presidio east of Fronteras on the cordon. Agua Nueva was one of the garrisoned haciendas north of Chihuahua City. Guajoquilla, far south, stood within the limits of today's Ciudad Jiménez. The Marqués de Rubí visited them all. For descriptions, see Lawrence Kinnaird, ed., *The Frontiers of New Spain, Nicolás de Lafora's Description, 1766-1768* (Berkeley, 1958).

47. Built and manned in 1742, the presidio of Terrenate was located in Sonora on the headwaters of the Río San Pedro some twenty miles due south of present-day Fort Huachuca, Arizona. At the very time that the Bustamante-Vildósola expedition was operating on the upper Gila, Captain Francisco Elías of Terrenate was pursuing a destructive band of Gila Pimas farther downstream to the west. Father Baltasar heard about this expedition too from another Jesuit chaplain. Arthur D. Gardiner, ed., "Letter of Father Middendorff, S.J., Dated from Tucson, 3 March 1757," *The Kiva*, vol. 22 (1957), pp. 1-10.

48. South of Fronteras in the valley of the river now called the Moctezuma, formerly the Río de Oposura, there lived a large Spanish population.

49. The Sierras de Pitaicachi, Embudos, Espuelas, and Enmedio seem to have been close to or parts of the present Sierras de la Cabellera and San Luis lying along the state line between Sonora and Chihuahua just south of the international border, while the Sierra de las Ánimas was the Ánimas Range of extreme southwestern New Mexico.

50. Father Sáenz used the word *ranchería* to refer both to a group of Apache and to the temporary villages or camps in which they lived.

51. In the Playas region south of Lordsburg.

52. Likely the Pyramid Mountains immediately south of Lordsburg.

53. Early U.S. Army maps show the Ojo de Santa Lucía some six to ten miles up Mangas Creek from its confluence with the Gila. It is known today as Mangas Spring. Myers, p. 10.

54. The Jesuit seems to be describing the confluence of Turkey Creek, the northern or smaller fork, and the Gila proper, the larger southern fork, a dozen miles upstream from Cliff. From the top of a prominent peak on the north side of the river, evidently the one climbed by the Tarahumara, the ruggedness of both canyons can be seen. Just downstream from this confluence is the proposed Hooker Dam site.

55. The San Francisco River, a major tributary of the Gila, flows south from extreme west central New Mexico, crosses over into Arizona, and joins the Gila south of the town of Clifton.

56. For a brief general description of the ruins in this area, see A. F. Bandelier, *Final Report of Investigations Among the Indians of the South-western United States,* Part 2 (Cambridge, 1892), pp. 347-65. Neither Walter Hough's *Antiquities of the Upper Gila and Salt River Valleys in Arizona and New Mexico,* Bureau of American Ethnology, *Bulletin* 35 (Washington, 1907) nor his *Culture of the Ancient Pueblos of the Upper Gila River Region, New Mexico and Arizona,* United States National Museum, *Bulletin* 87 (Washington, 1914) covers the specific sector of the Gila traversed by Father Sáenz, though the various items of material culture discussed and illustrated presumably are similar to those mentioned by the Jesuit. See also Carl Sauer and Donald Brand, "Pueblo Sites in Southeastern Arizona," *University of California Publications in Geography,* vol. 3 (1930), pp. 415-58.

57. Like Todos Santos, La Casita had been suggested in 1746 as a possible presidial site. Navarro García, pp. 89-90. The ruins must have been considerable; some maps of the 1760's show a structure there. Captain Manuel de Echeagaray broke camp at "la Casita de Gila" on October 23, 1788. The very same day fifty-eight years later, Lt. W. H. Emory mentioned in the same area passing by "one of the long-sought ruins." *Notes of a Military Reconnoissance, from Fort Leavenworth, in Missouri, to San Diego, in California, Including Parts of the Arkansas, Del Norte, and Gila Rivers,* 30th Cong., 1st Sess., Sen. Exec. Doc. No. 7 (Washington, 1848), p. 64. La Casita stood in the vicinity of present Redrock, New Mexico.

58. Vestiges of ancient civilization along this stretch of the Gila seemed to stimulate the traveler's imagination. Ninety years after Father Sáenz, Emory commented in a similar vein: "We were now approaching the regions made famous in olden times by the fables of Friar Marcos, and eagerly did we ascend every mound, expecting to see in the distance . . . the fabulous 'Casa Montezuma.'" Emory, p. 64.

59. Near today's Duncan, Arizona. In this area Emory passed "the ruins of two more villages similar to those of yesterday." *Ibid.,* p. 65.

60. Evidently this was the "Cañada de Todos Santos" scoured by a detachment of the Cordero expedition in late November 1785. Thomas, p.

289. The canyon though deep is wide enough in places to afford ideal campsites. Much of it will be flooded if Hooker Dam is built.

61. The northernmost portion of the Peloncillo Mountains just across the state line into Arizona, or perhaps the nearby Whitlock Mountains.

62. In the vicinity of modern San Simón, Arizona, in the valley of the same name.

63. Speaking in 1796 of Apache raiding strategy, Lt. Col. Antonio Cordero asserted that "Once an offensive expedition has been decided upon . . . they choose in the interior of some mountain range of the district a rugged terrain which is defended by nature, provided with water and wild fruits, where they leave their families in safety with a small escort. They leave this place divided into small parties . . . and they come together again at the time and place agreed upon, near the country which they have decided to invade." Daniel S. Matson and Albert H. Schroeder, eds., "Cordero's Description of the Apache—1796," NMHR, vol. 32 (1957), p. 345. It would be difficult to imagine a more desirable base of operations from the Apaches' standpoint than the rocky, almost impenetrable Chiricahuas of southern Arizona.

64. In the mid-1770's the presidial garrison of Fronteras was moved north temporarily to San Bernardino, a site west of Douglas, and evidently just south of the international border. During the early Mexican period, raiding Apache caused the abandonment of a large cattle ranch in the area. For a description of "the ruins of the hacienda of San Bernardino" in 1851, see John Russell Bartlett, *Personal Narrative of Explorations and Incidents in Texas, New Mexico, California, Sonora, and Chihuahua*, vol. 1 (New York, 1854), pp. 255-56.

65. On the 1784 map by Rocha, the Cañada de Guadalupe is a pass through the mountains just east of San Bernardino, the same Guadalupe Pass through which Cooke's emigrant road later wound its way. Bartlett called it "a frightful cañon." *Ibid.*, pp. 252-55; illustration following p. 254.

66. San Luis was on the eastern side of the Sierra de Embudos, part of the present Sierra de San Luis.

67. This would seem to be an accurate rendering in the context of the report, yet the Spanish reads: *De las Sierras la maior mas corpulenta y aspera parece ser la de Mogollon, aunque hasta aora estaba en inteligencia de que lo era Chiguicagui, pero el mismo no ser manantial de Aguas en Parage tan frio parece que no la haze tan recomendable á esta, fuera de que á la vista solo se manifiesta ser un espinazo largo y encumbrado, como 15 leguas.*

68. The Apaches' "principal delicacies," according to Cordero, "are the mescal. There are various kinds taken from the hearts of the maguey, sotol, palmilla and lechuguilla; and it is used by cooking it with a slow fire in a

subterranean fireplace, until it acquires a certain degree of sweetness and piquancy." Matson and Schroeder, pp. 338-39.

69. Father Pfefferkorn who served for more than two decades as a missionary in Sonora described the Indians' preparation and consumption of *péchita* in *Sonora: A Description of the Province*, trans. by Theodore E. Treutlein (Albuquerque, 1949), pp. 71-72.

70. The *Matalote*, perhaps the hump-back sucker or the Colorado River squawfish, was recorded in New Mexican waters from the early seventeenth century. For a discussion of it and other native fish, see *The Memorial of Fray Alonso de Benavides, 1630*, trans. by Mrs. Edward E. Ayer (Chicago, 1916; reprint, Albuquerque, 1965), pp. 261-62, n. 41. While excavating Santa Cruz de Quíburi on the San Pedro, a major tributary of the Gila, archeologists found the vertebrae of large fish, presumably eaten by both Indian and Spanish residents of the area. These were identified "as belonging to the Colorado River squawfish (often called Colorado 'salmon'). . . . a predatory minnow . . . attaining a reported length of 6 feet and a weight of 100 pounds." Dr. Robert R. Miller, quoted in Charles C. DiPeso, *The Sobaipuri Indians of the Upper San Pedro River Valley, Southeastern Arizona* (Dragoon, Arizona, 1953), p. 236. Early Anglo-American travelers were impressed by the abundance of fish in the upper Gila. Emory described a trout-like fish, without scales, that tasted more like catfish. Emory, p. 62; illustration facing p. 62. The Apache, however, were not fish eaters, reported Cordero, "but they kill them also and keep the bones [spines] for different uses . . ." Matson and Schroeder, p. 345.

71. As for the beaver, the Apache esteemed it, wrote Cordero, both "for the taste of its flesh [*sic*] and the usefulness of its hide." *Ibid.* By the mid-1820's the first of a long succession of trappers had begun to exploit the beaver supply on the upper Gila. James Ohio Pattie described at length his party's good hunting. Flint, pp. 71-106.

72. "They likewise make a sort of grits or pinol of the seed of hay or grass which they reap with much care in its season, although in small quantities (since they are not by nature farmers) . . ." Cordero in Matson and Schroeder, p. 339.

73. *Jigüite* is a common name for the Mexican rubber plant, or gua-yule, and for the related low, bushy mariola found in the Southwest. The name jiguite may also have been applied to the desert rosewood, or as a variant of *jegüite* to some sort of range grass. Apache girls did make grass dolls decorated with "jingles." Morris Edward Opler, *An Apache Life-Way: The Economic, Social, and Religious Institutions of the Chiricahua Indians* (Chicago, 1941), pp. 45-46.

74. The name Natage was more often applied to a group of eastern, buffalo-hunting Apache.

75. An allusion to the general campaign of 1747.

76. Juan Ignacio Flores Mogollón served as New Mexico's governor from 1712 to 1715.

77. Just why this range became "a majestic monument to the memory of Governor Mogollon" seems to have been entirely forgotten. T. M. Pearce, *New Mexico Place Names: A Geographical Dictionary* (Albuquerque, 1965), p. 102.

78. Cuchuta, some ten miles due south of Fronteras, was one of the two visitas looked after by the missionary of Cuquiárachi.

FRIARS, BUREAUCRATS,

AND THE SERIS OF SONORA

JOHN L. KESSELL

THE OLD friar's hemorrhoids were killing him. "Full of years and the most painful afflictions," Father President Mariano Buena had no choice but to give up. Four years earlier, in 1768, the strong-willed veteran had led fourteen of his brethren from the Franciscan missionary college at Querétaro, in central Mexico, north a thousand miles by land and sea to the frontier province of Sonora. They had taken over secondhand missions left vacant by the Jesuit Expulsion. They had endured arrogance and apathy from their neophytes and from government bureaucrats; they had lived with drought and flood, epidemics, heat, and squalor; they had seen Apache arrows stuck in the doors of their churches. As superior in the field Fray Mariano had seen it all. Soon, God willing, he would walk again in the gardens of the College.

A younger man, tall and austere, his gray habit hanging loosely on his slender frame, stood nearby. Forty-four-year-old Juan Crisóstomo Gil de Bernabé, chosen by the College to succeed Father Buena, had ridden down to Ures in the valley of the Río Sonora with a prayer on his lips and an emptiness in the pit of his stomach. For almost four years he had persevered at Los Santos Ángeles de Guevavi, a run-down adobe compound in the mesquite ten miles northeast of today's Nogales, Arizona. He had done his best through an interpreter to instruct his Pimas and Pápagos. He had felt an abiding compassion for them, but he had hardly reached them.

Fray Juan, a fervently penitential Christian, had come to the Indies from a severe mountain-top monastery in Aragón, where a crucifix bled and spoke with a friar. He wore a hair shirt, scourged his flesh, and wept while saying Mass. Gil's impact had been greater on the culturally Hispanic mixed-breeds of the nearby Tubac garrison. Few Indians could comprehend such seemingly pointless suffering.

Now at Ures in the spring of 1772 Juan Gil listened intently as Buena, propped up in his cell, recounted the most critical issue facing him as the new Father President—what to do about the Seri Indians.[1]

NEVER more than a few thousand individuals in all, the Seris of Sonora had stubbornly resisted domestication. Roaming the bone-dry, two-hundred-mile-long gulf coast north from Guaymas, loosely organized bands of these primitive fishermen and gatherers had clashed with Spaniards for a century. Though the Jesuits had lured some of them into inland missions, Seri-Spanish relations had consisted in the main of raids, retaliation, treachery, deportation, escape, and mutual loathing. "This nation, of all the Indian nations known up to now," wrote a Spanish officer, "has been and is without doubt the most inconstant, bellicose, stubborn, ungrateful, and cruel. . . . They are the ones who with unthinkable savagery poison their arrows, setting a bad example to the other tribes, and thereby assure that the slightest wound is fatal."[2]

By the mid-1760's the Seris, joined by rebel Pimas in the incredibly stark and hostile Cerro Prieto region due north of Guaymas, cast a menacing shadow across the province. For Spanish cattlemen, miners, and missionaries it meant a two-front war—with the Seris on the west and the relentless Apaches to the north. In 1768 the greatest military expedition in Sonora's history had gathered at Pitic, present-day Hermosillo, to attack and pursue the Seris, in the words of the obese Governor Juan de Pineda, "until their total extinction."

In two massive assaults Pineda and Colonel Domingo Elizondo commanding over a thousand armed men—veterans from Mexico, frontier presidials, and native auxiliaries—had failed to dislodge an estimated two hundred families. After that, they resorted to guerrilla tactics.[3]

In the meantime, the king's brilliant, egocentric minister extraordinary to New Spain, José de Gálvez, hoping to further fragment the hostiles and to reap personally the glory of victory, had offered an alternative to extermination. Writing from Baja California in March 1769, he requested Father President Buena to let the Seris and their allies know—without disclosing Gálvez' part in it—that pardon was theirs if they would surrender upon the Visitor General's arrival. When that failed, and nearly cost the life of a friar, Gálvez beneficently proclaimed a general amnesty. Yet by summer only a few dozen hungry Seris had straggled into the concentration camp at Pitic. Some devilish Pimas, it seemed, had spread the lie that the Spaniards meant to murder the Seri headmen and throw the rest into the sea.[4]

Determined to break the impasse, iron-fisted Gálvez himself had reined up in Pitic October 1, 1769. Father Buena was with him, ready even then to found a mission for the Indians the Visitor had vowed to humble. But Gálvez had been driving himself too hard. At Pitic he suffered a complete mental breakdown. Instead of riding off the conqueror, the "new Balboa," as the *gacetas* had begun to call him, profoundly depressed, he let himself be carried to Ures where for five months Buena served the most powerful official in New Spain as priest, protector, and analyst. The Father President had not been shy about asking for favors. All he had received in return was a courteous letter and some oil for the altar lamp.[5] That, Buena told his successor, was the problem: government officials kept demanding a Seri mission, but when the friars asked for help the bureaucrats sat on their hands.

The dismal contest had dragged on for two more years. Spanish search-and-destroy units disappeared into the arid fastness of Seriland, and small groups of beaten, sick, and starving natives emerged to give themselves up. Measles and smallpox stalked the hostiles' camps. Turncoat Seris like Crisanto, who had become the Spaniards' chief ally, emissary, and scout, made the rounds telling their desperate relatives of the rations and respite to be had at Pitic. By April 1770 one hundred and fifty-one pitiful refugees had turned themselves in, and more were on the way.[6]

A year later Crisanto and three of his fellows, wearing their pelican-skin robes and shell necklaces, had traveled under escort to Mexico City where they appeared at the viceregal palace to swear undying Seri allegiance before the Marqués de Croix and a smug José de Gálvez. These Indians assured Spanish officials that they themselves would deal with the holdout called Marcos and with the Seris still at large on Tiburón Island.[7] By the summer of 1771 Colonel Elizondo and his veterans had been recalled, not because they had gained total victory in Sonora but because the viceroy feared war with Great Britain. Marcos gave up that winter, and the Tiburones sent word of their desire for peace.[8]

While naked Seri POWs stood in line at Pitic for rations their captors debated what to do with them. Some Spaniards could never forget past atrocities. They urged that the savages be split up and exiled. At first the king listened to them. Colonel Elizondo objected. Indicting previous governors of Sonora for their bungling and treachery, he told how he and Pineda had struggled to win the Seris' confidence. Were they now to walk up to Crisanto and the others and announce their exile? Never again would an Indian trust a Spaniard. Besides, the Seris would rather die than leave the land of their fathers. Rather than exile, Elizondo proposed subsidies. Give them arable land, seed, plows, and oxen. Once the Seris learned how satisfying agriculture could be, the government could cut off the dole. To instruct them in the Faith the colonel asked for a missionary, an extremely able and patient one, since these Indians were, in his words, "more atheistic than heathen." In due course the king concurred.[9]

Just before he decamped late in April 1771, Elizondo had sat two long nights parleying with Seri headmen at Pitic. They had agreed on a site for their settlement "a short musketshot" from the garrison. It was, the commander believed, "the most suitable we could have hoped for. . . . From the willingness to work I observe and from their diligence in acquiring a few reales to clothe their families, I am convinced that they will continue in good faith."

On their way back from Mexico City the Seri delegation had stopped at Álamos, two hundred miles southeast of Pitic, to call on Intendant Pedro Corbalán, a Gálvez appointee who became interim governor after Pineda suffered a stroke. Corbalán had urged exile, but he quickly changed his stance when the idea lost favor. The Indians presented don Pedro with an order from the Marqués de Croix: "You will see to it that the Seris are established in a formal town and doctrina on the site agreed upon with Colonel Domingo Elizondo at the Indians' own request, naming it Nuestra Señora de Guadalupe." The intendant-governor was also to arrange with Father President Buena for a missionary to the Seris.[10]

The proposed Pitic settlement was no ordinary doctrina. The government had spent hundreds of thousands of pesos to congregate a few hundred Seris. When the defense of New Spain dictated, the viceroy had pulled back Elizondo and his regulars. Because of the high initial investment and commitments elsewhere, word came down: whatever it takes, keep the Seris quiet. And no matter how logically the Franciscans argued against coddling these Indians, Pitic remained the peace symbol, a far cheaper way than war to deal with the Seris.

Everything depended on bringing water to the settlement. Without irrigation the Seris would never become self-sufficient, the government would have to keep feeding them; without food they would flee back to their coastal haunts and the whole costly business would begin again. Hence Intendant Corbalán gave the matter highest priority. He went to Pitic himself in the spring of 1771. There he commissioned Lieutenant Francisco Mesía to repair an acequia nearly two miles long, from the Río Sonora to the *hornos de munición*, near which he ordered fields cleared. That fall, as the project neared completion, Corbalán had written to Father President Buena in a tone the friar thought imperious.

Buena should dispatch a missionary to Pitic at once. He could live temporarily in the house built for Gálvez and at least get started. Since the Seris had been denied the benefit of religion for so many years, the Padre must proceed prudently and refrain from punishing them for fear of provoking a new outbreak. He must incline his charges toward agriculture and encourage them to work on the all-important ditch. If "by some unlikely chance" the ditch were not completed, there would be little hope of holding the Seris at Pitic.[11]

No sooner had Corbalán fired off his letter to Buena when distressing news arrived from Lieutenant Mesía. The flooding Río Sonora had cut its channel more than a vara deeper: the entire acequia would have to be dug out to that depth, which, according to Mesía, was economically infeasible. There was simply too much rock. He had therefore let his Pima and Ópata Indian work gangs return to their missions while he sat down to await further orders.

Corbalán exploded. Why had the problem not been anticipated months before and a different site chosen for the ditch or for the settlement? Mesía would have to work out the least expensive alternative with the Seris and the friar who, in Corbalán's words, "I am convinced will soon arrive there."[12] On that score too, the intendant-governor was soon disabused.

Father Buena had responded with his usual candor. At Ures a missionary for Pitic was standing by, awaiting only the word "to enter upon this arduous, extremely difficult undertaking." Buena would have sent him at once had not Corbalán himself stressed the uselessness of the site if the irrigation project failed. Now that it had failed, the Father President took the opportunity to lecture the intendant on the perils to and the requisites for a missionary to the Seris.

If these Indians, reduced at such great cost, should break away and return to the Cerro Prieto, whatever the reason, the missionary would reap the blame. If he so much as mentioned work to them he would incur their "total aversion, or, considering their savage and indomitable nature, their irreconcilable hatred." When to set them an example he went out into the fields with a hoe they would laugh at him or turn their backs and take off "to roam the wilds, which is the only thing they are inclined to do from their scabrous cradle on." If the friar challenged their voracious consumption of everything including oxen, they would despise him all the more; if not, there would soon be nothing left. Therefore let someone else make them work and teach them respect for property.

Even more serious, Father Buena asserted, was the Seris' casual sex life. No padre could close his eyes to polygamy. Here the Father President urged Corbalán to use the authority of his office to remove "this great and utter obstacle to their conversion" *before* the missionary arrived. Furthermore, there must be a church, if only of straw, and all the religious paraphernalia, including at least a painting of the Virgin of Guadalupe.[13]

Two months later Corbalán forwarded a copy of Buena's letter to a new viceroy, the able Antonio María Bucareli, so that he could see for himself "the obstacles the said Father President puts in the way of sending a religious to administer the Seris." Clearly Father Buena was as negative about the Seris as Colonel Elizondo was positive. Bucareli demanded further reports. He ordered Corbalán to do everything in his power to get water to the Seris.[14] And he instructed and sent north to Sonora a new governor, the frail, not-so-able Mateo Sastre. With Sastre, loose-living former sergeant major of the Infantry Regiment of Navarre, the ardent Fray Juan Gil would have to take up the Seri issue. Buena wished him luck.

As IF there were not enough already to confound the new Father President, Fray Juan would have to reckon with a bitter, high-level rivalry. Pedro Corbalán, relative of the Marqués de Croix, intendant, and guardian of the royal treasury at Álamos, represented the Gálvez-Croix tradition. He worked to consummate their bold designs. Mateo Sastre, delegated by a more conservative but no less forceful viceroy, wanted more than anything else to make a name for himself. An ill-defined division of powers between the experimental intendancy and the governorship heightened the tension. Both men sought the distinction of pacifying the Seris once and for all.[15]

While Governor Sastre made his way slowly up from the south, Intendant Corbalán tried desperately to finish the ditch. He entered into a contract with Teniente Político Juan Honorato de Rivera who guaranteed to see the job through for thirteen hundred pesos. By midsummer it appeared that he might.[16]

Sweaty and uncomfortable, Governor Sastre finally reached Pitic in the muggy heat of July 1772. He inspected the ditch and reported to the Minister of the Indies in Spain, "I am encouraging the work from time to time in person on horseback. I shall serve as overseer until its conclusion, which I feel certain will occur on August 8." The Seris themselves seemed content. "The only cause for regret is that they are living without religion—they do not confess, receive the sacraments, or hear the word of God—in sum, they are living like idolaters." When the governor admonished Crisanto, the Indian professed that all his people wanted to be Christians, but that they had neither priest nor church. As a token of their good intentions the males had already given up all but their woman of longest standing.[17]

When labor troubles and torrential rains halted work on the acequia, Sastre rode on north along the muddy Río San Miguel to his capital, the unpretentious presidential town of Horcasitas. Here he straight-away suffered an attack which temporarily paralyzed his right side. Here Father President Juan Gil came to pay his respects.

Why, the governor demanded, had the friars not placed a missionary at Pitic? Did they not wish to minister to the Seris? They did, vowed Gil, but until the ditch was done, until Mexico City allocated funds for a church, their hands were tied.[18] While at Horcasitas, Gil learned "by chance" that Sastre was withholding news of an auspicious event, apparently because he intended to take all the credit himself.

Two Tiburón Indians, Cazoni and Tumuzaqui, had come in to welcome the new governor and swear obedience. "Having thanked them warmly for their courtesy," Sastre bragged, "I tried to counsel and persuade them to accept reason and embrace our Holy Faith. It would seem that they valued my advice and the personal way in which I spoke to them, for as a result of this they presented me with the attached memorial." The paper they had marked with crude crosses said that they earnestly desired salvation, ministers, and a church—on Tiburón Island. Before these heathens could change their minds the anxious Sastre, fancying himself subduer of the Tiburones, sent Lieutenant Manuel de la Azuela and eight soldiers to reconnoiter the island and designate the most approprite site for a mission. Juan Gil went along "on his own."[19]

Jagged Tiburón, a three-hundred-thousand-acre piece of Sonoran Desert broken off from the mainland, had long been home to the Tiburones, one of a half dozen Seri subgroups recognized by the Spaniards. To their would-be conquerors it became a symbol of the Seris' barbarous freedom, a last stronghold, the final obstacle to pacification. Gálvez had wanted to invade it, occupy the few waterholes, take off the people, and thereby "rid this interior gulf of a real barrier to free navigation."[20] Later when a Tiburón delegation had begged the Spaniards' pardon and promised not to harass mainland residents they had been given leave to stay, but "warned that at the least violation troops would come and put them to the sword."[21]

At Carrizal, a meager waterhole on the sandy coastal plain opposite the island, Lieutenant Azuela and Father Gil met with Cazoni and some twenty families. Once Azuela, in the name of Governor Sastre, had created the Tiburón chief captain general of his nation and instructed him to raise a hundred warriors in the king's service, Gil asked, through the Indian interpreter Francisco, whether they were willing to give up their heathen ways. They answered yes, but there were conditions.

First, the mission must be founded at Carrizal, where all the island dwellers, estimated at more than five hundred, would congregate. And second, Fray Juan himself must be their missionary "until death." The Franciscan, displaying more zeal than good sense, agreed. He and Azuela then crossed over to the island to parley with the others, who approached them unarmed carrying makeshift crosses. The conditions were the same.

The very night he returned to Horcasitas, Juan Gil wrote the governor. To show Sastre just how much the Franciscans did want to minister to the Seris, the Father President outlined a bold new economic base for a mission at barren Carrizal.

Since the place was, in the friar's words, "utterly useless for any kind of planting" and the land "pure sand and alkali," he proposed a salt works and fishing as mission industries. For the first he would need twenty or twenty-five of the army surplus mules left behind by Elizondo, and for the second, one of the government-owned launches at Guaymas. To reduce further the cost of maintaining himself, a missionary companion, and the neophytes at Carrizal, Gil suggested the appropriation of two additional sites, thirty and forty-five miles away, for a dry farm and a stock ranch, the first at a place called Tenuaje and the second "between Siete Cerritos and the Cerro del Guzguz." He also asked for some of the excess oxen at Pitic and for seed. The next day, September 17, Sastre forwarded Gil's letter to the viceroy, admitting that the friar's recommendations were not without merit.[22]

Intendant Corbalán in the meantime had begun to get on Sastre's nerves. He continued to direct the Pitic project from Álamos as if he were still governor. He wrote asking Sastre to persuade the Seris to clear fields for winter wheat. He announced that he had commissioned his subdelegate Pedro Tueros to divide up Seri holdings, once the acequia was operable, into family plots, commons, and church land for Mission Nuestra Señora de Guadalupe "which is what the pueblo is to be called." He told Juan Antonio Meave, agent in charge of the government dole, to make plows and oxen available. And, remembering the deceased

Father Buena's refusal, he again urged Viceroy Bucareli to see that a friar be named for the Seris.

At Pitic contractor Rivera struggled to finish the ditch. When all the Indian *tapisques* deserted him, he kept the job going with a half dozen Pimas from the presidio. He applied for more workers to Sastre, who took no action for a month. He fought rain and boulders. Then on September 18 he made a cautious prediction to Corbalán—the Seris could begin planting October 1.[23]

Father President Gil recognized the implications. No longer was Buena's hard line tenable. In their reports to Bucareli both Sastre and Corbalán were putting pressure on the Franciscans. Gil kept the College informed, and in mid-October, just as water finally reached the Seris at Pitic, the friars made their bid with the viceroy. The College was destitute. Funds for church, padres' quarters, and maintenance would have to come from the government. Support for two missionaries was essential since the College's closest mission was sixty miles from Pitic and "because these Seris have given ample proof of their inconstancy, no less of their cruelty, and therefore one must fear, with more than enough cause, a sudden uprising."[24]

While the viceroy's fiscal considered the friar's request, Fray Juan Gil accompanied the inspection party on a tour of the completed irrigation project. All agreed. It was strong, well-built, and carried an abundance of water. Resolved now to found a mission, the Father President went begging: wine, wax, whatever people would give. Because he himself was committed to the Tiburones, he named thin-faced young Matías Gallo missionary to the Seris at Pitic.[25]

For a year and a half Intendant Pedro Corbalán had anguished over the Pitic ditch. Now, while he fussed about the way in which his underlings had terminated the contract with Rivera, Sastre stepped in and stole the show.[26]

Just back from the Cieneguilla placers, the ailing governor summoned his strength and rode to Pitic, arriving November 16. He had decided to so do, he later informed Corbalán sarcastically, "so that neither you nor I would be thought negligent." Finding the Seris lolling about, but allegedly wanting to work, Sastre ordered ten fully rigged plows and as many yokes of oxen turned over to them on the spot.

> At once I [Sastre] moved on to the inspection of the lands accompanied by the Reverend Father Fray Juan Crisóstomo, President of these missions. At the same time I also designated their community lands, marking out for the Indians a half league in each of the four directions with the center point at the Cerro de la Conveniencia, situated that same distance from the pueblo. I commissioned the aforesaid Father to make the distribution to each individual family in the presence of Governor Crisanto, War Captain José Antonio, and some of the other caciques, which pleased them very much. The following day I had the pleasure of seeing the soil broken by their plows and a half fanega of wheat planted.[27]

Government agent Meave was conspicuously absent that day. He had provided no place in the pueblo for the friars to stay. Still, on November 17, 1772, in the name of the College of Querétaro and in the utmost poverty, Fathers Gil and Gallo founded the Seri mission, calling it San Antonio de Padua. Nuestra Señora de Guadalupe—the choice of Gálvez, Croix, and Corbalán—became an alternate patroness. The same day, November 17, Viceroy Bucareli authorized the construction of a church at Pitic at royal expense. He also politely rebuffed the friars. So long as the Seris maintained good faith, one missionary would be sufficient, one who could manage newly pacified Indians, treat them gently, and incline them toward agriculture.[28]

Before the governor left Pitic a group of Tiburones showed up. They still wanted to settle at Carrizal. Sastre summoned Father Gil. Then and there he arranged with the friar to take them seed and rations, to remove them from the island, and to set a date when plows and oxen should be delivered, or so Sastre told the viceroy. According to Franciscan sources, the governor compelled Fray Juan to go ill-provisioned into the wilderness. Whatever the case, it cost the Father President his life.[29]

NOT ALL the Tiburones wanted a mission. Some had spoken against Cazoni, against appeasing Spaniards in any way. Yet a crowd came over from the island for the founding at Carrizal November 26. They accepted gifts and pozole and stood around as Fray Juan went through the curious ritual of the Mass. Some helped put up the large ramada that served as a church. They built a hut of poles and brush for the Father and others for Captain General Cazoni, Governor Hernando Nanos, and War Captain Pavacot. But few came to catechism. Mission Dulcísimo Nombre de Jesús was little more than a token.[30]

Gil, left with only his young acolyte, kept hoping that approval of his plan would arrive from Mexico City. While he waited he taught some of the children to cross themselves and tried to get the men to catch more fish than they ate. Until he could offer them tangible benefits, the Tiburones would continue to roam and hunt turtles, ignorant that Jesus Christ had died for them.

While Father Gil endured at Carrizal, bureaucrats Corbalán and Sastre kept up their feud. The intendant bitterly resented the governor's thinly veiled charge of negligence. In the matter of the Seris he would stand on his record. Agent Meave and Subdelegate Tueros dutifully minimized Sastre's role: the governor had only stayed at Pitic a day; he had accomplished nothing new; and the Seris were not all of a sudden happily plowing fields. When Apaches struck at his capital, Sastre withdrew all but a handful of the Pitic garrison to Horcasitas. Fray Matías Gallo left. Until there were a church and quarters for him he preferred to live at Ures and commute. Corbalán proposed to the viceroy that Seri crops be meted out by the friar or an agent. If, as Sastre had suggested, they were divided immediately on a family basis the Indians would wolf them down or sell them. Though Bucareli continued to enjoin cooperation between intendant and governor, he feared that their discord might wreck the Seri peace.[31]

From time to time Fray Juan Gil emerged from the wilderness to satisfy the demands of his office. Whenever the Father President was in Horcasitas the people knew it. They jammed the church to hear a one-man revival. As far as don Miguel Joseph de

Arenibar, the absentee parish priest, was concerned, the Franciscan zealot could inveigh against sin till the whole bawdy populace repented. Once, the licentious Sastre invited Father Gil to stay in the governor's quarters. Whatever his host did, it so scandalized the friar that he left in a huff. Opponents of the governor saw to it that word of the incident reached the viceroy.[32]

Sastre was sick. Late in December Bucareli admonished him for not reporting on a number of urgent matters. "The signatures on my letters," Sastre pleaded on February 1, 1773, "will prove to Your Excellency the deplorable state of my suffering." Father Gil wrote from Carrizal. He still had not received all the promised supplies, or approval of his proposals. It appeared that the bureaucrats looked upon Carrizal as no more than a half-way station. They seemed to expect the Tiburones to come in from there to Pitic. No matter. Wretched and forsaken, Gil was content. All he wanted was to end his life in the company of his Tiburones. On March 7, with little warning, he got his wish.[33]

The night before, a Tiburón lad named Ixquisis, evidently put up to it by the anti-Spanish faction, started a rumor at Carrizal. Rebel Pimas, he said, were on their way to murder the missionary and the Indians who had invited him. Not waiting for verification, Gil and his neophytes cleared out. About midnight from a hill nearby they looked down to see flames leaping from the huts.

On the morning of the seventh Father Gil sent Cazoni to round up the people while he and the acolyte started back down. Part way Ixquisis and three youths blocked their path. Fray Juan greeted them. He took tobacco from the sleeve of his habit and started to hand it to them. When one stooped to pick up a big rock Gil yelled at his assistant to run.

It hit the friar square in the chest smashing the crucifix he carried. As he cried out condemning his tormentors another rock caught him on the forehead. He went down. Even after they had beaten him lifeless, the acolyte recalled, they kept on pounding the corpse. Then they ran.

When Cazoni and the others found the body they carried it back to the smouldering mission. As they were setting up an army tent to cover the grave, someone recognized two of the assailants. Cazoni executed them on the spot. With their severed heads and some of the sacred objects from the church he set out for Pitic.

Word had already reached Horcasitas. Lieutenant Azuela rode at once. At Pitic he met Cazoni. Thanking the native leader for his loyalty, he asked him to return to Carrizal ahead of the soldiers to calm his people. Only the guilty parties had cause to fear.

As the column drew near, all the Tiburones who had not fled to the island, children and adults, came out to meet it, weeping for Fray Juan, noted the lieutenant. The soldiers marveled at the tent, "a sign of the Indians' veneration, a deed most admirable among these heathens." Much to their relief, Cazoni had already captured Ixquisis. Azuela heard the testimony of both Indians and took custody of the prisoner. Then, exhorting the Tiburones not to let this heinous crime lead to general rebellion, he rode in haste for Horcasitas. Governor Sastre was dead.[34]

SIX WEEKS after the murder of Juan Gil, Bucareli sent his condolences to the College and requested that the friars name another Father President. No friend of Gálvez' intendant system, the viceroy had already passed over Pedro Corbalán and designated veteran Captain Bernardo de Urrea interim governor and judge in the case against Ixquisis. Even though "this inhuman and horrible crime . . . cries out for the most severe and exemplary punishment," he insisted on due process of the law. Because Sonora lacked lawyers, he forwarded detailed instructions. Nothing must be done to alienate the rest of the Tiburones. Cazoni should be rewarded. The viceroy ordered the remains of Father Juan Gil exhumed and transferred to the closest church.[35]

The Tiburones were torn. "Under no circumstances are these Indians to be forced," read the instructions to Sastre's successor, "nor are those who might move [away from Carrizal] to be restrained."[36] Just when it appeared that Fray Juan had died in vain, Cazoni presented himself before Captain Urrea saying that his people wanted a settlement and lands like those of their relatives at Pitic. That could be arranged, the interim governor allowed, at a site called Torreón, a league west of Pitic.[37]

Late in September Urrea and Father Arenibar, who had thought Gil a fool in the first place to trust the barbaric Tiburones, rode out to Carrizal to redeem the martyr's bones. They found the tent intact. When the grave was opened they noticed no foul odor. They placed the bones in a wooden box along with the relics the Indians had buried with the body—the missionary's rosary, medals, and cross, the broken crucifix, and the book he was carrying when slain, the *Mística Ciudad* of Venerable María de Ágreda. Back at Horcasitas the box was placed temporarily in the church on a table shrouded in black and surmounted by four candles. The people came and wept. A week later Fray Matías Gallo and Fray Francisco Antonio Barbastro carried it to Ures for burial.[38]

DURING the decade after Gil's death, the Seris reverted. Reports of their "fine carpet of ripe wheat" and their delight with free clothes were offset by reports that they were selling their rations and trafficking with bad Indians. Bureaucrat Corbalán held up construction of the Pitic church, first because there was no precedent for building a mission church in Sonora at the king's expense, and second for lack of an architect. Captain Urrea remitted to Mexico City the evidence in the Ixquisis case, but before final judgment was rendered the defendant died in jail.[39] A new governor, don Francisco Antonio Crespo, listened cautiously for a time to the blandishments of the Tiburones. At their invitation he even rode out to Carrizal, to find the place deserted. He then reported to Bucareli:

> The settlement they had at Carrizal during the time of my predecessor . . . was no more than show, without the least stability. By and large they opposed the presence of the friar. Although the general, Ignacio Cazoni, and a few others acted then, and even to the present, in good faith, this Indian enjoys neither the authority nor the respect necessary (as I have already told Your Excellency) for us to hope with any basis in fact for the desired end.[40]

Detail from a stylized eighteenth-century portrait of Juan Gil.
Courtesy Museo Municipal, Querétaro

W. J. McGee, "The Seri Indians,"
Bureau of American Ethnology *Annual Report* no. 17 (1898)

Cazoni, who did settle near Pitic with forty-seven Tiburones, accused Crisanto of witchcraft and the murder of one of Cazoni's daughters. Crisanto then murdered Cazoni and escaped.[41]

In view of the Seris' "perverse habits" Bucareli approved a second missionary and a guard detail at Pitic. But the tide had turned. A few at a time they slipped away. Then the bloody raids resumed, and Spaniards began counting up the times these Indians had rebelled—fourteen, some said.

By 1780 frontier commanders had once again put the blame for all Sonora's woes squarely on the vile, unregenerate Seri nation. Pedro Corbalán, again elevated to the position of intendant-governor when Gálvez became minister of the Indies, admitted that after a decade of experience with the Seris he could only conclude that "very little or nothing at all has altered their perverse way of thinking or reformed their depraved inclinations toward idleness, sloth, and licentiousness." Let the savages die in the field or surrender and be exiled, "the males twelve years and older to Havana and the women and children to the Californias." He had used the same words nine years before.[42]

Gálvez, too, revived an earlier plan. In March 1782 he emerged from an audience with the king and announced:

> His Majesty believes that to chastise the Seris and their relatives of Tiburón Island it would be advisable as soon as possible [i.e., when the war with Great Britain was over] to mount a vigorous and well-planned expedition against this island in an effort to annihilate all its perfidious inhabitants capable of bearing arms.[43]

THE SERI fiasco of the early 1770's could hardly have been averted. It had happened before, and it would happen again. Yet in the effort to pacify Sonora and to civilize and save souls, they all had to try—the grand Gálvez, the enlightened Elizondo, the bureaucrat Corbalán, realistic, outspoken Father Buena, desperate Sastre, and the self-mortifying Fray Juán Gil. When extermination failed, they tried to make the Seris Christian peasant farmers, to assimilate them by force. If Corbalán suggested stock raising and Gil a fishing cooperative they did so only as half-way measures.[44] The ideal remained the same.

But the Seris, Sonora's only totally non-agricultural people, refused to fit the mold. A few hundred survive today. They fish and carve. They still do not farm.

NOTES

1. Fray Francisco Antonio Barbastro, Compendio de lo más notable que han trabajado en Sonora los hijos del Colegio de la Santa Cruz . . . desde el año de 1768 hasta él de 1783, Babiácora, Sept. 10, 1788; Fr. Marcellino da Civezza Collection, Antonianum Library, Rome (Civ. Col.), 202.35, microfilm, Mission San Xavier del Bac, Tucson, Arizona. The College chronicler, Fray Juan Domingo Arricivita, based most of what he wrote about the missions and missionaries of Sonora on Barbastro's account. *Crónica seráfica y apostólica del Colegio de Propaganda Fide de la Santa Cruz de Querétaro en la Nueva España*, segunda parte (México, 1792), pp. 515-19. Barbastro and Arricivita, apologists for the friars, consistently laid the blame for the Seri fiasco on government officials. Buena died later that year in the Real de San Antonio, seventy-five miles southeast of Ures. Gil de Bernabé, a native of Alfambra (Teruel), had crossed from Spain in the "mission" of 1763. Despacho de embarcación, Cádiz, July 18, 1763, *et al.*; Archivo General de Indias, Sevilla (AGI), Contratación, leg. 5545A. John L. Kessell, "The Making of a Martyr: The Young Francisco Garcés," NMHR, vol. 45 (1970), pp. 186-89.

2. Jacobo Ugarte y Loyola to Teodoro de Croix, Horcasitas, Jan. 15, 1780; AGI, Audiencia de Guadalajara (Guad.), leg. 272. W. J. McGee's "The Seri Indians," *Annual Report*, Bureau of American Ethnology, no. 17 (Washington, 1898), has been supplemented by A. L. Kroeber, *The Seri*, Southwest Museum Papers, no. 6 (Los Angeles, 1931); William B. Griffen, *Notes on Seri Indian Culture, Sonora, Mexico*, School of Inter-American Studies, Latin American Monographs, no. 10 (Gainesville, 1959); and other recent studies. See also Edward H. Spicer, *Cycles of Conquest: The Impact of Spain, Mexico, and the United States on the Indians of the Southwest, 1533-1960* (Tucson, 1962), pp. 105-17. Some excellent photographs, showing the Seris in the mid-twentieth century,

116

are reproduced in William Neil Smith, "The Seri Indians and the Sea Turtles," *The Journal of Arizona History*, vol. 15 (1974), pp. 139-58.

3. Pineda, Decreto contra la rebelión del Cerro Prieto, Horcasitas, Sept. 10, 1768; Archivo General de la Nación, México (AGN), Provincias Internas (PI), vol. 47. Elizondo to Viceroy Marqués de Croix, Pitic, Feb. 3, 1771; *ibid.*, vol. 81. Matías de Armona, Breve informe, Nov. 29, 1769; AGI, Audiencia de México, leg. 2477. See also Donald W. Rowland, "The Elizondo Expedition against the Indian Rebels of Sonora, 1765-1771," (unpublished Ph.D. dissertation, University of California, Berkeley, 1930).

4. Luis Navarro García, *Don José de Gálvez y la Comandancia General de las Provincias Internas del Norte de Nueva España* (Sevilla, 1964), pp. 148-85. Barbastro. Elizondo to Gálvez, Pitic, June 21, 1769; AGI, Guad., leg. 416.

5. Herbert Ingram Priestley, *José de Gálvez, Visitor-General of New Spain (1765-1771)* (Berkeley, 1916), pp. 267-95. Navarro García, p. 178. Buena had even censored the Visitor's mail, deciding which reports he should see and which might upset him. Buena to Pineda, Ures, Oct. 26, 1769; AGN, Historia, vol. 18. Barbastro. Gálvez to Buena, México, July 18, 1770; Civ. Col., 201.86.

6. Extracto historial de este expediente; AGI, Guad., leg. 416. Crisanto had just brought in the head of a Pima rebel, Extracto México, May 31, 1770; AGN, PI, vol. 81.

7. Elizondo to the Marqués de Croix, Pitic, April 8, 1771; *ibid.* Elizondo to Croix, Pitic, April 21, 1771; *ibid.* Extracto, México, May 27, 1771; AGI, Guad., leg. 416. Croix to Julián de Arriaga, México, Sept. 19, 1771; *ibid.*, leg. 512.

8. [The Marqués de Croix] to Elizondo, México, Jan. 18, 1771; AGN, PI, vol. 81. Francisco Bellido to Viceroy Bucareli, Pitic, Dec. 27, 1771; AGI, Guad., leg. 512. Pedro Corbalán to Bucareli, Álamos, Jan. 21, 1772; *ibid.* At the Spaniards' urging Crisanto and his Seri warriors had deceived and killed the notorious Pima malcontent Cueras.

9. [Arriaga] to the Marqués de Croix, San Lorenzo, Nov. 3, 1770; *ibid.*, leg. 416. Elizondo to Croix, Feb. 3, 1771. Croix to Arriaga, México, Feb. 27, 1771; *ibid.*, leg. 512. [Arriaga] to Croix, Madrid, July 5, 1771; *ibid.* Croix to Corbalán, México, June 12, 1771; AGN, PI, vol. 247.

10. Elizondo to the Marqués de Croix, April 21, 1771. Elizondo and Corbalán to Croix, Pitic, April 29, 1771; AGI, Guad., leg. 416. Croix to Corbalán, México, June 8, 1771; AGN, PI, vol. 247. Croix to Arriaga, México, June 27, 1771; AGI, Guad., leg. 416. Corbalán to Croix, Álamos, March 16, 1771; AGN, PI, vol. 93. [Croix] to Corbalán, México, June 12, 1771; *ibid.*

11. Corbalán reached Pitic in time to discuss the state of the province with Colonel Elizondo, just before the latter departed. Corbalán to the Marqués de Croix, Pitic, April 29, May 2, 28, 1771; *ibid.* Corbalán to Croix, Pitic, Aug. 2, 1771; AGI, Guad., leg. 512. Corbalán to Buena, Álamos, Oct. 17, 1771; AGN, PI, vol. 247.

12. Mesía to Corbalán, Pitic, Oct. 12, 1771; *ibid.* Corbalán to Mesía, Álamos, Oct. 21, and Nov. 7, 1771; *ibid.* Corbalán to Bucareli, Álamos, Dec. 24, 1771; *ibid.*

13. Buena to Corbalán, Ures, Oct. 29, 1771; *ibid.*

14. Corbalán to Bucareli, Dec. 24, 1771. Bucareli to Arriaga, México, Jan. 27, 1772; AGI, Guad., leg. 512. Bucareli to Corbalán, México, April 28, 1772; AGN, PI, vol. 247. The presidial captain at Pitic reported to Bucareli that treasury officials—by whom he must have meant Intendant Corbalán and his agents—were jeopardizing the Seri settlement by haggling over the cost of renewing work on the ditch. Bellido to Bucareli, Dec. 27, 1771.

15. For biographical sketches of Corbalán and Sastre, see Francisco R. Almada, *Diccionario de historia, geografía y biografía sonorenses* (Chihuahua, 1952), pp. 184-85, 732-33. Navarro García, pp. 256-57.

16. Rivera, *et al.*, Horcasitas, March 25, 1772; AGN, PI, vol. 247. Corbalán to Bucareli, Álamos, June 26, 1772; *ibid.* Bucareli to Arriaga, México, July 26, 1772; AGI, Guad., leg. 512.

17. Sastre to Arriaga, Pitic, July 29, 1772; *ibid.*, leg. 416. Sastre was later reminded that he should direct his reports to the viceroy, not to Spain. [Arriaga] to the governor of Sonora, El Pardo, March 5, 1773; *ibid.*, leg. 513.

18. Juan Honorato de Rivera to Corbalán, Pitic, Sept. 5, 1772; AGN, PI, vol. 247. Sastre to Bucareli, Horcasitas, Oct. 19, 1772; *ibid.*, vol. 81.

19. Sastre to Bucareli, Horcasitas, Sept. 4, 1772; *ibid.* Sastre to Arriaga, Horcasitas, Sept. 4, 1772; AGI, Guad., leg. 513. Memorial of Cazoni and Tumuzaqui; *ibid.*

20. Gálvez to the Marqués de Croix, Álamos, June 10, 1769; *ibid.*, leg. 416.

21. Extract for Council of the Indies of the Marqués de Croix to Arriaga, México, May 31, 1770; *ibid.*

22. Gil de Bernabé to Sastre, Horcasitas, Sept. 16, 1772; AGN, PI, vol. 81. Sastre to Bucareli, Horcasitas, Sept. 17, 1772; *ibid.*

23. Corbalán to Sastre, Álamos, Aug. 17 and 29, 1772; *ibid.*, vol. 247. Corbalán to Tueros, Álamos, Aug. 29, 1772, transmitting the detailed *Instrucción que ha de observar para el establecimiento de los Indios reducidos de la nación Seri en las inmediaciones del presidio del Pitic.* Corbalán to Meave, Álamos, Aug. 17, 1772; *ibid.* Corbalán to Bucareli,

Álamos, Aug. 17 and Sept. 5, 1772; *ibid.* Rivera to Corbalán, Pitic, Sept. 5 and 18, 1772. *ibid.*

24. Fray Romualdo Cartagena to Bucareli, Querétaro, Oct. 16, 1772; *ibid.*

25. Rivera to Corbalán, Pitic, Oct. 28, 1772; *ibid.* After the inspection Rivera turned the ditch over to the Administrador de Rentas Reales Francisco Antonio Dorronzoro. Dorronzoro to Corbalán, Pitic, Oct. 28, 1772; *ibid.* Barbastro. Arricivita, pp. 426-27. Matías Gallo had come from Spain in the mission of 1769. Lista de los cuarenta religiosos; AGI, Guad., leg. 369.

26. Corbalán to Dorronzoro, Álamos, Nov. 13, 1772, *et al.;* AGN, PI, vol. 247. Further inspection in December revealed one weak section of the ditch. A rubble levee to hold back the current of the Ríos Sonora and San Miguel was suggested. More about the ditch is in Testimonio de la junta celebrada en primero de febrero de este año [1776], informe que en su virtud hizo don Pedro Corbalán, y la que en su vista devolvió a celebrar en primero de agosto; *ibid.*

27. Sastre to Corbalán, Horcasitas, Dec. 6, 1772; *ibid.* Extracto, México, Feb. 24, 1773; AGI, Guad., leg. 513. Corbalán had cautioned Tueros to respect the nearby hacienda administered by the Benedictine friar Benito Monserrat. When Sastre dictated the bounds of Seri lands Fray Benito claimed that all or most of the area lay within the hacienda grant. Testimonio del cuaderno tercero formado sobre el establecimiento de los Indios Seris en el Pitic y pretensión del P. F. Benito Monserrat; AGN, PI, vol. 247.

28. Bucareli, letters to Sastre, Corbalán, and Cartagena, México, Nov. 17, 1772; *ibid.* Bucareli to Arriaga, México, Nov. 26, 1772; AGI, Guad., leg. 416. Both Barbastro and Arricivita (pp. 427-28) refer to an unjustified and bitter complaint from the viceroy, who, on the basis of Governor Sastre's reports, charged that the friars did not want to minister to the Seris. Fearing another such attack, the College ordered Fray Juan Gil to go ahead prematurely with the Carrizal mission.

29. Sastre to Bucareli, Horcasitas, Nov. 29, 1772; AGN, PI, vol. 247. Barbastro. Arricivita, pp. 427-28, 520-21. Francisco Antonio Dorronzoro had written that Tueros requested him to store 500 fanegas of wheat or maize and aid Meave so that Father Gil "does not lack the slightest thing for planting at Tenuaje with these Tiburón Seri Indians, all of which I shall do." Dorronzoro to Corbalán, Oct. 28, 1772.

30. For a recent description of Carrizal, see Paul M. Roca, *Paths of the Padres through Sonora* (Tucson, 1967), pp. 174-75. More than a century after Gil's death it was said in Hermosillo that the ruins of his poor mission could still be seen near Pozo Escalante. Fortunato Hernández

claimed to have found fragments of it in 1902. See his *Las razas indígenas de Sonora y la guerra del Yaqui* (México, 1902), p. 21. McGee, pp. 19, 80-82.

31. Corbalán to Sastre, Álamos, Dec. 22, 1772; AGN, PI, vol. 247. Meave to Corbalán, Pitic, Dec. 8, 1772; *ibid.* Tueros to Corbalán, Cieneguilla, Jan. 14, 1773; *ibid.* Gov. Francisco Crespo to Bucareli, Horcasitas, Nov. 30, 1773; *ibid.*, vol. 81. Corbalán to Bucareli, Álamos, Feb. 11, 1773; *ibid.*, vol. 247. Bucareli to Arriaga, México, Dec. 27, 1772; AGI, Guad., leg. 416.

32. Almada, p. 733. Testimony in the cause of Juan Gil, Horcasitas, Oct., 1782; Franciscan General Archive, Rome, vol. XI/34, no. 36.

33. [Bucareli] to Sastre, México, Dec. 30, 1772; AGN, PI, vol. 81. Sastre to Bucareli, Horcasitas, Feb. 1, 1773; *ibid.* Barbastro.

34. Extracto, México, April 26, 1773; AGI, Guad., leg. 513. Testimony of Cazoni; quoted in Arricivita, pp. 428-29. Barbastro. According to Fray Matías Gallo's burial entry in the Pitic register, Xavier, a mulatto *paje*, and interpreter Francisco, a Guaymas Indian, buried the body in the Carrizal cemetery March 8. Gallo, March 22, 1773, in register of Mission San Antonio de Padua del Pitic; Archivo de la Mitra de Sonora, Hermosillo.

35. Bucareli to Father Guardian of the Colegio de la Santa Cruz de Querétaro, México, April 21, 1773; AGI, Guad., leg. 513; quoted in Arricivita, pp. 429-30. Bucareli to Urrea, México, April 21, 1773; AGI, Guad., leg. 513. Bucareli to Arriaga, México, April 26, 1773; *ibid.*

36. Nota de los asuntos que se hallan pendientes en las Provincias de Sinaloa y Sonora, México, July 3, 1773; AGN, PI, vol. 81. [Melchor de Peramás] to Crespo. México, Aug. 4, 1773; *ibid.*

37. Crespo to Bucareli, Horcasitas, Dec. 2, 1773; *ibid.*

38. Barbastro. Testimony in the cause of Juan Gil.

39. Bucareli to Arriaga, April 26, 1773. [Bucareli] to Crespo, México, Sept. 7, 1773; AGN, PI, vol. 81. Crespo to Bucareli, Horcasitas, Dec. 2 and 7, 1773; *ibid.* Crespo to Bucareli, Horcasitas, Jan. 23, 1774; *ibid.*, vol. 96. Manuel de la Azuela to Crespo, Pitic, Nov. 22, 1775; *ibid.*, vol. 237. Corbalán to Sastre, Álamos, Feb. 15, 1773; *ibid.*, vol. 247. Corbalán to Bucareli, Álamos, Feb. 22, 1773; *ibid.* Details of constructing the Pitic church are found in several expedientes in AGN, PI, vol. 247.

40. Crespo to Bucareli, Horcasitas, Sept. 20, 1774, *et al.; ibid.*, vol. 96. Earlier the governor had characterized Cazoni in these words: *aunque de buena índole es torpísimo e ignorante.* Crespo to Bucareli, Horcasitas, May 11, 1774; *ibid.*

41. Juan Bautista de Anza to Teodoro de Croix, Horcasitas, June 30, 1777; AGI, Guad., leg. 515.

42. Corbalán to Teodoro de Croix, Arizpe, Jan. 9, 1780, *et al.; ibid.* leg. 272. Corbalán to the Marqués de Croix, March 16, 1771. Navarro García, pp. 325-33. See also Max L. Moorhead, *The Apache Frontier: Jacobo Ugarte and Spanish-Indian Relations in Northern New Spain, 1769-1791* (Norman, 1968), pp. 49-52.

43. [Gálvez] to Teodoro de Croix, El Pardo, March 6, 1782; AGI, Guad., leg. 271. Cf. Gálvez to the Marqués de Croix, June 10, 1769.

44. Corbalán to the Marqués de Croix, Pitic, May 2, 1771; AGN, PI, vol. 93. Gil de Bernabé to Sastre, Sept. 16, 1772.

SOURCES FOR THE HISTORY
OF A NEW MEXICO COMMUNITY:
ABIQUIÚ*

"WRITING ABOUT ABIQUIU," F. Stanley confesses, "is like picking at a tassle. Any strand you pick up ultimately proves a story." And Stanley, author of dozens of privately printed village "stories," should know.

It is easier to write about Elizabethtown, the nineteenth-century New Mexico boomtown, where one theme and one culture predominated, and where only a ghost survives. Abiquiú, a living community where manifold themes and at least three cultures have shared the stage, holds out the challenge and the savor of variety. An academic, secure in one field or in one period, may back off. Yet if we aspire, as we say we do, to grasp the interaction of cultures through time, what better "laboratory" than Abiquiú? Besides, the story is bound to entertain.

Set in a many-colored landscape of stunning natural beauty forty-five miles northwest of Santa Fe, Abiquiú has been from the beginning a string of settlements sharing that five- or six-mile stretch where the Chama River meanders from west to east. La Puente, Santa Rosa, Santo Tomás, and the others—their history is inseparable.

The sources abound. I have admitted some secondary works less for their texts than for their notes and bibliographies, and I have excluded others readily found therein. The categories, artificial at best, are intended only to dress the ranks. A list of abbreviations is appended.

---

*I have accented the word Abiquiú throughout for the benefit of the reader from Peoria (Abbey-cue, *not* A-bee-cúe or A-bee-coo-you).

Since a good many of the sources cited suggest further sources, I make no claim to comprehensiveness. This is a working document not a final product, a beginning not an end.

I. General histories, local studies, bibliographies

A demonic plague of witches, Indian raids and treaties, the departure or return of an expedition, a sensational crime—only a community's moments of high drama rate mention in the general histories. Still, by using such moments as clues, the way a tracker uses "sign," following index entry to text to note and to primary source, a researcher can close on his subject very quickly.

Hubert Howe Bancroft, *History of Arizona and New Mexico, 1530-1888* (San Francisco: History Co., 1889; reprinted ed., Albuquerque: Horn and Wallace, 1962), is still the place to start. Basing his histories on his vast collection of books and manuscripts (nucleus today of the Bancroft Library at the University of California, Berkeley), Bancroft set the standard for western regional history. For years others followed, even copied. Compare, for example, Bancroft's note on p. 737, listing agents at the Abiquiú Indian agency, with Ralph Emerson Twitchell, *The Leading Facts of New Mexican History*, 5 vols. (Cedar Rapids, Iowa: Torch Press, 1911-17; reprinted ed., 2 vols., Albuquerque: Horn and Wallace, 1963), II (1963):447n. To his credit, Twitchell acknowledged his debt to Bancroft and to others and from New Mexico archives added much to the story. Half a century later, Frank D. Reeve, *History of New Mexico*, 3 vols. (New York: Lewis Historical Publishing Co., 1961), offered a new synthesis. He included more on Abiquiú than either Twitchell or Bancroft, but he rarely cited specific sources. A textbook with no Abiquiú entry in the index is Warren A. Beck, *New Mexico: A History of Four Centuries* (Norman: University of Oklahoma (OU) Press, 1962). In 1979, despite the appearance recently of several brief treatments, among them Marc Simmon's readable *New Mexico: A Bicentennial History* (New York: W. W. Norton, 1977), New Mexico still lacks a good, up-to-date general history.

Drawing the circle closer to Abiquiú, Frances Leon Swadesh, *Los Primeros Pobladores, Hispanic Americans of the Ute Frontier*

(Notre Dame: University of Notre Dame Press, 1974), examines settlement up the Chama Valley and into the San Juan Basin, development of community life, and the adjustments demanded by United States conquest. Alvar Ward Carlson, "The Rio Arriba: A Geographic Appraisal of the Spanish-American Homeland (Upper Rio Grande Valley, New Mexico)" (Ph.D. diss., University of Minnesota, 1971), devotes a chapter to "Abiquiu: A Village on One of the Last Existing Community Grants." Somewhat revised, this surfaces as "Spanish Colonization and the Abiquiu Grant, New Mexico, 1754-1970," in, of all places, *The Philippine Geographical Journal* 20 (Apr.-June 1976): 61-68.

F. Stanley (Stanley Francis Louis Crocchiola), compiling whatever he could get his hands on, sketches *The Abiquiu (New Mexico) Story* (c. 1960) in a thirty-five-page booklet, from pre-Spanish pueblos to the mining of dinosaur bones at Ghost Ranch in the late 1940s. Another short publication, a good-humored blend of folk tradition and history by a native of the community, is Gilberto Benito Córdova's *Abiquiú and Don Cacahuate: A Folk History of a New Mexican Village* (Los Cerrillos, N.M.: San Marcos Press, 1973).

Popular articles, which may contain a high concentration of romantic gush, are worth a look nevertheless, if only to suggest topics and provoke questions. Three examples are: Frank C. Spencer, "Old Abiquiu, Crossroads of History," *New Mexico Magazine* (NM) 26 (May 1948): 22-23, 31, 33; Betty Woods, "Trip of the Month, Abiquiu," NM 27 (Aug. 1949): 6; and Alice Bullock, "Peaceful Community May Harbor a Curse," *Pasatiempo*, Santa Fe *New Mexican*, Oct. 12, 1969. Was gold discovered near Abiquiú in 1830 or not? Was "Molleno," famed nineteenth-century santero, really from Abiquiú? Are buried treasure, bandido, and curse pure fiction? If so, who invented them, under what circumstances, and why?

Two bibliographies, less specialized than others listed below, deserve mention here. The first is Lyle Saunders, *A Guide to Materials Bearing on Cultural Relations in New Mexico* (Albuquerque: University of New Mexico (UNM) Press, 1944), and supplemented in the feature, "A Guide to the Literature of the Southwest," *New Mexico Quarterly* 12-24 (1942-54). And the second is Part II of Marta Weigle, ed., *Hispanic Villages of Northern*

New Mexico (Santa Fe: Lightning Tree, 1975). These are particularly helpful as guides through the maze of post-1930, government and grant-supported studies by scholar-bureaucrats reveling in the applied social sciences. Among current multidisciplinary listings, none is more useful than the on-going bibliographical section of the *SMRC-Newsletter* published since 1967 by the Southwestern Mission Research Center, Tucson.

To enter the teeming world of dissertations and theses the most painless way is through the free bibliographies published by University Microfilms International, Ann Arbor, Michigan. Begin with those on Spanish-surnamed populations, minorities, and Latin America. UMI also offers Datrix II, a computer search and retrieval system for dissertations and theses. Approached with keywords—Abiquiú, Chama River, Rio Arriba County, etc.—and $15.00, Datrix II will spit out up to 150 pertinent titles (10¢ for each additional one).

The marriage of computers and standard reference tools, which has spawned data bases, handy terminals, "on-line" searches and "off-line" printouts, let no man put asunder, least of all at the American Bibliographical Center, Santa Barbara, California. ABC-Clio, publisher since 1965 of *America: History and Life*, an annual of classified abstracts of periodical literature, indices of book reviews, and American history bibliography, is now computerized. The University of New Mexico General Library's On-line Search Service already is plugged into more than seventy data bases. The trick for the historian is to learn "search strategy."

II. Prehistory and Indians of the Abiquiú region

Doubtless the first of his pueblo to visit Washington, D.C., an entire skeleton, tenderly removed in 1874 from a prehistoric ruin close-by Abiquiú, arrived at the Army Medical Museum in a crate. Acting Assistant Surgeon H. C. Yarrow told of his pioneering archaeology, complete with a ground plan of the ruin, in the *Annual Report of the Chief of Engineers for 1875*, 44th Cong., 1st sess., House Executive Document (HED) 1, Part 2 (Serial 1676), pp. 1059-68. Thereafter the doctor got good mileage from his report, publishing excerpts in several places, including "Notice of a Ruined Pueblo and an Ancient Burial-Place in the Valley of the

Rio Chama" in *Report upon United States Geographical Surveys West of the One Hundredth Meridian*, vol. 7, Archaeology (Washington, D.C.: Government Printing Office (GPO), 1879).

Evidently the Chama Valley served the ancestors of the Pueblo Indians as an avenue of migration between Mesa Verde and the Rio Grande Valley. Adolph F. Bandelier, who stood outside the Abiquiú church because of the feast-day crowd on August 30, 1885, noted that the modern town was built almost on top of an early Pueblo ruin. In his *Final Report of Investigations among the Indians of the Southwestern United States, Carried on Mainly in the Years from 1880 to 1885*, 2 parts (Cambridge, Mass.: Archaeological Institute of America, 1890-92), II: 54-58, Bandelier distinguished between this ruin, on the south side of Abiquiú proper, and Dr. Yarrow's ruin, three miles east on the bluff above La Puente. Two installments of Bandelier's journals, recently published with copious annotations, mention Abiquiú: *The Southwestern Journals of Adolph F. Bandelier, 1883-1884*, ed. Charles H. Lange and Carroll L. Riley (Albuquerque: UNM Press, 1970), and *1885-1888*, ed. Lange, Riley, and Elizabeth M. Lange (Albuquerque: UNM Press, 1975).

Aiming in 1910 to sort out the place names, particularly the Tewa Pueblo Indian names, in a much wider area, the irrepressible John Peabody Harrington dedicated to Abiquiú and vicinity a map and a dozen pages in "The Ethnogeography of the Tewa Indians," *Twenty-Ninth Annual Report*, Bureau of American Ethnology (BAE), 1907-08 (Washington, D.C.: GPO, 1916). Although he came up with some interesting names, for example, "owl excrement pile arroyo," Harrington failed to locate or label positively the ruin on the bluff at La Puente. In 1919, however, a Smithsonian archaeological expedition did both. J. A. Jeancon, "Excavations in the Chama Valley, New Mexico," BAE, *Bulletin 81* (Washington, D.C.: GPO, 1923), reported a remarkable variety of Indian pottery and not a thing Spanish. This seemed to confirm the Tewa tradition that "great trade fairs" were held here before European colonization.

Perhaps the Pueblo people who moved out before Juan de Oñate moved in downriver in 1598 were the shadowy Asa, perhaps of Tewa ancestry. Such a people, according to Jesse Walter Fewkes,

"Tusayan Migration Traditions," *Nineteenth Annual Report*, BAE, 1897-98 (Washington, D.C.: GPO, 1900): 573-633, departed the Abiquiú area and migrated from pueblo to pueblo all the way to Hopi country, where some of them may have been recruited in the mid-eighteenth century by Spanish Franciscans and resettled as *genízaros* in the Abiquiú area. Scattered references to the Asa and to Abiquiú occur in other publications of the BAE, among them Frederick Webb Hodge, ed., *Handbook of American Indians North of Mexico, Bulletin 30* (Washington, D.C.: GPO, 1907-10). W. David Laird's impressive *Hopi Bibliography, Comprehensive and Annotated* (Tucson: University of Arizona (UA) Press, 1977) may suggest more. It is likely, too, that the Spanish documents contain further evidence of this intriguing Hopi connection.

Some among reports of archaeological surveys and digs in the Abiquiú region, in chronological order, are Frank C. Hibben, *Excavation of the Riana Ruin and Chama Valley Survey* (Albuquerque: UNM Press, 1937); Fred Wendorf, *Salvage Archaeology in the Chama Valley, New Mexico* (Santa Fe: School of American Research, 1953); Stewart Peckham, "Salvage Archaeology in New Mexico, 1957-58: A Partial Report," *El Palacio* (EP) 65 (1958): 161-68; and John R. Van Ness, "The Archaeology of the Chama River Drainage, New Mexico: A Review of the Literature" (MA thesis, University of Pennsylvania, 1968). For several summers the University of New Mexico's archaeological field school, based at Ghost Ranch and presided over by Prof. Florence Hawley Ellis, conducted hot and thirsty on-the-job training at Sepawi and other Chama drainage sites. No overall account of the results has yet appeared.

As for "historic" Indians, the nearby Tewa pueblos of Santa Clara and San Juan have produced two anthropologists of note, Edward P. Dozier and Alfonso Ortiz, who in turn have each written a book, *The Pueblo Indians of North America* (New York: Holt, Rinehart, and Winston, 1970) by Dozier and *The Tewa World: Space, Time, Being, and Becoming in a Pueblo Society* (Chicago: University of Chicago Press, 1969) by Ortiz, that together serve to introduce both the people and "the literature."

Ortiz also is editing the volume on the Southwest in the revised *Handbook of American Indians*, forthcoming from the Smithsonian Institution.

A good place to meet Abiquiú's other Indian neighbors and those who have written about them is the *American Indian Ethnohistory Series*, ed. David Agee Horr (New York: Garland Publishing, 1974), especially in the following volumes: *Apache Indians I* and *VI-IX*, *Navajo Indians I-III*, and *Ute Indians I-II*. These are gatherings of the written testimony of experts before the U.S. Indian Claims Commission, much concerned with aboriginal land-use areas and heavily documented. In addition Norman A. Ross has compiled an *Index to the Expert Testimony before the Indian Claims Commission: The Written Reports* (New York: Clearwater Publishing Co., 1973). Mention here of a single notably comprehensive work, Francis Paul Prucha, *A Bibliographical Guide to the History of Indian-White Relations in the United States* (Chicago: University of Chicago Press, 1977), makes unnecessary the enrollment of individual tribal bibliographies on Navajos, Utes, and Jicarillas.

III. Spanish colonial

Even though don Juan de Oñate settled first in the vicinity of San Juan pueblo, less than twenty miles southeast of Abiquiú, in 1598, Spanish occupation of the middle Chama Valley waited for the eighteenth century. The place name Abiquiú appears in the documents at least as early as the 1730s.

Surely Spaniards passed that way in the 1600s. France V. Scholes's solidly documented studies of seventeenth-century New Mexico, most of which ran serially in the *New Mexico Historical Review* (NMHR), should be mined for leads. A seemingly unsupported allegation by Twitchell (*Leading Facts*, III: 521 n. 322)—"Diego de Vargas campaigned in all this section in 1694 and especially mentions Abiquiu"—warrants archival investigation. Fact is, Vargas's "journals," scattered about in all the pertinent major archives, and J. Manuel Espinosa's *Crusaders of the Río Grande: The Story of Don Diego de Vargas and the Reconquest and Refounding of New Mexico* (Chicago: Institute of Jesuit History,

1942) present a well-defined path into archival waters. All this, of course, presumes the ability to swim—to read and understand Spanish paleography.

A. *Archival sources*

The joys of travel aside, he who rushes first to Mexico or Spain to find all there is on Abiquiú has about as much chance as Columbus had of finding the Earthly Paradise on the Orinoco. Before getting his shots and plunging into foreign archives, the researcher ought to digest Richard E. Greenleaf and Michael C. Meyer, eds., *Research in Mexican History: Topics, Methodology, Sources, and A Practical Guide to Field Research* (Lincoln: University of Nebraska Press, 1973) for Mexico, and the *Guía de fuentes para la historia de Ibero-América conservadas en España*, 2 vols. (Madrid: Dirección General de Archivos y Bibliotecas, 1966-69) for Spain.

For both Spain and the Americas, including the United States, Lino Gómez Canedo's *Los archivos de la historia de América, período colonial español*, 2 vols. (México: Instituto Panamericano de Geografía e Historia, 1961), offers a guided tour of dozens of archives. One of three references in the index to the second volume under Abiquiú is to documents in the Edward E. Ayer Collection, Newberry Library, Chicago. Evidently these are private papers that once belonged to José María Chávez, Pablo González, and other Abiquiú notables. They date from the eighteenth, nineteenth, and twentieth centuries and have much to do with local land ownership and manipulation. Today microfilm (3 rolls) of Newberry material resides at the State Records Center and Archives, Santa Fe (SRC), only forty-five miles from Abiquiú.

Familiarity with archival guides and with the holdings of nearby institutions can save a researcher valuable time and, alas, on occasion, a trip to Spain. A large part of the known documentation for the history of colonial New Mexico has in fact been copied and brought together (in volumes of bound photostats, on microfilm, and in transcript) in one place—Special Collections, Zimmerman Library, University of New Mexico (SC-UNM). The Library of Congress and the Bancroft also have copies of much of this material. This is not to say that further searching—in the Cathedral Archives at Durango, Mexico, or among the Casa

Amarilla materials now being catalogued by the Archivo General de la Nación, Mexico City, or in a hundred other places—will not yield new finds, only to say, first things first.

Two complementary collections, the Spanish Archives of New Mexico (SANM) and the Archives of the Archdiocese of Santa Fe (AASF), one largely civil-military and the other ecclesiastical, head the list. Both focus on the post-1680 colony. Both have been microfilmed, and there are published guides.

Much more than a simple finding device, Ralph Emerson Twitchell's *The Spanish Archives of New Mexico*, 2 vols. (Cedar Rapids, Iowa: Torch Press, 1914; reprinted ed., New York: Arno Press, 1976), features summaries of some entries and translations of others. Volume Two inventories the documents spirited to Washington, D.C., in 1903 and returned to New Mexico in 1923, known today, with certain additions, as SANM, Series II. When the State Records Center microfilmed Series II (22 rolls)— containing, among other items of interest, mention of the bloody Ute attack on Santa Rosa de Abiquiú in 1747 (no. 497 which supplied the details was missing) and of the community's effort to oust Father Teodoro Alcina in 1820—Myra Ellen Jenkins et al. prepared a helpful little *Guide to the Microfilm of the Spanish Archives of New Mexico, 1621-1821* (Santa Fe: SRC, 1967) and a *Calendar of the Spanish Archives of New Mexico, 1621-1821* (Santa Fe: SRC, 1968). The latter, which has no index, is cross-referenced to Twitchell, which has.

During Territorial days sundry documents from the SANM found their way into the hands of collectors. Some were lost, others retrieved, and still others preserved in out-of-state libraries. Fray Angelico Chavez, "Some Original New Mexico Documents in California Libraries," NMHR 25 (1950): 244-53, lists what there is at the Huntington Library, San Marino, in the Ritch Collection, including a 1789 Abiquiú church inventory, and at the Bancroft Library among "New Mexico Originals" collected by A. L. Pinart (BL, NMO), including a detailed c. 1790 census of the Abiquiú district and much about Fray Juan José Toledo and the notorious Abiquiú witchcraft case of the 1760s.

To back up, Volume One of Twitchell's *Spanish Archives* describes the loose, numbered land documents segregated in 1855 for use by the Surveyor General of New Mexico and known today as SANM, Series I. These supplement the land grant files of the Surveyor General and the Court of Private Land Claims, files made up of Spanish grant papers and Anglo proceedings in such cases as the Town of Abiquiú, Juan José Lobato, La Polvadera, La Piedra Lumbre, Bartolomé Sánchez, and a dozen others close-by or overlapping. The lot, while in custody of the U.S. Bureau of Land Management in Santa Fe, was microfilmed by UNM and listed by Albert James Diaz in *A Guide to the Microfilm of Papers Relating to New Mexico Land Grants* (Albuquerque: UNM Press, 1960). Since then the originals have made their way back to the State Records Center. Only by close study of the land documents, which continue on through the Mexican period, can anyone hope to sort out the geography and plot the ebb and flow of settlement in the area about Abiquiú.

A goodly part of the church record—everything from fragmentary Abiquiú baptismal, marriage, and burial registers, censuses, even trials and land transfers, to a note congratulating the guest preacher on the feast of Santa Rosa for limiting himself to fifteen minutes—has been catalogued by Fray Angelico Chavez in *Archives of the Archdiocese of Santa Fe, 1678-1900* (Washington, D.C.: Academy of American Franciscan History, 1957). The astute historical tracker will follow the index beyond Abiquiú to nearby missions, notably Santa Clara, San Juan, and San Ildefonso, which from time to time served the Chama Valley settlements. Housed in the main office of the archdiocese in Albuquerque, these documents can also be consulted on microfilm in SC-UNM and at the SRC.

Another prime source, closely related to the AASF, is the so-called Archivo Franciscano at the Biblioteca Nacional, Mexico City (BNM). "Discovered" and hastily catalogued by France V. Scholes in 1927-28, the New Mexico materials in these bundles from the old Franciscan provincial archives contained, to single out one treasure among many, Fray Francisco Atanasio Domínguez's meticulous and embarrassing description of New Mexico in 1776, which had been filed away with a sarcastic note and forgotten. Although the entire collection has been recatalogued and microfilmed by the Mexican government, one can still use to advantage Scholes's brief "Manuscripts for the History of New Mexico in the National Library in Mexico City," NMHR 3 (1928): 301-23, together with the bound photostats in SC-UNM.

Two more foreign archives rate special mention: the Archivo General de la Nación, México (AGN), and the Archivo General de Indias, Sevilla, Spain (AGI). Copies in one form or another of thousands and thousands of document pages from each are available in SC-UNM. The Bancroft Library boasts the largest U.S. holding of AGN and AGI microfilm, as well as numerous transcripts in the Bolton Research Papers. Two dated guides still serve: Herbert E. Bolton, *Guide to Materials for the History of the United States in the Principal Archives of Mexico* (Washington, D.C.: Carnegie Institution, 1913; reprinted ed., New York: Kraus, 1965), and Charles E. Chapman, *Catalogue of Materials in the Archivo General de Indias for the History of the Pacific Coast and the American Southwest* (Berkeley: University of California Press, 1919; reprinted ed., Ann Arbor: University Microfilms, 1970). More detailed aids for some sections of these huge depositories have been printed, among them those appearing in the *Boletín* of the AGN and those tallied by José María de la Peña y Cámara in his *Archivo General de Indias de Sevilla, guía del visitante* (Madrid: Dirección General de Archivos y Bibliotecas, 1958).

Finally, a salute to the most active copier of Spanish documents before photocopying, Adolph F. Bandelier. Although much of the Bandelier material can still be found in the above-mentioned archives, certain of the originals he transcribed in New Mexico for the Hemenway Southwestern Archaeological Expedition have evidently since vanished. Fifteen volumes of transcripts endure in the library of the Peabody Museum, Harvard University. An idea of how much they contain can be had from "The Bandelier Collection of Copies of Documents Relative to the History of New Mexico and Arizona" in *Report of the United States Commission to the Columbian Historical Exposition at Madrid, 1892-93* (Washington, D.C.: GPO, 1895). Numbers 26-30 and 34 deal with the successive repeopling of Abiquiú. There are also signed Bandelier transcripts in the Thomas B. Catron Collection, SC-UNM (see Lange, Riley, and Lange notes to Bandelier, *Journals, 1885-1888*). Charles Wilson Hackett edited the copies made by Adolph and Fanny for the Carnegie Institution and published them under the cumbrous title *Historical Documents Relating to New Mexico, Nueva Vizcaya, and Approaches Thereto, to 1773, Collected by Adolph F. A. Bandelier and Fanny R. Bandelier*, 3 vols. (Washington, D.C.: Carnegie Institution, 1923-37). Volume Three is the most pertinent.

Going Bandelier one better, the Documentary Relations of the Southwest (DRSW), an ongoing project at the Arizona State Museum, University of Arizona, aims not only at publication of a multi-volume, bilingual series of selected documents but also at harnessing the computer. During the process of selection, done in the old way, in the archives, document-by-document, categories of specific information—e.g., all ethnic groups, important persons, and place names mentioned—are noted and later fed into a master computer index. To explain the project and to aid those who would use its products, a preliminary *The Documentary Relations of the Southwest Project Manual, 1977*, compiled by Charles W. Polzer, Thomas C. Barnes, and Thomas H. Naylor (Tucson: Arizona State Museum, 1977), has already appeared. See also Polzer, "The Documentary Relations of the Southwest," *Hispanic American Historical Review* 58 (1978): 460-65.

Although the DRSW has not come yet to New Mexico, the Southwest is understood to be the area of analogous cultures contained within the 94th and 122nd meridians and the 22nd and 38th parallels. The possibilities are just as broad. Imagine a computerized biographical dictionary of the Spanish Southwest. Bandelier would have loved it.

After this section was all set down came Henry Putney Beers, *Spanish and Mexican Records of the American Southwest: A Bibliographical Guide to Archive and Manuscript Sources* (Tucson: UA Press, 1979), to put flesh on the bones. Not only does Beers's remarkable new compendium describe where the sources are, but also how and when they got there and who was responsible. It is essential.

Settlement, exploration and trade beyond, mission and missionaries, and a witch hunt: selected secondary sources

Relatively rich bottomlands along a perennial stream and feed for stock on a thousand hills and mesas drew Hispano settlers up the Chama Valley early in the eighteenth century. By the 1730s they were living close-by Abiquiú under the patronage of Santa Rosa de Lima. J. Richard Salazar, who documented the site for nomination to the National Register of Historic Places, demonstrates with "Santa Rosa de Lima de Abiquiú," *New Mexico Architecture* 18 (Sept.-Oct. 1976): 13-19, the kind of study necessary to piece together the local settlement puzzle. Some of his findings are at odds with those of Swadesh, *Los Primeros Pobladores*, cited above but not by Salazar. Who these first families were—the Trujillo, Martín Serrano, Montoya, et al.—Fray Angelico Chavez suggests in *Origins of New Mexico Families in the Spanish Colonial Period* (Santa Fe: Historical Society of N.M., 1954; reprinted ed., Albuquerque: University of Albuquerque, 1973) and later installments in *El Palacio*. Marc Simmons, "Settlement Patterns and Village Plans in Colonial New Mexico," *Journal of the West* 8 (1969): 7-21, sets them in a broader context.

As for numbers, beginning with Fray Juan Miguel Menchero's 1744 estimate of twenty families at Santa Rosa (BNM, New Mexico Documents, legajo 8, no. 17), a fairly complete list of colonial censuses appears in Appendix I of John L. Kessell, *Kiva, Cross, and Crown: The Pecos Indians and New Mexico, 1540-1840*, National Park Service (Washington, D.C.: GPO, 1979). Alicia V. Tjarks, "Demographic, Ethnic and Occupational Structure of New Mexico, 1790," *The Americas* 35 (1978): 45-88, discusses some of the earlier censuses and squeezes all she can out of the one for 1790, but she misses the local reports from the Abiquiú district (BL, NMO).

How war and peace with Navajos, Utes, and Comanches affected the peopling and repeopling of the Chama Valley is a theme worth pursuing. Frank D. Reeve's articles in NMHR on Navajo-Spanish relations and two of Alfred Barnaby Thomas's works, *The Plains Indians and New Mexico, 1751-1778* (Albuquerque: UNM

Press, 1940) and *Forgotten Frontiers: A Study of the Spanish Indian Policy of Don Juan Bautista de Anza, Governor of New Mexico, 1777-1787* (Norman: OU Press, 1932, 1969), point the way to the documents. Other studies of the Provincias Internas, by scholars like Elizabeth A. H. John, Max L. Moorhead, and Luis Navarro García, are cited in the bibliography of Kessell, *Kiva, Cross, and Crown.*

Trade between Abiquiú and the Utes during the Spanish period, which holds up through the Mexican years and beyond, may have been "a small-scale, individual, and rather shabby affair," as David J. Weber suggests in *The Taos Trappers: The Fur Trade in the Far Southwest, 1540-1846* (Norman: OU Press, 1971), but it made a mark, largely because the readiest commodity was captive Indian women and children. Three articles on the subject, relying for the most part on the same trial records of illicit traders, are: William J. Snow, "Utah Indians and Spanish Slave Trade," *Utah Historical Quarterly* (UHQ) 2 (1929): 67-73; Joseph J. Hill, "Spanish and Mexican Exploration and Trade Northwest from New Mexico into the Great Basin, 1765-1853," UHQ 3 (1930): 3-23; and S. Lyman Tyler, "The Spaniard and the Ute," UHQ 22 (1954): 343-61. L. R. Bailey's book *Indian Slave Trade in the Southwest, A Study of Slave-taking and the Traffic of Indian Captives* (Los Angeles: Westernlore Press, 1973) adds nothing.

Several smallish exploring and trading parties—hardly pageants in the wilderness—jumped off from Abiquiú. The unpublished journals of Juan María Rivera, who led at least two of them in the year 1765, repose in the Biblioteca Central Militar of the Servicio Histórico Militar in Madrid. Donald C. Cutter hints at their contents in "Prelude to a Pageant in the Wilderness," *Western Historical Quarterly* (WHQ) 8 (1977): 5-14. The better-known Domínguez-Escalante expedition of 1776, which outward bound laid over a day at the mission of Abiquiú, two hundred years later gave the state of Utah something to celebrate. Out of the Bicentennial came *The Domínguez-Escalante Journal, Their Expedition through Colorado, Utah, Arizona, and New Mexico in 1776*, trsl. Fray Angelico Chavez, ed. Ted J. Warner (Provo: Brigham Young University Press, 1976), bilingual successor to earlier English translations by Herbert S. Auerbach and Herbert E. Bolton. Anglo-American interloper Zebulon Montgomery Pike, according to *The Journals of Zebulon Montgomery Pike*, ed. Donald Jackson, 2 vols. (Norman: OU Press, 1966), in 1807 descended the Agua Caliente to the Chama, thereby just missing Abiquiú, which nevertheless, misspelled and mislocated, found a place on his map.

Back in 1754 the brash and capable Gov. Tomás Vélez Cachupín knew exactly what a *genízaro* was when he authorized the mission of Santo Tomás for Indians of that designation, some of them Tewa-Hopis already living in the Abiquiú area. Two hundred and two years later, Fray Angelico Chavez was at considerable pains to define the term in "Comments Concerning 'Tomé and Father J. B. R.'," NMHR 31 (1956):68-74. It takes some doing, lest one end up with the usual "detribalized, Hispanicized, mainly non-Pueblo, erstwhile captive," which sounds rather like an eighteenth-century test-tube baby. This matter of racial makeup is not purely academic. If the descendants of *genízaros* are mostly Indian, why, some people ask, should they not receive free schooling and health care?

Mission Santo Tomás de Abiquiú, the only *genízaro* mission, came into being at a tense time in New Mexico. With the "barbarians" at the gates, missionaries damned governors and governors damned missionaries. Missionaries also damned bishops. The scene is well set in Henry W. Kelly, *Franciscan Missions of New Mexico, 1740-1760* (Albuquerque: UNM Press, 1941), and Eleanor B. Adams, *Bishop Tamarón's Visitation of New Mexico, 1760* (Albuquerque: UNM Press, 1954), both of which were featured serially in NMHR. Both authors made extensive use of BNM, New Mexico Documents.

"A man with an extraordinary awareness of the ordinary," Fray Francisco Atanasio Domínguez captured the scabby, sometimes hilarious, and often insecure essence of life in the colony in 1776. He drew word pictures of Abiquiú's mission plant and of the lesser chapel of Santa Rosa de Lima, right down to the last viga and the wig belonging to Our Lady of the Conception. He told of a lively trade fair for the Utes. And he was hard on the *genízaros*, if his string of "they are weak, gamblers, liars, cheats, and petty

136

thieves" can be considered hard. In 1956 the apt team of Adams and Chavez resurrected this eighteenth-century New Mexico classic under the too-modest title *The Missions of New Mexico, 1776: A Description by Fray Francisco Atanasio Domínguez with Other Contemporary Documents* (Albuquerque: UNM Press, 1956, 1975).

Secure in its place as bible of the subject, George Kubler's *The Religious Architecture of New Mexico in the Colonial Period and Since the American Occupation,* 4th ed. (Albuquerque: UNM Press, 1972), has sections on Abiquiú but he, like so many others, confuses the site of La Puente with that of La Capilla de Santa Rosa. In *The Missions of New Mexico Since 1776* (Albuquerque: UNM Press, in press), John L. Kessell grapples with the question, What has become of all these structures in the two centuries since Domínguez? Finally, Gilberto Benito Córdova, native Abiqueño, completed in 1979 a specialized study called "Missionization and Hispanicization of Santo Tomás Apóstol de Abiquiú, 1750-1770" (Ph.D. disseration, UNM).

We may never grasp just how missionization worked at Abiquiú, but surely the witches of the 1760s have something to tell us. Marc Simmons, *Witchcraft in the Southwest: Spanish and Indian Supernaturalism on the Rio Grande* (Flagstaff: Northland Press, 1974), who devoted a paragraph to the subject, followed Twitchell who followed Bancroft who had the trial proceedings in his library. Another part of the record is in the AGN, Sección de Inquisición, tomo 1001. Women possessed by the Dragon of Hell, exorcism, a network of sorcerers, stone idols in caves—all are here.

IV. Mexican

Santa Fe's conspicuous celebration of Mexican independence may have made news in Mexico City, but it signaled few overnight changes. Granted, the few Missouri traders on hand that January of 1822 can be seen as harbingers of an economic revolution, but even that took time. Most everyone embraced the epithet "Mexican citizen" with gusto. Still, things Mexican flowed gradually out of things Spanish.

As the fiber of familiar institutions went limp, which it had begun to do before independence, locals took up the slack. Armed hit and miss, militiamen far outnumbered regulars. Community brotherhoods managed the social and spiritual business of the church as old priests died off, and few were replaced. Rico families got richer in partnership with Anglos who came and stayed and married their daughters. Reacting to the instability of government at higher levels, district officials took the law more and more unto themselves. More and more people were counted on censuses, and more and more settlements. Never had New Mexicans moved around so much. And in all this Abiquiú had a part.

Some of the sources mentioned in the previous section pull up arbitrarily at 1821-22; others, like the current of events, flow through uninterrupted. On the Mexican period per se, Lansing B. Bloom, "New Mexico under Mexican Administration, 1821-1846," *Old Santa Fe*, serially in vols. 1-2 (1913-15), endures as the standard work. David J. Weber of Southern Methodist University is presently at work on a careful comparative study of Mexican Texas, New Mexico, Arizona, and California for the Histories of the American Frontiers series (UNM Press). Meantime, he gives us a rundown of printed sources in "Mexico's Far Northern Frontier, 1821-1854: Historiography Askew," WHQ 7 (1976): 279-93, and "Mexico's Far Northern Frontier, 1821-1845: A Critical Bibliography," *Arizona and the West* 19 (1977): 225-66.

The Mexican Archives of New Mexico (MANM) is to 1821-46 what SANM, Series II, is to the colonial years, except for Twitchell. Most of the originals have their abode in Santa Fe at the SRC where they were microfilmed (42 rolls) in 1969. Myra Ellen Jenkins's short *Guide to the Microfilm Edition of the Mexican Archives of New Mexico, 1821-1846* (Santa Fe: SRC, 1969), which notes a number of complementary private collections, and her *Calendar of the Microfilm Edition of the Mexican Archives of New Mexico, 1821-1846* (Santa Fe: SRC, 1970), define the categories of documents. A partial, item-by-item card catalogue of MANM, as photographed and bound pre-Jenkins, is at hand at SC-UNM, but only for the years 1821-32. Recently Malcolm Ebright dipped into MANM to come up with an 1832 quarrel between Abiquiú's Manuel and Ramón Martínez in "Manuel Martínez's Ditch Dispute: A Study in Mexican Period Custom and Justice," NMHR 54 (1979): 21-34.

The Archives of the Archdiocese of Santa Fe and Chavez's guide to them run sequentially through the Mexican years. To these should be added a stray, the parish baptismal register of Santo Tomás de Abiquiú, 1832-61, on microfilm at Zimmerman Library, UNM.

Two archives in Mexico City that bear looking into, besides the obvious AGN, are the Archivo Histórico Militar Mexicano of the Secretaría de la Defensa Nacional and the Archivo Central of the Secretaría de Relaciones Exteriores. Before taking off on Aeroméxico, however, the researcher should check the holdings of copies at SC-UNM and the Bancroft Library, then read the pertinent sections in Greenleaf and Meyer, *Research in Mexican History.*

Private collections and family papers, like those of Manuel Álvarez, Donaciano Vigil, L. Bradford Prince, and a dozen others at the SRC may contain bits and pieces of the Abiquiú story. These keep turning up. In a small collection in SC-UNM, "New Mexico Documents, 1770-1876," one finds the last will and testament of José Manuel Martínez of Abiquiú, dated in 1843.

Among published censuses of Mexican New Mexico the Antonio Narbona count of 1827, in H. Bailey Carroll and J. Villasana Haggard, *Three New Mexico Chronicles: The Exposición of Don Pedro Bautista Pino 1812; the Ojeada of Lic. Antonio Barreiro 1831; and the additions by Don José Agustín de Escudero, 1849* (Albuquerque: Quivira Society, 1942), has Abiquiú and environs with 3,557 souls, of whom 508 are farmers, 48 craftsmen, 6 merchants, a school teacher, and 301 day laborers. The 1845 census of Abiquiú, El Rito, and Ojo Caliente by priest and enumerator Eulogio Valdez, printed in typescript in Virginia L. Olmstead, *Spanish and Mexican Colonial Censuses of New Mexico: 1790, 1823, 1845* (Albuquerque: N.M. Genealogical Society, 1975), gives names, ages, and marital status of heads of household and spouses.

By the late 1820s Abiquiú had become something of a little Taos. Here at a half dozen posts, traders and trappers rendezvoused and outfitted for ventures north and west. Many of the big names were in and out of Abiquiú. Cerán St. Vrain put Jacob P. Leese in charge of his store here, and Manuel Álvarez maintained local ties. LeRoy R. Hafen, aided by an impressive stable of scholars, called the roll in *The Mountain Men and the Fur Trade of the Far West*, 10 vols. (Glendale: Arthur H. Clark, 1965-72). Weber's *Taos Trappers* provides continuity.

"The longest, crookedest, most arduous pack mule route in the history of America" is how LeRoy R. and Ann W. Hafen described the 1,200-mile *Old Spanish Trail: Santa Fé to Los Angeles* (Glendale: Arthur H. Clark, 1954). Santa Fe may have been the New Mexico terminus, but Abiquiú was both jumping-off place and port of entry. Beginning in 1829-30 with Antonio Armijo's round trip and lasting well into the 1840s, New Mexican woolens went west and California horses and mules came east. Horse thieving and slaving were sidelights. Two earlier articles by Eleanor Lawrence, cited in Weber's critical bibliography, complement the Hafen book. And today, as fate would have it, Abiquiú's Rafael Rivera, a member of Armijo's company who got lost for a couple of weeks, is being touted as the first non-Indian to gaze on the site of Las Vegas, Nevada.

Trading and raiding—the former mostly with Utes and the latter mostly by and against Navajos—pretty much summed up Mexican Indian affairs in the Chama Valley. Part I of Frank McNitt's *Navajo Wars: Military Campaigns, Slave Raids, and Reprisals* (Albuquerque: UNM Press, 1972) portrays a cycle of events that became facts of life. But it was never black and white. In the fall of 1844 the Utes who gathered near Abiquiú were in a surly mood. Loudly demanding compensation for past wrongs, they descended on Santa Fe and roughed up the governor. Ward Alan Minge reveals the outcome in "Mexican Independence Day and a Ute Tragedy in Santa Fe, 1844," *The Changing Ways of Southwestern Indians, A Historic Perspective*, ed. Albert H. Schroeder (Glorieta, N.M.: Rio Grande Press, 1973), pp. 107-23. All winter Abiquiú feared war.

As a birthplace of notables, few communities of similar size can match Abiquiú. Chief among those who came to prominence during Mexican rule and stayed on as burs under the Anglo saddle was Antonio José Martínez, priest, educator, and champion of his people. Martínez, who served the parish of Santo Tomás briefly in 1826 before moving to Taos, has been vilified in fiction by Willa

Cather and only grudgingly recognized by Paul Horgan. He awaits a biographer. In the meantime, we have one good article by E. K. Francis, "Padre Martínez: A New Mexican Myth," NMHR 31 (1956): 265-89. Another unforgettable priest, a son of the Abiquiú Gallegos clan, was José Manuel Gallegos, New Mexico's delegate to Congress in 1855-56 and 1871-73.

As if one congressman were not enough for any town, Abiquiú in 1843 produced another, Francisco Antonio Manzanares, the Las Vegas merchant who served in 1884-85. Brief biographical sketches of New Mexico's national legislators can be found in Dorothy Woodward's *New Mexico, Land of Enchantment*, rev. ed., 87th Cong., 2nd sess., Senate Doc. 155 (Washington, D.C.: GPO, 1962). Don Devereux, "Julian Chavez, An Early Rio Arriba Emigrant," EP 74 (Winter 1967): 35-36, follows another Abiqueño overland about 1830 to California where, after a memorable career as ranchero and politician, he leaves his name on Chavez Ravine, home of the Los Angeles Dodgers.

Don Julián's distinguished brother, José María, stayed home and was breveted general of volunteers during the Civil War. Even famed Ute Indian leader Ouray, according to J. M. Manzanares, "Colorado Recollections of a Centenarian," *The Colorado Magazine* (CM) 10 (1933): 114-15, was born of a Ute mother and an Apache father at Abiquiú where he later worked for the Manzanares and Martínez families.

V. Territorial

If the adjective "bustling" ever fit Abiquiú, it was during the Territorial years. Military post, Indian agency, mercantile, ranching, and mining center, cradle of emigrants—the community was all these and more. To set the place in context it would be well to consult the Goldentree bibliography by Rodman W. Paul and Richard W. Etulain, *The Frontier and the American West* (Arlington Heights, Ill.: AHM Publishing Corp., 1977), which has sections on all these topics and more.

A. *Military post*

Unquestionably the most prideful and foolhardy boast made by the United States occupation forces in 1846 was that they would protect the locals from injury by hostile Indians. So spoke Maj.

William Gilpin who reined up at Abiquiú late in September. Contemporary John T. Hughes alluded to Gilpin's actions in *Doniphan's Expedition and the Conquest of New Mexico and California*, ed. William Elsey Connelley (Kansas City: Bryant and Douglas, 1907). McNitt put them in context in *Navajo Wars*. And Pvt. James Austin had the time of his life. Writing to his brother from Abiquiú on October 23, 1846, he told of a soldier's happy camp life. A photostat of the letter is on file at the Museum of New Mexico, Santa Fe (MNM). "We live together like brothers," crowed Austin, who shared quarters with five others, "and if you could see us about eating time you would say we were the happiest set of poor devils you ever saw." A few months later James Austin died in action at Taos.

By April of 1849 Capt. John Chapman and Co. A Vols., Santa Fe Guard, seventy-eight strong, occupied the post at "Albiquin." Under that misspelling, the post returns from April 1849 to October 1851, minus June-December 1849 when the volunteers pulled out, are preserved at the National Archives, Washington, D.C. (NA), in Record Group (RG) 94, Records of the Adjutant General's Office, 1780s-1917. Microfilmed as part of Returns from United States Military Posts, 1800-1916 (Microcopy No. 617), roll 12, they are present and accounted for in SC-UNM and elsewhere. Equally fruitful for the military historian is RG 393, Records of United States Army Continental Commands, 1821-1920. Whatever the record group, two publications will help: *Guide to the National Archives of the United States* (Washington, D.C.: General Services Administration (GSA), 1974) and *National Archives Microfilm Publications* (Washington, D.C.: GSA, 1974).

The sparse details of post returns can often be fleshed out with correspondence and inspection reports. George Archibald McCall, *New Mexico in 1850: A Military View*, ed. Robert W. Frazer (Norman: OU Press, 1968), found a company of dragoons paying $183-a-month rent in Abiquiú. Because there was no hospital, the half-dozen sick men were being treated in their quarters. "The climate of this region of [the] country," ventured Colonel McCall, "is considered a very healthy one (the only cases of disease now existing being venereal)." In 1851 the rent, as revealed to Congress (32nd Cong., 1st sess., HED 2, Serial 634, pp. 235-41), was up to $280.

Abiquiu Peak, looking westerly. J. S. Newberry, "Geological Report." *Report of the Exploring Expedition from Santa Fe, New Mexico to . . . the Great Colorado of the West, in 1859.* 1876. Plate 1, opposite p. 69.

Familiar military sources like Francis B. Heitman, *Historical Register and Dictionary of the United States Army, From Its Organization, September 29, 1789, to March 2, 1903*, 2 vols. (Washington, D.C.: GPO, 1903; reprinted ed., Urbana: University of Illinois Press, 1965), will serve to trace an officer's career, but to find out that Abiquiú commander Lawrence P. Graham was an incompetent sot may require recourse to the unofficial commentary of men who did duty with him, like Cave Johnson Couts, *Hepah, California! The Journal of Cave Johnson Couts from Monterey, Nuevo Leon, Mexico to Los Angeles, California during the Years 1848-1849*, ed. Henry F. Dobyns (Tucson: Arizona Pioneers' Historical Society, 1961). Pvt. James A. Bennett remembered his time at Abiquiú in *Forts and Forays, A Dragoon in New Mexico, 1850-1856*, ed. Clinton E. Brooks and Frank D. Reeve (Albuquerque: UNM Press, 1948; serially in NMHR, 1947), although McNitt, *Navajo Wars*, measuring him against the official record, had to make adjustments for slippage.

The local tradition that Negro troops manned the Abiquiú post, most unlikely before the Civil War, nevertheless deserves investigation. Another lead worth checking out concerns artist Edward M. Kern, who served the detachment as forage master from July 1850 until the following spring. Although Robert V. Hine, *Edward Kern and American Expansion* (New Haven: Yale University Press, 1962) holds out no such hope, it would be grand to discover a Kern portfolio of Abiquiú scenes.

B. *Indian agency*

If they understood the Army's boast to control them, the Navajos, Utes, and Jicarilla Apaches at first simply scorned it. Aided in their self-determination by United States civil and military authorities who could not agree on Indian policy and by an ungenerous, preoccupied Congress, the tribes did pretty much as they had done under previous regimes. They raided as it suited their interests, and they came in to places like Abiquiú for trade, gifts, and an occasional treaty-signing ceremonial.

To reconstruct the Abiquiú agency molehill one must go into the mountains of the National Archives, into Record Group 75, Records of the Bureau of Indian Affairs, and into RG 48, Records of the Office of the Secretary of the Interior. Pertinent sections already microfilmed include the Records of the New Mexico Superintendency of Indian Affairs, 1849-80 (T21, 30 rolls), Letters Sent by the Indian Division of the Office of the Secretary of the Interior, 1849-1903 (M606, 127 rolls), and Interior Department Territorial Papers, New Mexico, 1851-1914 (M364, 15 rolls). Lively narratives by the New Mexico superintendent and/or Abiquiú agent show up in the Annual Report of the Commissioner of Indian Affairs, which in turn shows up in the Annual Report of the Secretary of the Interior and also separately.

The early years of the Abiquiú "agency," from 1849 until the mid-1850s, are something of a blur, with special agents like Lafayette Head and José Antonio Manzanares fading in and out of the picture. At Abiquiú in 1849 James S. Calhoun, New Mexico's first superintendent of Indian affairs (1849-52) and territorial governor (1851-52), entered into a treaty with the Utes. Its text is printed in Charles J. Kappler, ed., *Indian Affairs: Laws and Treaties*, vol. 2 (Washington, D.C.: GPO, 1904; reprinted ed., New York: Interland Publishing, 1972), also in Twitchell, *Leading Facts*, III. Annie Heloise Abel collected and edited *The Official Correspondence of James S. Calhoun* (Washington, D.C.: Office of Indian Affairs, 1915) and followed that with "The Journal of John Greiner," *Old Santa Fe* 3 (1916): 189-243, and "Indian Affairs in New Mexico under the Administration of William Carr Lane, from the Journal of John Ward," NMHR 16 (1941): 206-32, 328-58.

Again Frank McNitt's *Navajo Wars*, taken with Frank D. Reeve's "The Federal Indian Policy in New Mexico, 1858-1880," NMHR, serially in vols. 12-13 (1937-38), can be used as an initiation. Both scholars did toilsome research in the National Archives. Today their extensive collections of notes, transcripts, photoprints, microfilms, and maps are available to scholars, McNitt's at the SRC in Santa Fe and Reeve's in SC-UNM in Albuquerque.

From Bancroft's listing of Abiquiú agents, one gets the impression that they were the usual mix—grafters and honest visionaries, political hacks and adventurers, good administrators and bad. At least one, an enterprising Scotsman who lasted from 1858 to

1861, also held an appointment, says Laura C. Manson White in "Albert H. Pfeiffer," CM 10 (1933): 217-22, as captain, Co. A, Abiquiu Mounted Volunteers of Militia. Another, responsible during his tenure for about 1,100 Wiminutche Utes, 700 Capote Utes, and some Jicarillas west of the Rio Grande, got up on a soap box and delivered an open *Report on the Apaches and Navaho Indians of Abiquiu Indian Agency, to President Grant*, September 23, 1869 (printed pamphlet, Harvard College Library, Cambridge). This was a man of strong convictions, well characterized by Lawrence R. Murphy in *Frontier Crusader—Willliam F. M. Arny* (Tucson: UA Press, 1972). Three years later, in 1872, a successor of Arny's moved the agency north to the abandoned buildings of Fort Lowell near Tierra Amarilla, where the last rations were doled out in 1881.

C. *Mercantile, ranching, and mining center*

Sharing the understandable bias of Anglo miners bound for the bonanza, Richard Sopris pictured Abiquiú as "a miserable Mexican village with supplies, and the very worst starting point." Others disagreed, notably promoter Charles Baker and his cohorts, six Anglos and five Hispanos, who in 1861 secured a charter as the Abiquiu, Pagosa, and Baker City Road Company to operate a toll road north to the San Juan mining district. That winter of 1860-61 miners crowded into Abiquiú. St. Vrain & Co., Denver, shipped in supplies. Santa Fe and Denver newspapers reported the excitement, as did Virginia McConnell in "Captain Baker and the San Juan Humbug," CM 48 (1971): 59-75. A photocopy of the toll-road company's charter is in SC-UNM.

Ever since 1852 Abiquiú had boasted an on-again-off-again post office. Sheldon H. Dike, *The Territorial Post Offices of New Mexico* (Albuquerque: Dikewood Corp., 1958), gives dates and names of some of the postmasters. The *Colorado, New Mexico, Utah, Nevada, Wyoming and Arizona Gazetteer and Business Directory, 1884-5*, vol. 1 (Chicago and Detroit: R. L. Polk and Co. and A. C. Danser, 1884), credits the village with a church and a district school. "The shipments comprise wool, pelts and hides. Population, 300. Mail, tri-weekly. Alexander Douglas, postmaster." Twelve entries follow—three proprietors of general stores, with only Douglas's name in bold type, one justice of the peace, and the rest cattle and/or sheep breeders. Although the population holds steady, J. A. Carruth, *Business Directory of Arizona and New Mexico for 1897* (Las Vegas, N.M.: Daily Examiner Printing and Binding, 1897) offers some additional information: "Española and Chamita nearest railroad points, mail daily, school 4 months, banking at Santa Fe, Catholic church services regularly, principal resources, agriculture, fruit and mining." Henry Grant is now postmaster and Grant Bros. the only general store. Allen David lists himself as miner.

Prospectors had been lured into the rugged country around Abiquiú for as long as anyone could remember. They had found copper early on, in Cobre Canyon eight or nine miles north. Bernardo de Miera y Pacheco labeled "El Cobre" on his maps in the 1770s (see, e.g., the detail of his 1779 map in Domínguez, *Missions*, p. 44). A U.S. exploring expedition poked up the canyon for a look in 1859. Although J. N. Macomb got his name on the *Report of the Exploring Expedition from Santa Fé, New Mexico, to the Junction of the Grand and Green Rivers of the Great Colorado of the West, in 1859*, Engineer Department, U.S. Army (Washington, D.C.: GPO, 1876), Dr. J. S. Newberry's geological section formed the bulk of it. Newberry described the countryside and the mines, and he made a sketch of "Abiquiu Peak, Looking Westerly," which J. J. Young transformed into a handsome color rendering. Next a travel writer, William M. Thayer in *Marvels of the New West* (Norwich, Conn.: Henry Bill Publishing Co., 1887) picked up Newberry's account of climbing Abiquiú peak, complete with the illustration in black and white, and attributed it wrongly to Macomb. For those today who marvel at the colorful scenery in the area and wonder what is tufa and what is not, Harold T. U. Smith, "Tertiary Geology of the Abiquiu Quadrangle, New Mexico," *The Journal of Geology* 46 (1938): 933-65, has the answer.

The chalcocite copper ore of the Abiquiú Mining District "occurs as rounded grains and nuggets up to 5 in. in diameter," writes Stuart A. Northrop, *Minerals of New Mexico*, rev. ed. (Albuquerque: UNM Press, 1959), who lists Las Minas de Pedro and Las Minas Jimmie on the east side of the canyon within the Plaza Colorada Grant. The record of Pedro Jaramillo vs. John Johnson (Rio

Arriba County District Court, Civil Case 455, 1890-91, SRC) over copper in the Abiquiú district, proves that someone thought it was worth going to court over.

The machinations of lawyers and land brokers, imperceptible at first to the people on the land, eventually came home as fences went up across grazing grounds and forests traditionally open to all, and as farming plots were quietly acquired and blocked up. How they went about it is well illustrated by Herbert O. Brayer, *William Blackmore: The Spanish-Mexican Land Grants of New Mexico and Colorado, 1863-1878* (Denver: Bradford Robinson, 1949; reprinted in *Spanish and Mexican Land Grants*, New York: Arno Press, 1974), and by Victor Westphall, *Thomas Benton Catron and His Era* (Tucson: UA Press, 1973). Catron, who owned outright or had a piece of at least thirty-four grants including the Cañón de Chama, Piedra Lumbre, and Tierra Amarilla, also had dealings with Abiquiú rico Pablo González. The Abiquiú documents at Newberry Library, cited above in the Spanish colonial section, should shed light on their relationship. So might the Catron Papers in SC-UNM.

D. *Cradle of emigrants*

For every well-known emigrant Abiquiú contributed to other communities—Martínez to Taos, Chávez to Los Angeles, Gallegos to Albuquerque, Manzanares to Las Vegas—there were dozens of less conspicuous souls who for one reason or another risked a new start elsewhere. "The gradual contiguous spread of Hispano colonists during the nineteenth century is a little-known event of major importance," asserts geographer D. W. Meinig in his provocative and closely knit *Southwest: Three Peoples in Geographical Change, 1600-1970* (New York: Oxford University Press, 1971).

Some made it to California. Recognizing the truth in the saying "it takes one to know one," southern California ranchers recruited Abiquiú *genízaros* to guard their herds against other New Mexicans and Indians. Their story is told by Joyce C. Vickery in *Defending Eden: New Mexican Pioneers in Southern California, 1830-1890* (Riverside: University of California at Riverside, 1977).

But mostly they migrated northward out of Abiquiú, colonizing such grants as the Tierra Amarilla and then, as Apaches, Utes, and Navajos were gradually contained, venturing into the San Juan Basin west of the mountains and into the San Luis Valley on the east. Hundreds of their descendants live today in the southern counties of Colorado. Alerted by Swadesh's *Los Primeros Pobladores*, no Abiquiú historian should lose sight of this intimate Colorado connection.

Through censuses, parish and county archives, and newspapers one can measure the heartbeat of a given community and follow the pulse of its influence outward. The 1850 census, edited and printed in typescript by Margaret Leonard Windham, *New Mexico 1850 Territorial Census*, 4 vols. (Albuquerque: N.M. Genealogical Society, 1976), is tough to use for Rio Arriba County because town headings are omitted. Record Group 29, Records of the Bureau of the Census, NA, contains the documentation for this and the progressively more detailed federal censuses that followed. Microfilm of the schedules for relevant New Mexico and Colorado counties is listed in *Federal Population Censuses, 1790-1890, A Catalog of Microfilm Copies of the Schedules* (Washington, D.C.: GSA, 1978).

Parish records, whether stored in the Archives of the Archdiocese of Santa Fe in Albuquerque or kept in the parishes themselves, abound with vital data to complement censuses in a largely Roman Catholic area. Fray Angelico Chavez, whose published guide to the AASF runs to 1900, is now cataloguing the more recent materials. For Abiquiú per se the researcher should examine not only what exists at the parish of Santo Tomás and its present missions but also the records at the parish of San Juan Nepomuceno in El Rito, of which Abiquiú was a mission for nearly fifty years. Three commemorative publications by Chavez help sort out parishes and missions: *The Old Faith and Old Glory, 1846-1946* (Santa Fe: Santa Fe Press, 1946), *Lamy Memorial, Centenary of the Archdiocese of Santa Fe, 1850-1950* (Santa Fe: Schifani Bros., 1950), and *The Lord and New Mexico* (Albuquerque: Archdiocese of Santa Fe, 1975).

Unfortunately the annals of Rio Arriba County are fragmentary at best. In the late 1930s and early 1940s when WPA Historical Records Survey teams were compiling inventories of county archives, they missed Rio Arriba. What noncurrent records survive, dating hit and miss from the late 1840s to the 1930s, are housed at the State Records Center in Santa Fe. Here are registers, books, and papers concerning civil and criminal district court cases, assessments, voting rolls and elections, justices of the peace (including the Abiquiú book, 1896-1915), vital statistics, the sheriff, schools, probate estates and guardianships, coroner's inquests, and the like. Current records repose in the Rio Arriba County Courthouse at Tierra Amarilla, county seat since 1880.

Although no one in town published a newspaper, items datelined Abiquiú turn up from time to time in the territorial press— when a killing occurs, when a contract is let or a land grant surveyed, when the church of Santo Tomás burns or a fierce wind damages the place. A few partial indices of New Mexico papers exist, usually in the town of publication, for example, at the History Library, MNM, in Santa Fe. Roman Catholic newspapers, like *Revista Católica* and *The Southwestern Catholic*, should not be overlooked. Pearce S. Grove, Becky J. Barnett, and Sandra J. Hansen have led us to water in *New Mexico Newspapers: A Comprehensive Guide to Bibliographical Entries and Locations* (Albuquerque: UNM Press, 1975), but they cannot help us drink. Newspaper research, for all its value, is just plain tedious.

VI. Twentieth century

With world-renowned artist Georgia O'Keeffe living in José María Chávez's house, water skiers and picnickers cavorting at Abiquiu Lake, and all sorts of enlightened human interaction going on at Ghost Ranch Presbyterian Conference Center, it is no wonder that old timers scratch their heads in disbelief. They have seen their relatives leave the valley in search of work. They have seen the highway paved and sewer pipes installed. They have seen the Town of Abiquiú Grant lost for nonpayment of taxes and repurchased for them by the federal government. Even the Penitentes are back in the priest's good graces.

A. *Economics, land, federal assistance, and social science*

The story of Abiquiú's rude initiation into the twentieth-century world of wage labor and commercial land ownership has been outlined by Alvar Ward Carlson and touched upon in dozens of studies from the 1930s and 40s cited by Weigle, yet much remains to be said. All the local sources mentioned in the previous section, plus oral history, should be mined right on up through the Depression and War years.

Although rural poverty becomes an overriding theme, the *New Mexico Business Directory* (Denver: Gazetteer Publishing Co.), published more or less regularly between 1903 and 1942, focuses on some of the people who were making it. Of the seven hundred persons assigned to Abiquiú and vicinity in the 1903-04 edition, twelve were cattlemen-farmers; two each were cattlemen-freighters, just plain freighters, attorneys, notaries public, general merchandisers, saloon keepers, and shoemakers; and one each barber-blacksmith, justice of the peace, and miner. Beginning in the late 1940s publications from the Bureau of Business Research, UNM, take up the wartime slack. Things get tense. Marlowe M. Taylor, *Rural People and Their Resources, North-Central New Mexico*, Agricultural Experiment Station Bulletin 448 (Las Cruces, N.M.: State University, 1960), and Margaret Meaders, "The Economy of Rio Arriba County: The County Background Series," *New Mexico Business* 18 (Apr. 1965): 1-25, (May 1965): 1-29, carefully analyze a situation about to get out of hand.

Armed assault on a courthouse in peacetime America was bound to make national headlines. That it happened at Tierra Amarilla, not forty-five miles from Abiquiú, insured it and the events surrounding it an immediate place in local legend. First the defiant acts of grant heirs calling themselves the Abiquiu Corporation, nervously reported in the New Mexico press, then the rise of Reies López Tijerina, and finally the courthouse shootout. The people of Abiquiú have strong and divergent feelings about all this, feelings worth recording.

Two books aiming to present the facts with a minimum of legend are Peter Nabokov, *Tijerina and the Courthouse Raid* (Albuquerque: UNM Press, 1969), and Richard Gardner, *¡Grito! Reies Tijerina and the New Mexico Land Grant War of 1967* (New York: Harper and Row, 1971). Nabokov has already deposited his research materials, including taped inteviews, in SC-UNM, and Gardner says he will do the same. The State of New Mexico has proffered suggestions for reforming the land grant mess in a *Land*

Title Study (Santa Fe: State Planning Office, 1971), a partial response to the challenge of Tijerina and his Alianza Federal de Mercedes. Another partial response, for those who want to get down to the legal nitty gritty, is Michael Roch and Luella G. Rubio's "A Bibliography of Spanish and Mexican Law Relating to Land Grants in New Mexico," typescript (New Mexico Legal Rights Project, 1975), copy in SC-UNM.

No overall account of federal assistance in the Abiquiú area has yet been compiled. On September 10, 1941, *The Albuquerque Journal* ran a story it headlined "FSA to Determine Needs of Abiquiu, May Help Redeem Land From State, Says Chavez." Item 207 in Saunder's *Guide* is a typewritten report by the Farm Security Administraion, "Land Purchase Proposal for the 'Town of Abiquiu Grant,' Rio Arriba County, New Mexico." A check of RG 96, Records of the Farmers Home Administration (successor of the FSA), NA, would probably turn up further documentation. The same with RG 114, Records of the Soil Conservation Service, NA. A couple of brief typescript SCS reports, both dated April 22, 1946, reside in SC-UNM: "Program for Abiquiu-Vallecitos Soil Conservation District, New Mexico," and "Work Plan for Abiquiu-Vallecitos Soil Conservation District, New Mexico." The Santa Fe *New Mexican* (June 11, 1964) shared news of the grant to construct an Abiquiú sewage treatment plant. There must also be records of local OEO and HEW programs.

Three diverse yet not-so-diverse works will serve to demonstrate the social scientists' enduring interest in northern New Mexico as "a country within a country." Nancie L. González in *The Spanish-Americans of New Mexico: A Heritage of Pride* (Albuquerque: UNM Press, 1969) aims at "an up-to-date synthetic account of the sociocultural system." Alfredo Jiménez Núñez shows that Spaniards are mindful of their New Mexican kin with *Los hispanos de Nuevo México* (Sevilla: Universidad de Sevilla, 1974), a community study centered on Española. In advocating "A Unified Approach to the Anthropology of Hispanic Northern New Mexico: Historical Archaeology, Ethnohistory, and Ethnography," *Historical Archaeology* 10 (1976): 1-16, Paul Kutsche, John R. Van Ness, and Andrew T. Smith use Abiquiú as an example in posing several plausible hypotheses. The names of other prominent social scientists—Clark S. Knowlton, Olen E. Leonard, and a dozen more—turn up over and over in the bibliographies cited earlier.

B. *Folklife, Penitentes, and modern intrusions*

But for the Works Progress Administration's Federal Writers' Project, launched in 1935, Rosario O. Hinojos might never have had her retelling of "The Murder of Tomás Martínez" set down on paper, nor Amalia Chávez her song "Sobre las Olas." These are a couple of Abiquiú items from hundreds of folk contributions collected in northern New Mexico during the project. Lorin W. Brown's posthumous *Hispano Folklife of New Mexico, The Lorin W. Brown Federal Writers' Project Manuscripts*, ed. Charles L. Briggs and Marta Weigle (Albuquerque: UNM Press, 1978), features an extended and integrated bibliography, already a trademark of Weigle's. Further access to this remarkable storehouse is provided by a card file in the History Library, MNM, and by Gilberto Benito Córdova's annotated *Bibliography of Unpublished Materials Pertaining to Hispanic Culture in the New Mexico WPA Writers' Files* (Santa Fe: N.M. Department of Education, 1972). Córdova, who has lived and listened in Abiquiú most of his life, in "A Hispano Tale from Abiquiú, New Mexico," *Aztlán* 1 (Fall 1970): 103-10, shares one of Steven Suazo's delightful parables about an honest stepdaughter and a spiteful daughter who in their respective encounters with the Blessed Virgin come away with signs on their foreheads, the first with a star and the second a horn.

Two other Abiquiú Suazos, Sóstenes and Valentín, were among the ninety-eight storytellers Juan B. Rael relied on for his *Cuentos Españoles de Colorado y Nuevo México (Spanish Folk Tales from Colorado and New Mexico)*, rev. ed., 2 vols. (Santa Fe: MNM Press, 1977). J. Manuel Espinosa, "Spanish Folklore in the Southwest: The Pioneer Studies of Aurelio M. Espinosa," *The Americas* 35 (1978): 219-37, concludes this tribute to his father with a listing of the elder Espinosa's writings. Taken with Weigle's bibliographies, which show further bibliographies, with *The New Mex-*

ico Folklore Record, published irregularly since 1946-47, and with the works of Arthur L. Campa and John D. Robb, the above references are enough to divert any serious academic historian.

No aspect of Hispano folklife in New Mexico has been more gawked at and more distorted than the Brotherhood of Our Father Jesus, commonly known as the Penitentes. Responding first to virtual abandonment by the Roman Catholic Church and second to the culture shock of Protestant occupation, village laymen in Abiquiú and elsewhere pooled their resources and their resourcefulness to provide community social services and religious expression.

Marta Weigle, in *Brothers of Light, Brothers of Blood: The Penitentes of the Southwest* (Albuquerque: UNM Press, 1976), goes a long way toward correcting the distortion. At the same time she offers *A Penitente Bibliography* (Albuquerque: UNM Press, 1976) meant, in her words, to "serve as the obituary for the seemingly endless stream of irresponsible, secondary, sensational palaver about the Brotherhood and a substantial refutation to anyone who publishes yet another 'exposé' of the 'hitherto unknown' and 'secret' cult about which 'so little has been written'." Herein she pays her respects to Dorothy Woodward whose *The Penitentes of New Mexico* (Ph.D. diss., Yale University, 1935; reprint, New York: Arno Press, 1974) remains the "standard scholarly source," and whose papers are found in the SRC, Santa Fe.

Weighing the evidence prudently, Weigle concludes that the Penitente phenomenon was a regional lay adaptation of New Mexico's long Franciscan tradition. Fray Angelico Chavez, "The Penitentes of New Mexico," NMHR 29 (1954): 97-123, and review of Weigle, NM 54 (June 1976): 21, heartily disagrees. He sees the Penitentes not as an outgrowth of the Franciscan Third Order but as a relatively late transplant from Mexico.

An eyewitness account of Holy Week in Abiquiú, Alice Corbin Henderson's *Brothers of Light: The Penitentes of the Southwest* (New York: Harcourt, Brace and Co., 1937; reprinted ed., Santa Fe: William Gannon, 1977) is at once evocative and sympathetic.

There are two *moradas*, or Penitente meeting houses, in Abiquiú: east, properly La Morada del Alto, and south, La Morada del Moque. Richard E. Ahlborn made them and their furnishings the subjects of his *The Penitente Moradas of Abiquiú*, Contributions from the Museum of History and Technology, Paper 63 (Washington, D.C.: Smithsonian Institution Press, 1968). Many of the religious images and artifacts so carefully photographed here were subsequently stolen, but then recovered, which is another story worth telling. Today La Morada del Alto is on the New Mexico State Register of Cultural Properties and La Morada del Moque is well-nigh fortified.

Worthy of note in a paragraph by itself is E. Boyd's massive and richly illustrated *Popular Arts of Spanish New Mexico* (Santa Fe: MNM Press, 1974), the altarscreen-to-zaguan of the subject.

Georgia O'Keeffe, whose powerful canvases each command more money than most artists make in a lifetime, is a modern intrusion any community would welcome. Although she has of choice remained aloof, some of her paintings betray her attachment to the local scene. *Georgia O'Keeffe* by Georgia O'Keeffe (New York: Viking Press, 1976) is a stunning tour of her work with the artist as guide. An excerpt, "O'Keeffe," appeared in NM 54 (Dec. 1976): 29-44, and a long review by Stanford Schwartz in *The New Yorker* (Aug. 28, 1978).

Ghost Ranch and Abiquiu Dam, nearby attractions that bring a lot of people to buy gas and to poke around the village, are probably looked upon by a majority of Abiquiú natives with mixed emotions. Naturalist and philanthropist Arthur Newton Pack, developer of the former, writes informally about the place and some of the people who have come under its spell in *We Called It Ghost Ranch* (Abiquiú: Ghost Ranch Conference Center, 1965). Out of the New Mexico Geological Society's twenty-fifth field conference there, October 10-12, 1974, came *Ghost Ranch: Central-Northern New Mexico*, Silver Anniversary Guidebook, ed. Charles T. Siemers (Socorro: N.M. Geological Society, 1974).

The twenty-one-million-dollar, 325-feet tall, 1,540-feet long, earthfill, flood-control and sediment-retention Abiquiu Dam, raised up between 1956 and 1963, is described briefly in the U.S. Army Corps of Engineers Southwestern Division's serial publication *Water Resources Development by the U.S. Army Corps of Engineers in New Mexico* (e.g., Dallas, 1963). The Corps took plenty of ribbing from the Santa Fe *New Mexican* in 1962-63 when the big tub did not fill up as rapidly as predicted. Plans are now afoot to make it bigger.

VII. Graphics, historical archaeology, and oral history

Like love, graphic material is pretty much where you find it. Many of the published works named above contain appropriate illustrations and most of the archives reproducible documents. Andrew K. Gregg, *New Mexico in the Nineteenth Century, A Pictorial History* (Albuquerque: UNM Press, 1968), features pictures—not photographs—from "nearly three hundred books, newspapers, or magazine articles," including one of Agent Arny and his Utes and Jicarillas. There are a number of ideas for illustrating the Spanish colonial period—signatures and portraits of notables, map illuminations, pottery designs, all manner of artifacts, early woodcuts and title pages, the seal of the Mexican Inquisition—in Kessell's *Kiva, Cross, and Crown.*

For historic photographs the first place to look is the Photo Archives, MNM, where the vast array includes copy prints from collections all over the country. The SRC and SC-UNM are good second bets. Córdova in *Abiquiú and Don Cacahuate* thanks "Joseph and Robert Grant for their willingness to share their extensive Abiquiu photo collection." There may be other such. Photos can be fun; two natives of the area, within months of each other, published the same shot of the chapel of Santa Rosa reversed and with different dates—Salazar, "Santa Rosa," and Córdova, "A Rose in the Desert," NM 54 (July 1976): 34-35.

As for maps, the MNM, purchaser of a 1760 Bernardo de Miera y Pacheco "original," is in the process of acquiring copies of all known maps of colonial New Mexico. The Frank McNitt Collection, SRC, contains an impressive run of nineteenth-century maps, many from the NA, many of the Navajo country and adjacent points, among them William H. Bell's "Map of a reconnaissance for a wagon road from Abique to the mouth of the Arroyo Tunicha," 1859.

When the old church of Santo Tomás, which photographs show first with a flat roof and then with pitched tin roof, came down in 1937 to make room for a new one, nobody thought to indulge in salvage archaeology or an environmental impact study. There is one thing, however. John Gaw Meem's architectural drawings (1935) of the new "Pueblo revival" church survive, in the Meem Collection, Zimmerman Library, UNM.

Although not much that resembles archaeology has ever been done in Abiquiú proper, Frank C. Hibben once dug a stratigraphic trench at Santa Rosa de Lima. Others "potted" that exposed and easily accessible site, and lo, the State Highway Department paved New Mexico 84 right across the south end of it. Herbert W. Dick of Adams State College in Alamosa, Colorado, made a surface survey and a partial field sketch, and with Wesley R. Hurt contributed "Spanish-American Pottery from New Mexico," EP 53 (1946): 280-88, 307-12.

Today Santa Rosa de Lima is on the National Register of Historic Places. A model, locally run archaeological project, under the field supervision of Charles M. Carrillo, has captured the community's imagination. Melissa Noland, "Abiquiu's Roots: Villagers Unearth Their Past," EP 83 (Winter 1977): 31-34, and Betsy Petrick, "Abiquiu Rebuilds Its Heritage," Suntrails USA 1 (Mar. 1978): 18-19, 47, tell of the excitement.

The time seems right, while there are still people around who remember what happened to the vigas from the old Santo Tomás church, to revive the oral history program initiated by Gilberto Benito Córdova in 1967. Perhaps, too, an invitation should be extended to those persons who have documents hidden away in trunks and cigar boxes to bring them out for copying. What better gift to the next generation than a library of tapes and family papers.

There is no lack of sources for the history of Abiquiú. F. Stanley's analogy, with which this essay began, is surely a good one. Yet he who would write the story, beware. Just picking at the tassle will never do.

Abbreviations

AASF	Archives of the Archdiocese of Santa Fe, Albuquerque
AGI	Archivo General de Indias, Seville
AGN	Archivo General de la Nación, Mexico City
BAE	Bureau of American Ethnology, Smithsonian Institution
BL	The Bancroft Library, University of California, Berkeley
BNM	Biblioteca Nacional, Mexico City
CM	*The Colorado Magazine*
EP	*El Palacio*
GPO	Government Printing Office
GSA	General Services Administration
HED	House Executive Document
MANM	Mexican Archives of New Mexico, SRC
MNM	Museum of New Mexico, Santa Fe
NA	The National Archives of the United States, Washington, D.C.
NM	*New Mexico Magazine*
NMHR	*New Mexico Historical Review*
NMO	New Mexico Originals, BL
OU	University of Oklahoma
RG	Record Group, NA
SANM	Spanish Archives of New Mexico, SRC
SC-UNM	Special Collections, Zimmerman Library, UNM
SRC	State Records Center and Archives, Santa Fe
UA	University of Arizona, Tucson
UHQ	*Utah Historical Quarterly*
UNM	University of New Mexico
WHQ	*The Western Historical Quarterly*

Detail of the 1656 Texeira plan of Madrid showing the Vargas houseblock and the parish church of San Pedro el Real, lower left.

160

DIEGO DE VARGAS: ANOTHER LOOK

JOHN L. KESSELL

N OT FOR NEARLY FIFTY YEARS, since the extraordinary, painstaking work of historian J. Manuel Espinosa, have we looked closely at Diego de Vargas (1643–1704), governor and recolonizer of New Mexico.[1] It is time we did.

Vargas is slipping out of focus. A recent popular history of the Southwest had this to say about him:

> He was lean, resilient, and exquisitely elegant, his thin face adorned with hairline mustaches and a narrow goatee. Although he had married into a family as illustrious as his, he was unhappy. At the age of thirty-one he walked out on his wife and sailed to New Spain. Because divorces were impossible in Catholic Spain, the adored woman he found in Mexico City, mother of three of his children, remained unwed. He added grandly to his already immense fortune, and in 1688 offered to return the lost province to Mexico at his own expense.[2]

Unfortunately, this graphic description is more than a little distorted. Vargas was endlessly in debt. He missed his family in Spain. He had a broad face. And he lisped.

He was born in Madrid, capital of the Spanish empire. Although the family spent part of the year at the big house in Torrelaguna, seat of Vargas rural properties north of the city, Madrid was home. Baptized on 8 November 1643, Diego Joseph de Vargas Zapata y Luján Ponce de León y Contreras hardly knew his parents.[3] María Margarita de Contreras, his mother, died when he was five.[4] The following year his father, Capt. Alonso de Vargas Zapata, knight of the Order of Santiago, left him and his older brother Lorenzo in the care of a paternal great-grandmother and set off as alcalde mayor, or district officer, of Chiapas in the jurisdiction of Guatemala. They never saw him again. At least the boys were not uprooted. Surrounded by aunts and uncles and cousins, they continued living where they always had, in the principal upstairs apartments of the Vargas home "on the street that leads down from the Puerta de Moros to [the parish church of] San Pedro."[5]

Diego de Vargas grew up with the amenities of his class—the middle-ranking nobility of the capital. When Lorenzo died, about 1660, Diego became his father's heir. At the age of eighteen, he secured from the crown license to administer don Alonso's estates. The settlement of accounts with his legal guardian of the previous two years suggests what occupied a young man of his station in Madrid in the early 1660s.

A notary recorded the expenses routinely: for his grammar lessons (eighteen months at 20 reales per month) and schoolbooks (235 reales), his dancing lessons (ten months at 24 reales per month), his manservant (100 reales a month), food for the two of them (120 reales a month), and twenty-two pairs of shoes (11 reales each) plus two plain pairs for the dancing lessons (10 reales each). He dressed and slept well. The itemization included everything from shirts to sheets, silk stockings to hats, a velvet suit, an ordinary black suit, and others for winter, spring, and summer; gloves, handkerchiefs, ribbons, and incidentals. In the spring of 1661 Diego de Vargas had fallen ill. The cure, which included artificially opening a small wound to evacuate fluids, cost 375 reales for "two physicians and a surgeon who attended him, medicine, and other things for his comfort." Over a sixteen-month period, don Diego also spent 322 reales on bullfights, theatrical performances, and other "minor expenses."[6]

Early in November of 1662, the nineteen-year-old Vargas signed a power of attorney in favor of his great-uncle Sebastián de Vargas, a Jesuit residing at the Colegio Imperial de San Pedro y San Pablo, "because I need to go to continue my studies to the University of Valladolid for which I am about to leave."[7] Eighteen months later, on 5 May 1664, in the monumental Gothic church of Santa María

Magdalena at Torrelaguna, Father Sebastián celebrated his nephew's marriage to Beatriz Pimentel de Prado Vélez de Olazábal, twenty-two. The principal house of the Pimentel almost adjoined that of the Vargas on the Plaza del Coso: Diego and Beatriz had known each other since childhood.[8]

The young couple wasted no time. Entries in the parish baptismal register at Torrelaguna record five children in six years. The first, Isabel María Polonia, born nine months and four days after the wedding (9 February 1665), would through a tragic chain of circumstances become her father's inheritor. But she was not, as has been suggested, his only legitimate child. Juana Viviana, who outlived them all and was still alive in 1740, followed (2 December 1666), then María Antonia (18 December 1667), who died in infancy, and finally the two boys, Francisco Antonio, also called Francisco Iván (4 October 1669) and Juan Manuel (20 December 1670). Beatriz's brother Gregorio Pimentel de Prado, knight of the Order of Santiago, stood as godfather to all five.[9]

News of the death of Maestre de Campo Alonso de Vargas on 15 August 1665, in the city of Santiago de Guatemala, reached Madrid in 1666. A widower when he sailed for the Indies, don Alonso had remarried a much younger woman than he in Guatemala and was the father of three more children. His will, however, left no doubt. Diego inherited. Only in the event of Diego's death without immediate heirs would the Vargas properties pass to Alonso's firstborn American child, Pedro Alonso, who at the time of his father's death was only three years old.[10]

For the next half-dozen years, from the summer of 1666 when he took legal possession of his inheritance until the summer of 1672 when he embarked for the Indies, Diego de Vargas personally managed the family properties and the family lawsuits, residing most of the time in Torrelaguna. Once at least, he traveled to Granada to inspect holdings there. Although the Vargas *mayorazgos*, or entailed estates, of Madrid, Torrelaguna, and Granada were fairly diversified—houses, vineyards, olive groves, enclosed pastures, farm lands, and a variety of rents and privileges from religious and secular corporations—taken together, they were not profitable. There were a thousand minor details, and more debts than income. Later he would refer to his properties repeatedly as

The only known portrait of Diego de Vargas, Capilla de San Isidro, Pretil de Santiesteban, 3, Madrid (detail).

"mis miserables mayorazgos."[11] Don Diego was, without question, a noble and landed Spanish gentleman. But the roof leaked.

In 1667 he petitioned the crown for permission to further encumber his estates. "Because of limited maintenance and the ravages of time," the houses in Madrid and Torrelaguna were sadly run-down. Put in shape, he reasoned, the complex in Madrid would provide additional rental income and the mill at Torrelaguna could be returned to production. At the Madrid place the apartments at the corner of the Calle del Almendro and the street leading down to the parish church had to be rebuilt from the foundations up. Elsewhere tile roofs, drain gutters and spouts, brick floors, cracked walls around windows and doors, the three kitchens, the water pipes: all were in urgent need of repair. Even the "secret stairway" down to the latrines was sinking.[12]

It was hard for don Diego to reconcile the traditional luster of the house of Vargas and the hard times that engulfed him. *"Los Vargas son gavilanes,"* the poet had sung. "The Vargases are hawks!" "Have Vargas see to it," the Catholic Kings had ordered—*"Averíguelo Vargas"*—and Tirso de Molina made that the title of a play. Diego de Vargas Zapata y Luján, only male heir of his direct line, knew the history. Warrior-knights, bishops, counselors to kings, his forebears had won honor and fame in the Catholic reconquest of Spain and in the expansion of empire. He had grown up in old Madrid amid the lore and the shrines of San Isidro Labrador, St. Isidore the Farmer, patron saint of the city. He knew that in the twelfth century his ancestor, the knight Iván de Vargas, was Isidore's employer and that the future saint had met his wife, Santa María de la Cabeza, while tilling Vargas land at Torrelaguna. Years later, as Diego de Vargas proclaimed the reconquest of New Mexico for God and crown, he did not have to invent the rhetoric. Outlandishly misplaced in time and space, like Don Quixote, Diego de Vargas was the warrior-knight.

Still, the contrast between the brilliance that once was Spain, between the appearances kept up at court, and the disenchanting realities of life in the mid-seventeenth century—the depressions, bread riots, and military reverses—cannot have escaped him. The year Vargas was born, French artillery had routed Spain's legendary pikemen at Rocroi in the Low Countries. An unstable economy and the disruption of agricultural production at home forced cash-poor landed families like his deeper and deeper into debt. The year Vargas's first daughter was born in Torrelaguna, King Philip IV died and Charles II, "a sickly child, retarded by rickets, and mentally subnormal," succeeded to the Spanish throne, "the last, the most degenerate, and the most pathetic victim of Habsburg inbreeding."[13]

His decision to go to the Indies was calculated. The royal service offered regular pay for honorable employment, and the get-rich-quick aura of America held out prospects of fortune. Besides, he had matters to attend to in Guatemala. His father, it seems, had been party to business deals there. At home the Vargas properties were heavily mortgaged. The debt service and inflation were getting beyond him. His father and his father's father had responded similarly to the family's straitened circumstances. Lorenzo de Vargas Zapata, who secured appointment in 1649 as corregidor of Zacatecas, New Spain's fabled silver city, had died before embarking. Alonso de Vargas Zapata had served with distinction and died in Guatemala. Hope of restoring the family's fortune still lay in America. Now it was up to don Diego.[14]

That summer of 1672, he saw to the details. He made a will, describing himself as native of Madrid and resident of Torrelaguna. His older son Francisco Iván, not yet three, would succeed him in the event of his death.[15] To identify himself as legal and sole heir of Alonso de Vargas, he had proof of his legitimacy drawn up in due legal form. Four witnesses testified. They knew him personally. He was, they agreed, "a young man of medium stature, straight hair, and broad face, who lisps somewhat and cannot pronouce certain words."[16]

He was going to America, he stated in a power of attorney to Sebastián de Vargas, S.J., to settle his father's affairs and to claim the inheritance that belonged to him.[17] At a court notorious for its ostentation and its intrigues, he had obtained appointment as *gentilhombre del aviso*, royal courier to the viceroy of New Spain and to the president of the Audiencia de Guadalajara. At Torrelaguna, don Diego compiled a detailed inventory of the Vargas properties, named Gabriel Pimentel overseer, anticipated as best he could the immediate needs of his family, and took his leave.[18]

In mid-August he rode south from Madrid, bound for the port city of Cádiz. A week later in the capital a spectacular fire consumed numerous houses on the Plaza Mayor, but not the one belonging to his aunt Juana de Vargas with its twelve and a half balconies, which he would inherit.[19]

Delayed in Cádiz more than six months, Diego de Vargas made the crossing in 1673. Later the same year Viceroy, the Marqués de Mancera, granted him the post of alcalde mayor of Teutila, a mining zone southeast of Mexico City in the dense, rugged mountains of Oaxaca.[20] To the new district officer from Madrid, it was an exotic place, worlds away from home. Here he learned of the death of his wife doña Beatriz, the mother of his four small children, at Torrelaguna on 10 July 1674. She had died so suddenly that she had not received the sacraments. She was thirty-two.[21]

Although his penmanship was bad and his syntax worse, Diego de Vargas wrote home. An incomplete collection of his personal letters, retained today in two parts by descendants, shows him to have been a loving and solicitous head of the family, always anxious about money, always seeking advancement, always homesick. There is, of course, no way to judge with perfect certainty how sincere don Diego was in his frequent professions of loneliness and nostalgia. After all, he had in a sense escaped his burdens in Spain; he seemed to relish at times, particularly during the reconquest of New Mexico, the excitement of the Indies; and he sired a New World family. Yet it was the house of Vargas in Madrid, more than anything else, that continued to define his identity.[22]

As early as 1675, in a letter to Gregorio Pimentel, he was contemplating return to Madrid "after having been in this kingdom, missing my homeland and toiling continually over different terrains and roads whose ruggedness I can scarcely exaggerate to you, and living among Indians, which is the same thing as existing in a desert." He asked his brother-in-law to place his two girls in the Franciscan Conceptionist convent at Torrelaguna and to arrange for the boys to stay with their grandmother.[23]

Vargas's tenure at Teutila lasted two years. When it ended, he underwent the prescribed review and was judged an exemplary official. He may have gone to Guatemala to attend to matters there, an objective he had expressed to Gregorio Pimentel, and then returned to Mexico City, where evidently from the mid-1670s he maintained a residence. In 1679 the viceroy, Archbishop Fray Payo Enríquez Afán de Rivera, named him alcalde mayor of the mining district of Tlalpujagua in the high, pine-forested mountains of eastern Michoacán, no more than three or four days' ride from the capital. Its administration occupied don Diego for the next decade, until almost the eve of his departure for New Mexico. In 1690, even after a successor had taken over at Tlalpujagua, Vargas was still trying to collect from local mine owners for his allotments to them of mercury, an essential ingredient in the patio process of silver refining and a crown monopoly.[24]

The seventeen years Vargas experienced in New Spain, from the time he delivered the royal dispatches to Viceroy Mancera in 1673 until he rode north in November of 1690 to assume the governorship of New Mexico, are an unwritten chapter of his life. By 1679 or before, judging by the age of the eldest natural child whom he recognized in his final will of 1704, Diego de Vargas, a widower in his thirties, had met the mother of his American family. He did not marry her, but he had by her at least three children: Juan Manuel (born 1679–80)—the same name as his second son in Spain; Alonso (1681–82); and María Teresa (1685–86).[25] They may have occupied a residence in Mexico City on the Plazuela de las Gayas.[26]

Meanwhile in Madrid, his older daughter married well. On 13 December 1688, Isabel María wed don Ignacio López de Zárate y Alvarez de Medina, knight of the Order of Santiago, minister of the Council of Italy, and fiscal for the Council of War. He was forty-one, a second son, and she was not quite twenty-three, mistress of the house of Vargas. He moved in with her.[27] Vargas knew the family, well-placed bureaucrats all of them. He was elated by the match. What chagrined and perplexed him for years was the dowry he wished to provide. He simply did not have the money. He tried paying in installments, then drew up a power of attorney in favor of López de Zárate, assigning to his son-in-law the administration and income of all his properties in Spain.[28] That proved no blessing.

The family estates were, as usual, in sorry shape. The reports depressed Vargas. "I can do no more in life," he wrote to Isabel María from El Paso, "than to have given up my homeland, my properties, and the love of being in your company. . . . I recognize

168

from the papers and accounting that my son lord don Ignacio sends me the bad management there has been and that the estate is more encumbered now than when I left it." From six thousand miles away he tried to advise his son-in-law, addressing him as always in the third person, the polite form in Spanish, on crops and improvements and lawsuits. "My devotion," he vowed, "can express itself to no greater degree than that of having exiled myself to this kingdom, last on earth and remote beyond compare, in order to seek in this far place the means once and for all to be relieved in my desire to make good Your Lordship's dowry."[29]

In his unrelenting effort to make a career in America pay, Diego de Vargas sought preferment wherever he could find it. A son-in-law at court seemed providential. Although Vargas's bid for a promotion from the New Mexico post, which he pressed for at least a decade—to Guatemala, he suggested in 1698, or Buenos Aires, or Panamá, or Chile, or Cuba[30]—never was successful, López de Zárate's advocacy helped secure his reappointment to New Mexico and the title *marqués*.

During the unhappy, thirty-five-year reign of Charles II, the Spanish crown created as many noble titles of Castile as it had in the previous two hundred years—five vizcondes, seventy-eight condes, and 209 marqueses. At least Vargas's was not simply bought. He earned it by his deeds, a rarity in those unheroic times. The name was up to him. As early as 1692 he had thought of Marqués or Conde de los Caramancheles, after certain family holdings near Madrid. In Spain there was no hierarchical distinction between marqueses and condes. In the end he combined the names of two Vargas rural properties north of the city of Granada near Ignalloz, the *cortijos* of La Nava and Barcinas, to become first Marqués de la Nava de Barcinas.[31]

There was another thing Diego de Vargas thought he deserved: membership in the still prestigious military order of Santiago. His father had been a knight of Santiago, and his grandfather, and his great-grandfather. His son-in-law and his three brothers-in-law were knights of Santiago. Writing from Santa Fe in 1697, and evidently consulting a manual on knighthood he had with him in New Mexico, he asked López de Zárate, who sat on the Council of the Orders, to obtain a decree providing that a knight of Santiago invest him in the nearest church and that he be allowed an absence from New Mexico of a hundred days for the purpose.

"I am resolved in this," Vargas explained, "because in two years on the feast of Santiago [25 July], I have won two decisive victories of greatest importance, which I attributed to miracles from heaven." He had vowed, if he returned to Spain, to make a pilgrimage to Santiago de Compostela. Along with the decree, he wanted his son-in-law to send a habit of Santiago made in Madrid and a dozen of the red dagger-cross insignias of the order, "both large ones for cloaks and small ones to put on jackets."[32] Whatever the impediment—family enemies, lack of material wealth, charges pending against him in Mexico City—the recolonizer of New Mexico failed to gain membership in the Order of Santiago.

News from López de Zárate was not always depressing. With some regularity his letters brought glad tidings of grandchildren. Beginning in 1690 Isabel María gave birth to at least four: Rosoléa Gregoria, Diego Joseph, Francisca María, and María Manuela. She and don Ignacio favored long strings of baptismal names. In the parish church of San Pedro el Real on 11 October 1700, for example, their third was baptized Francisca María Teresa Antonia Rafaela Juliana Juana Ignacia.[33] From America, Diego de Vargas conveyed his sentiments. "My heart will rejoice," he confessed to Isabel María after the birth of the first, "to know that you are well and also my beloved granddaughter to whom I send lots of kisses and give my blessing." He had a favor to ask. He wanted portraits of the family, and also of his son Juan Manuel.[34]

Vargas's elder son, Francisco Iván, had died sometime between 1675 and 1685. That made his other son, Juan Manuel, his father's sole male heir and successor. Although the boy was less than two years old when don Diego last saw him, he doted on him. He must have been an attractive youth, for he had become a queen's page at court. Vargas implored his son-in-law to treat Juan Manuel not as a brother but as a son, to see to the young man's proper upbringing, to favor and protect him. When word reached don Diego in 1690 that Juan Manuel, now almost twenty, wanted to join him in America, the governor-elect of New Mexico disapproved vigorously. His son should continue to serve at the palace and learn discipline. In time he could join a cavalry unit and become a man.

"The Indies are fine for those who sell in a store," Vargas admonished, "but not for men whose object is to flee the trades, and thus it is dangerous ground." Because the viceroys, inundated by recommendations, had only so many posts to fill, there were already many humiliated nobles in America.[35]

He came anyway, nine years later, without his father's knowledge. Embarking at Cádiz in July 1699 with his weapons and his two servants—one round-faced with dark curly chestnut hair and the other with hawk face and short blond hair—Cavalry Captain Vargas Pimentel had given as the purpose of his passage "to seek don Diego de Vargas Zapata, my father, who is in the City of Mexico."[36] But Diego de Vargas was not in Mexico City. He was confined in Santa Fe by order of his successor in office. This, Juan Manuel scolded his brother-in-law, was all López de Zárate's fault for not having forwarded promptly his father's reappointment to the governorship of New Mexico. Juan Manuel had had an interesting visitor—the other Juan Manuel, a student, "as big as I am and very like me in appearance. There is another small one, and their mother sent to welcome me and to offer their house. But I shall not see her."[37]

When Diego de Vargas, released on orders from the viceroy, finally reached Mexico City on 29 October 1700, he looked so fit, Juan Manuel reported, that those who knew of his ordeal could scarcely believe it. Father and son had the first sight of each other three leagues from the capital. "On seeing me," wrote Juan Manuel, "he was so overcome that for a long time he spoke not a word to me." They went for an audience with the viceroy, the Conde de Montezuma, who received the elder Vargas with demonstrations of affection and respect, "false, as is his custom," added Juan Manuel.[38]

By early 1701, the young Vargas wanted to return to Spain. He had achieved his "fond purpose" of finally knowing his father. But there was a war on, and the fleet sat anchored at Veracruz for fear of the English and Dutch navies. So while don Diego—who now signed "el Marques de la naba de Brazinas" even in letters to Isabel María—prepared his defense against charges of malfeasance in office, Juan Manuel enjoyed himself in the capital. When at last the fleet, some twenty laden vessels escorted by a like number of French warships, sailed in June 1702, he was aboard.[39]

The report that his son had died on the return voyage struck Vargas to the core of his being. The entire fleet and every ship of the French escort had been burned, sunk, or captured in the sea-land battle of Vigo, 22–23 October 1702, a signal disaster in Spanish naval history. More than two thousand Spaniards and Frenchmen, as close as anyone could estimate, had perished, among them Capt. Juan Manuel de Vargas Pimentel. They held a service for him at Torrelaguna and the priest entered a note in the parish burial book. Only later did his father get word in Mexico City via Havana. He could scarcely comprehend that his dear son, "the idol of my affection," to whom he had just entrusted all his properties, was dead. All his hopes for the house of Vargas, which he had so recently adorned with the title of marqués, had vanished in the horror of Vigo.[40]

But he had to pull himself together, to guard his honor, and to continue the struggle to repair his fortune "in order that my plight not expose me to the perpetual captivity of my remaining in this damned kingdom lost for not being able to leave it and trapped by my debts." Faced by such weighty considerations, it was well, he thought, that he open his eyes "to the recognition of thirty years misspent, from August 11, 1672, when I left that kingdom and my beloved homeland, that delightful villa of Madrid, crown of all the world."[41]

He hated the thought of a return to New Mexico. He wanted a promotion, but none came. Once acquitted on all counts, a blessing he attributed to the fairness of the recently arrived viceroy, the Duque de Alburquerque, Vargas saw no other alternative. He had to exercise his reappointment to the frontier province. There was also the matter of an eleventh-hour encomienda, a grant by the crown to Diego de Vargas of 4,000 pesos annually for two lifetimes to be collected as tribute, in goods, from the Pueblo Indians of New Mexico. As an institution, the encomienda at this late date was being phased out all over the empire. Although Vargas seems wisely not to have pressed its imposition, his heirs later succeeded in having the grant converted to a pension.[42]

Then in his sixtieth year, he cannot have relished the thousand-mile ride. Back in Santa Fe in November 1703, Diego de Vargas had only a short time to live. He must have had a premonition. In mid-January he wrote individual letters to his brother-in-law, his sister, both sons-in-law, both surviving daughters, and a long-time family employee, putting his affairs in order. The next letter they received from America, dated in Santa Fe on 20 April 1704, came from Juan Páez Hurtado, Vargas's most trusted lieutenant. The Marqués de la Nava de Barcinas was dead.

He had died pursuing Apaches in the Rio Grande Valley south of present-day Albuquerque, not from battle but from sickness. So ill that he could not ride, he had been carried from downriver to Bernalillo on the shoulders of Pueblo Indian auxiliaries. Páez Hurtado rode south from Santa Fe with medication. The governor had a long history of recurrent bouts with *tabardillo,* "the spotted fever," or typhus.

This time he had not responded. He had dictated his last will, professed in the Franciscan Third Order of Penitence, and about five in the afternoon of 8 April 1704, he gave up his soul. Describing Vargas's fatal illness to the family in Spain, Páez Hurtado called it *"un grave accidente de calenturas por habérsele resfriado el estómago."* It may have been dysentery.[43]

Diego de Vargas, who relied on his own strength of character and on the disunity of the Pueblo Indians to recolonize New Mexico in the 1690s, was a loving and lonely family man cursed all his adult life by reduced circumstances. The notion that he was wealthy, based in part on his landed status in Spain and in part on his claim to have reconquered the province at his own expense, is ill-founded. He did underwrite the relatively inexpensive expedition of 1692 and the recruitment of one group of colonists. Another look suggests a revision of the passage quoted at the beginning of this article.

> On the eve of his departure for America, he was a young man of average height, straight hair, and broad face, with a speech impediment. Although he had married well, the chronic indebtedness of the Vargas properties weighed heavily upon him. At the age of twenty-eight, in hopes of restoring his family's financial welfare, he

took leave of them and set out for New Spain. His wife died soon after. A widower, he chose not to marry the woman in Mexico City who bore him three more children. He added scarcely a peso to his already encumbered assets and in 1688, the year of his appointment as governor of New Mexico, wanted nothing so much as to go home.

The parish church of Santa María Magdalena, Torrelaguna (Madrid), where Diego de Vargas was married, his children baptized, and his wife baptized and buried.

NOTES

1. J. Manuel Espinosa, *Crusaders of the Río Grande: The Story of Don Diego de Vargas and the Reconquest and Refounding of New Mexico* (Chicago: Institute of Jesuit History, 1942), is the standard narrative. Seven articles by him about the recolonization are listed in the bibliography. His *First Expedition of Vargas into New Mexico, 1692* (Albuquerque: University of New Mexico Press, 1940), vol. 10 of the Coronado Cuarto Centennial Publications, includes a scholarly English translation of Vargas's campaign journal and correspondence of 1692 and five related documents. The current, long-term Vargas Project at the University of New Mexico, funded in part by the National Historical Publications and Records Commission and the National Endowment for the Humanities, has as its goals: (1) bringing together all available documentation bearing on New Mexico during the pivotal period 1680–1710, (2) entering the vital information in a model computer data base, and (3) publishing in English translation a six-volume scholarly edition of the Journals of Diego de Vargas.

2. David Lavender, *The Southwest* (New York: Harper and Row, 1980), pp. 59–60.

3. Archivo Histórico Nacional, Madrid (AHN), Sección de Ordenes Militares, Casamientos, Santiago, núm. 10.461. A certification of Vargas's baptism is included in the proof of good lineage required of his daughter Isabel María when her husband Ignacio López de Zárate, knight of the Order of Santiago, was elevated in 1694 to the Consejo de las Ordenes. Licenciado Pedro de la Carra had performed the baptism, according to the certification, "for the parish priest of San Ginés and San Luis," but it does not say where. The baby's maternal grandparents, Diego de Contreras and Beatriz de Arraiz, became his godparents. Since his father, grandfather, and forebears were members of the parish of San Pedro el Real, a stone's throw from the ancestral home, it is probable that Diego was baptized there. The original entry, written in a baptismal book of the parish of San Luis, seems not to have survived the burning of that church in 1936. (*Guía de los archivos de Madrid* [Madrid: Dirección General de Archivos y Bibliotecas, 1952], p. 462). The certificate and related genealogical material is printed in José Pérez Balsera, *Laudemus viros gloriosos et parentes nostros in generatione sua* (Madrid: privately printed, 1931), copy in the History Library, Museum of New Mexico, Santa Fe. Another genealogy, by Diego de Vargas's grandson, is Diego Joseph López de Zárate Vargas, *Breve descripcion genealogica de la ilustre, quanto antiquissima casa de los Vargas de Madrid* (Madrid: privately printed, 1740), copy in the Real Academia de la Historia, Madrid.

4. Doña María Margarita, who died on 17 April 1649, was only twenty-six. She was laid to rest in the Vargas chapel of the church at the Franciscan Convento Grande in Madrid. Not quite seven months later, on 13 November 1649, Vargas's paternal grandfather Lorenzo de Vargas Zapata also died (Relación de D. Diego de Vargas Zapata y Luján, Madrid, 30 June 1670, con nota posterior, Archivo General de Indias, Sevilla [AGI], Indiferente, 123).

5. Nombramiento de tutora y curadora a la señora D.ª Juana Ponce de León y otros, Madrid, 8 April 1650, Archivo Histórico de Protocolos de Madrid (AHPM), Protocolo (P.) 7.214. To provide for the boys in case of their great-grandmother's death, don Alonso named a succession of five more guardians. A superbly detailed plan of Madrid, drawn in 1656 when Diego de Vargas was not yet thirteen, shows the Vargas houseblock, no. 153 on later plans, and the nearby parish church of San Pedro with its mudéjar tower, block no. 152 ("Topographía de la Villa de Madrid descrita por don Pedro Texeira, año 1656," Nueva edición [Madrid: Ayuntamiento de Madrid, 1980]). See also Miguel Molina Campuzano, *Planos de Madrid de los siglos XVII y XVIII* (Madrid: Instituto de Estudios de Administración Local, Seminario de Urbanismo, 1960).

6. Ajustamiento de cuentas, D. Diego de Vargas y D. Joseph de Castro su curador, Madrid, 29 August 1662, AHPM, P. 10.120.

7. Carta de poder, Madrid, 4 November 1662, AHPM, P.10.120. Later Vargas took some pride in having been a student at Valladolid (Espinosa, *Crusaders of the Río Grande,* p. 28).

8. Matrimonios, Libro 3 (1628–66), Parroquia de Santa María Magdalena, Torrelaguna. Almost two years Diego's senior, Beatriz was born on 8 January and baptized on 22 January 1642. Bautismos, Libro 4 (1638–66), Parroquia de Santa María Magdalena, Torrelaguna. The couple's marriage contract, dated 1 April 1664, is preserved in the Archivo de Notarías, Torrelaguna. The Vargas house, or Palacio de Salinas, is at present a Guardia Civil barracks: only the handsome sixteenth-century facade is original. The Diputación Provincial de Madrid has published a booklet, accompanied by color slides and tape cassette recording, *Guía de la Provincia de Madrid: Torrelaguna,* describing the once-walled medieval town. Today its chief claims are as birthplace of Santa María de la Cabeza, and of Francisco Jiménez de Cisneros, and as site of the formidable fifteenth- and sixteenth-century "semi-cathedral" of Santa María Magdalena.

9. Bautismos, Libros 4 (1638–66) and 5 (1667–1701), Parroquia de Santa María Magdalena, Torrelaguna. López de Zárate Vargas, *Breve descripcion,* pp. 15–16.

10. Testamento del Maestre de campo D. Alonso de Vargas, Ciudad de Santiago de Guatemala, 14 August 1665, photocopy in the Archivo del Marqués de la Nava de Barcinas, Madrid (AMNB).

11. Memorial de toda la hacienda, Torrelaguna, 9 August 1672, AMNB.

12. Facultad para imponer sobre los bienes hasta en cantidad de 4,000 ducados, Madrid, 23 July 1667, etc., AHPM, P. 9.012.

13. John Lynch, *Spain under the Habsburgs,* 2 vols. (Oxford: Basil Blackwell, 1981), 2: 249. On Spain in the seventeenth century, see also Antonio Domínguez Ortiz, *La sociedad española en el siglo XVII,* 2 vols. (Madrid: Consejo Superior de Investigaciones Científicas, 1964); V. Vázquez de Prada, *Historia económica y social de España,* vol. 3, "Los siglos XVI y XVII" (Madrid: Confederación Española de Cajas de Ahorros, 1978); Henry Kamen, *Spain in the Later Seventeenth Century, 1665–1700* (London: Longman, 1980).

14. Relación de D. Diego de Vargas, 30 June 1670.

15. Testamento de D. Diego de Vargas Zapata, Madrid, 21 June 1672, AHPM, P. 10.125.

16. Prueba, Madrid, 21 June 1672, AHPM, P. 10.956. Repeating the same description, almost word-for-word, the witnesses saw don Diego as *"un moço de mediana estatura pelo lacio y cara ancha algo ceceoso que no puede pronunciar algunas raçones."* This must have been a speech defect, an identifying feature like a scar, not simply the *ceceo* of regional Spanish utterance.

17. Poder, Madrid, 21 June 1672, AHPM, P. 10.125.

18. Memorial de toda la hacienda, 9 August 1672.

19. Ramón de Mesonero Romanos, *El antiguo Madrid*, 2 vols. (Madrid: La Ilustración Española y Americana, 1881), 1: 277.

20. On Teutila, see Peter Gerhard, *A Guide to the Historical Geography of New Spain* (Cambridge: Cambridge University Press, 1972), pp. 300–305. Relación de D. Diego de Vargas, 30 June 1670.

21. Difuntos, Libro 2 (1664–1712), Parroquia de Santa María Magdalena, Torrelaguna. They had buried doña Beatriz in the cavernous parish church, in the Vélez family chapel of San Gregorio, a fine example of Gothic fabric and Renaissance adornment. The burial entry gave no clue to the cause of her death.

22. Preserved in the archive of the Marqués de la Nava de Barcinas (AMNB) and that of Rafael Gasset Dorado (ARGD) in Madrid, these Vargas letters, 55 in all, present the recolonizer of New Mexico in a different light. Only 1, a fragment, is from the 1670s. There are 2 from the 1680s, 20 from the 1690s, and 32 from the period 1700 to 1706. Forty-four are by Vargas (2 of them incomplete) and the rest by relatives (2 incomplete). Not properly a part of the official Journals of Diego de Vargas, this collection of family letters is being translated and prepared for publication separately by John L. Kessell in collaboration with Eleanor B. Adams.

23. Vargas to Gregorio Pimentel de Prado, Teutila, 22 October 1675, ARGD. The first part of the letter, in which he must have commented on the death of doña Beatriz, is missing.

24. Vargas to Ignacio López de Zárate, México, 14 June 1690, AMNB. Relación de D. Diego de Vargas, 30 June 1670. He seems to have had the title justicia mayor first and then alcalde mayor. For a description of Tlalpujagua, see Gerhard, *Guide*, pp. 318–20.

25. Testamento del Marqués de la Nava de Barcinas, Bernalillo, 7 April 1704, Spanish Archives of New Mexico (SANM), State Records Center and Archives, Santa Fe, Series I, no. 1027. Although the baptismal books of the Sagrario parish in Mexico City exist for this period, it would be difficult to identify these children. As issue of unmarried parents, they would appear only as *hijos de la iglesia* without the names of mother or father.

26. Parroquia de la Asunción, Sagrario, México, Padrones (1670–1824), vol. 7, Genealogical Library, Church of Jesus Christ of the Latter-day Saints, Salt Lake City, Utah, microfilm 036,415. A census of the Sagrario parish in 1689 shows a "Cassa de Diego de bargas" on the Plazuela de las Gayas. Manuel de Vargas is

the first of seven persons enumerated. Another "Cassa de Bargas" on the same plazuela has no enumeration.

27. Pérez Balsera, *Laudemus viros gloriosos*.

28. Vargas to López de Zárate, México, 8 February 1690, AMNB.

29. Vargas to Isabel María de Vargas Pimentel, Paso del Río del Norte, 23 September 1691, and to López de Zárate, Paso del Río del Norte, 25 September 1691, and 9 April 1692, AMNB.

30. Vargas to López de Zárate, Santa Fe, 9 October 1698, ARGD. He was at this time, he told his son-in-law, a prisoner of his successor in office, Pedro Rodríguez Cubero.

31. Vargas to López de Zárate, Santa Fe, 30 September 1698, ARGD. Domínguez Ortiz, *Las clases privilegiadas en la España del Antiguo Régimen* (Madrid: Ediciones ISTMO, 1973), pp. 71, 77. Vargas's royal concession of title was dated 15 June 1699. Although he spelled Barcinas, or Barzinas, correctly before he left Spain, he misspelled it Brazinas consistently in America.

32. Vargas to López de Zárate, Santa Fe, 4 January 1697, AMNB. The manual, Joseph Micheli y Márquez, *Tesoro militar de Cavallería: Antiguo, y moderno modo de armar cavalleros, y professar, según las ceremonias de qualquier Orden Militar* . . . (Madrid: Diego Díaz de la Carrera, 1642), was listed in the post-mortem inventory of Vargas's books in 1704 (Eleanor B. Adams, "Two Colonial New Mexico Libraries, 1704, 1776," *New Mexico Historical Review* [*NMHR*] 19 [April 1944]: 150).

33. AHN, Ordenes Militares, Casamientos, Santiago, núm. 10.461. López de Zárate Vargas, *Breve descripcion*, p. 15.

34. Vargas to Isabel María de Vargas Pimentel, México, 4 November 1690, and Paso del Río del Norte, 23 September 1691, and to López de Zárate, Paso del Río del Norte, 25 September 1691, AMNB.

35. Vargas to López de Zárate, incomplete [late 1690], AMNB.

36. Capt. Juan Manuel de Vargas Pimentel, 1699, AGI, Contratación, 5459, núm. 20.

37. Vargas Pimentel to López de Zárate, México, 2 November 1699, ARGD.

38. Vargas Pimentel to López de Zárate, México, 7 April 1701, AMNB.

39. Vargas Pimentel to López de Zárate, 7 April 1701.

40. Vargas to López de Zárate, México, 31 December 1702–4 April 1703, ARGD. Oficio, 23 November 1702, Difuntos, Libro 2 (1664–1712), Parroquia de Santa María Magdalena, Torrelaguna. Cesáreo Fernández Duro describes the battle of Vigo in some detail in *Armada española desde la unión de los reinos de Castilla y de Aragón*, 9 vols. (Madrid: Sucesores de Rivadeneyra, 1895–1903), 6: 23–45.

41. Vargas to López de Zárate, 31 December 1702–4 April 1703.

42. Lansing B. Bloom, "The Vargas Encomienda," *NMHR* 14 (October 1939): 366–417.

43. Páez Hurtado to López de Zárate, Santa Fe, 20 April 1704, AMNB. Espinosa, *Crusaders of the Río Grande*, p. 358 n. 25, discusses Vargas's death. See also Vargas correspondence, 1702–1703, AMNB and ARGD.

The Vargas Portrait:
By Whom and When Was It Painted?

JOHN L. KESSELL

Self-assured in court dress and attended by the attributes of a military career, the subject of the full-length painting is undoubtedly don Diego de Vargas. At present, however, there are unanswered questions about the portrait. By whom and when was it painted? Was it painted from life? If not, did the artist use an earlier likeness of don Diego? Who commissioned the painting and when?

Perhaps a Spanish art historian, by close study of the Vargas portrait and its companion (of Juan Antonio López de Zárate), will be able to identify the artist. As yet, no specific mention of the paintings in wills or other family documents—at least not in Vargas' generation or that of his children—has come to light. Inventories of the furnishings in the private chapel of San Isidro, where the paintings hang—if such

John L. Kessell is associate professor of history in the University of New Mexico and author of several books, including *Kiva, Cross, and Crown: The Pecos Indians and New Mexico 1540–1840* (1979, reprinted 1987) and *The Missions of New Mexico Since 1776* (1980), and numerous articles on the Spanish Southwest. He is also editor of the long-term documentary Vargas Project in the University of New Mexico, which is collecting, editing, and publishing in ten volumes the primary sources for the Spanish recolonization of New Mexico in the 1690s. The first volume of the series, *Remote Beyond Compare: Letters of don Diego de Vargas to His Family from New Spain and New Mexico, 1675–1706*, edited by John L. Kessell, Rick Hendricks, Meredith D. Dodge, Larry D. Miller, and Eleanor B. Adams, is forthcoming later this year from the University of New Mexico Press.

Don Diego de Vargas, as portrayed in a drawing by José Cisneros from Cisneros' *Riders Across the Centuries* (1984). This evocative modern drawing is closely based on the portrait of Vargas reproduced in color on the cover of this issue, and again on page 306. Note the addition of the dagger cross insignia of the military Order of Santiago on his jacket. Despite the inscription on the original painting concerning Vargas' membership in this order, researchers for the Vargas Project have ascertained that he was never admitted to the order. Courtesy of Texas Western Press of the University of Texas at El Paso.

inventories still exist—could provide clues. Even better would be a copy of the contract between the artist and his client or clients.[1]

Vargas did know a famous artist. In the summer of 1670, two years before he left Madrid for the Indies, don Diego leased for four years an apartment in the renovated Vargas family complex to court painter Francisco de Herrera, the Younger, a native of Seville trained in Italy. The flamboyant don Francisco had loaned Vargas money, and the lease served as security.[2]

The association is interesting, but the relatively inferior quality of the two paintings in question, obvious even to an untrained eye, rules out Herrera as the artist. It is possible, of course, that Herrera did paint a portrait of Vargas, a different one, or arrange for an apprentice or someone else to do so. A brief physical description of don Diego, recorded in 1672, is not at notable variance with the man pictured on the surviving canvas.[3]

Surely don Diego, bidding farewell to his wife and children, would have wished to leave them his portrait, along with his will and the inventory of his holdings. Vargas understood the value of a picture as remembrance. Nineteen years later, from El Paso, he would beg his elder daughter and son-in-law to send him portraits of the family.[4]

The two portraits in the chapel of San Isidro today seem, on the

---

1. In none of his three extant wills did Diego de Vargas list paintings of any kind or, for that matter, other household furnishings. Diego de Vargas, Wills: Madrid, June 21, 1672, Protocolo 10.125, Archivo Histórico de Protocolos de Madrid, Madrid, Spain; Mexico City, June 1, 1703, Notaría 692, Archivo General de Notarías del Distrito Federal, Mexico City; Bernalillo, April 7, 1704, I:1027, Spanish Archives of New Mexico. Neither did he include such details in the 1672 inventory of his holdings. Diego de Vargas, Listing of the entire estate, Torrelaguna, August 9, 1672, Archive of the Marqués de la Nava de Barcinas, Madrid, Spain. His son-in-law and daughter made no mention of paintings in their wills. Ignacio López de Zárate to Isabel María de Vargas Pimentel and Juan Antonio Pimentel, Power of attorney to make a will, Madrid, October 28, 1706, Protocolo 14.570, Will of Isabel María de Vargas Pimentel, Madrid, January 22, 1718, Protocolo 14.868, Archivo Histórico de Protocolos de Madrid.

2. Contract between Diego de Vargas and Francisco de Herrera, Madrid, July 31, 1670, Protocolo 11.431, Archivo Histórico de Protocolos de Madrid. Herrera, first appointed court painter by Felipe IV, was reappointed in 1672 by Carlos II, who later made him Assistant Keeper of the Palace Keys and Royal Architect. Herrera died in Madrid in 1685. See Jonathan M. Brown, "Herrera the Younger: Baroque Artist and Personality," Apollo, 84 (July 1966), 34–43.

3. Diego de Vargas, Proof of legitimacy, Madrid, June 21, 1672, Protocolo 10.956, Archivo Histórico de Protocolos de Madrid.

4. Diego de Vargas to Isabel María de Vargas Pimentel, September 23, 1691, and Diego de Vargas to Ignacio López de Zárate, September 25, 1691, Archive of the Marqués de la Nava de Barcinas. There is no evidence that don Diego ever received the family portraits he requested.

basis of circumstantial evidence, to have been painted about 1740, long after the deaths of two men whose memories they perpetuate. It is likely that Vargas' grandson, don Diego José López de Zárate Vargas Pimentel Zapata y Luján Ponce de León Cepeda Alvarez Contreras y Salinas, Marqués de Villanueva de la Sagra and Marqués de la Nava de Barcinas, commissioned them. What better way to memorialize the first holders of the two titles he had inherited: Juan Antonio López de Zárate, first Marqués de Villanueva de la Sagra, and Vargas, first Marqués de la Nava de Barcinas.[5]

For at least twenty years, don Diego José had been petitioning the Spanish crown for payment in arrears of the four thousand-peso annual revenue awarded to his grandfather for two heirs in succession. Finally successful in 1737, López de Zárate Vargas must have received a considerable sum. "Very possibly," writes historian Lansing B. Bloom, "it was this sudden affluence which enabled the Marquis to publish in Madrid in 1740 his genealogical history of the illustrious Vargas family."[6] This same affluence may also have motivated don Diego José to commission the two paintings.

The inaccurate legend on the Vargas portrait appears to be a scrambled version of the entry for don Diego in his grandson's privately printed genealogy. Using the same phrases, the author of the legend combined the fact that Vargas had rescued sacred vessels during his reconquest of New Mexico and the fact that he had died at Bernalillo while on campaign. The resulting juxtaposition has don Diego dying in open warfare during an attempt to rescue the sacred vessels at

---

5. Juan Antonio López de Zárate (1646–1698), knight of the Order of Santiago, was serving in the important capacity of Secretario del Despacho Universal, responsible for the promulgation of royal decrees, when he died. Although he provided for the disposition of several unspecified engravings or paintings in his will, don Juan Antonio listed no portrait of himself. Will of Juan Antonio López de Zárate, Madrid, February 5, 1698, Protocolo 12120, Archivo Histórico de Protocolos de Madrid. Because he had no children or grandchildren, Juan Antonio bequeathed his noble title of Castile, which he had enjoyed since 1686, to his younger brother, Ignacio López de Zárate (1647–1707), Diego de Vargas' son-in-law. With Ignacio's death, the title passed to his son, Vargas' grandson, Diego José López de Zárate Vargas.

Granted in 1698, Diego de Vargas' own noble title, after his death in 1704, descended on his elder daughter, Isabel María (1665–1718), and then, after her demise, on Diego José (1691–1745), the first person to hold both titles. For additional biographical detail, see José Pérez Balsera, *Laudemus viros gloriosos et parentes nostros in generatione sua* (Madrid: Tipografía Católica, 1931).

6. Lansing B. Bloom, "The Vargas Encomienda," *New Mexico Historical Review*, 14 (October 1939), 414. Diego José López de Zárate Vargas, *Breve descripción genealógica de la ilustre, quanto antiquíssima casa de los Vargas de Madrid* (Madrid: n.p., 1740).

Bernalillo.[7] If the family in Spain learned of Vargas' earlier heroics at the mining town of Teutila in Oaxaca, where he rushed into the burning parish church in 1676 to save the sacred images, their retelling of that episode may explain in part the confusion about the details of his death.[8]

Evidently the two portraits were executed by the same artist. The lettering of the legends on both appears to be that of one person. Yet the treatment of the subjects is understandably different, even stereotypical. Vargas is represented as a noble military figure, while Juan Antonio López de Zárate assumes the stance of a noble lawyer and councilor of the king. It may be that an expert in seventeenth and eighteenth-century dress can provide clues to when the paintings were done, pointing out, for example, some detail or other only in vogue at a certain time.

In 1741, when don Diego José drew up the draft of a will in his own hand, he stated that he was adding to the Vargas entail in Madrid three religious statues so that they would always remain in the family's oratory, or private chapel. His mother, before her death in 1718, had asked him to do so. The images, made in Naples, were of San José, San Isidro Labrador, and Santa María de la Cabeza. Unfortunately, he said nothing about paintings or other furnishings of the chapel.[9]

After Diego José López de Zárate Vargas died in 1745, his entails and his two titles passed to his eldest son, Antonio María. With the latter's death in 1792, they devolved upon don Diego José's second son, Ignacio. When Ignacio dictated his will in 1803, he reiterated his father's provision that the three statues be entailed and kept in the oratory, for which, he added, he had borne the cost and obtained a bull from the pope. He then listed other items that should be included

----

7. The relative passages from the genealogy are: "libertadose las Santas Imagenes, y Vasos Sagrados . . . en cuya Conquista proseguia su infatigable zelo, quando el año de 1704, perdió la vida en Campaña Rasa, en el Sitio de Bernalillo" ("having saved the holy images and sacred vessels . . . during which campaign he carried on with indefatigable zeal, when, in the year 1704, he lost his life in open warfare at the site [or, in the siege] of Bernalillo"). López de Zárate Vargas, *Breve descripción genealógica*, 12–13. The legend on the painting, however, reads: "perdio la Vida en Canpaña Rasa por libertar los Vasos Sagrados en el Sitio de Bernalillo, año de MDCCIV."

8. Payo de Rivera Enríquez, Exemption from tribute, Mexico City, March 6, 1677, Indios 25:232, Archivo General de la Nación, Mexico City, Mexico.

9. Will of Diego José López de Zárate Vargas, Madrid, April 6, 1741, Protocolo 15.840, Archivo Histórico de Protocolos de Madrid; Pérez Balsera, *Laudemus viros gloriosos*, 91–97. On page 116, Pérez Balsera states that, according to a document in his possession, López de Zárate's ancestors serving in Italy commissioned noted Neapolitan sculptors to fashion the statues of San Isidro Labrador and Santa María de la Cabeza.

183

in the family's Madrid entail: two relics—a cord of San Francisco de Paula and a staff of San Pedro de Alcántara—and "the portraits of my ancestors."[10]

The need for further study is obvious. A more pressing need, however, is for conservation, particularly of the Vargas portrait. In the late 1980s, the crackle is severe in places. Perhaps a reader of the *New Mexico Historical Review* will underwrite the costs of study and conservation. After all, it would be a great shame to allow the deterioration of the only known portrait of don Diego de Vargas, by whomever and whenever it was painted.

---

10. Will of Ignacio López de Zárate Vargas y Gaitán, Madrid, July 11, 1803, Protocolo 23.011, Archivo Histórico de Protocolos de Madrid. Don Ignacio, who died in 1804, named as his heir the only surviving child of his first marriage, don Isidro López de Zárate y Gamarra. On the chapel of San Isidro, which took its present form in the 1850s, see Pérez Balsera, *Laudemus viros gloriosos,* 112–16.

Eleanor B. Adams and her family, ca. 1925: her father, Charles
W. Adams, M.D.; mother, Faustina; brother, Charlie; and sister,
Virginia. Courtesy of Sally M. Fesler.

Eleanor Burnham Adams: Woman of Letters, 1910–1996

JOHN L. KESSELL

Her younger brother Charlie, a student at Harvard University in the late 1940s, recalls an occasion in Cambridge when Eleanor was home from New Mexico. He asked her to look over a term paper he was writing. "Dead," she pronounced. "No life. Write it over. I only have time to read it once more. Bring it to me in the morning." He spent the rest of the day and all night rewriting. The revision she judged only a little better, but her sisterly chiding earned him a decent grade.[1]

Editor of the *New Mexico Historical Review* from 1964 to 1975 and historian of colonial Spanish America, Eleanor B. Adams ranked among the few women scholars of her day to achieve international acceptance in the historical profession. To introduce the appended list of her publications and to honor her memory, I offer this brief biographical sketch of a distinguished woman of letters.

Born in Cambridge, Massachusetts, on 14 May 1910 to Faustina Burnham and Charles Waldron Adams, M.D., Eleanor was the first of three children, two girls and a boy. As they grew up, the family maintained close contact with the Burnhams of Grand Manan Island, New Brunswick, and the Adamses of Provincetown at the tip of Cape Cod. A good many of their ancestors had been Loyalists during the American Revolution. As she would point out with undisguised irony, they were among the *other* Adamses.

Living at home at 27 Garfield Street, Eleanor attended Cambridge Latin School and Radcliffe College, studying Romance languages and literature and graduating cum laude in 1931. She then booked passage to Spain with a group of students from Smith College. During her year

Professor emeritus of History at the University of New Mexico, John L. Kessell has served as interim editor of the *New Mexico Historical Review* from August 1999 to July 2000.

abroad, she studied at the University of Madrid and Centro de Estudios Históricos. Young and idealistic in republican Spain, she never forgave the reactionary forces that subsequently overthrew that noble experiment.[2]

At home again in Cambridge by the fall of 1932 during the worst of the depression, Adams went to work temporarily as an enumerator for the U.S. Bureau of the Census. Graduate school was financially out of the question, so she found something that suited her equally well. In the autumn of 1934, venturing "past the shrunken heads on the fifth floor . . . to the end of a crooked office corridor" in Harvard's Peabody Museum, she secured a secretarial position with the esteemed Post-Columbian Section, Division of Historical Research, Carnegie Institution of Washington. She could walk to work. She resumed her study of ballet and modern dance, appeared in performances, and rowed a shell on the Charles River.[3]

At No. 10 Frisbie Place on the Harvard campus, which she and some of her fellow workers jokingly termed Frisky Place, twenty-four-year-old Eleanor entered the heady interdisciplinary world of historians, anthropologists, archaeologists, and linguists all concentrating their studies on Spanish colonial Yucatan. Historian France Vinton Scholes, who had already begun publishing in the *New Mexico Historical Review* his fundamental documentary histories of seventeenth-century New Mexico, became her mentor. Their collaboration lasted a lifetime.

Adams was a quick study. Scholes taught her Spanish history, paleography, the origin and nature of historical documents, and how to find them in the archives. So astute was she at paleography that he came to trust her reading of difficult passages over his own. Soon, he admitted proudly that her position was "rather more that of an investigator than a secretary."[4]

It was in the former capacity that the Carnegie Institution sent Adams to Mexico in 1938. Arriving by ship at Vera Cruz, she traveled by Pullman to Mexico City and checked into the Hotel Geneve, her home for the next seven months, from July 1938 until February 1939. During that time, the young American woman from Massachusetts worked assiduously in the Archivo General de la Nación, transcribing or ordering microfilm of documents on lists supplied by Scholes. During March and April, she visited the Mayan ruins of Chichén Itzá, in Yucatan, happily observing the Carnegie Institution's archaeological expedition in the field. By mid-May, she was back at Frisbie Place.[5]

Eleanor Adams never married. She came closest in 1939. Her beau, a dentist, was a member of a prominent Mexican family. And although his mother opposed his engagement to a North American woman, Alfredo and Eleanor planned to be married. She wrote in May to Scholes, who was then in Mexico City, that she hoped by special arrangement to remain in Cambridge even though the Post-Columbian Section was scheduled to remove to Carnegie headquarters in Washington, D.C., when Scholes returned.

> As I have already told you, I hope it will be possible for me to go on with as much of my work as possible after I am married, not only because I shall need the extra money but because, as you know, I find my work very interesting (on the whole!) and it would be a wrench to give it up entirely.[6]

Scholes foresaw difficulties. "Your work and mine," he explained, "will be so closely interrelated that we should be in the same place— for day-to-day discussions, allocation of work, etc." He did not want to rush her. Whenever she and Alfredo decided on their plans, Scholes and archaeologist Alfred Vincent Kidder, chairman of the Division of Historical Research, would "give the question the fullest and most earnest consideration deserved by your abilities, your interest in the work, and your services to the historical program and your whole-hearted and able collaboration in that program."

He closed by passing on favorable comments about their two-volume, co-edited *Don Diego Quijada, Alcalde Mayor de Yucatán*, recently published in Spanish in Mexico City by José Porrúa Turanzas and Sons. Silvio Zavala, dean of Mexican historians, liked it, while his colleague Vito Alessio Robles said he could see the English under the Americans' translation of the introduction. "But if that is the worst he can say," allowed Scholes, "then I'm very happy."

The Porrúas had presented him with certain other volumes he had inquired about. The gift, he told Adams, "should have been to you!" So cordial were relations with the publishers that Scholes was negotiating for a documentary series of one or two small volumes each year. "Don't die of heart failure," he teased Adams, "you'll not have to carry the proof reading!!!"[7]

For whatever reasons, Alfredo and Eleanor parted company. In 1940, she moved to Washington, rented an apartment, and threw herself single-mindedly into her career as scholar. Her friend Margaret A. L. Harrison also remembers Eleanor tea dancing at the Mayflower Hotel. She was not a good social dancer; she disliked having to follow.

*   *   *

France Scholes, meantime, had received an invitation from University of New Mexico President James F. Zimmerman to return to UNM, where he had taught and headed the Department of History during the 1920s. He accepted, at first part time, beginning in the summer of 1941. Although he had long since fulfilled course requirements for the Ph.D. at Harvard, he had never bothered to submit a dissertation. This he did finally in 1943, combining previously published studies as "Church and State in New Mexico in the Seventeenth Century."[8]

At Scholes's behest, the Carnegie Institution provided that Eleanor Adams join him on detached duty at UNM. She made the move to Albuquerque in 1941, arriving several months before the Japanese bombed Pearl Harbor. Soon after, she joined a group of women who had volunteered to knit scarves for the armed services. Staying at first in apartments, then with her friend Eupha Morris, whose lawyer-husband Harry was overseas during the war, Eleanor lived successively in the homes of two absent UNM faculty members.[9]

Adams had never been to New Mexico before. Almost every weekend when gasoline was available, Scholes would take wife Lillith, daughter Marianne, and Eleanor on excursions by car around the state. Even as he served as dean of the Graduate School, then as academic vice-president at UNM, Scholes and Adams kept producing works on colonial Yucatan, New Spain, and New Mexico, publishing some together and others separately.

In 1949, when a new director of the Carnegie Institution terminated the Division of Historical Research, Scholes arranged a position for Adams as curator of the rapidly growing microfilm collection of Hispanic manuscripts at the University of California's prestigious Bancroft Library in Berkeley, of which their long-time friend and colleague, George P. Hammond, was director. While in California in 1950 and 1951, she explored the Monterey Peninsula, taking the weekend train to Pacific Grove, which brought back memories of her family's summer place at Brant Rock in Marshfield south of Boston.

At Berkeley, Adams inventoried and organized the Spanish and Mexican microfilm while continuing her own research, though she despised the bureaucracy of the UC main library that made requisitioning even pencils an ordeal. Later in 1951, after training Vivian C. Fisher as a successor, she returned to UNM with the title of Research Associate in History. It was then that Eleanor purchased the comfortable, flat-roofed Southwestern bungalow at 413 Bryn Mawr, S.E., that remained her home for the rest of her life. She especially enjoyed boiling lobster and entertaining friends and colleagues on her patio, which was overhung with trumpet vine.

She and Scholes at once resumed work on the documentary volumes for the Porrúas, their friends and publishers in Mexico City. Seven appeared between 1955 and 1961, prime sources for the institutional and social history of sixteenth-century New Spain. In response to praise for their partnership, Scholes often remarked graciously that "the lady had done most of the work."

Professor Scholes's occasional forgetfulness had resulted in an awkward coincidence that turned out famously. In the cache of Franciscan documents for the history of New Mexico he had discovered in Mexico City in 1928, he had noted particularly the long and telling report compiled in 1776 by fray Francisco Atanasio Domínguez. No document revealed more about the eighteenth-century colony.[10] Not remembering he had suggested to Adams that she transcribe and translate it, Scholes proposed the same task to Franciscan historian Fray Angélico Chávez. Each labored long hours and months without knowledge of the other's efforts.

Soon after Adams returned from the Bancroft, however, they discovered their momentous duplication. Fray Angélico volunteered gallantly to turn everything over to her. She refused, they became fast friends, and together they created a doubly valuable work, *The Missions of New Mexico, 1776: A Description by Fray Francisco Atanasio Domínguez with Other Contemporary Documents*, published first in 1956 and again in 1976. Their dedication read simply "France Vinton Scholes. His Book."[11]

In the summer of 1957, Adams planned another of her frequent research trips to Mexico City, this time inviting her teenage niece Sally Maddux to accompany her. They rented rooms in the home of a Mexican general and his family. Sally had the time of her life, recalling forty years later that her aunt:

Eleanor B. Adams, France V. Scholes, and Fray Angélico Chávez, 1956, at the publication of *The Missions of New Mexico, 1776.* Courtesy of the late Roland F. Dickey.

traveled with style and flair, interested in everything, taking advantage of opportunities to see and learn and show her favorite places, making the effort to meet and know people and maintain relationships over the years. She had many interesting friends.[12]

Eleanor Adams's eleven-year editorship of the *New Mexico Historical Review* began with the July issue in 1964, when she took over from ailing long-time editor and New Mexico historian Frank Driver Reeve; it ended with the July 1975 issue, after which she retired from UNM. Working with her close friend Roland F. Dickey, master book designer and director of UNM Press, she gave the *Review* a quiet and elegant "new look" in January 1965. In addition to her keen intuition, exacting standards, and broad array of scholarly talents, she brought to the craft of editing a clarity and discernment soon reflected in the journal's pages.[13]

I first met Adams in 1965 when I stopped by the *NMHR* office with an article for her consideration.[14] During the next three years as I pursued a Ph.D. in history at UNM, I often came to her with questions. Then, between 1970 and 1972, I enjoyed the privilege of working closely with her as assistant editor of the *Review*. At the same time, she directed my search for primary sources relating to Pecos Pueblo for a study I was preparing on contract with the National Park Service.[15] We collaborated on several other projects, and over the years, I began to think of myself almost as a surrogate son.

Numerous authors, colleagues, and students sought her counsel and friendship. With patience and good humor, she taught us to scrutinize historical documentation, to appreciate the editor's role, and to write and think more clearly. She coaxed France Scholes, who had formally retired in 1962, to submit the last of his dozens of seminal contributions to the colonial history of New Mexico, the two-part "Royal Treasury Records Relating to the Province of New Mexico, 1596–1683."[16]

Midway through her tenure as editor of the *Review*, Eleanor Adams found herself in a fight and refused to back down. Her nontraditional career path made her vulnerable professionally. Adams had been hired under special conditions, had no advanced degree, and carried no classroom teaching load. With Scholes no longer on campus, several faculty members of the Department of History tried to have her removed. Others in the department rallied staunchly to her defense, pointing out that her reputation as a scholar and her list of publications far exceeded those of her detractors. She not only was retained but promoted to Research Professor-at-Large.[17]

Honors continued to come her way. None meant more than the degree of Doctor of Humane Letters conferred by Tulane University in 1984. The citation from Tulane's president, Eamon M. Kelly, to "Eleanor Burnham Adams, Researcher, Author, Scholar," read in part:

> Your meticulous research and lucid writing have shed light on the complexities of Colonial Mexican and Southwest American History, and your numerous published works have played a central role in the development of an entire academic specialty. . . . Indeed, we owe you a debt of gratitude for the rich legacy you have provided American scholarship. . . . We seek, too, to

recognize and commend the humane values that inform your work; you demonstrate that the true scholar is committed equally to increasing our storehouse of knowledge and to transmitting that knowledge so that others may develop their own insights from it.[18]

*   *   *

Adams was increasingly affected over the years by osteoarthritis, requiring her use of first one "stick," as she called it, then two, and finally hip replacements. Nevertheless, for several years after retiring, she gamely continued to travel to Mexico and to visit family in Massachusetts and Maine. At home, she read *The New Yorker* and mystery novels, delighted in figure skating, golf, and tennis on television, and spoiled her regal Maine coon cats.

By the early 1990s, as her condition worsened, she became subject to falls. I remember a telephone call one Christmas Eve several hours before dawn. Eleanor had fallen but managed to pull the phone down beside her. When I arrived, I found her kneeling by her bed, unable to get up. Solemnly but softly, I intoned, "Bless you, my child. Do rise; your sins have been forgiven." Once she was propped back up in bed, she chuckled.

Eventually unable to remain at home, Adams entered a nursing home in 1994 and, after an especially bad fall, a rehabilitation hospital. In the summer of 1995, she left Albuquerque for good, when relatives came and escorted her by train back to Massachusetts. On the morning of 15 January 1996, Eleanor Burnham Adams died peacefully in the town of Norwell. She is buried in the family plot at the lush, rolling Mount Auburn Cemetery in Cambridge, the first garden cemetery in North America.[19]

In her research and writing about colonial New Mexico, Eleanor Adams concentrated on the eighteenth century, just as France Scholes had on the seventeenth. "I am convinced," she wrote in 1963,

that post-Reconquest history is fully as interesting and significant as that of the pre-Revolt period. I feel that my work should result in an important contribution to historical scholarship, and that the better understanding of New Mexico's past should have some bearing on the understanding of her present.[20]

None of us has said it better.

194

Eleanor B. Adams in 1984, when Tulane University conferred upon her the degree of Doctor of Humane Letters.

NOTES

1. Charles W. Adams to John L. Kessell, Hanover, Mass., 16 August 1999, Eleanor B. Adams Papers (EBAP), Center for Southwest Research, Zimmerman Library, University of New Mexico, Albuquerque.

2. A University of New Mexico "Biographical Record," completed by Adams on 31 July 1962, listed "Univ. of Liverpool Summer School, 1931," presumably en route to Spain. EBAP.

3. Sally M. Fesler, "Thoughts on the Life of Eleanor Adams [1910–1996]," prepared for a memorial at the Mount Auburn Cemetery, Cambridge, Mass., 14 May 1996, EBAP. Eleanor B. Adams, "The Historical Society of New Mexico Honors France Vinton Scholes," *The Americas* 27 (January 1971), 228-32 (quotation, 228). See also Richard E. Greenleaf, "Eleanor Burnham Adams: Historian and Editor," *New Mexico Historical Review* 60 (January 1985), 4-9.

4. France V. Scholes to Eleanor B. Adams, Mexico City, 24 May 1939, and Adams to Scholes, Cambridge, Mass., 2 August 1939, EBAP.

5. Monthly Financial Statements, Division of Historical Research, Carnegie Institution of Washington, covering 1 May 1938–10 May 1939, EBAP. In brief periodical reports, Scholes chronicled the historical component of Carnegie's Yucatan project in the *Annual Report of Carnegie Institution of Washington: Yearbook*, vols. 30-48 (1930–1949). Historian Lewis Hanke would write in 1973: "The most sustained and important cooperative research project carried on by a United States institution in Latin America during the twentieth century was probably the Yucatan program of the Carnegie Institution of Washington." Quoted by Greenleaf, "Eleanor Burnham Adams," 6-7.

6. Adams to Scholes, Cambridge, 17 May 1939, EBAP.

7. Scholes to Adams, 24 May 1939.

8. Adams, "The Historical Society of New Mexico," 230.

9. Adams appeared between 1942 and 1946 in *Hudspeth's Albuquerque City Directory* (El Paso, Tex.: Hudspeth's Directory Co., 1942–1945/46), but was not listed in Albuquerque city and telephone directories from October 1948 until 1952. During part of this time, she returned to Cambridge to be with her ailing mother, who died in 1949. Subsequently, she took the job at Berkeley.

10. France V. Scholes, "Manuscripts for the History of New Mexico in the National Library in Mexico City," *New Mexico Historical Review* 3 (July 1928), 301-23.

11. Eleanor B. Adams and Fray Angélico Chávez, eds., *The Missions of New Mexico, 1776: A Description by Fray Francisco Atanasio Domínguez with Other Contemporary Documents* (Albuquerque: University of New Mexico Press, 1956, 1976).

12. Fesler, "Thoughts on the Life."

13. Although her name did not appear formally on the masthead until she assumed the editorship in 1964, at least as early as mid-1962, she listed herself as associate editor. "Biographical Record," 31 July 1962.

14. John L. Kessell, "The Puzzling Presidio: San Phelipe de Guevavi, Alias Terrenate," *New Mexico Historical Review* 41 (January 1967), 21-46.

15. John L. Kessell, *Kiva, Cross, and Crown: The Pecos Indians and New Mexico, 1540–1840* (Washington, D.C.: National Park Service, 1979).

16. France V. Scholes, "Royal Treasury Records Relating to the Province of New Mexico, 1596–1683," *New Mexico Historical Review* 50 (January and April 1975), 5-23, 139-64.

17. Her academic titles at UNM were: Research Associate in History (1951–66), Research Associate Professor (1967–74), and Research Professor-at-Large (1974–75).

18. Quoted by Greenleaf, "Eleanor Burnham Adams," 5-6. Among her other honors were: corresponding membership in the Academy of American Franciscan History (1951), alumna membership in the Radcliffe chapter of Phi Beta Kappa (1956), Award of Merit from the American Association for State and Local History (1973), the Governor's Award of Honor for Historic Preservation (1984), and the Historical Society of New Mexico Board of Directors' Award for a lifetime of distinguished achievement (1990).

19. "Preserving the Records of Mount Auburn Cemetery," *Annotation: The Newsletter of the National Historical Publications and Records Commission* 27:2 (June 1999), 1, 19.

20. Eleanor B. Adams to Harold Enarson, Albuquerque, 11 April 1963, EBAP.

The Published Works of Eleanor Burnham Adams

AS SOLE AUTHOR:

"Two Colonial New Mexico Libraries, 1704, 1776." *New Mexico Historical Review* 19 (April 1944), 135-67.

"Note on the Life of Francisco de Cárdenas Valencia." *The Americas* 2 (July 1945), 21-29.

"The Chapel and Cofradía of Our Lady of Light in Santa Fe." *New Mexico Historical Review* 22 (October 1947), 327-41.

"A Bio-Bibliography of Franciscan Authors in Colonial Central America." *The Americas* 8 (April 1952), 431-73; 9 (July 1952), 37-86. Reprinted as *A Bio-Bibliography of Franciscan Authors in Colonial Central America.* Bibliographical Series, 2. Washington, D.C.: Academy of American Franciscan History, 1953.

"An English Library at Trinidad, 1633." *The Americas* 12 (July 1955), 25-41.

"Viva el Rey!" *New Mexico Historical Review* 35 (October 1960), 284-92.

"Fray Silvestre and the Obstinate Hopi." *New Mexico Historical Review* 38 (April 1963), 97-138.

"The Franciscan Inquisition in Yucatan: French Seamen, 1560." *The Americas* 25 (April 1969), 331-59.

"The Historical Society of New Mexico Honors France Vinton Scholes for Outstanding Achievement in Spanish Colonial History, 1970." *New Mexico Historical Review* 45 (July 1970), 245-50. Reprinted in *The Americas* 27 (January 1971), 228-32.

"Jurisdictional Conflict in the Borderlands." In *The Roman Catholic Church in Colonial Latin America*, edited by Richard E. Greenleaf. New York: Alfred A Knopf, 1971. [Excerpts from her introduction to *Bishop Tamarón's Visitation of New Mexico, 1760.*]

"Fray Francisco Atanasio Domínguez and Fray Silvestre Vélez de Escalante." *Utah Historical Quarterly* 44 (Winter 1976), 40-58.

"History of the Southwest: Personalities and Discoveries." In Donald C. Dickinson, W. David Laird, and Margaret F. Maxwell. *Voices from the Southwest: A Gathering in Honor of Lawrence Clark Powell.* Flagstaff, Ariz.: Northland Press, 1976.

"The New Mexico Martyrs' Book." *New Mexico Historical Review* 75 (July 2000), 414-22.

As Co-author:

With France V. Scholes. *La iglesia en Yucatán, 1560–1610.* Washington, D.C.: Carnegie Institution, 1938.
————. "Books in New Mexico, 1598–1680." *New Mexico Historical Review* 17 (July 1942), 226-70.
With France V. Scholes and Ralph L. Roys. "History of Yucatan." *Carnegie Institution of Washington Yearbook* 43 (1944), 178-84.
With France V. Scholes, Ralph L. Roys, and Robert S. Chamberlain. "History of Yucatan." *Carnegie Institution of Washington Yearbook* 45 (1946), 217-21.
With Doris Z. Stone, "Conversion of Gaymí and Darién and its Indians." In Samuel K. Lothrop, *Archaeology of Southern Veraguas, Panama. Memoirs of the Peabody Museum of Archaeology and Ethnology, Harvard University* 9:3 (1950), 97-103.
With John E. Longhurst. "New Mexico and the Sack of Rome: One Hundred Years Later." *New Mexico Historical Review* 28 (October 1953), 243-50.

As Sole Editor:

"Bishop Tamarón's Visitation of New Mexico, 1760." *New Mexico Historical Review* 28 (April, July, October 1953), 81-114, 192-221, 291-315; 29 (January 1954), 41-47. Reprinted as *Bishop Tamarón's Visitation of New Mexico, 1760.* Publications in History, vol. 15. Albuquerque: Historical Society of New Mexico, 1954.
"Letter to the Missionaries of New Mexico, Fray Silvestre Vélez de Escalante," and "Writings of Fray Silvestre Vélez de Escalante." *New Mexico Historical Review* 40 (October 1965), 319-35.
"A Sidelight on the Santa Fe Trade, 1844." *New Mexico Historical Review* 46 (July 1971), 261-63.

As Co-editor:

With France V. Scholes. "Documents Relating to the Mirones Expedition to the Interior of Yucatan, 1621–1624." *Maya Research* 3 (1936), 153-76, 251, 276. [Reprinted under the same title. Culver City, Calif.: Labyrinthos, 1991.]

With France V. Scholes. *Documentos para la historia de Yucatán*:
1. *Primera Série, 1550–1561*. Mérida: Carlos R. Menéndez, 1936.
2. *La Iglesia en Yucatán, 1560–1610*. Mérida: Carnegie Institution, Diario de Yucatán, 1938.
3. *Discurso sobre la Constitución de las Provincias de Yucatán y Campeche, 1766*. Mérida: Carnegie Institution, Diario de Yucatán, 1938.
———. *Don Diego Quijada, Alcalde Mayor de Yucatán, 1561–1565*. 2 vols. *Biblioteca Histórica Mexicana de Obras Inéditas*, 14, 15. Mexico City: Antigua Librería Robredo de José Porrúa e Hijos, 1938.
With Ralph L. Roys and France V. Scholes. "Report and Census of the Indians of Cozumel." *Contributions to American Anthropology and History*, Carnegie Institution of Washington, 4 (1940), 1-45.
With France V. Scholes, Ralph L. Roys, and Robert S. Chamberlain. *The Maya Chontal Indians of Acalán-Tixchel: A Contribution to the History and Ethnography of the Yucatan Peninsula. Publications*, 560. Washington, D.C.: Carnegie Institution, 1948. Reprint, Norman: University of Oklahoma Press, 1968.
With France V. Scholes. *Proceso contra Tzintzicha Tangoaxan, el Caltzontzin, formado por Nuño de Guzmán, año de 1530*. Mexico City: Porrúa y Obregón, 1952.
———. "Inventories of Church Furnishings in Some of the New Mexico Missions, 1672." In *Dargan Historical Essays*. Edited by William M. Dabney and Josiah C. Russell. Publications in History, 4. Albuquerque: University of New Mexico Press, 1952.
———. *Documentos para la historia del México Colonial*. Mexico City: José Porrúa e Hijos, 1955–61:
1. *Relación de las encomiendas de indios hechas en Nueva España a los conquistadores y pobladores de ella. Año de 1564*. 1955.
2. *Advertimientos generales tocantes al gobierno de Nueva España que los Virreyes dejaron a sus sucesores, 1590–1604*. 1956.
3. *Ordenanzas del Hospital de San Lázaro de México. Año de 1582*. 1956.
4. *Información sobre los tributos que los indios pagaban a Moctezuma. Año de 1554*. 1958.
5. *Sobre el modo de tributar los indios de Nueva España a Su Majestad, 1561–1564*. 1958.
6. *Moderación de doctrinas de la Real Corona administradas por las Ordenes Mendicantes, 1623*. 1959.
7. *Cartas del Licenciado Jerónimo Valderrama y otros documentos sobre su visita al gobierno de Nueva España, 1563–1565*. 1961.

With Fray Angélico Chávez. *The Missions of New Mexico, 1776: A Description by Fray Francisco Atanasio Domínguez with Other Contemporary Documents*. Albuquerque: University of New Mexico Press, 1956, 1975.

With Ralph L. Roys and France V. Scholes. "Census and Inspection of the Town of Pencuyut, Yucatan, in 1583, by Diego García de Palacio, Oidor of the Audiencia de Guatemala." *Ethnohistory* 6 (Summer 1959), 195-225.

With France V. Scholes. *Relación Histórica Descriptiva de las Provincias de la Verapaz y de la del Manché, escrita por el Capitán don Martín Alfonso Tovilla, Año de 1635, publicada por primera vez con la Relación que en el Consejo Real de las Indias hizo sobre la pacificación y población de las provincias del Manché y Lacandón el Licenciado Antonio de León Pinelo*. Guatemala: Universidad de San Carlos, 1960.

With Keith W. Algier. "A Frontier Book List—1800." *New Mexico Historical Review*. 43 (January 1968), 49-59.

With John L. Kessell. Reeve, Frank D. "Navajo Foreign Affairs, 1795–1846." Part I, 1795–1815. Part II, 1816–1824. *New Mexico Historical Review* 46 (April, July 1971), 101-32, 223-51. Reprinted as *Navajo Foreign Affairs, 1795–1846*. Tsaile, Ariz.: Navajo Community College Press, 1983.

With John L. Kessell, Rick Hendricks, Meredith D. Dodge, and Larry D. Miller. *Remote Beyond Compare: Letters of don Diego de Vargas to His Family from New Spain and New Mexico, 1675–1706*. Albuquerque: University of New Mexico Press, 1989.

In addition: sundry book reviews, notes, encyclopedia entries, translations, and annotations.

Reinstalling the Spanish Component

THE JOURNALS OF DON DIEGO DE VARGAS, NEW MEXICO, 1691–1704

John L. Kessell

C ould he trust them? Characteristically, he was laying himself open, taking a grave but calculated risk. Amid some one hundred and fifty allied Pueblo Indians marching behind Gov. Diego de Vargas and dozens of armed Spaniards came a sullen contingent of Jemez fighting men he had vanquished in battle not six weeks before. Yet on this day, Vargas needed every man. He had struck a deal with these Jemez. He would free more than three hundred of their women and children held hostage in Santa Fe if the men would join him in a final assault on defiant Tewas and Tanos fortified atop Black Mesa. All previous efforts had failed. This time, however, beating back parties of enemy skirmishers and threatening to denude their planted fields below the mesa, the Spanish governor prevailed. Tewa and Tano spokesmen, after negotiating a schedule and exchanging gifts, pledged that the people would

Professor Emeritus of History at the University of New Mexico, John L. Kessell is founding editor of the Vargas Project. His most recent book is *Spain in the Southwest: A Narrative History of New Mexico, Arizona, Texas, and California* (Norman: University of Oklahoma Press, 2002, ISBN 0-8061-3407-0). He would like to thank his colleagues on the Vargas Project at the University of New Mexico, especially Rick Hendricks, as well as Larry D. Miller and Meredith D. Dodge, for their valuable suggestions in revising this essay. This piece will appear, in essentially this form, as the afterword to the sixth and final volume of the Vargas Series: John L. Kessell, Rick Hendricks, Meredith D. Dodge, and Larry D. Miller, eds., *A Settling of Accounts: The Journals of don Diego de Vargas, New Mexico, 1700–1704* (Albuquerque: University of New Mexico Press, 2002).

come down peaceably and reoccupy their pueblos. Two days later in Santa Fe, true to his word, Vargas released the Jemez women and children.

Above all, he was a risk taker, which explained in large part how he waged war and peace. Deep-seated character traits — arrogance, valor, dogged determination, and devotion to honor — governed the career of Diego de Vargas, working often to his advantage but finally against him. As reconqueror of New Mexico during the 1690s, Vargas not only presided over the third and final phase of the Pueblo-Spanish War begun in 1680, but also lent his name to an era. For much of this time, officials in Mexico City and Madrid rightly considered New Mexico a war zone and debated the level of military spending. Meanwhile, colonist families, Spanish officers and men-at-arms, Franciscan friars, Pueblo Indians who sided with them, and Pueblo Indians who fought tenaciously against them lived a day-at-a-time existence and shifted to survive. By the end of Vargas's abbreviated second term, for better or for worse, the colony had been restored to the Spanish empire.

Son of a middling and financially encumbered nobleman of Madrid, don Diego grew up in Spain with the amenities of his class and a large extended family. His mother died when he was five, and his father, Capt. Alonso de Vargas Zapata, a year later took an overseas assignment in Guatemala, where he eventually remarried. Young Vargas never saw him again. Evidently because of a congenital speech defect, the boy did not follow his father as a *menino*, or noble page in the royal household. Instead, when he had acquired requisite age and skill, he enrolled in the palace guard. In 1664, then twenty, he married Beatriz Pimentel de Prado, whom he had known since childhood. With the death of his older brother in Spain and his father in Guatemala, don Diego assumed responsibility for the debts and maintenance of the Vargas estate, a role that gave him no pleasure. Beatriz, during the first six years of their marriage, bore him five children, one of whom died in infancy. Then in 1670, resolved to end the family's long tradition of indebtedness and secure a share of his father's New World legacy, Diego de Vargas, citing the notable services of his father and grandfather, petitioned the crown for an appointment in the Spanish Indies. He sailed in 1672.

Finding favor at the viceregal court of the Conde de Paredes in Mexico City, don Diego won appointments successively as *alcalde mayor* of Teutila in Oaxaca and Tlalpujahua in Michoacán, while keeping a residence and friends in the capital. Vargas's heroics in both outlying posts, especially his economic revitalization of the Tlalpujahua mining district, earned him high marks as an administrator. Shortly after receiving the sad word that Beatriz had

DIEGO DE VARGAS, THE ONLY KNOWN PORTRAIT, IN THE CAPILLA DE SAN
ISIDRO, MADRID, SPAIN.
(*Photo courtesy Palace of the Governors, Santa Fe, New Mexico, neg. no. 11409.*)

died in Spain, the young widower found a companion. Her name may have been Nicolasa Rincón. He did not marry her. Nor, evidently, did he pursue other women. Between 1679 and 1686, the couple produced two natural sons and a daughter. Through an agent at court in Madrid, Diego de Vargas contributed twenty-five hundred pesos and received royal title to the low-ranking governorship of New Mexico, a remote colony in exile. Fortuitously, the new viceroy, another able madrileño, took don Diego's part at every turn. From the day of his accession at brutish El Paso, Vargas knew there would be no restoration of New Mexico without the patronage of the Conde de Galve.[1]

VICEROY THE CONDE DE GALVE (1688–1696).
(*From Manuel Rivera Cambas*, Los gobernantes de México [*Mexico City: Imprenta de J. M. Aguilar Ortiz, 1872*], 265.)

Loss of the kingdom and provinces of New Mexico dated from 1680, when fifteen to twenty thousand Pueblo Indians, all but united, had struck and killed or expelled twenty-five hundred Spanish colonists. The affront cried out for vengeance. Galve made restoration of New Mexico a matter of first order. Native peoples in silver-rich Nueva Vizcaya and Sonora had also risen, emboldened by the Spaniards' seeming inability to humble the Pueblos. Equally apparent in terms of imperial rivalry was the French threat of invasion from the east following the Sieur de La Salle's landing on the Texas coast in the mid-1680s. Religion gave further cause. Thousands of Pueblo Indian souls, apostates from Spanish Catholicism, must be absolved and reconciled. Hence—even in the shadow of Carlos II's uncertain reign and European wars, rapacious pirates in the Caribbean, and riots in Mexico City—the recolonization of New Mexico stood out.[2]

From the moment of his accession, Vargas's challenge was evident. How, given the paltry human and physical resources of this exiled colony, could he effect the triumphant reconquest he envisioned? Enduring the tribulations of his first eighteen months in office, a resolute don Diego pleaded again and again for aid from Viceroy Galve. His armed reconnaissance without women and children late in 1692, and the Pueblo Indians' assent to ritual repossession, convinced Vargas that these erstwhile rebels would accept restoration of the Spanish colony peaceably. In Mexico City, Galve and his court toasted a fait accompli. Don Diego bid for early promotion. But all were deceived, especially the hundreds of colonists who joined their governor on the tardy recolonizing expedition of 1693. Admonishing them to look beyond immediate hardship and any fear of Pueblo Indian opposition, he anticipated resettling New Mexico with plow, seed, and livestock. Forced instead to fight in the snow for Santa Fe, certain of the colonists came to despise the strutting Diego de Vargas.

The future looked bleak. Hardly any of the Spanish men, women, and children crowding into Santa Fe's close quarters the last two days of 1693 had bargained for what lay ahead. The viciousness of the reconquest—of hand-to-hand combat, executions, dismemberment, theft of livestock and stored maize, destruction of crops in the field, and hostage-taking—rose as a crescendo from the battle for Santa Fe in 1693, through the assaults of 1694, to the uprising of 1696 and its bloody aftermath.[3] This was no black-and-white struggle between cruel Spanish invaders and noble Pueblo resistors. Both peoples were deeply rent by the experience.

Pueblo Indians, never able to regain the near unity of 1680, fought and died on both sides of every major encounter. Factionalism among the Pueblos, when related by Spaniards, regularly came down Eurocentrically to one question: Are they for us or against us, our king, and our Catholic faith? On occasion, Spanish documents picked up dissenting Pueblo voices, but always transmitted in non-Pueblo terms. The Christian God, in one instance, had enlightened certain members of the outlying and resistant Zuni nation to preserve images of Jesus Christ. Whatever power such effigies possessed for the individuals who secreted them, Spaniards were loath to believe that the Indians' action might have resulted not from veneration but from internal dissension among Zunis. Pueblo peoples had reasons enough of their own to accept or oppose returning Spaniards, that is, to use them or items of their material culture in one way or another. Pueblo animosities and loyalties — personal or kinship affairs; maintenance of territorial, occupational, or trade boundaries; disputes over sacred or profane leadership — such motivations gave Pueblos ample justification to ally themselves with or contest a renewed Hispanic presence.

Whatever their reasons, Pueblos defied Pueblos, splitting not only close-built individual communities like Pecos and Taos, but also language groups. That Keresan-speaking Zia, Santa Ana, and San Felipe, brutalized during two previous Spanish entradas, sided irrevocably with Spaniards under Vargas (while their linguistic kin of Cochiti and Santo Domingo vacillated between fight and flight) likely owed less to intimidation than to the prospect of enlisting Spanish allies against their long-time, encroaching Towa neighbors of the Jemez pueblos. On this occasion, moreover, there reappeared a leader of commanding presence.

Bartolomé de Ojeda, an *indio ladino* literate in Spanish but also a Keres war captain, had fought the Spaniards at Zia in 1689, suffering nasty wounds, capture, and abduction. Recovering from the trauma, he had lived three years among Hispanic refugees in the El Paso district. There, Ojeda made up his mind, for reasons he did not share, to rally certain of his own people to the Spanish side, perhaps to spare them during the inevitable recolonization. Without Ojeda, Domingo of Tesuque, Juan de Ye of Pecos — all of whom, in Roman Catholic terms, Vargas embraced as compadres — and others like them who interpreted, negotiated, and recruited Pueblo allies, the disruption might have lasted years longer.

At the same time, other Pueblo principal men fought valiantly against Spanish reoccupation, earning both Vargas's grudging admiration and his

A ZUNI MAN, PHOTOGRAPH BY EDWARD S. CURTIS, 1903.
(*Photograph courtesy Palace of the Governors, Santa Fe, New Mexico, neg. no. 143712.*)

enmity. Cacique Diego Umviro of Pecos thought of Spaniards as a different species and justified killing them if they again invaded the Pueblos' world. As in 1680, Vargas's men-at-arms recognized mixed-blood leaders among their Pueblo antagonists. Of Indian and mulatto descent, Lucas Naranjo, a Santa Clara war captain, seeking to put himself at the head of a purge of Spaniards in 1696, died instead when a soldier's musket ball struck him in the Adam's apple and came out the nape of his neck.

While the Spanish recolonizers, united by the task of restoring a common sovereignty, might have appeared almost monolithic, no level of their society was exempt from dispute. At the top, two contending peninsular Spaniards set a poor example.[4] Considering himself a proprietary conqueror, Vargas doggedly refused to accept the end of a governor's standard five-year term without promotion or reappointment. That put him and his legally appointed successor at dagger points in 1697. Although socially inferior, Pedro Rodríguez Cubero, newly wielding the authority of the office, refused to abide don Diego's obstructions. He brought suit and imprisoned him. Colonists by the dozens, eager to vent their spleen or ingratiate themselves with Rodríguez Cubero, rendered a litany of malfeasance, immorality, and financial irregularities against Vargas and his inner circle. Others professed their loyalty. The internecine legal wrangling cost don Diego six years and heavy expense before he at last gained reappointment in 1703, only to die in office the following year. Still, through it all, the Hispanic polity of distant New Mexico held together, attesting to the maturity of the colonial system.

Not only did the Vargas era demonstrate the resilience of a governorship in contention, but also the full range of Spanish royal justice that bound a far-off colony to the empire. From the governor's appointed alcaldes mayores in every district of New Mexico and the Santa Fe cabildo, or town council, on up to the Audiencia of Mexico City and the Council of the Indies in Madrid, a citizen had recourse, at least in theory. Even during Vargas's rule, which critics considered despotic, colonists through the cabildo in 1696 and 1697 won a new viceroy's approval to send Capt. Lázaro de Mizquía to Mexico City with their suggestions for better government. Yet at every level, favoritism, whom one knew or had influence with, weighed heavily. It is doubtful that viceregal authorities would have considered such complaints against Vargas during the administration of the Conde de Galve, don Diego's friend and sponsor.

In the New Mexico colony, privileged members of Vargas's staff, several of whom he brought with him from Mexico City or Tlalpujahua, responded in their own ways to the dangers and opportunities of the recolonization.[5] Their behavior ranged from the unquestioned fealty of Juan Páez Hurtado to the opportunism of Antonio de Valverde Cosío. Unlucky Alfonso Rael de Aguilar, veteran secretary of government and war, and a family man with pregnant wife and six children, found himself caught in the crossfire between Vargas and Rodríguez Cubero. Despite scurrilous threats by the former governor's partisans, Rael eventually confessed to spying for don Diego. Most of these ranking retainers, younger than their patron, stayed on with their families after his death, competing for power and prestige and ending their lives in the restored colony.

Relatively few in number, the Franciscans exercised a spiritual and sacramental monopoly in restoration New Mexico, as they had since the colony's founding. Both remoteness and tradition contributed to this unusual situation. Faithful Roman Catholics throughout most of the Spanish Indies could resort not only to members of more than one religious order, to Jesuits, Dominicans, and others, but also to the diocesan clergy. In New Mexico, however, Franciscans ministered to everyone. Colonists alienated the friars at their own risk. For pastoral care, baptisms, marriages, and burial of their infants or parents, they had no other choice. After Diego de Vargas had resolved in his favor a dispute over church property in the El Paso district, the governor got on well enough with most of the Franciscans. He reinstalled the blue-robed friars at Pueblo Indian missions as circumstances permitted. He relied on them as military chaplains, and certain of them sided openly with him against Rodríguez Cubero.

It was, however, the hundreds of colonists themselves who—along with the Pueblo Indians—determined the outcome of the Vargas era. Four distinct groups of culturally Hispanic settlers made their toilsome way up the Rio Grande Valley in the 1690s.

The refugees—native New Mexican men and women who had lived through the revolt of 1680 and the children born to them during the colony's exile—were coming home. Most, having endured a dozen years of hand-to-mouth existence in the several El Paso settlements, were impoverished. On a muster roll, Governor Vargas noted the case of veteran Sgto. Mayor Sebastián González, whose household numbered fourteen but who claimed to own not even a shirt. Although they accepted similar incentives of land and status, these survivors resented the newer recruits. No one who had not shared the experience could ever understand the depths of their suffering. As reminders, too, these New Mexicans had among them several dozen former captives ransomed during Vargas's reconnaissance of 1692, most of them children who had grown up with the Pueblos since 1680 and knew them intimately.

A second contingent, rugged young men, some with families, Vargas had recruited in 1693 from the mining districts of northern New Spain to serve in the presidio of restored Santa Fe. On occasion, he referred to them loosely as the one hundred Spanish soldiers. These two bands—returning New Mexicans and military recruits, numbering altogether eight or nine hundred souls—appeared first in Governor Vargas's train late in 1693 and fought in winter for Santa Fe.

Another 220 or 230 persons, sixty-odd families who considered themselves better than the other colonists, composed the third group. Enlisted with considerable fanfare in and around Mexico City, these self-proclaimed españoles mexicanos, many of them artisans, reached New Mexico in June 1694 and, after a miserable, crowded winter in Santa Fe, found themselves transplanted to Villa Nueva de Santa Cruz de la Cañada. Predominantly urban dwellers, few had experience farming or raising stock.[6]

Finally came a mixed company of about 145 individuals gathered in Zacatecas, Sombrerete, and vicinity in 1694 and 1695 by Juan Páez Hurtado: men, women, and children, some legitimate families and others pushed together fraudulently so Páez could collect more in government subsidies.[7] Throughout Vargas's remaining years and long thereafter, these four groups, socializing and often marrying within, appear to have maintained separate identities and not always harmonious relations.[8]

A rough and resilient militia captain who lived to be eighty exemplified the disapproving returnees. Francisco de Anaya Almazán II, born in New Mexico about 1633 and widowed after 1663, had then married a sister of his brother's wife, but lost her, his children, and all his possessions in the uprising of 1680. He persevered during the El Paso years, married a third wife, and joined the restoration. Picking up practically where he left off, Sargento Mayor Anaya Almazán served again as alcalde mayor in the Galisteo district and as an officer of the colony's Confraternity of La Conquistadora. He received a modest land grant from Governor Vargas and bought a house in Santa Fe. Don Diego relied on Anaya and fellow returnees like Roque Madrid and Juan Ruiz de Cáceres who knew Pueblo languages. At times, Vargas and subsequent governors heeded the counsel of these experienced New Mexicans and, at others, they pointedly ignored them. Regardless, Anaya, born and bred in the colony, personified a continuity that bridged the entire, continuous, three-act Pueblo-Spanish War, from 1680 through 1696.[9]

Of the military recruits, none was more ambitious or successful than Antonio de Valverde Cosío, a peninsular Spaniard from Santander who had cast his lot with Vargas at Sombrerete in 1693. He soon became the governor's favorite, accused by detractors of sharing all don Diego's excesses. Valverde's ascent from adjutant to economic, political, and social overlord of the El Paso district had no precedent in the colony. Parleying his entrée into an influential, transatlantic association of men from Santander and a trip to Spain as don Diego's agent in the late 1690s, don Antonio became captain-for-life of the El Paso presidio and the area's alcalde mayor. His diversified farming, livestock, and brandy- and wine-producing property known as San Antonio de Padua—truly a hacienda—operated on a scale unknown in the extreme north. Largely because of the entrepreneurship of Valverde and his extended family, El Paso proved more viable economically during the first half of the eighteenth century than any of the upriver villas of Santa Fe, Santa Cruz de la Cañada, and after 1706 Albuquerque. When he died in 1728, having served as governor of New Mexico between 1717 and 1722, Antonio de Valverde left an estate worth tens of thousands of pesos.[10]

On up the Rio Grande Valley, Hispanic mechanical and popular arts took new and lasting root with the transplanted artisans dispatched from the vice-regal capital under Capt. Cristóbal Velasco and fray Francisco Farfán in 1693. Even as they learned to farm, they did not abandon their trades. Along with blacksmiths, cartwrights, cobblers, masons, millers, tailors, and weavers came a filigree maker, coppersmith, sculptor, musician, and two painters. The only chandler listed, Juan de Góngora, had died before the company's departure from Mexico City. His widow, however, Petronila de la Cueva y Almonacid, then thirty-seven, along with two sons and three daughters, relocated without him. Of medium build with aquiline face, large eyes, and the scar of an old wound on her left cheek, she soon met Juan de Chaves Medina of Zacatecas in the close quarters of Santa Fe. Uncharacteristically, she remarried outside the group of españoles mexicanos and remained with her children and new husband in Santa Fe. Twenty years later, neighbors accused her of malicious gossip.[11]

The last of Vargas's four imports of settlers materialized in 1695 and buoyed the restoration to a degree. Resourcefully recruited in northern New Spain by Juan Páez Hurtado, they came on the scene after the fierce campaigns of 1694 but before the Pueblo uprising of 1696. Robust, thirty-year-old Francisco Montes Vigil, with curly chestnut hair and a scar under his left eye, and his wife María Jiménez de Enciso, both natives of Zacatecas and considered españoles, had gone to sign up with their five children and a free mulatto servant. Instead of appearing on the muster roll as one large family unit of eight persons entitled to the maximum family subsidy of 320 pesos, Páez had them distributed among three units, evidently so that he and they might collect more. The list showed Francisco and María with two children, a fictitious uncle with their other three, and the mulatto as part of a third unit. These paper families, meant to hoodwink royal officials in Zacatecas, may not have dictated how the company traveled to New Mexico.

RAFAEL GARCIA, BORN IN BELEN, NEW MEXICO, ON 2 MAY 1804, GREAT-GREAT-GRANDSON OF RAMON GARCIA JURADO, WHO ARRIVED IN SANTA FE AS A TEENAGED COLONIST IN 1694.
(Photograph property of author, courtesy James, Estevan, and Dominic García, Albuquerque, New Mexico.)

Later, in 1697 and 1698, during Rodríguez Cubero's denunciations of Vargas and Páez Hurtado, Francisco Montes Vigil testified that he had aided in the deception. He and another recruit frequented gambling houses in Zacatecas, picking up vagabonds and taking them to the treasury office to enlist for New Mexico under made-up names. For each, Páez allegedly received 100 pesos, paid the man off with 4 to 6 pesos, discharged him, and kept the balance. Several dozen people on the list never left Zacatecas. Such accusations seem to have been true, at least partially, although no record of a conviction has come to light.[12]

It hardly mattered. Regardless of how or in which of the four immigrant parties they had come to the colony, and regardless of how long they adhered socially, most of the twelve or thirteen hundred Hispanic men, women, and children put down roots, had babies, and became New Mexicans. Together, by their expanding presence, they reinstalled the Spanish component in New Mexico's evolving cultural universe.

On the surface, little had changed. Restoration New Mexico looked very much like the prewar colony. The Vargas era had introduced few evident new technologies. No innovative tool, item of horse gear, or weapon changed how jobs got done. No flood of currency altered the largely barter and credit economy. People dressed and furnished their homes similarly, ate the same foods, and passed a normal day in familiar pursuits, mostly farming, tending livestock, and raising families. Daily dealings between Hispanic settlers and Pueblo Indians—for purposes of exchange, service, and social contact, both forced and consensual—resumed almost as soon as the fighting ceased. And as in the previous century, the two neighboring peoples coexisted pragmatically, giving and taking articles of material culture, useful customs, nouns from their languages, and blood through ethnic crossbreeding, all the while heedfully maintaining the lines of their parallel societies.

It is too simple to say that lessons of the Pueblo-Spanish War, which resulted as much from the environmental crises of the 1670s as from colonial oppression, taught the two peoples to make common cause. Other forces, external and internal, offer better explanations. Heightened pressure from surrounding nonsedentary nations compelled Pueblo and Hispanic agriculturalists to join in their mutual defense, especially after the 1720s when Comanches added themselves to the prewar array of Apaches, Navajos, and Utes. Demography, too, corrected an old imbalance. Before the war, Hispanic colonists survived as a nervous and high-handed minority. After the

214

restoration, their numbers grew steadily, reaching parity around 1750 with a diminished but stable Pueblo population—at about ten thousand each. Whether a pervasive new respect, engendered by the war years, grew between peoples culturally Pueblo and Hispanic is debatable.

In contrast to many areas of colonial Latin America, New Mexico did not produce a new race born of Spaniards and Indians, even though the two peoples coincided as near neighbors in the Rio Grande Valley. The colony, however, lacked an exploitable natural resource. Hence, despite its relatively large sedentary population of Pueblo Indians, there was little to attract non-Indian immigrants or to set Indians at mining, gathering, or growing. Except for a few families, Hispanic and Pueblo New Mexicans were poor. Neither group had reason to envy or want to be part of the other. Few Spaniards, and fewer Franciscans, learned any of the half-dozen Pueblo languages, which, more than any other circumstance, left the Indians free to preserve their culture. So, as the two peoples worked out their modus vivendi, each allowed the cultural identity of the other.

From a historical perspective, the Pueblo-Spanish War and Vargas era most assuredly thrust up a watershed between the seventeenth- and eighteenth-century colonies. Even though the government, religious life, and defense of resource-poor New Mexico continued to run on subsidies from the royal treasury, Spain's fundamental justification for providing them shifted. Defense of empire replaced evangelism. For most of the earlier century, missionary rationale subsumed the territorial imperative, and Spanish kings kept funding the Franciscans' city of God on the Rio Grande until the Pueblos tore it down in 1680. And while the restored friars still depended on their government stipends, military spending on New Mexico increased dramatically after 1700 as Spain fought to hold western North America against a rising tide of adversaries.

Much else changed in New Mexico, almost imperceptibly. For one thing, the eighteenth-century colony was decidedly more secular. The Franciscans never regained after 1680 the sway they exercised before. No longer did they wield the authority of the Holy Office of the Inquisition so indisputably. Most New Mexicans still had spiritual recourse only to the friars, but a few diocesan priests took up residence first in the El Paso area, then in Santa Fe, and three bishops of Durango carried out visitations of New Mexico in the eighteenth century.[13] Economically, too, the friars lost ground. Before the war, they had controlled the colony's principal supply service, while the combined wealth of their mission lands, labor force, and flocks always overshadowed that of the secular community. Neither circumstance survived.

215

Encomiendas, grants to Spaniards of Indian tribute, which operated to sustain a corps of armed Spanish captains in the prewar colony, were not reinstated. Governor Vargas's eleventh-hour award, in effect a government annuity, implied no burden on the Indians of New Mexico. Paid officers and soldiers of the Santa Fe and El Paso presidios took the place of encomenderos in rallying able members of New Mexico's citizen militia and the Pueblo auxiliary fighting men who regularly outnumbered them.

Diego de Vargas had a vision, and to that end, against all odds, he bent his will. Encouraged by Viceroy Galve, Vargas proposed to transplant to New Mexico a reliable, sturdy class of settlers recruited in the heartland of New Spain. Responding to incentives of land, status, and a new start, these people, Governor Vargas believed, would willingly become small landholders in the reestablished colony. Presidios at El Paso and Santa Fe would protect this civilian base population. Don Diego wanted at least five hundred such colonist families, some two or three thousand men, women, and children, as well as enough government funding to settle them permanently in New Mexico's hostile environment.

When far fewer families volunteered and expenses soared, Vargas watched his carefully conceived program founder. He felt betrayed. Economy-minded bureaucrats in Mexico City seemed bent on compromising his plan as originally conceived and approved. His demands of the viceregal government grew more strident. Only when the heartland of New Spain dried up as a source did he send Páez Hurtado recruiting in the mining districts of the near north. Next, the Pueblo uprising of 1696 intervened. In 1697, with his project still sadly deficient, don Diego bridled against the appearance of a successor. Rodríguez Cubero seemed not to care, and while their struggle further undermined the plan, Governor Vargas's vision had lasting effect.

Returning New Mexicans woke up to the changes reluctantly. They had expected not only to reoccupy positions of leadership in the restored colony, but also to reclaim their families' prewar properties. Instead, they received scant preferment from Governor Vargas. Members of his retinue, meanwhile, wasted no time marrying daughters of old-line New Mexican families, adding social acceptance to their advantage as don Diego's favorites. More distressing to the returnees was the new governor's land policy. Vargas could not regrant to surviving heirs the large estancias of the previous century and still have sufficient productive land to distribute to the hundreds of new settlers he continued to expect. Thus, as a result of his plan and the eventual growth of the Hispanic population in a limited arable and pastoral landscape, the average farm and ranch in the postwar colony was smaller. By resisting the claims of New Mexico's prewar elite, Vargas had assured a somewhat more egalitarian eighteenth century. Difficult to discern at any one moment, such reforms put a new face on colonial New Mexico.

Although don Diego de Vargas died about five o'clock Tuesday afternoon, 8 April 1704, likely in Fernando Durán y Chaves's house at Bernalillo, the Vargas era lived on. His lieutenants provided political continuity. The governor's office passed smoothly to Juan Páez Hurtado as acting governor in 1704 and from him to the next man appointed from Mexico City. The process, in fact, appeared to be operating more effectively on the periphery of empire than in Spain itself where the War of the Spanish Succession had embroiled most of Europe. In distant New Mexico, Vargas's people and policies prevailed.

Three of don Diego's retainers succeeded him as governor. Like their patron, all were Spanish-born. These peninsulares and their households, even when not occupying the governor's palace, remained the cream of New Mexico's rude society, almost as if they had been blood relatives and heirs of the Reconqueror. As mayordomos of the Conquistadora Confraternity, preferred godparents, marriage sponsors, invited guests, and persons of influence, they retained their class superiority, graciously or not. Two, Páez Hurtado (1704–1705, 1717) and Antonio de Valverde (1717–1722), committed early to the business of the colony, lived full lives, and died in New Mexico, the latter in El Paso in 1728, the former at Santa Fe in 1742. The third, Félix Martínez (1715–1717), a member of Vargas's officer corps and longtime captain of the Santa Fe Presidio, did not consider himself a New Mexican, returning several times to Mexico City and dying there in 1731. Martínez and Valverde, never scrupling to profit from the governorship, recalled the Hapsburg mentality of public office as commodity. Neither anticipated the dawning code of the Bourbons, and both, as did Diego de Vargas, found themselves under investigation for malfeasance in office.

Military affairs proceeded as well with officers who had trained and fought under Vargas. They commanded the presidios of El Paso and Santa Fe, maintained the order of drill, escort, and guard duty, and, up until the reforms of Inspector Gen. Pedro de Rivera in the mid-1720s, manipulated presidial supply and payroll to their own benefit. When occasion demanded, they led columns in pursuit of Apaches, Navajos, Comanches, and Frenchmen. Veteran captains like Roque Madrid and Juan de Ulibarrí further distinguished themselves.[14] At don Diego's side, they had shared the strategic advantage of cohorts

of mixed Pueblo auxiliaries. They adhered, therefore, to his policies of request-
ing quotas of fighting men from individual pueblos based on population and
of sharing spoils in equal parts. Throughout the eighteenth century, campaign
rolls regularly revealed more Pueblo Indians than Hispanic men-at-arms.

Franciscans reinstalled in Pueblo communities by Governor Vargas kept on
ministering to their mission congregations and to an increasing number of non-
Indian families who lived nearby. Most adopted a more tolerant attitude than
their prewar brethren toward acts that appeared to their eyes as traditional Pueblo religious practice, so long as they did not interfere with the daily regimen
of Christian instruction, worship, and work. The crisis of 1696, during which
five friars had died violent deaths at the hands of Pueblo Indians, deeply impressed them. Passionately, as fears mounted, they had debated the nature of
martyrdom and what was worth dying for. To protect consecrated objects of
their faith from insolent, mocking unbelievers, or to teach the ultimate object
lesson of Christ's sacrifice, the majority agreed, were good reasons; to foolishly
go among threatening peoples was not. Fortunately for the missionaries in the
years after Vargas, death rarely loomed with such immediacy.

Experience elsewhere in New Spain had taught Diego de Vargas the ef-
ficacy of treating with Indians in a face-to-face, no-nonsense manner. He
embraced Indians physically and showed them respect. He stood as godfather
to the children of Pueblo leaders, which bound these principal men to him
as compadres, whatever this ritual may have meant to them. When circumstances permitted, Vargas negotiated in person. Parties who sat across from
him recognized in the Spanish governor a man of action, as quick to reward
as to punish. Whether his policies benefited or distressed them, don Diego
rarely failed to keep his word. Similar personal diplomacy permitted Antonio
de Valverde to avert a rebellion of Sumas in the vicinity of El Paso between
1711 and 1713 and, much later, distinguished such governors as Tomás Vélez
Cachupín (1749–1754, 1762–1767) and Juan Bautista de Anza (1778–1788).[15]

Vargas's cordiality with Pueblo leaders had worried covetous non-Indians.
In the minds of returning New Mexicans, it was bad enough that don Diego
had refused to regrant the large properties they had expected. Some in fact,
like the heirs of old Francisco de Anaya Almazán II, took their complaints to
subsequent governors and asked for additional acreage.[16] Worse in the long
run, because it effected many more colonists, was Vargas's evolving plan to
guarantee Pueblo Indian communities a fixed, measurable land base.

Long-established Pueblo towns already occupied in the 1690s twenty or
more sites with adjacent arable land along the Rio Grande and its tributaries

north and south of Santa Fe. Although Governor Vargas seemed initially unsure of how much land the law provided for such native corporations, by 1704,
the year of his death, he evidently had decided. That year, to resolve a land
dispute between San Felipe Pueblo and colonists at La Angostura, Sec. Alfonso
Rael de Aguilar supervised the measurement for the Indians of the equivalent
of a league (about 2.6 miles) in each direction, or four square leagues, some
17,350 acres. The so-called Pueblo league, ignored or challenged ever since
by the Pueblos' non-Indian neighbors, remains to this day one of New Mexico's most contentious land issues.[17]

Few would deny the consequence of the Vargas era. Documents now available in *The Journals of don Diego de Vargas* suggest not only topics of research
that will bring into sharper focus this great divide in the colony's history, but
also currents of inquiry flowing back through the seventeenth century and
forward toward the present. The challenge is to embrace, own, and learn from
all of the past. A clearer understanding of who we are in New Mexico today de-
pends on our response.

Notes

1. The initial volume of the Vargas Series, John L. Kessell, ed., *Remote Beyond Com-
    pare: Letters of don Diego de Vargas to His Family from New Spain and New Mexico,
    1675–1706* (Albuquerque: University of New Mexico Press, 1989) [hereafter RBC],
    is in the main biographical. Particularly revealing are the dynamics of Vargas's re-
    lations with the family in Spain. He is utterly devoted to his surviving son and elder
    daughter. He both admonishes and implores his influential son-in-law, whom he
    sees as the key to his own advancement. He confesses to a trusted brother-in-law. As
    the reader grasps the man's frustrations, his painful devotion to honor, his occasional
    joy, and his sadness, the bronze image cast for and by him in the public record is
    replaced by a more human figure.
2. The remaining five volumes of the Vargas Series, all published by the University of
    New Mexico Press in Albuquerque, chronicle the cultural give and take of the re-
    colonization, beginning with Vargas's accession in El Paso in 1691 and ending with
    his death at Bernalillo in 1704, but featuring largely the several thousand men, women,
    and children who defined the experience. John L. Kessell and Rick Hendricks, eds.,
    By Force of Arms: The Journals of don Diego de Vargas, New Mexico, 1691–93 (1992)
    [hereafter BFA]; John L. Kessell, Rick Hendricks, and Meredith D. Dodge, eds., *To
    the Royal Crown Restored: The Journals of don Diego de Vargas, New Mexico, 1692–
    94* (1995) [hereafter RCR]; John L. Kessell, Rick Hendricks, and Meredith D. Dodge,
    eds., *Blood on the Boulders: The Journals of don Diego de Vargas, New Mexico, 1694–
    97* (1998) [hereafter BOB]; John L. Kessell, Rick Hendricks, Meredith D. Dodge,
    and Larry D. Miller, eds., *That Disturbance Cease: The Journals of don Diego de*

Vargas, New Mexico, 1697–1700 (2000) [hereafter TDC]; and John L. Kessell, Rick Hendricks, Meredith D. Dodge, and Larry D. Miller, *A Settling of Accounts: The Journals of don Diego de Vargas, New Mexico, 1700–1704* (2002) [hereafter ASA]. For a comparison with a wholly contemporary Vargas-era enterprise, undertaken in a very different human and physical environment, see Grant D. Jones, *The Conquest of the Last Maya Kingdom* (Stanford, Calif.: Stanford University Press, 1998). Its leader, Martín de Ursúa y Arizmendi, gained promotion to the governorship of the Philippines, a post Diego de Vargas sought unsuccessfully.

3. For an assessment of warfare in this context, see Rick Hendricks, "Pueblo-Spanish Warfare in Seventeenth-Century New Mexico: The Battles of Black Mesa, Kotyiti, and Astialakwa," in *Archaeologies of the Pueblo Revolt: Identity, Meaning, and Renewal in the Pueblo World*, ed. Robert W. Preucel (Albuquerque: University of New Mexico Press, 2002), as well as RCR and BOB.

4. No longer do Vargas and Rodríguez Cubero emerge as so distinctly hero and villain. TDC, ASA, and Rick Hendricks, "Pedro Rodríguez Cubero: New Mexico's Reluctant Governor," *New Mexico Historical Review* 68 (January 1993), 13–39.

5. Rick Hendricks traces the roots of a number of prominent New Mexicans back to Tlalpujahua, an interesting sidelight on Vargas-era patron-client relations, in "La presencia de Tlapujahuenses en la reconquista de Nuevo México," *Relaciones: Estudios de historia y sociedad* (El Colegio de Michoacán) 70 (Primavera 1997), 193–206.

6. José Antonio Esquibel and John B. Colligan, *The Spanish Recolonization of New Mexico: An Account of the Families Recruited at Mexico City in 1693* (Albuquerque: Hispanic Genealogical Research Center of New Mexico, 1999).

7. John B. Colligan, *The Juan Páez Hurtado Expedition of 1695: Fraud in Recruiting Colonists for New Mexico* (Albuquerque: University of New Mexico Press, 1995).

8. To what degree (and for how long) the four immigrant groups of the 1690s can be identified as discrete social entities remains to be determined.

9. The idea of a protracted, three-phase Pueblo-Spanish War—the 1680 Pueblo Revolt, the impasse of the El Paso years from 1681 to 1691, and the recolonization of the 1690s—is suggested by John L. Kessell, "Spaniards and Pueblos: From Crusading Intolerance to Pragmatic Accommodation," in *Columbian Consequences, vol. 1: Archaeological and Historical Perspectives on the Spanish Borderlands West*, ed. David Hurst Thomas (Washington, D.C.: Smithsonian Institution Press, 1989), 127–38.

10. Rick Hendricks, "Antonio de Valverde Cosío," in *American National Biography*, ed. John A. Garraty and Mark C. Carnes (New York: Oxford University Press, 1999), 22:148–49.

11. Fray Angélico Chávez, *Origins of New Mexico Families in the Spanish Colonial Period* (Santa Fe: Historical Society of New Mexico, 1954), 164.

12. Colligan, *Juan Páez Hurtado Expedition*, x–xii, 17, 39–40, 89–90, and BOB, 508–9, 510, 537, 560–62 n. 22.

13. Beginning in 1725, with Antonio de Valverde's request to the bishop of Durango for a secular priest to minister at Las Caldas to Suma Indians and workers on his hacienda of San Antonio de Padua, the Paso del Norte district became a focal point of

220

contention between the diocese of Durango and the Franciscans for spiritual control of the New Mexico colony. Several secular priests served in that area, and residents of the downriver communities found themselves not as bound to the Franciscans as were most New Mexicans. Rick Hendricks, "The Church in El Paso del Norte in the Eighteenth Century," in *Seeds of Struggle, Harvest of Faith: Papers of the Archdiocese of Santa Fe Catholic Cuarto Centennial Conference on the History of the Catholic Church in New Mexico*, ed. Thomas J. Steele, S.J., Paul Rhetts, and Barbe Awalt (Albuquerque: LPD Press, 1998), 107–10.

14. See, for example, Alfred Barnaby Thomas, ed., *After Coronado: Spanish Exploration Northeast of New Mexico, 1696–1727* (Norman: University of Oklahoma Press, 1935), and Rick Hendricks and John P. Wilson, eds., *The Navajos in 1705: Roque Madrid's Campaign Journal* (Albuquerque: University of New Mexico Press, 1996).

15. For Valverde and the Sumas, see Rick Hendricks, "Spanish-Indian Relations in El Paso del Norte in the Early Eighteenth Century: The Rebellion of 1711," in *Proceedings of the Ninth Jornada-Mogollon Conference*, ed. Raymond P. Mauldin, Jeff D. Leach, and Susan Ruth, Publications in Archaeology, 12 (El Paso, 1997), 167–78.

16. In 1714, children of Francisco Anaya Almazán II attempted to expand the boundaries of the grant Vargas had made to Francisco, protesting to Gov. Juan Ignacio Flores Mogollón that they wanted what had been promised instead of the smaller grant their father had received. To their disgust, Flores Mogollón validated the original grant without expanding the boundaries. Joaquín and Juana Anaya Almazán, Petition and revalidation of grant by Gov. Juan Ignacio Flores Mogollón, Santa Fe, 20 August 1714, Spanish Archives of New Mexico I: 497, cited in Malcolm Ebright and Rick Hendricks, *Pueblo Indian Land in New Mexico* (Albuquerque: University of New Mexico Press, forthcoming).

17. The evolution of the Pueblo league is detailed by Ebright and Hendricks, *Pueblo Indian Land*.

Juan Bautista de Anza, Father and Son
PILLARS OF NEW SPAIN'S FAR NORTH

John L. Kessell

The news stung. Shouted from horseback, blurted in cantinas, whispered at mass, it fell on disbelieving ears. For as long as most could remember, Juan Bautista de Anza, captain for life of the garrison at Fronteras, had been their protector. Yet on 9 May 1740, Anza lay dead, victim of an Apache ambush.

The event seemed so improbable. The captain was much too savvy a campaigner. Had he not recently lectured Sonora's governor about just such ambushes? Still, according to a Jesuit visitor who heard the story over a decade later, our only source today, Anza was concluding a routine patrol through Pima mission villages in the Santa Cruz River Valley of present-day southern Arizona. For whatever reasons, he rode out ahead of his men. Apaches, bows drawn, had sprung from cover, loosing their arrows and felling the forty-six-year-old Spaniard from his horse. Apparently they tore off the crown of his scalp as a trophy and were gone. Respected veteran Juan Mateo Manje, whom Captain Anza had known well, likened the practice of scalp taking among Sonora's Indians to the European seizure of enemy battle flags. The swiftness of Spanish retaliation—three days after Anza's

John L. Kessell is Professor Emeritus of History at the University of New Mexico. This article also appears in the newly published anthology *Western Lives: A Biographical History of the American West*, ed. Richard W. Etulain (Albuquerque: University of New Mexico Press, 2004).

death, thirteen were killed and fourteen taken captive—implied that punishment might have been inflicted on a nearby camp of friendly Apaches.

In the captain's quarters at Fronteras, thirty miles south of today's Douglas, Arizona, his mourning widow gathered about her the two girls from her late husband's previous union along with their own four children: Francisco Antonio, fifteen; María Margarita, thirteen; Josefa Gregoria, eight; and Juan Bautista the younger, not yet four, who was most like his father. To be certain—from the year 1718, when the elder Anza, a Basque from Spain, first appeared in the records of Sonora, for seven decades thereafter, until 1788, with the burial of his American-born namesake—the sequential careers of this venturous father and son amply illustrate the vitality of colonial New Spain's far northwestern frontier, today's American Southwest.

For two centuries before the Anzas, realities and mirages commingled north of the city of Mexico, beckoning the restless. Eyewitness reports by Alvar Núñez Cabeza de Vaca and fray Marcos de Niza, embellished in a climate of wonder, had set in motion one of North America's great false starts. The grandly medieval exploration carried out between 1540 and 1542 by the several units under Francisco Vázquez de Coronado had begun with banners waving and ended in disgrace. More than three hundred European horsemen and footmen, heirs of the Spanish *Reconquista* yet carrying among them Native wooden and obsidian weapons, led forth a thousand imposing Mexican Indian fighters. They had lost no battle. Defeated instead by an endless topography that offered no hope of immediate return, they had at least experienced the vastness of the continent. And they had met face-to-face a medley of its scattered Native peoples, from the Yumas of the Colorado River in the west to the Wichitas of present-day central Kansas. Then they withdrew, and colonization stalled.

Not for the next 185 years did another notable Spaniard travel as broadly as Coronado in the far north. A military bureaucrat, Insp. Gen. Pedro de Rivera, and his staff went out from Mexico City in 1724 and came back in 1728, neither with much fanfare. Rivera rode eight thousand miles, reviewed two dozen garrisons, installed Juan Bautista de Anza the elder at Fronteras, proposed cutting defense costs by more than one third, and drew up a needed code of reforms that were largely ignored. Colonization, meanwhile, given time and chance, had streamed northward.

The biggest incentive at first was silver. An especially bountiful strike in the late 1540s at Zacatecas, 350 miles northwest of Mexico City, set off a series of bonanzas financed in large part by Basque venture capitalists. Hu-

223

manity, hybrid in race and estate, swarmed the camps. Free and slave laborers, mining engineers, bakers, whores, blacksmiths, homeless vagrants, jugglers, and children jostled for space. Storekeepers stocked a surprisingly wide array of hardware, dry goods, and confections. The insatiable demand for meat, hides and tallow, wool, wheat, and eggs brought stockmen and farmers. Such frantic intrusion also brought war.

Spaniards called them *Chichimecas*. A generic term of deep derision, it served to reduce the various culturally distinct seminomadic Native groups of the high desert simply to enemies. The European invaders thought first

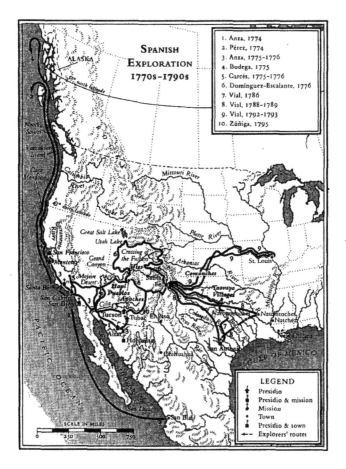

SPANISH EXPLORATION, 1770S TO 1790S
From John L. Kessell, *Spain in the Southwest: A Narrative History of Colonial New Mexico, Arizona, Texas, and California* (Norman: University of Oklahoma Press, 2002), 284.
(Courtesy University of Oklahoma Press, copyright 2002)

224

to stamp them out, hunting them on search-and-destroy missions, placing bounties on male heads, and selling their families into slavery. But the Chichimecas fought back, forming confederations, learning to ride, and becoming ever more nomadic. Exasperated, the Spaniards set out salaried frontier garrisons, or presidios, and fortified nearly all their built spaces, even to experimental wagons meant for protection of supplies to the mines and silver to Mexico City. Nothing seemed to work. By the 1580s and 1590s, astute captains, taking advantage of a prolonged drought and the slow attrition of Chichimeca fighting men, had evolved a welfare program. In exchange for peace, the Spanish government agreed to provide foodstuffs, clothing, axes, copper kettles, bolts of cloth, and other assistance and ban slaving. Delegations of Chichimeca headmen, escorted to Mexico City, gawked at what Spaniards had wrought. In the long run, peace by purchase proved cheaper than war.

Given the profusion of mines fanning northward across Nueva Vizcaya, roughly the modern Mexican states of Durango and Chihuahua, prospectors counted on the progression to continue at higher latitudes. Yet they were wrong. Studying the U.S.-Mexican border on a map today, starting at the Pacific shore and trending more east than south, the surveyors' dead-straight line is inconvenienced slightly at the Colorado River, then proceeds with only three corrections until it is swept along with the current and big bends of the Rio Grande all the way to the Gulf of Mexico. No Spanish colonial miner could have known that beyond that line, in New Spain's far north, mining would count for practically nothing. Even the modest mines operated in the latter-day Mexican state of Sonora during the 1720s and 1730s by the first Juan Bautista de Anza lay below that line.

Juan de Oñate had to see for himself. Affluent son of a major Basque developer of the Zacatecas district, don Juan got together a consortium in the 1590s to invest in pacification of the town-dwelling and clothed peoples inhabiting a northern land optimists had already begun calling the new Mexico. By terms of a contract negotiated with the viceroy in Mexico City, Oñate was exalted as proprietor and first governor of New Mexico in turn for outfitting, transporting, and settling there its first two hundred soldier-colonists and their families. When in the summer of 1598 they came among the Pueblo Indians with all their baggage, dependents, and hungry animals, this motley train of settlers contrasted sharply with the martial cavalcade of Coronado. Yet Oñate met every challenge, among them fierce battles with Pueblo Indians and desertion of most of his colonists, while prospecting at every turn. Assay results, however, belied the vast mineral potential he kept reporting to Mexico City. Finally after a decade, lamenting his expenditure of six hundred thousand pesos, Juan de Oñate resigned.

Wise counselors urged that New Mexico be abandoned. In reply, the colony's Franciscan missionaries swore abruptly to having administered Christian baptism to upward of seven thousand Pueblo Indians. Surely a gross exaggeration, it served. The Spanish government straightaway converted the kingdom and provinces of New Mexico from proprietary to crown colony, assuming costs, appointing a salaried governor, and subsidizing a continued Franciscan ministry to seemingly tolerant Pueblo Indians. Because of New Mexico's unusual status as a missionary project, the friars wielded uncommon authority. Exercising a spiritual monopoly as the colony's only Roman Catholic priests, they also controlled the triennial supply caravans. Their dozens of missions, taken together, occupied the best arable lands, employed most Pueblo Indians, and ran more sheep than anybody else. Santa Fe, the colony's only chartered municipality, never amounted to more than a few hundred residents. Others lived in valleys as far north as Taos and especially downriver on several large properties, or *estancias*. While periodic epidemics and Apache raiding steadily dragged down Pueblo Indian numbers, the small Hispanic community of cousins procreated.

All alone in the far north, the friars' city of God on the Rio Grande, contested from within by governors and colonists who coveted Indian land and labor, endured for three generations until mission Indians tore it down. Driven to desperation by drought and colonial persecution, they rose in the monumental Pueblo Revolt of 1680, putting to death twenty-one Franciscans and hundreds of colonists. The surviving two thousand Hispanic men, women, and children, still greatly outnumbered, fled down the Rio Grande to El Paso. Exactly one hundred years later, the second Juan Bautista de Anza governed New Mexico.

During the 1690s, while Spaniard Diego de Vargas fought grimly to restore upriver New Mexico, other colonies crossed the line into the far north. Like New Mexico, each spread up from the south over well-worn migration routes resembling the widespread fingers of a hand with its forearm at Mexico City. Into these fingers flowed culturally Hispanic families, provisions, and the mail, always south to north and back, with virtually no east-west contact among them. Although every one of these frontier colonies sustained the familiar reciprocal triad of Indian mission, presidio, and town and depended on limited farming and extensive herding, each had its origin in a different year and purpose: New Mexico (1598, 1609), mining, Franciscan missions; southern Arizona (1691), Jesuit expansion; Texas (1690, 1716), countering

French Louisiana; and Baja-Alta California (1697, 1769), securing the Pacific coast. And while the younger Anza bid heroically in the later eighteenth century to string webs of intercourse from one to another, colonial Santa Fe, Tucson, San Antonio, and Monterey remained firmly tied to the south, never to each other.

French colonial design, meanwhile, extending westward from the Mississippi Valley toward Texas and across the Great Plains in the direction of New Mexico, had goaded Spanish imperial strategists in Madrid and Mexico City to imagine New Spain's far north as a single, defensible outer frontier. The end of the European dynastic War of the Spanish Succession by treaty in 1714 assured efficiency-minded Bourbon Felipe V his throne and his empire. A half century later, when Great Britain replaced France as Spain's major rival for western North America, the enlightened Carlos III redoubled attention to the far north. And so it was during this eighteenth-century era of overarching imperial rivalry and everyday warfare with highly mobile Native groups that the Anzas, father and son, made their marks.

Inspector General Rivera liked young Anza. The resourceful Basque immigrant hailed from Hernani, a close-built cluster of three- and four-story stone houses half a dozen miles inland from Spain's animated north-coast port of San Sebastián. From there, Juan had likely sailed around 1712, toward the close of the War of the Spanish Succession. His father, Antonio, a pharmacist, businessman, and local officeholder, had lived his entire life in the same house. Juan's birth in that secure place on 29 June 1693, presented his parents a second child and, as time would tell, the eldest of four boys. As he grew, the lad took an interest in town affairs, learning at his father's side about property law and the court system and witnessing legal documents by age sixteen. Yet he sensed a wider world. Wandering about San Sebastián with a younger cousin, he visualized the marvels of the Spanish Indies. At the age of nineteen or twenty, Juan had emigrated. Within a decade, adhering to a centuries-old pattern, the cousin, Pedro Felipe de Anza, followed, joining Juan in the far north, where he oversaw the latter's mining and ranching interests.

Juan Bautista de Anza must have landed at humid Veracruz and made the ascent to New Spain's stunning viceregal capital, set in a bowl-like valley and lake and surrounded by perennially snow-clad volcanos. Passing through Guadalajara and on up the Pacific slope, a further land journey of seven hundred miles seems to have brought him to Culiacán in Sinaloa, where his mother had relatives. He cannot have stayed long. By 1718, he was fully invested with other old-country Basques four hundred miles farther north at a remote mining camp in the dry, gray-brown, mesquite-covered hinterland of Sonora.

The *real de minas* of Nuestra Señora de Guadalupe de Aguaje, a clutter of squat adobe structures, pole-and-mud huts, and tents, sat in a dusty depression between slopes punctured by hand-dug shafts. In January 1718, this restless camp was under inspection. Capt. Antonio Bezerra Nieto and his attendants examined, however diligently, account books and scales in Aguaje's ten stores or stacks of supplies, the shoring and condition of its seven mines, and payroll records. Most everything conformed to royal regulations, including the store and San Antonio Mine owned by Juan Bautista de Anza. Another inventory of goods, also in compliance, belonged to a woman, Rosa de Sierra.

Captain Bezerra's parting decree, witnessed and signed by the literate Anza, required at least four workers continuously at each mine, threatened livestock thieves with forced service at the presidio of Fronteras, and forbade residents of all classes to carry knives and machetes. Fines went toward completing the Aguaje jail. Bezerra may also have turned recruiter, discussing with the promising, twenty-four-year-old Anza a career in the frontier officer corps. The rare peninsular Spaniard, energetic and of proven nobility and blood purity, made an ideal candidate. Don Antonio may also have foreseen the young Basque as a son-in-law.

Four years later, Ensign Juan Bautista de Anza wed María Rosa Bezerra Nieto. "Well-built, light-complected, with full beard and straight hazel hair," Anza had enlisted and now lived at his father-in-law's well-fortified, fifty-man garrison of Janos in Nueva Vizcaya, thirty miles due south of New Mexico's present-day boot heel. Above the presidio and farming community of Janos, the road divided, one branch leading north and east to El Paso and the other west into the province of Sonora via the unkempt presidio of Fronteras. Already Anza, deeply involved in Sonoran affairs, had enemies, none more tenacious than don Gregorio Alvarez Tuñón y Quirós, the mostly absentee captain for life of Fronteras.

Few groups of European compatriots hung together more tightly in foreign parts than Basques and their descendants. Natural allies of the equally enterprising Society of Jesus, or Jesuits, whose founders were Basque, they formed an imposing economic and political ring in Sonora. To ambitious non-Basques, these unholy associates seemed bent on monopolizing the province and controlling access to Indian laborers for mines and ranches. Alvarez hated them, vowing that he would, in the words of a Jesuit superior, not rest until all of them were burden bearers in his mine. During near civil war in the early 1720s, Anza, labeled by the opposition a notorious trouble-maker, traveled to Mexico City as spokesman for the pro-Basque party. Previous complaints of malfeasance, meanwhile, had led to the arrest of Alvarez, then his acquittal. Recoiling, he turned up in 1723 with orders from the governor of Nueva Vizcaya to inspect the presidio at Janos, to which Anza had recently returned.

However smug the captain of Fronteras felt watching the mounted and fully armed troopers of Janos pass in review before him, he could find no ready fault with them, their commander, or Anza. They were a tough, effi-cient, battle-tested cavalry unit. Few presidios could measure up. The vice-roy in Mexico City, in fact, had heard so many damning reports about the corruption and ill success of the frontier military that he requested permis-sion from the crown for a general inspection. Royal authorization had come in 1724. As a result, in October 1726, Brig. Gen. Pedro de Rivera reined up at Janos. Except for the high price of goods deducted from the soldiers' sala-ries, he lauded the operation. If the inspector general was looking for an unfit officer of whom to make an example, he had to wait. He asked that Juan Bautista de Anza, now lieutenant of Janos, escort him and his party on to the presidio at Fronteras, still under nominal command of Gregorio Alvarez Tuñón y Quirós.

Fronteras lay in near ruin. Its captain had never lived on-site, choosing instead to reside far to the south at the headquarters of his mining hacienda. In effect debt peons, his demoralized troops rotated in service to him per-sonally. Worse, Alvarez had been pocketing for years the salaries of phan-tom soldiers. The others rarely ventured out of their run-down adobe complex. Apache raiding parties, relying on the garrison's unpreparedness, entered with impunity through nearby passes, causing frightened colonists and Jesuit mis-sionaries to complain loudly. Rivera listened. Formulating fifteen charges against Alvarez, the inspector general sacked him on the spot. Then—after composing a set of specific regulations that ranged from dress code, personal cleanliness, and attendance at mass to an order that troopers learn to use lances as the Apaches did—Rivera put Juan Bautista de Anza in command. Soon after lawyers in Mexico City lost Alvarez's case for a second acquittal, Sonora's deadly plague of 1728 struck down the Basque-Jesuit ring's most outspoken critic. At that, the crown imposed a posthumous indignity, ap-pointing Anza to attach the multifarious Alvarez estate and ensure payment of a huge fine into the royal treasury before other creditors had their day.

While the thirty-three-year-old Captain Anza put his shoulder to revitalizing Fronteras, the defensive, rapid-strike-and-retaliate warfare with Western Apaches never let up. Efforts to attract certain bands to peace with food and gifts, much as captains had done on the Chichimeca frontier a century and a half earlier, proved transient. As if Apaches were not enough, authorities informed Anza that pacification of the fiercely defiant Seri Indians also devolved upon him. Nonagricultural fishing and foraging inhabitants of the Gulf of California's seared Sonoran coast, two hundred miles southwest of Fronteras, Seris interfered with pearl fishing and killed trespassers. Hence in 1729, Captain Anza and thirty of his men joined the district officers of Sinaloa and Sonora, militia units, and Yaqui Indian auxiliaries in a campaign in which Anza commanded launches to invade the Seri refuge of Tiburón Island. A bold stroke, it hardly inconvenienced the Seris.

Besides warfare, the other constant in the captain's professional life was his special relationship with the Jesuits and his defense of their sprawling northwestern missionary enterprise. He knew the history. Beginning in 1591, stouthearted Jesuit missionaries had crossed the western Sierra Madre north of Culiacán. With their appealing material goods, faith, and charisma, they had proceeded relentlessly from one river valley to the next up the Pacific slope, converting to nominal Christianity a succession of Indian nations. The renowned Jesuit pied piper, explorer, and cartographer, Eusebio Francisco Kino, had reached today's southern Arizona exactly a hundred years later, in 1691.

Over the next two decades, Father Kino mounted dozens of expeditions, often escorted by Lt. Juan Mateo Manje, crisscrossing along Native trails a desert-and-jagged-mountain expanse called the Pimería Alta, land of the Upper Pima Indians. He ventured north as far as the valley of the Gila River and west to the Colorado, which with the aid of Native swimmers he crossed in a big basket balanced on a raft. Watching the sunrise over the head of the Gulf of California, Kino certified that Baja California was a peninsula, not an island after all. He envisioned a Spanish town where modern Yuma, Arizona, sprawls today. He urged that Jesuits advance northeastward to the Hopi Pueblo Indians, apostates from Franciscan Catholicism since the Pueblo Revolt of 1680. And he yearned to explore farther and cross on land to the Pacific coast of California.

Although Kino died in 1711, halting Jesuit expansion beyond the Pimería Alta, his protégé, testy old Father Agustín de Campos, imparted the vision to Juan Bautista de Anza. When Jesuits sought to reoccupy three mission stations that had been without resident priests since Kino's day, Anza smoothed the way, installing them in the spring of 1732: one at Soamca, just south of the Mexican-U.S. boundary; another at Guevavi, a few miles north; and the last at San Xavier del Bac, near present-day Tucson. Two years later, when mission Indians fled to the hills, Anza talked them back. He made the captain's quarters at Fronteras a hospice for sick Jesuits, where doña María Rosa attended them. She was pregnant with Juan Bautista the younger in 1736 when her husband took in distraught, sixty-seven-year-old Father Campos. The venerable priest had suffered a nervous breakdown, armed the Pimas of his mission, and vowed to fight to the death any superior who tried to force his retirement. Scandalously, he had also spoken ill of fellow Jesuits. Anza mediated a settlement, and Campos retired.

The two of them had talked long about Baja California, unique among provinces in the far north. Because the Society of Jesus had financed its occupation in 1697 and since then maintained it through a special Pious Fund, California belonged to the Jesuits. Inspector General Rivera had bypassed the presidio of Loreto since its captain and soldiers were Jesuit employees. All the same, the crown was pressuring the Jesuits to extend their sphere to the north and settle the bays of San Diego and Monterey as ports of haven for returning, Acapulco-bound Manila galleons. Kino and Campos had discussed how opening a supply route overland from Sonora could advance the project. Anza wanted that honor. When in 1734 desperate Pericú Indians at the southern tip of the peninsula rose and martyred two missionaries, the Jesuits were forced to look in the opposite direction. They requested that Captain Anza be put in command of a punitive expeditionary force. Sinaloa-Sonora's ambitious first governor, however, anxious to see what the Jesuits might be hiding in California, eventually crossed the gulf himself. Anza, meanwhile, hoped that the overland way to California might be paved with silver from a freak bonanza in 1736.

In October of that year, a startled Yaqui Indian prospector, Antonio Siraumea, combing rough hill country southwest of modern-day Nogales, came upon large, partially buried chunks of silver. Word got around the mining camp of Agua Caliente, about a dozen miles away, and others swarmed to the site, laying hands on more slabs, one weighing in excess of a ton. Eager to maintain order, the local deputy magistrate, who lived next to Agua Caliente at a place he called Arizona, notified his district superior, who at the time was Anza.

How to explain this rare phenomenon? Were these irregular pieces of silver someone's previously hidden treasure? Did they result from illegal

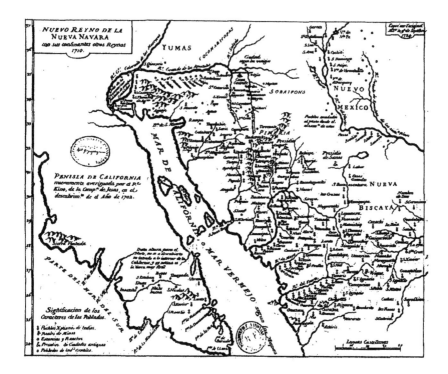

EUSEBIO FRANCISCO KINO'S CULMINATING 1710 MAP SHOWING THE LAND
PASSAGE TO CALIFORNIA.
Bibliothèque Nationale, Paris. From John L. Kessell, *Friars, Soldiers,*
and Reformers: Hispanic Arizona and the Sonora Mission Frontier,
1767–1856 (Tucson: University of Arizona Press, 1976).

smelting? Or were they ore from natural veins? The answer would determine the king's share. When Captain Anza and a column of soldiers arrived, he ordered as many of the lucky miners as had not yet slipped away to
appear, make declarations, and turn over the silver to him until Mexico City
rendered a decision. Although he entertained pleas that the precious metal
be returned, as presiding royal official he impounded it all and posted guards
at the source. The resulting array of documents, executed in the home of
Anza's deputy, bore Arizona as the point of origin. And because later officials
mistakenly transposed the phenomenal discovery to that place, not only did
the Basque word *Arizona* (the good oak) become synonymous with bountiful
mineral wealth, but also subsequently the name of the Grand Canyon state.

From Fronteras, Captain Anza forwarded to the viceroy samples of the
silver *planchas* or *bolas*, the documentary record, and a petition. He asked

232

that he be granted license to explore north and west toward California, which he still believed could be an island. While he awaited answers, Anza found himself drawn as protagonist into the bizarre revelation of a self-proclaimed Native prophet of the god Montezuma.

The episode had begun with a major disruption in central Sonora as Native workers deserted missions, mines, and ranches seeking the blessings of this supposed holy man and healer. Spies reported that the Indian Agustín Aschuhuli was preaching a new order. Indians and Spaniards would exchange roles, the former being raised to owners and the latter reduced to workers. Aschuhuli demanded of his worshipers gifts and food for him and for his six pretty young female attendants, and a black-shrouded idol rigged to appear as if it were smoking cigars. The accompanying wild mix of ritual had perverted certain Roman Catholic practices. Hastening halfway across Sonora to the port of Guaymas, Anza apprehended Agustín, who confessed, blaming the devil. Absolved, executed, and hung from a tall palm tree, Aschuhuli served as an example. Finally, at the center of the affected region, Anza and a Jesuit priest, proclaiming the folly of adherence to the false god Montezuma, ceremonially burned the idol.

Ordered back to the site of the mysterious silver trove with mining experts, Captain Anza renewed the inquiry, concluding that the slabs were in fact ore from several veins, not treasure. That limited the king's share to the standard fifth, which Anza dutifully collected before returning the impounded metal. He supervised as well the registration of mining claims, first to the Yaqui discoverer and then to others. In Mexico City, the viceroy's chief adviser took exception. He had assumed previously that the find was ancient Aztec treasure and as such should be shipped straightaway to Spain. Juan Bautista de Anza and his alleged experts were obviously incompetents. The case demanded further investigation. But by then, the discovery had played out. As late as May 1740, the viceregal bureaucracy still had under advisement Anza's California project and a possible royal commendation for his decisive action against the false prophet. But during that month, Apaches closed Anza's career.

His legacy was secure, for about twenty years, until his son and namesake undeliberately began to eclipse it. Young Anza rose to command a presidio, then to govern a province. He fought dozens of battles with Apaches, Seris, and other Native adversaries and made peace with some. He led colonists overland to California. Both father and son, devout Spanish Catholics, benefited the Jesuits, underwrote presidial chapels at their posts, and administered tithe collection in Sonora and New Mexico. And like his father, the younger Anza carried out most orders of his superiors with dispatch. One royal decree, however, conveyed in strictest secrecy and concerning the Jesuits, caused him unspeakable agony. The elder Anza might rather have died.

The second Juan Bautista de Anza had grown up in the financially and socially safe world of his father's making. The boy's godfather and first cousin once removed, Pedro Felipe de Anza, possessed the Midas touch. Wherever Pedro Felipe ventured, into mines, merchandise, ranch land, or cattle, whether alone or as partner of any of a dozen intermarried Basques, he made money. He and Agustín de Vildósola, godfather of young Juan's sister Josefa Gregoria, shared in lucrative joint ventures in western Sonora, with little respect for indigenous peoples. When the elder Captain Anza died, Vildósola, the overall commander of provincial militia, found himself largely responsible in 1740 as Yaquis and allied Native peoples in southern Sonora conspired in a prolonged and sometimes violent protest against the Jesuit missionary regime. Upon Vildósola's final negotiated settlement, a grateful viceroy made him governor of Sonora, a post he occupied until 1748. Anza's widow, María Rosa, with her younger children, other kin, and servants, meanwhile, seems to have resided alternately at the mining town of Basochuca north of Arizpe and on one of the family's ranch properties along the present-day Arizona-Sonora border.

This next generation was no less closely interlinked. When Juan was ten, his sister Josefa Gregoria married a Vildósola at Basochuca. Another home-country Basque, Gabriel Antonio de Vildósola, took a father's interest in Juan. The boy was confident and quick. Someone taught him an elegant, studied penmanship. Also to shoot. In his midteens, with an eye on the frontier officer corps, Juan enlisted as an unsalaried cadet. He cheered Gabriel Antonio's appointment as captain at Fronteras in 1754. A year later, just shy of his nineteenth birthday, Juan Bautista de Anza the younger assumed duties as lieutenant at the presidio where he was born.

Unlike his peninsular Spanish father, who had to learn the ways of the frontier upon arrival, son Juan was raised on them, a cultural heir of Sonora's Basque-Jesuit establishment. Born in America, a *criollo*, he sought continually to prove himself in the eyes of Spaniards from the old country, who always considered themselves superior. Day to day on the frontier, however, as officer and *patrón*, the younger Anza dealt naturally with peers whom the community considered *españoles*, with Indians at his side and those he fought, and with mixed bloods of European, Indian, and African extraction who served on campaigns under him or as mine workers or vaqueros on his ranches.

Back in the spring of 1752, the chastened leader of an uprising among mission Indians of the Pimería Alta had turned himself in to soldiers camped at a place called Tubac, twenty miles north of today's Nogales, Arizona. Cadet Anza, with Captain Vildósola, had tracked the offending Pimas, evidently the young man's earliest military experience. In 1753, while the governor of Sonora blamed the Jesuits for the recent rebellion and they blamed him, laborers had laid up at Tubac enough adobes to form the province's newest presidio, hardly a fortress. When Tubac's first captain, the Basque Juan Tomás de Beldarráin, died in September 1759 from wounds sustained on campaign against Seris in the south, the vacant post went to twenty-three-year-old Juan Bautista de Anza. Purchasing the captain's house from Beldarráin's heirs early in 1760, he moved his mother in with him.

Hispanic Sonora's two-front war, with Apaches across the north and Seris and other resisters to the south and west, added campaign after campaign to Anza's service record and luster to his reputation as a brave and sure leader. His personal life filled the spaces between. In October 1760, he grieved the loss of his mother, doña María Rosa. The following spring, the young captain petitioned his superiors for permission to marry. With license in hand, on the feast day of his name saint, 24 June 1761, in the church at Arizpe, Juan Bautista de Anza wed Ana María Pérez Serrano, daughter of a Basque business associate of his father. Jesuit Carlos de Rojas, the priest who had baptized the groom, officiated.

Talk of horses, drought, and Apaches occupied locals even while the imperial bounds of North America shifted. By the European treaty of 1763, French sovereignty no longer overlay midcontinent. Louisiana west of the Mississippi, including New Orleans, had passed to Spain. Great Britain's colonial sphere now extended west as far as the river. Spanish imperial strategists wanted to know how much of interior North America could be defended against Englishmen and the various non-Christian Indian nations already disputing expansion northward. It had been forty years since New Spain's far north had undergone gulf-to-gulf, on-site scrutiny. A new inspection, carried out between 1766 and 1768, fell to the high-ranking Marqués de Rubí.

Ever since the concurrent founding in 1718 of French New Orleans and Spanish San Antonio, families of Spaniards had ventured deep into forested and humid east Texas to people a log presidio and capital at Los Adaes right up against the territory of France. With Louisiana's transfer to Spain, the Marqués de Rubí would recommend the painful withdrawal of established settlers from east to central Texas. The provincial capital would follow them to semiarid San Antonio, a tight cluster of presidio, town, and five missions. La Bahía, another presidial community, lay about ninety miles southeast down the San Antonio River in watered and open brush country. Laredo, too, had attracted a growing population after a Spanish empresario colonized the lower Rio Grande Valley. Spanish Texas, sparsely settled and widely spaced, favored cattle over people. While the colony no longer served as outer barrier to a European rival, it remained an endless open range to Hispanic *tejanos* and their Indian trade partners and foes.

The Marqués de Rubí, his staff, and caravan crowded Tubac at Christmastime in 1766. In disbelief, having reprimanded a string of presidial commanders who gouged their men at the company store, Rubí noted that Captain Anza was selling supplies at discount. The garrison appeared well equipped and trained. Although Anza complained repeatedly of unmet government payrolls, he had access to loans through his Mexico City supplier's circle of fellow Basque financiers. Because he owned nearby ranches, people considered Captain Anza a local patrón. So many neighboring families, especially from properties to the south, had moved to Tubac for fear of Apaches that Rubí reckoned they could defend themselves. Hence he proposed that Anza's company be relocated farther north, a project undertaken at Tucson a decade later.

One of the few gripes of the soldiers at Tubac had to do with herding and guarding horses that did not belong to them. Anza, it seemed, had made a deal with the Jesuit priest at nearby Guevavi, a mission that supplied his presidio with beef and where his mother and Captain Beldarráin lay buried. The captain had offered to range the horses from Guevavi and two other missions with the presidial herd. The *marqués* decreed that the practice cease. Not long after the inspector departed, however, raiders made off with Guevavi's mares. Anza brought the rest of the mission horses back and put on a couple of Indian herders to care for them. Regulations be damned; neighbors came to understandings.

Like his father, Captain Anza recognized how intensely some of his acquaintances despised the Society of Jesus. Highly efficient, privileged, sometimes arrogant, Jesuits wielded disproportionate economic, political, and social power, especially in places like Sonora, where they were so concentrated. Earlier, in 1759 and 1764, the governments of Portugal and France, Spain's nearest neighbors, had banished all Jesuits from their dominions. But the Society was Spanish in origin. Surely Carlos III would resist his

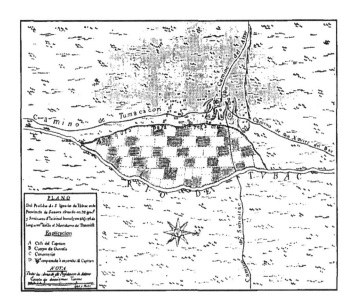

LT. JOSÉ DE URRUTIA'S 1766 PLAN OF THE PRESIDIO AT TUBAC
British Museum, London. From John L. Kessell, *Mission of Sorrows:
Jesuit Guevavi and the Pimas, 1691–1767* (Tucson: University of
Arizona Press, 1970).

reforming ministers who wanted to expel the Jesuits on the grounds of their
first loyalty to the pope and their abiding support of the old aristocracy.

An inscription across the sealed packet from Gov. Juan Claudio de Pineda
of Sonora read simply, "Do not open until July 23." The secretive operation,
begun with the king "locking away in his royal breast the reasons for his
decision" and spread to the far corners of the empire in mid-1767 with near-
infallible bureaucratic precision, now drew in Juan Bautista de Anza. The
governor, availing himself of the Anza family's close ties to Sonora's Jesuits,
ordered the captain of Tubac to Arizpe to arrest the father superior. Whether
it eased or made more difficult their encounter, Father Carlos de Rojas had
baptized and married don Juan. The captain's excuses made little sense as
he escorted Father Rojas from mission to mission, collecting Jesuits en route
south to Mátape, the designated detention center. There a royal official
waited to read to them formally the king's decree of expulsion. A number
would die in confinement, during a merciless voyage down the gulf, or on
their forced march across New Spain to Veracruz for deportation. Shaken,
Anza was back at his presidio by 1 September.

237

He still owed money to the exiled priest of Guevavi. Since the government meant to seize all Jesuit assets, who precisely was he supposed to pay? The temporary agent placed in charge at the mission so mishandled its slim resources that Anza demanded the keys. All over Sonora, similar scenes unfolded. The disruption caused by crushing at one blow the province's most diverse and thriving corporation persisted for years. As for conventional, government-subsidized, semiautonomous Indian missions, the reformers thought they had a better idea, something like collective farms. Franciscan replacements would be granted a spiritual ministry only, while civilian overseers managed material affairs and discipline. Reaching Sonora in 1768, the first Franciscans let circumstances dictate. Ill provided and sparsely populated, most frontier missions simply could not support two masters, nor did mission Indians understand who to obey. Consequently, within months, the surrogate missionaries had regained full management, and reformers called for further study.

Juan Bautista de Anza responded. One of a number of officials required in 1772 to comment on proposed reform of mission administration, Anza apologized for any lack of understanding. Then, based on twenty years of close observation, he damned the missions of the Pimería Alta. Assuming Hispanic assimilation of Native peoples as the goal, he had seen little progress. Worse, whereas mission Indians once had numbered in the thousands, only hundreds survived. He laid most of the blame on excessive work demanded in the missions of formerly seminomadic peoples. In contrast, nonmission Indians seemed to be increasing in numbers. Anza had nothing to say about measles or smallpox, infant mortality, punishment in the stocks, or psychological trauma, nor did he mention the more reliable food supply, appeal of Spanish Catholic ritual, or protection afforded by the missionaries. If the missions were to attract heathen peoples in the future, argued the captain, they must undergo radical change.

Settling Spaniards within mission pueblos, establishing schools to teach the children Spanish, allowing mission Indians off the reservation to trade and seek outside employment, allotting to them private property, and consolidating small mission villages in formal towns of eighty to a hundred families—by all these means, Anza suggested, mission Indians would emerge from their backwardness. Sharing in the benefits of Hispanic civilization, they would also abandon thoughts of rebellion. Whatever humanitarian concerns may have motivated Anza, his response was also self-serving. He and his associates had long wanted freer access to mission Indians as consumers and workers. At the same time, the captain of Tubac wrote what he sensed the new viceroy's lead counsel wished to hear. Two months earlier, that same official, a member of Anza's Basque support group in Mexico City, had endorsed his proposal to lead an expedition overland to California.

Another more powerful government agent, archreformer José de Gálvez, the king's special envoy to New Spain, already had his eye on the far northwest. Gálvez had enjoyed expelling the Jesuits. Next he threw himself into the revitalization of Sonora and California, more successfully on paper than in the field. Taking up temporary residence in Baja California, he busily mapped out Spanish occupation of Alta California, something the Jesuits had failed to realize. Russian sea otter hunters coasting down from Alaska and English seamen seeking a northwest passage had lent the required urgency. Gálvez loved logistics. By sea, he ordered two ships to beat against contrary winds and currents and put in first at San Diego and then Monterey. Simultaneously, a land party would mark the harsh six-hundred-mile track up the peninsula for Gov. Gaspar de Portolá, fray Junípero Serra, and their train to follow. When at last scurvy-racked survivors embraced on the shore of San Diego Bay, it was July 1769. Within six weeks, Captain Anza at Tubac knew that coastal Indians in California had seen Spaniards with long muskets.

Much as he wanted to investigate in person, Anza had his orders to take part in Gálvez's grand but ultimately unsuccessful offensive against the Seris. While the captain campaigned, a potentially troublesome Franciscan explored. The friar could have got himself killed. Earthy but shrewd, fray Francisco Garcés had taken over at San Xavier del Bac, the northernmost mission formerly administered by Jesuits. On several occasions, the missionary ventured all but alone to the banks of the Gila, then downriver to its junction with the Colorado, and finally beyond far enough to make out distant blue mountains. Natives by signs relayed further intelligence of Spaniards to the west. Brave or foolhardy, Garcés, it appeared, could take care of himself. When Anza petitioned the viceroy from Tubac in May 1772 to lead half his garrison by land to California, he asked that Father Garcés be allowed to join them.

Officials who deliberated at Mexico City and Madrid remembered the similar proposal of Anza's father and made it part of the record. Now, with the precarious Spanish beginnings at San Diego and Monterey in jeopardy for lack of supplies, the time seemed right. Of greatest concern, even more than funding, was that Anza's passing not harm Native peoples along the route. No new settlement was planned, only a reconnaissance. Again thanks to his Basque connections in Mexico City, don Juan secured the necessary loans. The expedition's forty men, broken into smaller units as circumstances demanded, were gone from Tubac the first four and a half months of 1774. At the strategic Colorado River crossing, Anza presented Yuma Indian headman Salvador Palma a medal stamped with the likeness of Carlos III. Garcés, a nonswimmer and unwilling to trust his horse, let Yumas carry him across. Matching every challenge of dry camps, rocky ravines, and curious Indians, the captain of Tubac covered more than five hundred miles in ten weeks to the mission at San Gabriel, within today's greater Los Angeles.

The feat earned Anza a gala hero's welcome in Mexico City and promotion to lieutenant colonel from the hand of the viceroy. Although Father Garcés convinced a new governor of Sonora that a better trail could be found by ascending the Colorado River north of the Yumas to the latitude of Monterey, momentum lay with Anza. He now set about recruiting colonist families in Sinaloa and Sonora, outfitting the lot, and plotting their way to southern California and then up along the coast range to people San Francisco Bay. This commission too he carried off with élan. Taking leave of Tubac in October 1775, Anza led an exodus of some three hundred men, women, and children, among them a soldier escort, wranglers, scouts, camp hands, and cooks, to San Gabriel in about the same time as his previous trip. Although his second-in-command subsequently conveyed the colonists to San Francisco in 1776, Juan Bautista de Anza had personally chosen the site and unknowingly immortalized himself as the city's founder.

That same year, 1776, José de Gálvez, elevated to minister of the Indies upon his return to Spain, observed with pleasure royal implementation of a long-considered defense project he had made his own. Recognizing that New Spain's far north lacked the wealth to support a full viceregal government, Gálvez urged a unified administrative and military jurisdiction to be known as the *Comandancia General de las Provincias Internas*, the General Command of the Internal Provinces. The governors of the six northernmost colonies—California, Sonora, Nueva Vizcaya, New Mexico, Coahuila, and Texas—would henceforth report not to the viceroy but to a commandant general. The new official would also assume overall command of the cordon of fifteen presidios set out roughly along the thirtieth parallel between the Gulf of California and the Gulf of Mexico. The presidial line, an expedient of the Marqués de Rubí, had been codified in the military regulations, or *Reglamento*, of 1772. Trouble was, virtually no roads going east or west bound the far north. Anza had made a start, joining Sonora and California. Yet he lived to see that linkage break and others come to nothing.

At a lavish reception in the viceroy's palace in early November 1776, powdered and bejeweled guests clustered around an odd attraction. Twice

JUAN BAUTISTA DE ANZA'S SECOND CALIFORNIA EXPEDITION SETS OUT
FROM TUBAC, OCTOBER 1775
Painting by Cal N. Peters.
(Courtesy Tumacacori National Historical Park)

the hero, Juan Bautista de Anza had brought with him to Mexico City the Yuma headman Salvador Palma, his brother, and two other Natives. Palma had been decked out at royal expense in a uniform of shiny blue cloth with gold-trimmed scarlet vest. Three months later, after religious instruction, the four Indians processed for baptism into Mexico City's cavernous cathedral, illuminated by thousands of candles. The service might have been mistaken for a meeting of the Royal Basque Society. The celebrant and all four godfathers were Basque. Lieutenant Colonel Anza and his own godfather, seventy-eight-year-old Pedro Felipe de Anza, bound themselves ritually to Palma and his brother. En route home, the Native foursome appeared again at the center of an ornate ceremonial during their confirmation in the cathedral of Durango. Meanwhile, Carlos III had appointed Juan Bautista de Anza governor of New Mexico.

He had been warned. In high summer 1778, at a meeting in Chihuahua hosted by Teodoro de Croix, first commandant general of the Provincias Internas, Anza listened to a litany of woes from New Mexico's outgoing

241

governor. He noted the facts. Including El Paso and its district, where the lieutenant governor resided, the province, with roughly twenty-five thousand souls dwelling in a recognizably Hispanic way, counted more than ten times the settled population of Texas, the Pimería Alta, or California. Increase in the eighteenth century had been natural for the most part, with little immigration. Collectively, New Mexicans, despite considerable racial mixing and blurring of class, saw themselves in two broad categories— españoles and Indians, the latter mainly inhabitants of twenty Pueblo Indian communities. New Mexico was poor. No mines or cash crops attracted outsiders or made rotations of Indian laborers a valuable commodity. Hence españoles and Indians lived and let live, each allowing the cultural identity of the other. Far removed from centers of power, exempt from sales tax, and battered by neighboring nonsedentary peoples, New Mexicans were a proud, self-dependent, and stubborn lot.

The new executive's caravan clogged the plaza in front of Santa Fe's mud-built palace of the governors in December 1778. Townspeople turned out to stare as this train of Sonoran Basques moved in. Although don Juan and doña Ana María had no children of their

own after seventeen years of marriage, a source of abiding sadness, his older brother Francisco Antonio, married to Ana María's sister, had brought their two young girls. The governor doted on his nieces. Other relatives, retainers, and servants swelled the household. Never before had New Mexicans been governed by a native of the far north, rarely by a criollo. A few years earlier, no one would have imagined such a thing. The Bourbon policy of merit over lineage, which had benefited even José de Gálvez, favored the rapid rise of the second Anza. His reputation as military hero and pathfinder had preceded him. Nevertheless, New Mexicans withheld judgment.

Of his new subjects, none proved a greater source of information than retired captain, tradesman, cartographer, painter, and carver Bernardo de Miera y Pacheco. A peninsular

PORTRAIT SAID TO BE JUAN BAUTISTA DE ANZA THE YOUNGE PAINTING FROM LATE NINETEEN' OR EARLY TWENTIETH CENTURY *(Courtesy Museum of New Mexico, neg. no. 50828)*

Spaniard who had shown up at El Paso in 1743 and subsequently moved to Santa Fe, Miera had served a succession of governors. Better than anyone, he knew the difficult terrain southwest of New Mexico toward Sonora, through which Anza intended to open a more direct trade route between Santa Fe and Arizpe. Miera had also ridden with the little party of Fathers Francisco Atanasio Domínguez and Silvestre Vélez de Escalante in 1776, hoping to find a northern way to Monterey. It still angered him that they had turned back. The new governor set Miera to work drawing a map of the colony, finished in 1779.

Miera's map of upriver New Mexico told the tale. Its legend listed by symbol not only chartered municipalities (Santa Fe, Santa Cruz, and Albuquerque), dispersed settlements of españoles, pueblos of Christian Indians, long-ruined pueblos, springs, and heathen villages, but also settlements destroyed by enemies. A lengthy headnote described how the Spaniards' haphazardly scattered houses invited death and destruction at the hands of Comanche and Apache raiders. To illustrate the point, Miera retold a storied 1760 Comanche assault on colonists in the Taos Valley. The defenders put up a good fight, killing dozens of their assailants, yet all fourteen died and sixty-four of their dependents, young and old, were carried into captivity.

Although Anza had never met a Comanche, he was thoroughly informed about them. First mentioned in the documentary record of New Mexico in 1706, they had since become peerless horsemen and masters of the teeming buffalo herds of the south plains. From the beginning, Comanches had raided and traded in New Mexico, depending on their needs. During the 1760s, a respectful New Mexico governor had achieved a balance of commerce and peace with various elements of the Comanche nation, but his successor failed to maintain it. Commandant General Croix had discussed with Anza the desirability of forming an alliance with Comanches against Apaches. Since then, however, Governor Anza had learned of an obstacle, the hardened Comanche war leader known to New Mexicans as Cuerno Verde, second of that name, for a green horn sticking out of his headdress. These circumstances called for a different approach.

Why not an offensive in force, during late summer, when farmers were assumed to be in their fields and most vulnerable? Anza took personal command of many more men than had ridden on any previous Comanche campaign—nearly eight hundred, a majority of them Pueblo, Ute, and Jicarilla Apache Indians with whom spoils were to be shared equally. They ventured north up the west side of today's San Luis Valley in southern Colorado, then passed through the mountains to the Front Range, where Comanches were not expecting them. Their success resounded. North of present-day Pueblo, on 31 August 1779, the New Mexican force surprised and overran a crowded, half-made Comanche camp. Soon after, an outmaneuvered Cuerno Verde put up a brazen defense and died fighting. Anza rode home with the headdress and cause for promotion to colonel.

Within months of the new governor's signal victory, New Mexicans were complaining about him to Commandant General Croix. In the name of defense, Anza was upsetting their very way of life. Dutifully on his 1779 map, Bernardo de Miera had paraphrased the governor's decree that dispersed colonists consolidate, "building their ample square plazas of at least twenty families each in the form of redoubts, the small ones with two bulwarks, and the large with four." Worse, Anza proposed to raze part of Santa Fe, displacing its residents, and to relocate the plaza with government buildings, presidio, and attached barracks. Croix listened to a large, socially mixed delegation of aggrieved New Mexicans at his new headquarters in Arizpe. Taking their petitions under advisement, he instructed Anza to suspend consolidation for the time being.

On another matter as well, the commandant general reined in his energetic New Mexico governor. Croix wanted the Hopi pueblos, which had broken away in 1680, returned to the Spanish Catholic fold. Aware that they had been weakened by two years of severe drought, Anza proposed to bring the Hopis down from their mesas by force. The king, Croix countered, would never consent. The governor's relief expedition found Hopi families in desperate straits. And some accepted his invitation to resettle in the Rio Grande Valley.

Next, Anza tried unsuccessfully to find that more direct passage from Santa Fe to Arizpe. Although his column got there, campaigning against Gila Apaches en route, the one-way trip took almost six weeks and traversed terrain not conducive to regular travel. Unhappily, the governor's return to New Mexico coincided with the worst outbreak of smallpox on record, locally manifesting a pandemic that overspread much of North America between 1779 and 1781. More than five thousand New Mexicans died.

So drastic a decline in the colony's population suggested to Governor Anza a measure of economy. Smaller church flocks needed fewer shepherds. Hence by attaching diminished congregations to larger ones, the number of 330-peso annual government stipends to New Mexico's Franciscan priests could be reduced proportionately from twenty-six to twenty. That, more than any other grievance the friars had with Anza, propelled their representatives to Arizpe in protest. But since cost cutting was regularly rewarded by Bourbon administrators, the plan appealed to Croix. His own budget had been frozen since 1779, when Spain had joined France in war against Great Britain. The additional funding he had requested for the Provincias Internas had gone instead to Spanish forces operating against British posts in the Mississippi Valley and on the Gulf of Mexico.

Wartime economics also ruptured Anza's road to California. Like other projects, the fully garrisoned presidio, missions, and gifts promised to Salvador Palma's Yuma Indians at the strategic Colorado River crossing had to be scaled back. During the winter of 1780–1781, a grumbling contingent of Spanish settlers and their ravenous animals, along with the disapproving Father Garcés and three other Franciscans, had taken up uneasy residence among some three thousand Yumas. Abuses accrued. When the exasperated Indians rose in the heat of July 1781, killing the missionaries and more than a hundred colonists, government officials blamed Anza and the deceased Garcés for misrepresenting the Yumas' goodwill. The vision of a land bridge to California had once again faded.

Scarcely a month before the Yumas retaliated, forty soldier-colonists and their families en route to settle the pueblo of Los Angeles and a presidio at Santa Barbara had crossed successfully. They were the last. Alta California now depended on the sea. All the same, during the isolated colony's dozen years of trial since 1769, a temperate coastal environment and fertile soils blessed it. Surviving a violent rising of Ipai Indians at San Diego in 1775, Father Serra's mission regime prospered. Substantial stone and adobe walls replaced initial wooden palisades. As producers of surplus foodstuffs, the California missions supplied presidios and towns. Members of Indian families, however, enticed or coerced from their villages into the artificial compounds, lived an average of only twelve years. Outside, the several hundred culturally Hispanic *californios*, taking advantage of an unusually low infant mortality rate, multiplied steadily. The government's later plans to force convict and orphan relocation to California by sea proved disappointing.

In more populous New Mexico, Governor Anza's efforts to enforce laws customarily ignored struck at people's livelihood, especially those drawn to the colony's outer edges. Unlicensed trafficking in sheep, horses, hides and meat, variety goods, and captives with the so-called wild Indians encircling New Mexico — Utes, Navajos, Apaches, and Comanches — had become a lifestyle, upon which Anza meant to impose Bourbon order. Other mandates, for the citizens' own good, simply rankled. Adults who did not possess a firearm were required by the governor's order in 1782 to provide themselves with a bow and twenty-five arrows or face two months in the Santa Fe jail. So as not to discourage travel, Anza directed that families dismantle roadside shrines to victims of Indian attack. When the righteous governor tried to hold Franciscans to strict observance of the ban on personal Indian labor in the missions, friars joined the outcry. Soon enough, disgruntled New Mexicans found a willing ear.

Croix's replacement as commandant general, peninsular Spaniard Felipe de Neve, detested the decorated, American-born Col. Juan Bautista de Anza. After meeting in Arizpe with another delegation from New Mexico, he wrote early in 1784 to José de Gálvez, accusing Anza of incompetence and recommending his dismissal. Furthermore, Neve demanded that Anza expunge from his service record that he had opened the overland road to California and had defeated Cuerno Verde. Since the next governor appointed in due course never reached New Mexico, Anza, who had requested reassignment, continued in office reluctantly. After Neve's death later in 1784, a succeeding commandant general set the record straight.

Anza's most enduring achievement was yet to come—a treaty of peace and commerce with the Comanche nation. Cuerno Verde's death had begun the process. Drought, smallpox, and worrisome intercourse between Anglo Americans and Plains Indian rivals heightened Comanche initiative. Assassination of an heir to Cuerno Verde and the insistence of New Mexico's governor in the summer of 1785 that he treat ultimately with a representative of the entire nation led to a huge Comanche rendezvous on the Arkansas River that fall. Widely hailed, Ecueracapa, by the authority of his people, would talk as an equal with Anza about formal commerce.

Neither lost face. The ritual solemnity of this midwinter summit eased now and again into spontaneous shows of emotion. With military personnel, the Santa Fe town council, and leading citizens arrayed in the cold, Ecueracapa dismounted in front of the governor's palace and greeted Anza for more than ten minutes. The tense business inside of reconciling Comanche and Ute leaders ended auspiciously in a ritual exchange of garments. Later, the concourse wended its way eastward, surely through snow, to the symbolic site agreed upon earlier by emissaries. The gateway pueblo of Pecos, long a target of Comanche raids, in February 1786 looked out upon a scene of fervent peacemaking. A crowd of Comanches, estimated at over two hundred, mobbed the Spanish governor with such intimate expressions of affection that his staff thought them unbefitting. Anza did not object.

Terms of the treaty called for cessation of hostilities and a new and lasting peace. Comanches were allowed to move closer to New Mexico. They would enjoy safe passage through Pecos to Santa Fe, which implied a regular distribution of gifts and free trade at Pecos. In turn, Comanches pledged to join Spaniards as allies in the war against common Apache enemies. And finally, Anza agreed to bestow on Ecueracapa symbols of authority to certify the peace to Comanches not present. Next day, an inaugural trade fair went off splendidly. As surety, late that spring, the Comanche chief sent his twenty-year-old third son to Anza for a Spanish education. Before the governor left New Mexico, he evidently arranged for the young man's schooling in Mexico City. More remarkable, long after the passing of Anza and Ecueracapa, the Comanche peace of 1786 endured.

Although the governor's subsequent treaty legalizing commerce with Navajos and engaging them against Gila Apaches did not last, Anza could credit a sharp decline in violent deaths to the colony's four allied tribes: Comanches, Jicarilla Apaches, Utes, and Navajos. A new viceroy, with earlier experience in the far north, codified in 1786 instructions for peace by purchase, reminiscent of the waning years of the Chichimeca War two centuries before. Again, accounts for Indian affairs listed piles and crates of raw sugar cones, hard trade bread, ribbons, blankets, hats, and metal tools in government warehouses at Santa Fe and elsewhere. From Texas to California, the last decade of the eighteenth century and the first of the nineteenth were years of relative prosperity as populations recovered, flocks and herds swelled, small industries like weaving started up, and trade of all kinds flourished.

The talk of making him governor of Texas or transferring him to Spain as colonel came to nothing. When finally, in November 1787, Anza knocked the dust of Santa Fe off his boots, he was leaving behind his older brother Francisco Antonio, who had died two years earlier. With the rest of his Basque household, don Juan made for Sonora, where he returned to active duty as commander of the presidio at Tucson and chief of military operations. Late the following year in Arizpe, anticipating a move to the presidio of San Miguel de Horcasitas in central Sonora, he sent doña Ana María, her widowed sister, and his two favorite nieces, now teenagers, ahead with an escort. He promised to follow in a few days. It was the last time they saw him. At midnight on 19 December 1788, Juan Bautista de Anza the younger, age fifty-two, died. The next day, while riders went to bring back his family, he was buried in the church at Arizpe.

News lagged. In November 1784, Governor Anza had reported to the commandant general that he had collected from New Mexicans 3,677 pesos in contributions to the war effort against Great Britain, unaware that diplomats in Paris had ended hostilities in due form more than a year earlier. By treaty, Great Britain had recognized the independence of its former colonies south of Canada, now the United States of America. Although Anza had been warned early in his governorship to watch for unauthorized Europeans on New Mexico's borders, he could not have foreseen the shadow these erstwhile British colonials would cast across the far north. A mere decade after Anza's death, however, in 1798, the governor of Spanish Louisiana did. Apropos of these Anglo Americans, Manuel Gayoso de Lemos had a vision:

> First, they become acquainted with the Indians, trade with them, and afterwards engage in contraband trade with the natives of Mexico. Some stay in the territories. . . . They are settled in sufficient numbers so that they will establish their customs, laws, and religion. They will form independent states, aggregating themselves to the Federal Union, which will not refuse to receive them, and progressively they will go as far as the Pacific Ocean.

Indeed they would, little appreciating that everything they sought others had sought before them.

Essay on Sources

Late in the twentieth century and early in the twenty-first, Juan Bautista de Anza, father and son, have a new champion who, like them, is of Basque ancestry. National Park Service historian Donald T. Garate is writing their biographies in two volumes of the University of Nevada Press Basque Series. Don generously provided me with a copy of his manuscript for the first volume, *Juan Bautista de Anza: Basque Explorer in the New World,* upon which I relied heavily. The book appeared subsequently in 2003. The author is at present working on the second volume. Garate's previous pertinent publications include "Who Named Arizona? The Basque Connection," *Journal of Arizona History* 40 (spring 1999): 53–82, and "Basque Ethnic Connections and the Expeditions of Juan Bautista de Anza," *Colonial Latin American Historical Review* 4 (winter 1995): 71–91. Seeking at the same time to introduce other scholars and enthusiasts of the Anzas to the culture of Sonora, Garate has been the moving force behind a series of World Anza Conferences held annually since 1996, most often in and around Arizpe, where the second Anza lies buried.

An older study, treating the elder Anza's special relationship with the Jesuits of Sonora, is Peter M. Dunne, "Captain Anza and the Case of Father Campos," *Mid-America* 23 (1941): 45–60. On military matters, the captain speaks for himself in "Juan Bautista de Anza Discusses Apache and Seri Depredations and the Need for a Presidio at Terrenate (1729–1735)," in *The Presidio and Militia on the Northern Frontier of New Spain: A Documentary History*, ed. Charles W. Polzer and Thomas E. Sheridan, vol. 2, part 1, *The Californias and Sinaloa-Sonora, 1700–1765* (Tucson: University of Arizona Press, 1997), 303–12.

Until we have Garate's inclusive biography of the second Anza, he will remain divided between Sonora, California, and New Mexico. While based in Sonora, he plays a prominent role in John L. Kessell, *Friars, Soldiers, and Reformers: Hispanic Arizona and the Sonora Mission Frontier, 1767–1856* (Tucson: University of Arizona Press, 1976). And from his post at Tubac, he takes a dim view in Kessell, ed., "Anza Damns the Missions: A Spanish Soldier's Criticism of Indian Policy, 1772," *Journal of Arizona History* 13 (spring 1972): 53–63.

Still at the head of the California list is Herbert Eugene Bolton's breezy *Outpost of Empire: The Story of the Founding of San Francisco* (New York: Knopf, 1931), supplemented by the diaries and other primary sources published in Bolton, ed., *Anza's California Expeditions*, 5 vols. (Berkeley: University of California Press, 1930). A library of popular retellings, authorization by Congress in 1990 of the Juan Bautista de Anza National Historic Trail (with its own newsletter, *Noticias de Anza*), and the launching in 1998 and recent development of the Web de Anza (http://anza.uoregon.edu) have made Anza's two-phase overland passage to California by far the best-known episode in the Spanish colonial history of the American Southwest.

Serving as New Mexico's governor for a tumultuous decade was notably hard on Anza. Alfred Barnaby Thomas, ed., *Forgotten Frontiers: A Study of the Spanish Indian Policy of Don Juan Bautista de Anza, Governor of New Mexico, 1777–1787* (Norman: University of Oklahoma Press, 1932), offers historical background and translated documents about Anza's dealings with Indian groups surrounding the colony. Rick Hendricks, "Church-State Relations in Anza's New Mexico, 1777–1787," *Catholic Southwest* 9 (1998):

24–42, explains how the governor offended New Mexico's Franciscan missionaries. The intended impact of administrative, judicial, military, and social reforms on all New Mexicans during the reign of Carlos III is examined in considerable detail by Carlos R. Herrera, "The King's Governor: Juan Bautista de Anza and Bourbon New Mexico in the Era of Imperial Reform, 1778–1788" (Ph.D. dissertation, University of New Mexico, 2000). Why the Bourbons' best-laid plans had so little effect, particularly on the colony's fringe populations, is evident in James F. Brooks, *Captives and Cousins: Slavery, Kinship, and Community in the Southwest Borderlands* (Chapel Hill: University of North Carolina Press, 2002).

Finally, to place the active careers of Juan Bautista de Anza, father and son, in the wider world of Spain's three-century-long colonial presence in North America, readers may wish to consult the text, notes, and bibliographies of David J. Weber, *The Spanish Frontier in North America* (New Haven, Conn.: Yale University Press, 1992), and John L. Kessell, *Spain in the Southwest: A Narrative History of Colonial New Mexico, Arizona, Texas, and California* (Norman: University of Oklahoma, 2002).

"To Stop Captain Merry"[1]

SPANISH EFFORTS TO INTERCEPT LEWIS AND CLARK

John L. Kessell

Although long a widower and reportedly somewhat slovenly in his dress, the august and learned third president of the United States bespoke confidence. This late fall day in 1802, Thomas Jefferson had invited Spain's minister to the United States, the marqués de Casa Yrujo (who previously had found Jefferson a cook), to the President's House at Washington. The two men sparred amiably. Then, with feigned nonchalance, Jefferson asked his guest a question. Would his majesty King Carlos take offense if the United States sent a small caravan of travelers to explore the course of the Missouri River with "no other view than the advancement of the geography?"

Yes, as a matter of fact, he would, replied the marqués. But why on earth, Jefferson wanted to know. The Spaniard did not flinch. He lectured the president about the folly of searching further for the fabled Northwest Passage "sought with so much anxiety by the most famous navigators of all the nations in the last two centuries." Later, reporting the exchange to Madrid, Casa Yrujo confided, "The President has been all his life a man of letters,

Professor Emeritus and founding editor of the Vargas Project at the University of New Mexico, John L. Kessell is author of *Spain in the Southwest: A Narrative History of Colonial New Mexico, Arizona, Texas, and California* (Norman: University of Oklahoma Press, 2002). He wishes to thank Primedia History Magazine Group for permission to publish here an annotated version of this article, which appeared as "Mission to Stop Lewis and Clark," *The Quarterly Journal of Military History* 18 (spring 2006): 6–14.

very speculative and a lover of glory, and it would be possible he might attempt to perpetuate the fame of his administration . . . by discovering . . . the way by which the Americans may some day extend their population and their influence up to the coasts of the South Sea [the Pacific]." Jefferson had not mentioned that he and his private secretary, Meriwether Lewis, anticipating a congressional appropriation, had already calculated the costs of such an expedition.[2]

For at least twenty years, Thomas Jefferson had visualized a route, by divine providence a waterway, across western North America to the Pacific. But European affairs seemed always to intrude. Most recently, in 1801, Napoleon had quietly bullied Spain into ceding Louisiana back to France. The rumors alarmed Jefferson. The United States wanted the vast, unmapped territory to reside in Spain's relatively weak domain, rather than pass to France, or be wrested away by Great Britain. In the vague hope that the United States might buy at least New Orleans, the president dispatched James Monroe to Paris. He then sent a confidential request to Congress, justifying Captain Lewis's mission in commercial terms. Jefferson also managed to obtain passports from the British and French ministers, but not from the marqués de Casa Yrujo. To Lewis the president told a half-truth: all three governments had been duly informed of his expedition and "such assurances given them as to it's objects, as we trust will satisfy them."[3]

With jarring clairvoyance, Spaniards had anticipated Jefferson. Fully fifteen years earlier, in 1788, the viceroy of New Spain, Manuel Antonio Flores, foresaw Lewis and Clark. The Americans, he believed, already lusted for a port on the Pacific. To make that happen, the United States, in Flores's words, would "try to sustain it [the port] by crossing the immense land of this continent above our possessions of Texas, New Mexico, and the Californias . . . and, in truth, it [the United States] would obtain the richest trade of Great China and India if it were to succeed in establishing a colony on the west coasts of America."[4]

When weather, yellow fever, and slave revolts in the Caribbean dashed Napoleon's dream of restoring French dominion in North America, he offered suddenly to sell not only New Orleans but all of Louisiana, lower and upper, extending north beyond St. Louis and westward from the Mississippi to who knew how far. Jefferson leapt at the chance. Before Lewis departed Washington in midsummer 1803, he knew of the startling deal. The Spanish governor at St. Louis wanted confirmation. Until word arrived from New

Orleans, he advised Lewis and party to remain on the American side of the Mississippi.

In early October 1803, an overly anxious Lewis had written Jefferson about a harebrained plan that must have shaken the president's confidence in his young protégé. Instead of wasting time in camp on the Mississippi, Lewis reckoned he would "make a tour this winter on horseback of some hundred miles through the most interesting portion of the country adjoining my winter establishment; perhaps it may be up the Canceze [Kansas] River and towards Santafee." He only wanted to help. He thought an eye-opening preview of western lands might silence congressional opponents of the expedition. Not until January 1804 did Lewis receive Jefferson's stern veto. "The object of your mission," the president scolded his captain, "is single, the direct water communication from sea to sea formed by the bed of the Missouri & perhaps the Oregon."[5]

The Missouri River, or Big Muddy, twenty-four hundred miles long, courses a greater distance than the Mississippi, into which it flows just above St. Louis. Only partially traced on maps of Jefferson's time, the river emerged out of the blank reaches of the northern Great Plains. Today, one can follow its bold sweep upriver west across Missouri, then northwest to clip Kansas, form the Nebraska-Iowa boundary, cut South Dakota in two, define a quarter of North Dakota, and finally straighten out west again across Montana to the base of the Rocky Mountains, about which Lewis and Clark had not a clue. The American president wished to know what marvels of nature lay along the river's vast drainage and beyond. Spanish claims be damned.

Already in 1804, a spy at New Orleans not only confirmed to Spanish authorities what Jefferson was up to, but also suggested what they should do about it. James Wilkinson, commanding U.S. general in the West, who at the same time collected pay from Spain as secret Agent 13, admonished the Spaniards that "An express ought immediately to be sent to the governor of Santa Fé, and another to the captain-general of Chihuaga [Chihuahua], in order that they may detach a sufficient body of chasseurs [light cavalry] to intercept Captain Lewis and his party, who are on the Missouri River, and force them to retire or take them prisoners."[6]

* * * *

Within the mud-built walls of Santa Fe's Palace of the Governors—some two thousand miles west and a little south of the Americans' as yet unloved capital on the Potomac—don Fernando de Chacón, Spain's ailing governor of New

Mexico, pondered his response. The dispatch from Com. Gen. Nemesio Salcedo, dated 3 May 1804, in Chihuahua, enclosed an urgent warning from New Orleans. Spain's agent for the transfer of Louisiana had events backward. He believed, incorrectly, that Jefferson had hastily planned Captain Lewis's trespass only after the U.S. purchase of Louisiana. "This step," he advised, "on the part of the United States at the same time that it took possession of the province of Louisiana; its haste to instruct itself and to explore the course of the Missouri whose origin they claim belongs to them, extending their designs as far as the South Sea [Pacific], forces us necessarily to become active and hasten . . . to cut off the gigantic steps of our neighbors . . . to arrest Captain Merry Weather and his party, which cannot help but pass through the [Native] nations neighboring New Mexico, its presidios or *rancherías*."[7]

Distance and poor judgment favored Lewis. Commandant General Salcedo, an intense, middle-sized man of stern countenance, knew he would be blamed. Salcedo's domain, the thinly inhabited Eastern Internal Provinces, sprawled from the Gulf of Mexico to the Rocky Mountains, four times bigger than present-day Texas. First, he reprimanded the New Orleans agent, who should never have sent his warning cross-country to Chihuahua. Conveying the message through Havana to Vera Cruz by sea and north by courier on the Camino Real would have been faster. Refusing to reshuffle priorities, the commandant general next ordered New Mexico's governor to carry on his military operations against warring Navajos.

As for "Captain Merry," Salcedo wanted Chacón to arrange with Comanche and other Indian allies for a Spanish party to reconnoiter eastward as far as the Missouri's near bank. The Indians would be well compensated for any useful information they provided. If veteran scout Pedro Vial would care to join the enterprise and keep a diary, so much the better. In sum, wrote Salcedo, "Nothing would be more useful than the apprehension of Merry, and even though I realize it is not an easy undertaking, chance might proportion things in such a way that it might be successful."

Now time and chance conspired. Governor Chacón decided on a gambit. He would wait and see what Indians friendly to Spain had to

SIGNATURE OF
FERNANDO DE
CHACÓN

254

say, which took the rest of May and all of June and July 1804. If he learned nothing that way, which evidently he did not, then he would organize a reconnaissance as far as the Missouri. So as not to arouse Lewis's suspicions, the Spanish party would set out under guise of searching for a fabled hill of gold in Comanche country.[9]

A few years earlier, Salcedo's predecessor as commandant general had disapproved of certain footloose, unattached frontiersmen who kept company with Indians, "since," in his words, "this class of wandering men love greatly the opportunity that facilitates their living among the barbarians in order to give free rein to their passions."[10] European morality aside, these were the very men Spain relied on to gather information about or confront Jefferson's Corps of Discovery. For that matter, Lewis and Clark's voyageurs fit the same mold. Pedro Vial, a Frenchman by birth, and thus always suspect in Spanish eyes, knew the Native peoples and trails of middle North America better than any man alive. His junior partner in the search for Merry possessed another valuable if rusty skill. He spoke English. José Jarvet had shed among Indians his Philadelphia Presbyterian upbringing and surname (perhaps Harvey) and boasted at least one Pawnee son.

Trailing north from Santa Fe, Vial, Jarvet, and soldiers from the local garrison, or presidio, added militiamen and Pueblo Indians at Taos until their party numbered fifty-two, almost precisely the size of Lewis's company at the time. It was early August 1804. Ten weeks prior, on 21 May, Lewis, his trusted co-commander Lt. William Clark, and a dozen soldiers, along with assorted hunters, boatmen, and interpreters, had pushed off from St. Charles near the mouth of the Missouri in a custom-built, cumbersome, fifty-five-foot keel boat and two pirogues.

No one worried much about Spaniards. On 3 August, Clark noted in his journal what an interpreter had told him, "that it will take a man 25 Days to go to St. a fee [Santa Fe] pass, the heads of Arkansas, round the Kansas head, across Some mountains from the top of which the City may be Seen." Spaniards had invited Indians from the Missouri to trade with them, and some Frenchmen and a few Pawnees had gone to Santa Fe that summer.[11] Rowing, poling, hauling, and occasionally sailing against the mighty Missouri's five-mile-an-hour current, the Americans had ascended well beyond the entry of the Platte River. They had covered over seven hundred miles.

The New Mexicans moved faster. On land they struck northeast, river hopping from the Purgatoire to the Arkansas to the Río Chato, or Platte. The first week in September, Pawnees feted them at a village in today's south-central Nebraska, seven hundred miles from Santa Fe. There, Vial conversed with "about twenty Frenchmen" who verified that Americans had taken possession of Louisiana. Traders in American employ, loaded with gifts for the Indians of the upper Missouri, had passed by. Worse, these interlopers were urging chiefs to surrender Spanish peace medals and all other ties with Spain. "I have charged the aforementioned chiefs of the country," wrote Vial in his diary, "not to give up the medals or patents, telling them they still do not know the Americans but in the future they will."[12]

Had the Frenchmen's intelligence been clearer to Vial, he and his men might have spurred north for two days and overtaken the waterborne Captain Lewis. Instead, while Vial addressed Pawnee and Oto principal men gathered in a council house on 15 September 1804, Lewis, perhaps 150 miles away, marveled at the fleetness of the white-tailed jackrabbit, a new species to him, whose leaps he measured the day before at twenty-one feet. A few days later, farther up the Missouri, Clark noted that Indians displayed the "Flags of Spane & the one we gave them yesterday." Vial, in the name of Governor Chacón, presented the Pawnee head chief a Spanish uniform with long coat and three-cornered hat, but he learned nothing to confirm the presence of Lewis and Clark. To cement further relations with the Pawnees, who had refused American medals and flags, Vial and Jarvet escorted another chief and eleven of his men back to Santa Fe, where all arrived on 5 November. Chacón forthwith presented the Pawnee leader with "gifts of clothing, a horse, rifle, powder, bullets, and a medal bearing the royal bust."[13]

Meanwhile, in Spain, Jefferson's emissary James Monroe offended the Spanish court. He proposed as the western boundary of Louisiana the Rio Grande all the way to its source in present-day southern Colorado. If Spanish ministers studied an available, up-to-date 1802 map of North America, they would have recognized that Monroe's "ambitious and exorbitant" claim would place New Mexico's capital in American territory. The resulting royal order set off a second probe for Lewis and Clark.

A younger man would take responsibility. In late March 1805, Fernando de Chacón surrendered the governorship of New Mexico to no-nonsense Lt. Col. Joaquín del Real Alencaster. The new governor, attempting to rein in semi-legal intercourse of New Mexicans with surrounding heathen Indians, barely averted a rebellion. At the same time, he planned the next sally "to acquire news and knowledge of the state of Captain Merri's expedition."[14]

In mid-August 1805, Joseph Whitehouse with Lewis and Clark in present-day Beaverhead County, Montana, understood Shoshones to say that Spaniards had a settlement only eight days south, "but that they have very little trade with them." Yet the men noticed horses with Spanish brands, mules obtained from Spaniards, a Spanish bridle, and "sundry other articles." The Indians informed Lewis, who had spent the day smoking with them, "that they could pass to the Spaniards by way of the yellowstone river in 10 days." They were not friends, however, since Spaniards forbade them to have guns or ammunition.[15]

Whatever the distance, real or imagined, Commandant General Salcedo's mistaken geographical notion that the Missouri bent menacingly southward toward New Mexico lent urgency to his instructions. Governor Real Alencaster must make every effort to cement relations with the Pawnees and other Indian nations, inviting their chiefs every year to Santa Fe for gifts and imbuing them with "a horror" of Englishmen and Americans. Thus, reasoned Salcedo, "when Captain Merri's expedition returns . . . they will intercept it, apprehending its members," and thereby eliminate the need to station Spanish troops on the Missouri. The Indians should be encouraged, at the very least, to take from the Americans any strong boxes and papers they might be carrying. That vision would have sent shudders down Jefferson's spine.

Despite Real Alencaster's detailed instructions, the second Vial-Jarvet parry came to sudden grief. About one hundred strong, the New Mexicans had camped on 5 November 1805, near the junction of the Purgatoire and Arkansas rivers in southeastern Colorado. Accompanying them were several foreigners, including trappers Baptiste LaLande and Laurent Durocher and American carpenter James Purcell, whom the governor had dispatched to St. Charles to spy on Americans. Signs were everywhere of numerous unidentified Indians. Vial put the camp on alert.

At midnight on the sixth, the unknown assailants attacked, using firearms, not bows, and yelling in a language no one recognized. They went straight for the New Mexicans' horses. While the defenders scattered in the dark to recover their animals three different times, the attackers pillaged the encampment, getting away with most of the supplies and gifts. After three hours of fighting, "we rushed them," wrote Vial, "until they were thrown into the river, shrieking, from which it is thought some harm was done them." But they came again, on foot and on horseback. Fully dressed in white, red, and blue with cloths tied on their heads, the unrecognized enemy harassed the retreating column for seven or eight miles, before finally breaking off and disappearing. Back in Santa Fe, Vial recommended a Spanish fort on the Arkansas, and Governor Real Alencaster saw in the aborted mission the evil hand of the United States.[16]

Half a continent to the northwest, on the very day the second Spanish counter-expedition began its retreat from the junction of the Purgatoire and Arkansas—7 November 1805—the fog was burning off over the lower Columbia River. As Lewis and Clark's men put full strength of their arms and backs into paddling canoes that raced with the river's current, a distant sight met their eyes. "Great joy . . . we are in *View* of the *Ocian*," proclaimed William Clark. No matter that it was really the Columbia estuary; they had spanned the Trans-Mississippi West. Despite the damp and tedious winter that lay before them in camp near present-day Astoria, Oregon, and a return who knew how, they had justified their president's faith.[17]

* * * *

Neither Jefferson nor Real Alencaster knew where Lewis and Clark were. No one in the civilized world did. Spain's two bootless attempts to gain intelligence about or an encounter with the outbound Americans did not, however, discourage further efforts. To stop Captain Merry would demonstrate to the Indian nations of the Great Plains that Spaniards were capable of policing the territories they claimed. Governor Real Alencaster, through Vial, Jarvet, and others, reminded Indian leaders that Spaniards as allies did not covet their lands, but Americans did. From Mexico City he ordered better quality medals and silver-headed canes, "similar to the medals and walking canes that the Americans have started to give them." The Kiowas, for example, did not much like the Spanish medals they received. "They want large and better engraved ones. . . . and to regale them I need more and finer things," the Spanish governor pleaded.[1]

He also asked for more troops, both to impress Spain's Native allies and to punish hostile bands. Moreover, salaried interpreter-agents should be sent out to live with the Pawnees and other nations of the plains. A Spanish fort on the Arkansas, Pedro Vial's suggestion, also would help keep the Indians within Spain's sphere of trade and influence. Finally, Governor Real Alencaster himself stood ready to lead an expedition upon Salcedo's approval. Unwilling to wait for the commandant general's reply, Real Alencaster sent Vial and Jarvet out again in April 1806, this time with three hundred men. Most were poor militiamen from La Cañada and Taos, just the sort

258

who resented the governor's strict rule. Besides, it was time for planting. Not far from home, they mutinied, deserting and streaming back to their villages. Disgusted, Salcedo approved Real Alencaster's discipline of conducting every tenth deserter to Santa Fe for trial.[19]

The same day the commandant general wrote from Chihuahua, 18 July 1806, the returning Captain Lewis and a small exploring party rode toward the Marias River beside vast, lumbering herds of buffalo in present-day northern Montana. "The musquetoes," Lewis had complained three days earlier, "continue to infest us in such manner that we can scarcely exist . . . my dog even howls with the torture he experiences from them."[20]

Never were mosquitos that bad in Santa Fe. Still, there was enough to complain about, especially through the eyes of a decorated, high-born Spanish career officer. They called this a capital? Most New Mexicans, so far as he could determine, lived in squalor like savages. Yet Salcedo had finally heeded Governor Real Alencaster's petitions, dispatching to Santa Fe in April 1806 Lt. Facundo Melgares and sixty Spanish dragoons. Short and thickly built, the thirty-year-old Melgares swaggered by nature. He had an uncle on the high court of New Spain, and his father-in-law served as the commandant general's adjutant.[21]

Melgares was present in May when the humiliated Pedro Vial and José Jarvet appeared before the governor to report on their third failed mission. Perhaps it was the Spanish lieutenant who suggested rounding up every tenth deserter for punishment. The two professional military men, Lieutenant Colonel Real Alencaster and Lieutenant Melgares, conferred earnestly about the next expedition, intending to mount a genuine show of force to awe Spain's Native allies. The two appeared together about town in the governor's carriage.

SIGNATURE OF
FACUNDO MELGARES

Billeting sixty dragoons in Santa Fe, with its population of just over five thousand, surely resulted in social excitement and endless fandangos. Always the bon vivant, Melgares took the lead.

The lieutenant had brought with him a communiqué from Salcedo to Governor Real Alencaster, along with relevant earlier correspondence copied at Chihuahua on 12 April 1806. The American president, unmoved by formal protests from Spain, simply insisted on violating Spanish sovereignty under the guise of scientific exploration. A letter of the previous July from the Spanish agent in New Orleans to the minister of state in Madrid lamented the unsuccessful efforts to halt the Missouri River exploration "under command of Captain Lewis Merry Whether, who already has made several shipments of plants, rocks, fossils, skins, and other curiosities of natural history, which are at present in possession of the Governor of this territory [Louisiana] to be sent opportunely to the President with another lot of live animals and birds that are to arrive within a few days."[22]

Of more immediate concern, however, was Jefferson's Red River probe, organized by William Dunbar and led by surveyor Thomas Freeman and botanist Peter Custis. Entering from the Mississippi in present-day Louisiana, they would travel up the Red, trending northwesterly along today's boundary between Oklahoma and Texas, cross the latter's panhandle, and threaten New Mexico. That, Salcedo argued, should not be permitted. Hence, Melgares's expedition must first cross the plains to the southeast, descend the Red, and with any luck arrest or turn back the Freeman-Custis party before proceeding north to the Arkansas and from there to the Pawnees.

Earlier in 1806, Manuel Godoy, the power behind the throne in Madrid, had reprimanded Salcedo regarding Lewis and Clark. The king wished to know why he had not been kept informed of the expedition's progress. "Likewise," wrote Godoy, "His Majesty desires to know how the said expedition has been permitted in territory of his domains, since it is well known that its designs should cause suspicion even though disguised with the appearance of being purely scientific."[23]

Melgares's impressive command—105 soldiers, dragoons and presidials; 400 New Mexican militiamen, and 100 Indian allies—would depart Santa Fe on 15 June 1806. Vial and Jarvet, despite their recent disgrace, likely went along as scouts. Lieutenant Melgares petitioned the governor to name Franciscan missionary José Pereyro chaplain, proffering a mule to carry the friar's religious paraphernalia and provisions.[24]

Toward the end of July, another Spanish force operating out of Nacogdoches in east Texas did intercept and block Freeman and Custis, who had ascended the Red River more than six hundred miles. The long column from New Mexico, evidently pressed hard by Melgares, had already veered north for the Arkansas River.

If we are to believe the subsequent account of Lt. Zebulon Montgomery Pike, who was taken into Spanish custody the following year, Melgares had faced down a mutiny. Weakened by short rations and exhaustion, someone dared question the Spanish lieutenant. Where was the expedition going?

"To this he haughtily replied, 'wherever his horse led him.'" Presented a few days later with a petition to return home, allegedly bearing the signatures or marks of two hundred New Mexican militiamen, Melgares exploded. "He halted immediately," wrote Pike, "and caused his dragoons to erect a gallows; then beat to arms. The troops fell in: he separated the *petitioners* from the others, then took the man who had presented the petition, tied him up, and gave him 50 lashes, and threatened to put to death, on the gallows erected, any man who should dare to grumble. This effectually silenced them."[25]

Pike liked Lieutenant Melgares, a true royalist, gallant, gracious, and generous to his own kind. As fellow officers, the two dined together in 1807, drank, and admired the comely women of New Mexico and Chihuahua, conversing eagerly in a mix of French and Spanish. Although Melgares's high style of travel offended Pike's Protestant sensibilities, the American could not help marveling. The Spanish lieutenant's "mode of living, was superior to any thing we have an idea of in our army; having eight mules loaded with his common camp equipage, wines, confectionary, &c."[26]

In 1806, however, before he had met Lieutenant Melgares and become his apologist, Pike had cast the Spaniard's summer expedition of that year in a somewhat different light. About 1 August, Melgares had ordered more than two hundred of his men to make camp on the Arkansas, evidently because Indians had stolen their reserve horses and mules. The rest, with or without Melgares, kept going, arriving late that month or early in September at the Pawnees' principal village on the south bank of the Republican River in extreme south-central Nebraska.

At the same time, on the near bank of the Missouri River, three hundred miles to the east, a group of riders was forming. Twenty-seven-year-old Lieutenant Pike commanded the company, his "Dam'd set of Rascels." A protégé of double-dealing Gen. James Wilkinson,

ZEBULON MONTGOMERY PIKE
Painting by Charles Wilson Peale
(Courtesy Independence National
Historical Park)

261

Pike had reconnoitered the upper Mississippi in 1805. Now, Wilkinson had instructed him to convey some Osage and Pawnee Indians home, help make peace between Kansas and Osages, perhaps contact Comanches, and explore the Arkansas and Red rivers—in short, do a bit of spying.[27]

Pike arrived at the same Pawnee village three or four weeks after Melgares's troops had left, reporting to U.S. secretary of war Henry Dearborn and to Wilkinson that the Pawnees displayed both Spanish and American flags. The Spanish commander, Pike told Dearborn, had remained on the Arkansas with the main body of his force. A lesser official, perhaps an ensign, had presented the Pawnees with documents of alliance issued in Santa Fe on 15 June 1806 and signed by Real Alencaster. These, the Indians had shown to Pike. "The chief further informed me, that the officer who commanded said party, was too young to hold councils, &c. . . . but that in the spring his superior would be here, and teach the Indians what was good for them." The Indians, who estimated the Spanish force at three hundred, informed Pike that the Spaniards had mustaches and whiskers, drums, and all the weapons of regular infantry and cavalry. Addressing Wilkinson, Pike presumed that the general would "be struck with some surprize, to perceive that so large a party of Spanish troops have been so lately in our territory."[28]

From the Pawnee village to where the Platte empties into the Missouri is, by the crow's flight, just over 150 miles. Lewis and Clark, anxiously en route home, had passed that place on 9 September 1806, likely while the Pawnees still entertained Melgares's bearded Spaniards. The next day, the returning Corps of Discovery learned from water-bound traders that Lieutenant Pike had set out from St. Louis to explore the Arkansas and Red rivers. Pike later claimed that the Melgares expedition had wanted to press on eastward, but the Pawnees had discouraged them.

As the tired and dispirited force from New Mexico retreated to Santa Fe, Captain Lewis recognized an old army buddy on a boat headed up the Missouri. John McClallen was full of a trading scheme to ascend the Platte, strike overland for Santa Fe, and cash in on the gold and silver he imagined awaited him there. Besides bluster, McClallen also made free with chocolate, whiskey, and news.

He told Lewis that Americans were worried. The president's Corps of Discovery had been gone more than two years. In the words of member John Ordway, "Mr. Mclanen informed us that the people in general in the United States were concerned about us as they had heard that we were all killed then again they heard that the Spanyards had us in the mines &c."[29]

Despite the boisterous folks of St. Louis who swarmed the returning heroes, Lewis found time to write to President Jefferson later the same day, 23 September 1806. "It is with pleasure that I anounce to you the safe arrival of myself and party at 12 Oclk. today at this place with our papers and baggage." Exhilarated, he poured forth a grand plan to harvest the inexhaustible beaver and otter furs of the upper Missouri and Columbia drainages and ship them from the Columbia's mouth direct to Canton in China. That would cut out the British, who were required by mercantile law to consign their furs first to London then transship them around Africa to China. Spanish objections to an American presence at the mouth of the Columbia seemed not to concern Meriwether Lewis.[30]

In Philadelphia, the marqués de Casa Yrujo, still Spain's minister to the United States, cursed news of the Americans' success. He reminded Madrid of his warning three years earlier. Yet, not all was lost. The outrageous trespass of Lewis and Clark on Spanish territory, Casa Yrujo believed, "will not immediately provide this government with any other advantages than the glory of having accomplished it." Spain must defend the mouth of the Columbia and "pluck the fruit from their discoveries," reserving for Spanish interests the precious China trade. Portly King Carlos, whose court never could envision the endless expanse of North America, chided those New World officials who had failed to stop Captain Merry, adding, "and they are ordered anew to do so if, as expected, the United States repeats the exploration."[31]

But the genie was out of the bottle. Thomas Jefferson already visualized an American West stretching to the Pacific.

Notes

1. Nemesio Salcedo to Joaquín Real Alencaster, Chihuahua, 11 February 1806, Twitchell doc. 1967, Spanish Archives of New Mexico II, New Mexico State Records Center and Archives [hereafter doc. T-number, SANM II]. This document is partially translated in Noel M. Loomis and Abraham P. Nasatir, *Pedro Vial and the Roads to Santa Fe* (Norman: University of Oklahoma Press, 1967), 202–3.
2. Casa Yrujo to Pedro Cevallos, Washington, 2 December 1802, in *Letters of the Lewis and Clark Expedition with Related Documents, 1783–1854*, ed. Donald Jackson, 2 vols., 2d ed. (Urbana: University of Illinois Press, 1978), 1:4–6. Jackson acknowledges his use of translations from A[braham]. P. Nasatir, ed., *Before Lewis and Clark: Documents Illustrating the History of the Missouri, 1785–1804*, 2 vols. (St. Louis: St. Louis Historical Documents Foundation, 1952).

   By far the most complete coverage to date of Spain's unsuccessful effort to thwart Lewis and Clark appears in Warren L. Cook's masterful *Flood Tide of Empire:*

Spain and the Pacific Northwest, 1543–1819, Yale Western Americana Series (New Haven, Conn.: Yale University Press, 1973), 446–90, wherein he comments, "Closer examination of the extant documentation suggests . . . that the Spanish made repeated efforts of considerable magnitude to intercept Lewis and Clark, and came surprisingly and dangerously close to achieving their objective" (pp. 460–61 n. 72). See also Stephen E. Ambrose, *Undaunted Courage: Meriwether Lewis, Thomas Jefferson, and the Opening of the American West* (New York: Touchstone, 1997), 77–78, 344–45.

3. Jefferson's Instructions to Lewis, Washington, 20 June 1803, in *Letters of the Lewis and Clark Expedition*, ed. Jackson, 1:61. Irregular spelling and grammar in English quotations have been retained without inserting [*sic*].

4. Flores quoted in Cook, *Flood Tide*, 130.

5. Lewis to Jefferson, Cincinnati, 3 October 1803, and Jefferson to Lewis, Washington, 16 November 1803, in *Letters of the Lewis and Clark Expedition*, ed. Jackson, 1:131, 137.

6. James Wilkinson's Reflections on Louisiana, New Orleans, March 1804, in *Letters of the Lewis and Clark Expedition*, ed. Jackson, 2:686. In a note, Jackson lends cautious credence to Warren L. Cook's treatment of Spanish efforts to counter Lewis and Clark.

7. Marqués de Casa Calvo to Nemesio Salcedo, New Orleans, 5 March 1804, in *Letters of the Lewis and Clark Expedition*, ed. Jackson, 1:185.

8. Salcedo to Fernando de Chacón, Chihuahua, 3 May 1804, in *Letters of the Lewis and Clark Expedition*, ed. Jackson, 1:187–88; and Donald Jackson, ed., *The Journals of Zebulon Montgomery Pike with Letters and Related Documents*, 2 vols., The American Exploration and Travel Series (Norman: University of Oklahoma Press, 1966), 1:412–13.

9. Chacón to Salcedo, Santa Fe, 16 May 1804, doc. T-1730, SANM II. For the belated search for a Cerro de Oro, see John L. Kessell, *Kiva, Cross, and Crown: The Pecos Indians and New Mexico, 1540–1840* (Washington, D.C.: National Park Service, 1979), 430–33.

10. Pedro de Nava to the Duke of Alcudia, Chihuahua, 3 November 1795, quoted in Cook, *Flood Tide*, 462 n. 77.

11. Gary Moulton, ed., *The Journals of the Lewis and Clark Expedition*, 13 vols. (Lincoln: University of Nebraska Press, 1983–2001), 2:439. After making the trip from Santa Fe to St. Louis in 1792, Vial reckoned the distance, if unimpeded by Indian hostility, at twenty-five days. Loomis and Nasatir, *Pedro Vial*, 390.

12. Vial quoted in Cook, *Flood Tide*, 463. Loomis and Nasatir, *Pedro Vial*, 423 n. 4, had not located Vial's diary of this trip, but Cook subsequently found it in Spain's Archivo General de Indias (Audiencia de Guadalajara 398).

13. Cook, *Flood Tide*, 464; Moulton, *Journals*, 3:73, 116; and Ambrose, *Undaunted Courage*, 166.

14. Cook, *Flood Tide*, 460, 465–70 (Real Alencaster quotation is on p. 467); Isidoro de Antillón's 1802 map, "La América Septentrional," in *Flood Tide*, end pocket; and Kessell, *Kiva, Cross, and Crown*, 434–35.

15. Moulton, *Journals,* 5:91, 92; 11:273, 275. Participant John Ordway also recorded the distance as eight days. Moulton, *Journals,* 9:205.

16. Cook, *Flood Tide,* 465–70. Real Alencaster's instructions, Vial's diary, and related correspondence are translated in Loomis and Nasatir, *Pedro Vial,* 428–40. Jackson, ed., *Journals of Zebulon Montgomery Pike,* 2:109–10 n. 2, 377 n. 2, surmises that the attackers may have been a Skidi Pawnee war party, even though Vial had excused Pawnees because they did not battle on horseback.

17. Moulton, *Journals,* 6:33; and Ambrose, *Undaunted Courage,* 310.

18. Real Alencaster quoted in Loomis and Nasatir, *Pedro Vial,* 429.

19. Salcedo to Real Alencaster, Chihuahua, 18 July 1806, doc. T-2001, SANM II; Cook, *Flood Tide,* 470–72; and Loomis and Nasatir, *Pedro Vial,* 447. No diary of the aborted mission is known by scholars to exist.

20. Moulton, *Journals,* 8:110; and Ambrose, *Undaunted Courage,* 385.

21. Arthur Gómez, "Royalist in Transition: Facundo Melgares, the Last Spanish Governor of New Mexico, 1818–1822," *New Mexico Historical Review* 68 (October 1993): 372. Eyewitness Thomas James, recalling his visit to Santa Fe in the winter of 1821–1822, derided Governor Melgares and the New Mexico militia: "He was five feet high, nearly as thick as he was long, and as he waddled from one end of the line to the other I thought of Alexander and Hannibal and Caesar, and how their glories would soon be eclipsed by this hero of Santa Fe." See Thomas James, *Three Years among the Indians and Mexicans,* Keystone Western Americana Series (Philadelphia: J. B. Lippincott Co., 1962), 95.

22. Casa Calvo to Pedro Cevallos, New Orleans, 18 July 1805, doc. T-1856, SANM II.

23. Godoy quoted in Cook, *Flood Tide,* 475 n. 106.

24. The governor mentioned a diary and his instructions to Melgares in a letter of transmittal, but neither has been located by scholars. Real Alencaster to Salcedo, Santa Fe, 8 October 1806, doc. T-2022, SANM II; Melgares to Real Alencaster, Santa Fe, 2 June 1806, doc. T-1992, SANM II; and Cook, *Flood Tide,* 475–77. Cook errs in calling the Melgares expedition "the largest Spanish force ever sent onto the Great Plains" (p. 477). That of Francisco Vázquez de Coronado in 1541 was three times as large, and Juan Bautista de Anza's sally onto the plains of present-day eastern Colorado in 1779 counted around eight hundred fighting men.

25. Jackson, ed., *Journals of Zebulon Montgomery Pike,* 2:58.

26. Ibid., 1:406–7.

27. Ibid., 1:viii–x.

28. Pike to Wilkinson, Pawnee Republic, 2 October 1806, and Pike to Dearborn, Pawnee Republic, 1 October 1806, in *Letters of the Lewis and Clark Expedition,* ed. Jackson, 2:148–53. Later, after Pike and Melgares had become friends, the American reported in his expanded journal that the Spanish lieutenant led his troops all the way to the Pawnee village, held councils, and presented the Indians "with the flags, medals, &c. which were destined for them" (vol. 1, p. 325). Pike also convinced himself that the Melgares expedition was looking for him. The evidence suggests, however, that Spaniards in Santa Fe had no information about Pike until well after

Melgares had returned to Santa Fe about 1 October 1806. See Cook, *Flood Tide*, 480–83.

29. Moulton, *Journals*, 9:361; and Ambrose, *Undaunted Courage*, 402–3.
30. Lewis to Jefferson, St. Louis, 23 September 1806, in *Letters of the Lewis and Clark Expedition*, ed. Jackson, 1:319–20; and Ambrose, *Undaunted Courage*, 406–9.
31. Casa Yrujo and King Carlos quoted in Cook, *Flood Tide*, 483–84.

•

Death Delayed

THE SAD CASE OF THE TWO MARÍAS, 1773–1779

John L. Kessell

W ord had finally reached Santa Fe. The executions should proceed.
Moreover, thundered lawyer Pedro Galindo Navarro, "the cadavers
should be left hanging there for an interval of several days so that those who
did not attend and see the sentence carried out may have this time after the
fact to see and convey the news to their pueblos, where it is likely to produce the salutary effect of terrifying and restraining wrongdoers."[1]

Violent death was commonplace in colonial New Mexico, but the spectacle of public execution was not.[2] This case was extraordinary. Pending for
five years, at times almost forgotten, its close now became a matter of unfinished business for Juan Bautista de Anza, the colony's famed incoming governor who evidently brought Galindo's legal opinion with him from
Chihuahua in the fall of 1778.[3]

* * * *

The crime scene had resembled the canvas of a twentieth-century Santa Fe
or Taos artist. Nothing on that spring Friday afternoon, 16 April 1773, bespoke the brutal murder about to take place. Three Pueblo Indians, a man
and two women, idled while a much larger group with tools in hand set out
from Cochiti Pueblo to labor at cleaning an irrigation ditch. The solitary
trio now made their way on foot up Peralta Canyon. They appeared to be in

Professor Emeritus and founding editor of the Vargas Project at the University of New Mexico,
John L. Kessell is the author of *Pueblos, Spaniards, and the Kingdom of New Mexico* (University of Oklahoma Press, 2008).

no hurry and were gone all day. About the hour of the evening angelus prayer, the two Indian women returned to the pueblo. The man did not.

Questioned over the weekend by neighbors, the women—the missing man's wife and his mother-in-law—rehearsed the story of how he had decided to stay and camp out in the countryside. Cochiti Indian Lorenzo Chaya, knowing that the man was from Tesuque Pueblo north of Santa Fe and unfamiliar with the local terrain, went looking for him. Picking up the threesome's trail, he followed it to the foot of the mountains where on top of a hill he found the man. Chaya did not touch the body but headed back toward the pueblo. Meeting six war captains on the trail, he led them back to where the dead man lay face down. Rather than disturb the body, they simply reported the death. On Monday, 19 April, a dozen young men carried the corpse down to the pueblo for burial. It bore unmistakable signs of foul play. The man had been murdered.

Initial investigation of reported crimes in colonial New México fell to the Spanish alcalde mayor. In this instance, the district officer was don José Miguel de la Peña, whose ranch lay some three miles south of Cochiti Pueblo on the opposite or east bank of the Rio Grande. Notified that a Cochiti mother and daughter had killed an Indian from Tesuque, Peña set in motion the legal process. Since no government-registered notary resided in New Mexico, he summoned two neighbors to serve as the required assisting witnesses: Nerio Antonio Montoya, his lieutenant alcalde mayor, who spoke the Keresan language of the pueblo; and Cristóbal Manuel Montoya.

At least one Franciscan missionary serving at the time in Peña's jurisdiction had a low opinion of the alcalde mayor. "This man set out to skin the Indians," wrote fray Joaquín de Jesús Ruiz, "demanding sheep, pregnant cows, maize, etc., in the governor's name, laying such a burden on the six pueblos under his command that the Indians cried out. The ministers were unable to speak up, because the officials are swollen with importance and the ministers unheard, and he who interfered in such cases came out with the decrees at his haunches."[4]

The alcalde's party reined up at Cochiti on Thursday, 22 April, nearly a week after the alleged murder. If he followed procedure strictly, Peña displayed his silver-tipped staff of authority, symbolizing at this time and in this place the desire of a distant king that all his subjects have recourse to royal justice. Verifying reports of the murder, the alcalde had the two women arrested. He then opened formal proceedings. First to testify through interpreter Montoya under oath and the sign of the cross was Lorenzo Chaya, who described finding the body. Pueblo governor Manuel Romero and his assistant Asencio declared further that the Tesuque man's name was Agustín. As soon as the young bearers had arrived in the pueblo with Agustín's corpse, they had reported to the father missionary and then buried the body.[5]

Alcalde mayor Peña next ordered the two accused women brought before him and his two assisting witnesses. Nerio Montoya continued to act as interpreter. Together, this preliminary tribunal heard the chilling initial testimony of María Josefa and María Francisca, mother and daughter. Asked straightaway if they had killed Agustín, they answered yes. Had he suddenly provoked them? The younger woman said no, admitting that the crime was premeditated, not a spontaneous act of passion or self-defense.

She tried to explain. As soon as she and Agustín had reached her mother's house at Cochiti, she had taken María Josefa aside and told her that she intended to kill her husband. At first the older woman protested. María Francisca insisted that he did not love her and, worse, if they did not kill him, he would take her away permanently to Tesuque — a genuine concern in matrilocal Cochiti. Pondering the almost certain abduction of her daughter, María Josefa had consented. The Friday of the murder, the three had hiked up to the foot of the mountains, where they climbed a hill and sat down under a pine tree. María Francisca offered to delouse Agustín, who untied the band that bound his braid and stretched out with his head on his wife's skirts.

When Agustín fell asleep, María Francisca took the band and wrapped it around her husband's neck like a noose. She held one end tightly, signaling to María Josefa to grab the other end and pull with all her might. With Agustín half choked, María Francisca pressed her mother to stab him with the knife they had brought along. When the point hit bone at the base of Agustín's neck, María Josefa slit his throat, then raised his jacket and stabbed him in the side. Somehow the old knife had turned up as evidence, and alcalde mayor Peña had it traced in the margin of the document.

Asked what pretense the two women had used to lure Agustín to his death, they testified that they asked him to go with them to dig squawbush root (*raices de lemitas*) for dying cloth. The band they had used to strangle him, what was it made of and where was it now? It was woven of typical new wool, they responded, and they had buried it down from where they killed Agustín. Last, María Francisca stated that late Saturday, the day after the murder, she had told Luis, a Cochiti war captain, that her husband had not returned to the pueblo, and Luis had sent out searchers who found the

DOCUMENT WITH ALLEGED MURDER KNIFE TRACED IN MARGIN
Spanish Archives of New Mexico II, doc. 673, folio 3 (*Courtesy the New Mexico State Records Center and Archives*)

body. If the two confessed murderers felt any remorse, it must have been lost in the translation.[6]

Before concluding his investigation, Peña petitioned fray Estanislao Mariano de Marulanda, the Franciscan missionary assigned to Cochiti, to have Agustín's corpse dug up to verify the wounds. There were only two: one in the neck three fingers wide, which slit the victim's gullet (enough by itself to have caused death) and the other below the ribs in his side the width of the knife, from which his intestines protruded. After examination the body was reburied in the same grave.[7]

That concluded the preliminary investigation. Signing the six-page dossier with his two witnesses, Peña remitted it, along with the two Cochiti women, to Gov. Pedro Fermín de Mendinueta in Santa Fe, who acknowledged receipt the next day, 23 August. The two female defendants were "put in secure confinement" in Santa Fe. Governor Mendinueta, who administered the colony from 1767 until 1778 — the lengthiest tenure of any Spanish governor of New Mexico — found himself sorely beleaguered, waging more war than peace with various divisions of the Comanche and Ute nations. Still, he took seriously the case of the two Marías.

First, Mendinueta ordered Peña to appoint and send to the capital two reliable interpreters: a Keres Indian who knew Spanish and a Spaniard who knew Keresan. By this means the governor sought to preclude "any fraud or deceit." Formal court proceedings began on 22 May 1773. Because María Francisca looked underage, Governor Mendinueta named Santa Fe citizen Pedro Tafoya to act as her guardian *ad litem* (*curador*). The court then swore in the two bilingual interpreters: Indian Gervasio Corís and lieutenant alcalde mayor Nerio Antonio Montoya. Immediately thereupon the governor summoned María Francisca.

The young widow listened as interpreter Corís explained in her language the gravity of the oath she was about to take and her obligation to tell the truth. María Francisca, who did not know how old she was, appeared to be between sixteen and eighteen. This, her second confession, in no way contradicted her earlier statement, yet it provided additional details regarding the women's motive for killing Agustín.

In the confidence of their home in Cochiti, her mother had asked María Francisca if Agustín had provided her with the customary minimum essentials: cloth for dresses, sash, and shoes (*mantas, faja, y zapatos*). She said no, and her mother pitied her, lamenting, "You poor little thing; he has given you nothing." When a Cochiti official notified María Francisca that she

271

must leave Cochiti with her husband the following Sunday (18 April), go back to Tesuque, and not return to her pueblo, she and her mother determined to kill Agustín. María Francisca admitted that it was she who had suggested the murder. Asked if there were other accomplices, she stated that there were not. Having nothing further to add, María Francisca ratified her confession, and interpreter Montoya signed it for her.[8]

María Josefa, sworn in under the same conditions as her daughter, declared that she was a native and resident of the pueblo of Cochiti, married, and unsure of her age. Nowhere in the record does the name or whereabouts of the older woman's husband appear. María Josefa looked to be forty. En route to the murder scene, she testified that the three of them had stopped in an orchard to eat peaches (an unlikely repast in mid-April, hinting at inaccuracies in the court translation). Asked if her son-in-law had died of the two knife wounds, María Josefa declared "that when she stabbed him he was already choked and she did it so he would not get up." Regarding her motive for conspiring with her daughter to murder her son-in-law, she said simply that Agustín wanted to take María Francisca to the pueblo of Tesuque.[9]

Hardly grounds for murder, Agustín had nevertheless spit in the face of a matrilocal society. He should have moved to her pueblo. A close reading of contemporary mission marriage registers might suggest the frequency of such mixed Pueblo unions across language boundaries; I suspect they were rare. Although not an issue in the trial proceedings, Agustín's Tewa-speaking community of Tesuque, closest pueblo to Santa Fe and long tightly linked to the Spanish capital, had become more accepting of the colonists' patrilineal and patrilocal ways.

Having heard their confessions, Governor Mendinueta formally charged María Francisca and María Josefa in the murder of Agustín. They were given six days to present any further evidence in their own defense. The younger woman already had recourse through the interpreters to her guardian. Because her mother was also deemed incompetent to prepare a defense and knew no one in the capital, the governor appointed citizen Julián de Armijo as her defense counsel (*defensor*). The interpreters did their best to make the women understand.

Six days later, Governor Mendinueta signed in receipt of guardian Tafoya's discovery of evidence for María Francisca. Tafoya had gone to the presidial jail (*cuerpo de guardia, cárcel*) with the Keresan interpreter to question her, trying to impress upon his young client the beauty of telling the truth. Given that she had already confessed to killing Agustín, Tafoya asked her what cause or motive she had for doing so.

María Francisca made known through the interpreter that she had only agreed to marry Agustín when he promised not to take her from her pueblo, to truly love her, and to care for her affectionately, none of which he had done. Instead, he spent "most of the time mad (*amostazado*)" at her. Surely Tafoya asked her what that meant—how did Agustín show his anger; did he beat her or otherwise abuse her?—yet his client offered no such incriminating evidence. Her husband's utter failure to provide the promised love and care had nurtured in her childish breast the inadvertent beginnings that would lead her to such an excess. She had married Agustín against her mother's will, not considering the long-term consequences of her act. Finding herself without her husband's protection or shelter, and living the bitter truth of her mother's opposition, she knew not where to turn. This had set her on the path to the ill-considered murder.

Whatever form Agustín's alleged abuse had taken—psychological or physical, or both—it ensnared María Francisca quickly. She had murdered him less than three months after their wedding. Not part of the court record, the marriage entry for the couple showed that fray Juan José de Llanos had officiated at their wedding on 26 January 1773 at the pueblo of Nambe, of which Tesuque was a visiting station.[10]

Armijo followed with his presentation of evidence in María Josefa's behalf. The older woman offered only that her daughter had told her how badly things were going in her marriage and that Agustín "was punishing her (*la castigaba*)." Again, the record offers no further explanation. Irrational, childlike, and persuaded by her daughter, María Josefa had committed this absurd act with no thought to the future. She had nothing further to say, and Armijo requested in her behalf that the governor exercise justice charitably.

Since neither Tafoya nor Armijo had asked for an extension, Governor Mendinueta provided them in turn with the trial record and ordered that each prepare within four days of receipt a formal defense of his client. Handed the documents on 29 May 1773, Tafoya presented his defense of María Francisca first.

Reviewing the proceedings, her guardian concluded that María Francisca, driven by inconsistent and illogical reasoning, seemed not to recognize the hideousness of her crime. He commented on his client's crass ignorance, citing the example of her telling war captain Luis that her husband had not returned to the pueblo. Even though who she was did not excuse her, she made Tafoya think of a girl deserving correction and punishment. The governor, with his understanding and charity, would know how to look upon this "simple neophyte" so lacking in reason. Tafoya ended his defense with a discussion of how fear could take hold of such a person.

Armijo, entrusted with the twenty-page trial record on 2 June, had an easier time than his colleague. He considered María Josefa only an accessory to the crime. When her daughter first proposed the murder, she had said no. Only after María Francisca had pressed her further did "the mother acquiesce to the daughter's accursed idea," thereby proving the old adage, "one parent for a thousand children, and a thousand children for one parent," that is to say, blood is thicker than water. "Had this evil daughter not dragged her mother along with her cunning, the ignorant mother, so lacking in speculative reason, would not have committed such a grave error." Nowhere else did Armijo or Tafoya allude to either woman's cunning. Armijo went on to cite God's law that thou shalt not kill, but also that he who pardons shall be pardoned. He pleaded that whoever decided María Josefa's fate take into account her utter lack of rationality and her obvious rusticity.

Governor Mendinueta chose not to decide the case without further legal advice. Because the defendants had no idea what a legal adviser (*asesor legal*) was or why such an opinion should be sought, the governor informed Tafoya and Armijo what he intended to do. Both men signed in assent, and on 11 June 1773, Mendinueta remitted the trial record to lawyer Juan Miguel Márquez in the city of Chihuahua or in his absence to another accredited legal expert.[11]

Ten months passed before New Mexico's governor had a reply. The two women, meanwhile, remained in confinement in Santa Fe. Had María Francisca been pregnant by Agustín, she would have delivered their baby by late 1773 or early 1774, yet no such baptismal entry appears in the registers of Cochiti, Nambe/Tesuque, or Santa Fe. Her mother, however, may have given birth. On 27 October 1773, fray Patricio Cuéllar of Santa Fe baptized Esteban Vicente, legitimate son of Antonio and María Josefa, both Indians of Cochiti. While there is no direct evidence that this María Josefa was María Francisca's mother, it is notable that the child of a Cochiti couple received baptism not in that pueblo but in Santa Fe. María Josefa could have been two- or three-months pregnant at the time of her arrest—hence even more desirous that her daughter remain with her in Cochiti—coming to term and delivering during her imprisonment in Santa Fe.[12]

The legal advice Governor Mendinueta had requested reached him in April 1774. No competent counselor had been present in Chihuahua, so the packet traveled hundreds of miles farther south to Durango, where lawyer Rafael Vallarta had studied the case the previous November and rendered a three-page opinion. The crime obviously horrified him, and, whatever his personal experience with Indians, he took an extremely dim view of their capacity. As if to demonstrate his attention to detail, Vallarta noted that the women's confessions contained two different words to describe the stab wound in the victim's right side, *costado*, the more general term, and *vacío*, the hollow beneath the rib cage. This inconsistency he attributed to the defendants' simplemindedness, a translation error, or the proximity of those two parts of the body. As for the proceedings, he opined that Mendinueta must correct several irregularities that could prejudice the case. The most important point had to do with María Francisca's precise age.

Neither María knew how old she was. From appearances, as recorded in their confessions, the mother looked to be forty and her daughter between sixteen and eighteen. Pointing out to Mendinueta that all Indians were minors before the law, Vallarta instructed the governor to name legal guardians for both women, not a defense counsel, as he had for the older woman. Still, age counted. If María Francisca were not yet seventeen when she committed the crime, her sentence would have to be mitigated; if, on the other hand, she were between seventeen and twenty-five, such mitigation would be at the judge's discretion, depending on the circumstances. Therefore, Mendinueta should determine the younger woman's age, providing a copy of her baptismal entry or some other certification as part of the record.

If with these amendments, the legal adviser continued, no further questions arose, and if the governor deemed further delay detrimental to public justice, he could, because of the hideous nature of the crime, sentence the two women to death. Depending on María Francisca's age, she would either die with María Josefa or serve ten years in a women's prison, having witnessed the public hanging of her mother. Before carrying out a death sentence, however, the governor should consult the audiencia, or high court, for confirmation or modification of its terms.[13]

Governor Mendinueta complied meticulously during the spring of 1774. He renamed María Josefa's defense counsel her guardian; presided in person as the defendants ratified their declarations without change; and, ordering a copy of María Francisca's baptismal entry, confirmed her age at the time of the murder. The Cochiti book of baptisms revealed that María

Francisca, legitimate daughter of Pedro and María Josefa, had received the sacrament on 6 April 1751, making her just over twenty-two at the time of the murder. (So, if the baby boy born in October 1773 was indeed her mother's, he was apparently María Francisca's half-brother, since her father had been Pedro not Antonio.)[14] Satisfied, the governor sent the proceedings back to Vallarta, who responded this time from Guadalajara, on 30 December 1774.[15]

Now the case was clear. The women's ratification of their open confessions left no doubt of their treachery in the deceitful, premeditated murder of a defenseless man. Hence, there should be no lessening of the twenty-two-year-old María Francisca's punishment. Vallarta stood by his previous opinion: Mendinueta could sentence them both to death as parricides (*con la calidad de parricidas*), killers of a close relative.[16] There would be no clemency on the basis of race, class, or gender; the two women had murdered a husband and son-in-law, assailing thereby the sanctity of the patriarchal family in Hispanic tradition. Before their execution, as a lesson to others, the condemned women might also be given two hundred lashes while led on beasts of burden through the streets of Santa Fe in the customary manner. This was Vallarta's legal opinion, not a sentence, and there is no evidence that the two Marías were ever whipped.[17]

For another four years, they languished in jail. We do not know whether family members or friends from their pueblo were allowed to visit them or if the two women were given work to do. In October of 1775, Mendinueta had directed their case to the viceroy of New Spain, who also served as president of the high court in Mexico City.[18] For unexplained reasons, no action was taken there for more than two years, and then, on the recommendation of another adviser, Viceroy Antonio María de Bucareli had the proceedings sent to Com. Gen. Teodoro de Croix in Chihuahua, who had jurisdiction over New Mexico.[19] Croix, of course, turned the matter over to his legal adviser, Pedro Galindo Navarro, who did not pronounce an opinion until 6 August 1778.

Galindo agreed fully with his colleague Vallarta. So heinous was the women's crime that their punishment should be conspicuously severe. To that end, Galindo endorsed the gallows. This spectacle, he added, would be especially fitting on a thinly garrisoned frontier subject to uprisings.[20]

By this time, the renowned Juan Bautista de Anza had assumed the governorship. Capital punishment for civilian crimes in colonial New Mexico was rare.[21] Yet it fell to Anza in January 1779 to pronounce sentence, which he ordered interpreted for the prisoners. The two Marías were made to understand and, as a routine sign of submission, to hold the document above their heads. The authorities would have provided that these convicted murderers receive absolution in the last rites administered by a priest, most likely fray Juan José de Llanos of the Santa Fe parish.[22]

Death by public hanging, as prescribed by Galindo, was a precise business to be carried out only by a trained executioner. Since no such professional was available, the two Indian women, at 11:45 on a winter's day, 26 January 1779—five years, nine months, and ten days after their crime—were shot, almost certainly by a firing squad from the Santa Fe presidio. Only then, on a gallows nearby, the dead bodies were hung.[23]

Lawyer Galindo Navarro had wanted the grisly reminders displayed for several days. Instead, at 3:00 PM, after only three hours, fray Juan José requested that the corpses be taken down and brought to the church. Obviously the ground was frozen outside, but why he gave the two women ecclesiastical burial inside the transept, normally considered a place of honor, is not recorded. Perhaps it was only a matter of convenience, or perhaps the friar remembered having married María Francisca and Agustín at Nambe some years earlier. He may not have recalled that 26 January 1779—the day of her execution for Agustín's murder—was precisely the couple's sixth wedding anniversary.[24]

Evidently, there was no backlash among Pueblo Indians. When Governor Anza led forth his celebrated 1779 campaign against Cuerno Verde and the Comanches six months later, 259 Pueblo fighting men, more than half of them from Cochiti and other Keresan towns, rallied to his banner.[25]

* * * *

One can only surmise what form the women's punishment might have taken if left solely to the officials of the pueblo of Cochiti.[26] Their fate might have been less severe, surely more rapidly decided, had their case not been referred to outside legal experts unfamiliar with New Mexico's unique Pueblo-Hispano culture. Despite a witch craze centering on the genízaro community of Abiquiu a decade earlier, there were no implications of witchcraft in the case of the two Marías.[27] On a broader stage, the 1770s came at the height of the Spanish enlightenment, when legally trained minions of King Carlos III sought to impose throughout the empire a uniform rule of law allowing few exceptions.

The women's crime was inexcusable, but what really drove two reticent Pueblo women to such an excess surely died with them. *Que descansen en paz las almas de Agustín y las dos Marías.*[28]

Notes

1. Pedro Galindo Navarro, Legal opinion, Chihuahua, 6 August 1778, doc. 690, fols. 2–3, Spanish Archives of New Mexico II, New Mexico State Records Center and Archives, Santa Fe [hereafter SANM II]. Photoprints and microfilm: r. 10, ff. 861–63, Spanish Archives of New Mexico II, Center for Southwest Research, University of New Mexico, Albuquerque [hereafter parenthetical citation, reel number, frame number, CSWR].

2. Charles R. Cutter, *The Legal Culture of Northern New Spain, 1700–1810* (Albuquerque: University of New Mexico Press, 1995), 138; and Marc Simmons, *Spanish Government in New Mexico* (Albuquerque: University of New Mexico Press, 1968), 178–79. See also Martina Will de Chaparro, *Death and Dying in New Mexico* (Albuquerque: University of New Mexico Press with the William P. Clements Center for Southwest Studies, Southern Methodist University, 2007).

3. The legal proceedings in the case are found on forty-five pages of docs. 673 and 690, SANM II (r. 10, ff. 752–88, 859–66, CSWR).

4. Ruiz quoted in Eleanor B. Adams and Fray Angélico Chávez, *The Missions of New Mexico, 1776: A Description by Fray Francisco Atanasio Domínguez with Other Contemporary Documents* (Albuquerque: University of New Mexico Press, 1956), 313 n. 6. On alcaldes mayores in general, see Cutter, *Legal Culture*, 82–93; and Simmons, *Spanish Government*, 170–92.

5. Lorenzo Chaya, Manuel Romero and Asencio, Declarations, Cochiti, 22 April 1773, doc. 673, fols. 1–2, SANM II (r. 10, ff. 753–55, CSWR). Ramón A. Gutiérrez, *When Jesus Came, the Corn Mothers Went Away: Marriage, Sexuality, and Power in New Mexico, 1500–1846* (Stanford, Calif.: Stanford University Press, 1991), 191, 205, misread the victim's name as Agustín de Girón, whom he took to be a Spaniard. Gutiérrez also erred in relating the gruesome details of the murder, the motive of the two Cochiti women, and their punishment. Robert J. Tórrez devoted a brief chapter to the case in *UFOs over Galisteo and Other Stories of New Mexico's History* (Albuquerque: University of New Mexico Press, 2004), 67–70. See also John L. Kessell, *Spain in the Southwest: A Narrative History of Colonial New Mexico, Arizona, Texas, and California* (Norman: University of Oklahoma Press, 2002), 289–92.

6. María Josefa and María Francisca, Declaration, Cochiti, 22 April 1773, doc. 673, fols. 2–3, SANM II (r. 10, ff. 755–57, CSWR). Tracing the knife used as a murder weapon in the margin of the document was apparently not an uncommon practice. Cutter, *Legal Culture*, 139, reproduces a similar document from 1803 with an outline of the knife wielded by a notorious Texas criminal.

7. José Miguel de la Peña, Proceedings of disinterment, Cochiti, n.d., doc. 673, fols. 3–3v, SANM II (r. 10, ff. 757–58, CSWR).

8. María Francisca, Confession, Santa Fe, 22 May 1773, and previous proceedings, doc. 673, fols. 4–6, SANM II (r. 10, ff. 759–63, CSWR). In colonial New Mexico, a *manta* was usually a nearly square piece of coarse cotton cloth about four feet on a side, two of which, sewn together, made a Pueblo Indian woman's dress, which was tied around the middle with a sash. Both men and women wore moccasins, re-

ferred to alternately as *teguas* or *zapatos*, the generic term for footwear. Marc Simmons, personal communication, 17 March 1993.

9. María Josefa, Confession, Santa Fe, 22 May 1773, doc. 673, fols. 6–7, SANM II (r. 10, ff. 763–65, CSWR).

10. Marriage of Agustín of Tesuque and María Francisca of Cochiti, Nambe, 26 January 1773, M-17, Nambe (Box 10), 1772–1862 (r. 27, f. 918), Archives of the Archdiocese of Santa Fe, Santa Fe, New Mexico [hereafter AASF]. Their witnesses were Joaquín el Coyote and his wife Juana María, both natives of Tesuque, and all the rest of the people of Nambe.

11. Proceedings, 22 May–11 June 1773, doc. 673, fols. 7–13, SANM II (r. 10, ff. 765–75, CSWR).

12. B-64, Santa Fe (Box 55), 1777–91 (r. 15, f. 295), AASF.

13. Vallarta to Mendinueta, Legal opinion, Durango, 19 November 1773, doc. 673, fols. 13v–14v, SANM II (r. 10, ff. 776–78, CSWR).

14. Fray Estanislao Mariano de Marulanda, Certification, Cochiti, 18 April 1774, doc. 673, fols. 18v–19, SANM II (r. 10, ff. 784–85, CSWR). The baby's father could of course have been Pedro Antonio.

15. Mendinueta, Transmittal, Santa Fe, 25 June 1774, doc. 673, fol. 19, SANM II (r. 10, f. 785, CSWR).

16. A parricide is defined in Joaquín Escriche, *Diccionario razonado de legislación y jurisprudencia*, 4 vols. (Bogota: Editorial Temis, 1977), 4:257, as "one who kills a parent, grandparent or great-grandparent, child, grandchild or great-grandchild, brother or sister, aunt or uncle, nephew or niece, husband or wife, father-in-law or mother-in-law, son-in-law or daughter-in-law, stepfather, stepmother, stepchild, or patron."

17. Vallarta to Mendinueta, Legal opinion, Guadalajara, 30 December 1774, doc. 673, fols. 20–21, SANM II (r. 10, ff. 786–88, CSWR).

18. Mendinueta, Transmittal, Santa Fe, 14 October 1775, doc. 673, fol. 21, SANM II (r. 10, f. 788, CSWR). This concludes doc. 673, which is entitled "*Causa criminal contra las reas M.a Fran.ca y M.a su madre sentenciadas a muerte con parecer del asesor.*" On the title page, pioneer archaeologist and ethnohistorian Adolph F. Bandelier noted, "See N.o 690. Ad. F. Bandelier." The case continues in doc. 690, where Bandelier wrote, "See N.o 673. Ad. F. Bandelier."

19. Bucareli to Croix, Transmittal, Mexico City, 17 June 1778, doc. 690, fol. 2, SANM II (r. 10, f. 861, CSWR).

20. Galindo Navarro, Legal opinion, Chihuahua, 6 August 1778, doc. 690, fols. 2–3, SANM II (r. 10, ff. 861–63, CSWR).

21. Charles R. Cutter, *The Protector de Indios in Colonial New Mexico, 1659–1821* (Albuquerque: University of New Mexico Press, 1986), 75, calls the execution of the two Cochiti women "a rare example of capital punishment."

22. Will, *Death and Dying*, 69–70. Anza, Pronouncement of sentence, Santa Fe, 22 January 1779; and José Maldonado, Notification, Santa Fe, 23 January 1779, doc. 690, fols. 3–4, SANM II (r. 10, ff. 863–65, CSWR).

23. Anza, Certification of execution, Santa Fe, 26 January 1779, doc. 690, fols. 4–4v, SANM II (r. 10, ff. 865–66, CSWR). Most historians have concluded that the women were hanged not shot.

24. Bur-48, Santa Fe (Box 26), 1726–80 (r. 40, f. 264), AASF.

25. Alfred Barnaby Thomas, ed. and trans., *Forgotten Frontiers: A Study of the Spanish Indian Policy of Don Juan Bautista de Anza, Governor of New Mexico, 1777–1787: From the Original Documents in the Archives of Spain, Mexico and New Mexico* (Norman: University of Oklahoma Press, 1932), 122.

26. Ethnographer Charles H. Lange, *Cochiti: A New Mexico Pueblo, Past and Present* (Carbondale: Southern Illinois University Press, 1959), 220, opting to omit legal affairs in which Spanish civil or ecclesiastical authorities were involved, reports no memory of this case in the pueblo. In 2007 Joseph H. Suina, former governor of Cochiti, inquired of knowledgeable members of the pueblo and found no one who remembered hearing of the two Marías' execution 228 years earlier.

27. Malcolm Ebright and Rick Hendricks, *The Witches of Abiquiu: The Governor, the Priest, the Genízaro Indians, and the Devil* (Albuquerque: University of New Mexico Press, 2006).

28. May the souls of Agustín and the two Marías rest in peace.

In Memoriam
DAVID J. WEBER (1940–2010)

John L. Kessell

On 20 August 2010, internationally acclaimed historian David J. Weber died in a Gallup, New Mexico, hospital, not far from his summer home, his *querencia* (the place where one's soul is most at peace), in the Zuni Mountains. Carol, his wife of forty-eight years, son Scott, and daughter Amy were with him. Together, the family had fought his multiple myeloma for nearly three years, never giving up hope of a remission. Even during the last days of his life, he continued dictating e-mails to Carol, ever sharing with colleagues and encouraging students.

Born in Buffalo, New York, on 20 December 1940, Weber graduated from the State University of New York, College at Fredonia, where he had changed his focus from music (he and Carol played the clarinet) to Latin American history. He earned both his MA (1964) and PhD (1967) in history from the University of New Mexico, the latter under the guidance of Prof. Donald C. Cutter. Weber's dissertation appeared in book form as *The Taos Trappers: The Fur Trade in the Far Southwest, 1540–1846* (University of Oklahoma Press, 1971). Between 1967 and 1976, he taught at San Diego State University, moving in fall 1976 to Southern Methodist University (SMU), his academic home for the next thirty-four years. There, Weber became Robert and Nancy Dedman Professor of History in 1986 and founding director of the William P. Clements Center for Southwest Studies in 1995.

Weber specialized in the Spanish Borderlands, Mexico, and colonial Latin America. More than any other scholar, he revitalized historical study of the Borderlands and led the field into the twenty-first century with style and grace. Comparisons with Herbert E. Bolton (1870–1953), pioneer promoter of the Spanish Borderlands and the epic of Greater America, are inevitable. I entitled a 1993 review essay of Weber's masterful *Spanish Frontier in North America* "A Bolton for the Nineties."[1] Inspired teachers, keen mentors, and prolific writers, both men lent themselves unselfishly to their profession. Bolton served as president of the American Historical Association in 1932; Weber became vice president of the Association's Professional Division in 2008. Bolton presided over a hub of research at the University of California's Bancroft Library; and Weber founded SMU's Clements Center, fostering fellowships, scholarly conferences, and academic publishing. Bolton wrote or edited some twenty-four books; Weber was working on his twenty-eighth and twenty-ninth when he died.

And while his formal bibliography runs to 124 entries, the conspicuous centerpiece is by all measures *The Spanish Frontier in North America* (Yale University Press, 1992; and *The Brief Edition*, Yale University Press, 2009).[2] Weber inherited the field in its third generation, by then greatly expanded in scholarly production if not in geographical area. Geographically, in fact, post-Bolton scholars had split the Borderlands between Spanish Florida and the Southeast on the one hand and Spanish California and the Southwest on the other. At SMU in Dallas, with half the field to the east and half to the west, Weber was perfectly situated to reunite and resynthesize the Spanish colonial history of North America.

That monumental undertaking he accomplished as never before. Mastering computer technology, Weber achieved unprecedented control over the enormous body of secondary and published primary sources, extending his interdisciplinary reach to archaeology, ethnohistory, and beyond. He mediated skillfully between the so-called "Black Legend" of unique Spanish cruelty and the no less distorted "White Legend" of Spaniards as civilizing saviors. Despite the daunting diversity of Native American peoples, their physical worlds, and their varied responses to Spaniards—all of which Weber considered with fresh insight and clarity—the Spanish imprint on the continent proved indelible. "However much Spaniards might eat Indian foods, wear Indian footwear, take Indian wives or concubines, produce mestizo children, learn Indian languages, or live beyond the civility of Spanish urban life," Weber concluded, "the core of Hispanic frontier culture and society remained recognizably Hispanic and clearly intact."[3]

Like Bolton, Weber was drawn to comparative studies. In a 1986 essay, "Turner, the Boltonians, and the Borderlands," which appeared in *The American Historical Review*, Weber wrote admiringly of scholars who had "moved well beyond the simple notion of the frontier as a line between 'savagery and civilization' to remind us that a variety of indigenous societies can exist in a frontier zone and that different host societies have different impacts on the cultures and institutions of intruders."[4] Already he was framing a challenge for himself, one he met grandly with *Bárbaros: Spaniards and Their Savages in the Age of Enlightenment* (Yale University Press, 2005).

Toward the end of the colonial era, a notably more secular time than earlier centuries, Spaniards cared less about saving Comanche souls than about enlisting Comanche fighters. As Weber pointed out, independent (as opposed to incorporated) Indians still held sway over more than half the land mass claimed by Spain in the western hemisphere. *Bárbaros* relates in engaging detail the many ways self-interested Spanish administrators, captains, and traders got on with equally self-interested, unconverted Indian peoples across multiple frontiers, from the Great Plains of Texas to the pampas of South America. More often than not, on-the-ground pragmatism trumped the Spanish Crown's vacillating policies. Telling quotations, a Weber trademark, abound. On the point of death, an old Araucanian Mapuche in Chile told a missionary priest, "Padre, do not tire yourself, because it is an inviolable custom and law of my forefathers not to believe anything that Spaniards say."[5]

In 2006, with a profound sense of fulfillment, Weber read in *The New York Review of Books* the qualities assigned to him by world-renowned historian of the Spanish empire J. H. Elliott, who referred to both *The Spanish Frontier* and *Bárbaros* as: "a mastery of the literature and impressive erudition; a capacity for the patient teasing out of the truth from sources that are often incomplete and partisan; and a lucid narrative style that carries the reader along. . . . To have subsumed so much information into so clear and comprehensive a survey is a formidable achievement."[6]

Weber's many achievements were widely recognized. Spain and Mexico, along with his native United States, inducted him into elite societies: the Real Orden de Isabel la Católica in 2002, the Orden Mexicana del Águila Azteca in 2005 (in both cases the highest honor bestowed on a foreigner), and the American Academy of Arts and Sciences in 2007. Fellows of the academy are recognized for "preeminent contributions to their disciplines and to society at large." Other inductees that year included former vice president Al Gore, Israeli biochemist and Nobel laureate Avram Hershko, former Supreme Court associate justice Sandra Day O'Connor, New York mayor Michael Bloomberg, and actor and producer Robert Redford.[7]

Yet none of this acclaim went to Weber's head. Always a thorough gentleman, David lent his soft-spoken assurance to all around him: students, colleagues, friends, and family. Less than a year before he died, he mailed me a copy of his latest book, *The Spanish Frontier in North America: The Brief Edition.* The generosity and warmth of his inscription celebrate the man:

"Inscribed for John Kessell, who has led me in the long journey to understand the Spanish frontiers in over 4 decades of friendship." Thanks, David, but you led us all.

Notes

1. John L. Kessell, "A Bolton for the Nineties—*The Spanish Frontier in North America*: A Review Essay," *New Mexico Historical Review* 68 (October 1993): 399–405.
2. David J. Weber, "Curriculum vitae academicae," http://faculty.smu.edu/dweber/CV.htm.
3. David J. Weber, *The Spanish Frontier in North America* (New Haven, Conn.: Yale University Press, 1992), 333.
4. David J. Weber, "Turner, the Boltonians, and the Borderlands," *The American Historical Review* 91 (February 1986): 71–72.
5. David J. Weber, *Bárbaros: Spaniards and Their Savages in the Age of Enlightenment* (New Haven, Conn.: Yale University Press, 2005), 126.
6. J. H. Elliott, "Barbarians at the Gates; *Bárbaros: Spaniards and Their Savages in the Age of Enlightenment*," *The New York Review of Books*, 23 February 2006, pp. 36–38.
7. "Historian David J. Weber Inducted into the American Academy of Arts and Sciences," http://smu.edu/newsinfo/releases/06159a.asp.

A Long Time Coming

THE SEVENTEENTH-CENTURY PUEBLO-SPANISH WAR

John L. Kessell

In his prize-winning book *When Jesus Came, The Corn Mothers Went Away, Marriage, Sexuality, and Power in New Mexico, 1500–1846* (1991), historian Ramón A. Gutiérrez implied that New Mexico's seventeenth-century Franciscan missionaries routinely abused their Pueblo Indian neophytes. "New Mexico's Indians," Gutiérrez informed us, "were conquered and made *mansos* [submissive] by a technique for which Fray Nicolás Hidalgo was renowned. In 1638 the friar beat Pedro Acomilla of Taos Pueblo and grabbed him 'by the member and twisted it so much that it broke in half.'" If, for a fact, grabbing Pueblo men's penises had been standard procedure in the missions, I dare say that the Pueblo-Spanish War, fought between 1680 and 1696, would have been not such a long time coming.[1]

So why, through three entire generations—born, lived out, and buried between the Spanish assault on Acoma in 1599 and the Pueblo siege of Santa Fe in 1680—was redemption so long in coming? Was the colonial regime not really so bad after all? Did the benefits of coexistence repeatedly undermine the urge to revolt, even as smallpox, measles, and flu cruelly reduced the Pueblo Indian population? Or were the Pueblos so deeply divided by traditional grudges—and by the new promise of settling old scores through alliance with Spaniards—that they simply could not rally themselves until 1680?

Professor Emeritus and founding editor of the Vargas Project at the University of New Mexico, John L. Kessell is the author of *Pueblos, Spaniards, and the Kingdom of New Mexico* (University of Oklahoma Press, 2008).

A united pre-Hispanic Pueblo world never existed. Taken together, rock and kiva art showing men in combat, projectile points embedded in human bones, mass graves, burned communities, and defensive works testify that this evolving island of town-dwellers was no native Eden before the advent of rapacious Europeans. Nor was this a constant war zone. Warrior gods appeared early in Pueblo creation stories, and evidently hunt and war societies formed to honor them and to feed and protect their people. Yet much of life went on peaceably as various groups exchanged edible, material, and even cultural resources. Cooperation and conflict ebbed and flowed at different times and different places (just as they would during the colonial period). Some late-thirteenth and fourteenth-century discord likely followed upon the introduction of the new kachina ceremonial system borne up from Mesoamerica, as it certainly did when a new Christian ceremonial system arrived two hundred years later.[2]

As Spaniards fastened their one true religion, common sovereignty, and lingua franca upon New Mexico, they took advantage of Pueblo disunion, enlisting Pueblo Indians to fight other Pueblo Indians. Soon enough, however, as encircling nomadic peoples threatened New Mexico's agricultural heartland, colonial authorities began to rely on mixed Pueblo Indian auxiliaries who on campaign regularly outnumbered Spanish men-at-arms.

More than once, numerically superior Pueblo Indian fighters sought retaliation not against the kingdom's nomadic enemies, but against the kingdom itself. Once Spaniards discovered the plots, these conspiracies broke apart, and the survivors took their grievances back underground. In 1680, however, the colony's recovery from environmental calamity and the emergence of ironfisted Pueblo leaders, at long last, produced the desired outcome. To stunned Spaniards, it was as if the familiar quotas of Pueblo auxiliaries set out one day on campaign and came back the next an angry, ordered, overpowering mob.

* * * *

Back in the mid-sixteenth century, Spaniards who first broke in on the Pueblo world were already well practiced in using Indian peoples against each other or as allies in common battles.[3] Francisco Vázquez de Coronado's reverberating entrada of 1540—upwards of four hundred mounted Europeans and three times as many formidable Mexican Indian auxiliaries—upset the prevailing Pueblo balance of power. Only the self-assured inhabitants at Cicuique, or Pecos, the populous easternmost gateway between pueblos and plains, sent a diplomatic mission to welcome the invaders. "Cicuye [Cicuique]," Coronado's chronicler Pedro de Castañeda de Nájera recalled, "is a *pueblo* of as many as five hundred fighting men. It is feared throughout that

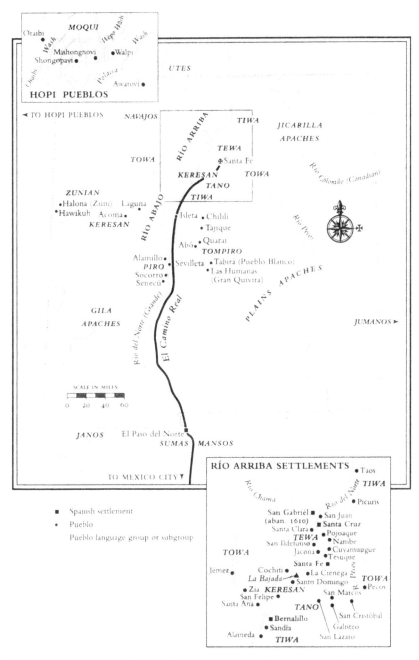

NATIVE GROUPS IN AND AROUND SEVENTEENTH-CENTURY NEW MEXICO
(Map drawn by Deborah Reade, Santa Fe, from John L. Kessell,
Pueblos, Spaniards, and the Kingdom of New Mexico, 2008, *courtesy*
University of Oklahoma Press)

14

287

whole land. . . . The people of this *pueblo* boast that no one has been able to subjugate them and that they subjugate [whichever] *pueblos* they want to."[4]

En route to Cicuique, Coronado's troop came upon "a fine, large *pueblo*, destroyed during their wars."[5] Although relations quickly soured when Spaniards took Cicuique hostages, Coronado testified at his trial in Mexico City that he had requested fighting men from Cicuique to help subdue Tiguex, the province of Southern Tiwas in the vicinity of modern-day Albuquerque. Cicuique's headmen envisioned a colonial scheme of their own. Their community, cramped by a short, high-elevation growing season and constricted farms, coveted Tiwa land in the lower-lying Rio Grande Valley. "They asked the general," Coronado's testimony states, "to give them a pueblo there, which they could settle with their people. And they said that they were coming to help in the war." But the Tiguex war ended, and the deal was never struck.[6]

Acoma, another seemingly aggressive pueblo, lacked the population of Cicuique but sat atop an all but unassailable height at the western gateway to the Rio Grande Valley. Its estimated two hundred warriors, characterized by Castañeda as "marauders feared throughout the land and region," could strike at others and withdraw to the safety of their natural stronghold.[7]

Spaniards who came after Coronado also noted inter-Pueblo hostilities. Antonio de Espejo's brash, fast-moving outfit, numbering at most a few dozen, was apparently the first expedition to use Pueblo Indian auxiliaries against other Pueblos in 1583. A contingent of Zuni men armed with bows and arrows volunteered to accompany the expedition to the Hopi pueblos. "Since about thirty of these friendly natives had come with us from the province of Sumi [Zuni], influenced by the Mexican Indian brothers, Andrés and Gaspar—two of those left by Coronado—and these warriors showed a fine spirit, saying they wanted to die wherever the Castillos died, we cut up pieces of red felt and put a colored sign on each man's head so that all could be recognized." Although this time the Hopis chose not to fight, no soldier who ever served in a foreign people's homeland would have failed to appreciate the red insignias that distinguished friendly Zunis from potentially hostile Hopis.[8]

Fifteen years later, in the summer of 1598, Pueblo lookouts sighted a larger column of Spaniards moving laboriously up the Rio Grande Valley. Bulky animals strained at overloaded carts, children and women walked beside or rode, while cursing men tried to keep livestock from straying. No mere adventurers, these were migrants looking for a new home.

Most of the Southern Tiwas, whose elders recalled their brutal strife with Coronado, simply vacated their pueblos and let these strangers pass by. Developer Juan de Oñate's many-hued colonists, six or seven hundred in all, finally moved in amidst the Tewas at the pueblo of Ohkay Owingeh, some twenty-five miles north of later Santa Fe. Oñate called the place San Juan Bautista. Hardly catching a breath, these new arrivals began to explore in every direction looking for mines and performing unintelligible acts of possession in Pueblo communities. Among the hollow benefits promised by Oñate was the *pax hispanica*, an end to conflict in the Pueblo world.[9]

Pecos, assaulted eight years earlier by the renegade entrada of Gaspar Castaño de Sosa, chose not to resist. Quizzical Pecos guides, hunters, and observers surely accompanied Vicente de Zaldívar and his metal men in September 1598 as they rode out from Pecos onto the plains to corral buffalo. The high and mighty Acomas, in contrast, did resist, throwing down the gauntlet later in 1598 by killing Juan de Zaldívar, Oñate's second-in-command and brother of Vicente, along with a dozen of his men. Rather than withdraw the vulnerable little colony—probably outnumbered at the time a hundred-to-one in the Pueblo world—a firm-jawed Oñate directed Vicente de Zaldívar and some seventy armed Spaniards to bring the Acomas to European justice. Neither he, nor poet Gaspar Pérez de Villagrá, said anything about enlisting Pueblo auxiliaries.[10]

Before the colony's restoration by Diego de Vargas in the 1690s, hardly anyone gave credit to allied Pueblo Indian fighting men. They might indeed have accompanied Vicente de Zaldívar's force, only to be ignored in formal accounts of the battle, just as Coronado ignored his massive contingent of Mexican Indians.[11]

At the very least, the vicious three-day fight at Acoma in 1599 must have attracted more than a few Pueblo spectators. Testifying in the wake of the Spaniards' numbing victory, Pérez de Villagrá swore that the Acomas had "wanted nothing more than to kill all the Spaniards in the army, and after disposing of them to kill the Indians at the pueblos of Zía, Santo Domingo, and San Juan Bautista, because they had failed to kill the Spaniards."[12]

The presence of Pueblo auxiliaries at Acoma in January 1599, however, would help to explain that improbable Spanish victory. And why should we not suppose that Oñate's Spaniards recruited Pueblo Indian allies for their major expeditions eastward across the plains in 1601 and westward to the Gulf of California in 1605, except that no Spaniard bothered to mention them?

A generation later, in 1634, Franciscan propagandist Alonso de Benavides observed that the Tewa nation, among which Oñate's colonists first settled, "is very attached to the Spaniards, and when a war breaks out they are the first to join and accompany them." Benavides gave credit to one of his fellow friars for establishing peace between Tewas and Jemez who had been previously, according to Benavides's excited account, "so hostile to the Christian Teoas [Tewas], their neighbors, that one of their captains wore around his neck a string of ears of the Christians that he had killed, and he was eating them."[13] In February 1632, Zunis at the pueblo of Hawikuh had risen and murdered Fray Francisco Letrado. Why would the Spanish punitive force that camped at El Morro a month later "to avenge the death of Father Letrado" not have included eager members of Tewa war societies?[14]

Pueblo men, traditionally good fighters, had their own reasons for joining the Spaniards. Besides a furlough from their missions and a chance to travel, campaigning alongside Spaniards allowed them to demonstrate their fighting prowess, to exact revenge on their own enemies, and to share in the spoils of war, including trophy scalps. The Spaniards' motives hardly mattered. Military campaigns often turned to trading or slaving, and commercial ventures sometimes broke into fights.

By enlisting Pueblo Indian auxiliaries against other Pueblo Indians, Spaniards kept pre-contact animosities alive or created new ones, thus preventing the Pueblo world's fighting men from joining forces against them. When, however, Spanish governors resorted to gathering quotas of Pueblo males from different communities and language groups to campaign together against common enemies of the kingdom, a notable shift occurred. Alien Pueblo war captains got to know each other and learned to fight shoulder-to-shoulder. Recruitment fell to New Mexico's half dozen alcaldes mayores, or district officers, who parleyed with local Pueblo leaders for the desired number of Pueblo fighters. Throughout the century, as the non-Christian, non-town-dwelling peoples who ringed the Pueblos' homeland—Apaches, Navajos, and Utes—increasingly raided from horseback, Spaniards grew ever more dependent on mixed Pueblo Indian allies.[15]

Corps of Native fighters could also be employed for personal gain. During the brief and raucous administration of Gov. Bernardo López de Mendizábal, New Mexico's Franciscans raised a chorus of protests. Rather than defend the kingdom from invading bands of heathens, López had turned its scant military resources toward taking slaves for sale in the mines to the south. "For this purpose of making captives," the friars complained to superiors in Mexico City, the governor in September 1659 "sent out an army of eight hundred Christian Indians and forty Spaniards, though there was evident risk at the time."[16] Even if the Franciscans exaggerated, a force of half that size would have included Indian men from many different pueblos.

To coordinate such a complex, polyglot enterprise, Governor López must have relied upon don Esteban Clemente, Native captain general of the eastern frontier and the most prominent, thoroughly Hispanicized Pueblo Indian in the kingdom. Distinguished by the honorific "don," military rank, and likely a written commission, cane of authority, and items of a Spanish officer's uniform, Clemente by all odds rode a horse and wielded a sword and arquebus.[17] Yet most of the hundreds of Pueblo Indians on the expedition of 1659 probably still walked—they could make twenty to thirty miles in a day—and camped a little way off from the Spaniards. Protected in combat by hide helmets, shirts, and shields, they relied for fire power on bows and arrows, at times on slings and dart-like spears, and at close quarters on a variety of clubs.[18]

The Spanish-speaking Clemente, raised in the Tompiro missions of the dry Salinas province a hundred miles south of Santa Fe, knew several Native languages and ran a trading operation to Plains Apaches. Both a business associate of the governor and a favorite of the Franciscans, Clemente got caught in the crossfire between church and state. The missionaries condemned Pueblo Indian kachina dances, while Governor López, who considered these ceremonials nothing more than harmless folk rituals, encouraged their revival. In 1660 the scandalized friars urged Clemente to dictate a statement condemning these "idolatrous" Pueblo rites. The kachinas, a dutiful Clemente swore, "are evil."[19]

POTSHUNO, A TEWA WARRIOR OF NAMBÉ *(Photograph by John K. Hillers, 1879, B. M. Thomas Collection (MNM/DCA), no. 55217)*

Toward the end of the 1660s, the kachinas and whatever other powers controlled the Pueblo universe seemed bent on revenge. Searing drought, famine, disease, crop and supply failures, and ever more frequent Apache raids scourged the kingdom. Hard-pressed governors appealed to the friars to empty their mission larders in support of defensive campaigns. Gov. Juan de Medrano y Mesía in the summer of 1669, hoping to lay waste the crops of western Apaches and Navajos, vowed to launch from the Jémez pueblos a force of fifty armed colonists and six hundred Christian Indians.[20]

To parry thrusts from eastern or Plains Apaches, Governor Medrano in 1670 appointed combat-scarred Capt. Juan Domínguez de Mendoza as field commander of thirty Spanish men-at-arms and three hundred Pueblo auxiliaries. Designating Abó, home pueblo of Esteban Clemente, as the staging area, the governor, not surprisingly, failed even to mention Clemente.[21]

291

Whether he came gradually to treason or decided all of a sudden, Clemente conspired to overthrow the colonial regime and win back the kachinas. The Spaniards' brutal crackdown on his Piro neighbors late in the 1660s may have contributed to the timing of Clemente's attempted revolt, probably around 1670.

The inevitably thick file of writs and declarations that described what Clemente tried to do has gone missing. All we have today is a statement made in 1681 by Diego López Sambrano, a tall, red-headed, and beady-eyed Hispanic native of Santa Fe, hated by the Tewa Indians.[22] According to López Sambrano:

> An Indian named Don Esteban Clemente, governor of all the Salinas pueblos, whom the whole kingdom secretly obeyed, launched another conspiracy which was general throughout the kingdom. He ordered the Christian Indians to drive all the horse herds of every district into the mountains, so as to leave the Spaniards afoot, and on Maundy Thursday night, as was attempted during the administration of General Concha [1649–53], to consume the entire body of Christians, sparing not a single friar or Spaniard. Having exposed this treason, they hanged said Indian, Don Esteban, and calmed the others, and when the property of said Indian was seized there was found in his house a great quantity of idols and whole pots of idolatrous powdered herbs, feathers, and other disgusting things.[23]

Clemente had fallen short. His revolt was simply not a long enough time coming. The eleventh chapter of 2 Samuel in the Christian Old Testament begins, "In the spring of the year, the time when kings go out to battle."[24] Both Clemente and his unnamed predecessor plotted to engage the Spaniards in the spring during Christian Holy Week. Would not mid-August, as all hands turned to the ripening harvest, have been a more opportune season? In retrospect we might also question an insurgency planned for the worst of times, when resources were scarce and everyone went armed. Chances were, when conditions improved, the Spanish ruling class would grow lax and less alert. After years of recruiting Pueblo Indian auxiliaries to accompany Spaniards on campaign, Clemente had apostatized to marshal the same Pueblo war captains against the colonial regime. Why would they have trusted him? He was too widely known, his connections too inclusive, and someone informed the Spaniards.

With the collapse of Clemente's project and the abandonment of the Salinas and some Piro pueblos in the 1670s, energy in the Pueblo world shifted notably from south and east to north and west, back to the heartland of the

Tewas and their Tano (or Southern Tewa) allies, along with an unsubmissive circle of outlying neighbors.

* * * *

Pueblo-Spanish relations pivoted on the year 1675. Combative Juan Durán de Miranda, ousted as governor in 1665 but reappointed in 1671, was finally leaving. By one of his last acts, Miranda commissioned Juan Domínguez de Mendoza to lead fifty-four Spanish men-at-arms and two hundred fifty Pueblo auxiliaries against Faraón Apaches in central New Mexico.[25] Whether they chose to admit it, by this time Spanish and Pueblo defenders of the kingdom had become codependent.

Not much of a record survives for the incoming governor Juan Francisco Treviño, except for one fateful episode. In 1675 the mission supply caravan returning to Mexico City carried not only former governor Miranda but also Franciscan superior Francisco de Ayeta, en route to appeal at the viceroy's court for aid to the desperate colony. The rumble of the wagons had scarcely faded when Treviño found himself in deep distress.

Again our best source is colonist López Sambrano, who stood center stage in the developing drama. At San Ildefonso Pueblo, northwest of Santa Fe, an Indian interpreter had accused Tewa "sorcerers" of bewitching long-suffering Fray Andrés Durán. The new governor, frightened by locals into condoning a witch hunt, dispatched his secretary Francisco Javier, along with López Sambrano, Luis de Quintana, and other vigilante riders, to sweep through Tewa country rounding up alleged sorcerers and confiscating ceremonial paraphernalia. It did not end there.[26]

Father Ayeta recalled later the "repeated and severe punishments" Spanish governors had inflicted on practitioners of Pueblo religion, in his words, most "recently in the year '75 . . . by Don Juan Francisco Treviño, who hanged four Indians in one day and had forty-three sentenced to whipping and being sold into slavery as convicted and confessed idolaters, sorcerers, and homicides."[27] The preemptive hangings took place among three different Pueblo language groups—Tewas, Keres, and Jemez—indicating a wider circle of unrest. Jailers whipped the prisoners, but before they could be sold, Tewa fighting men staged a daring coup.

López Sambrano picks up the story: "One morning more than seventy Indians armed with macanas [clubs] and leather shields entered the house where the said general [Treviño] was, filling two rooms." Keen observers of Spanish behavior, these Tewa men, like their fathers and grandfathers before them, carried token gifts. But they were armed, and an unflinching resolve shown in their eyes. They demanded that the governor pardon and release the prisoners or they would kill him and attack Santa Fe with reinforcements

293

waiting in the hills. Treviño caved. "Wait a while, children," he supposedly said, "I will give them to you and pardon them on condition that you forsake idolatry and iniquity."[28]

Bearing malice, the whipped and pardoned prisoner from Okhay Owingeh whom Spaniards would later accuse of plotting a general Pueblo revolt, had a notable advantage over Esteban Clemente—no Spaniard knew who he was. None of his accusers ever found out his Christian baptismal name. And when finally they did learn an approximation of his Tewa name, Po'pay, loosely "Ripe Corn," it was too late.

Meanwhile, in 1677, Father Ayeta reappeared with the convict-settlers and supplies he had wrung from the viceroy, and ineffectual Antonio de Otermín took over the governorship from a chastened Treviño. The Tewa coup of 1675 seemed all but forgotten. Defensive codependence resumed. The veteran Domínguez was back in the saddle in 1678, commanding fifty armed colonists and four hundred Pueblo auxiliaries against Navajos west of the Jemez Mountains.[29]

If Domínguez really did have four hundred Pueblo fighting men under his command, and the average quota per pueblo was forty, or more likely twenty, Pueblo males from ten or twenty different communities took part. In addition to the usual core of Tewas and Tanos, the force must have incorporated Keresan and Jemez men, and probably Northern Tiwas from Taos and Picuris, foreshadowing ominously the Rio Grande confederation of 1680.

Pedro Naranjo, a Keresan elder testifying in 1681, revealed how the anonymous Po'pay had established his command post in a kiva at Taos, the farthest pueblo north of Santa Fe and home to a fierce tradition of defiance. Naranjo did not say when Po'pay moved north or how long he conspired with conjured Native super-heroes.[30] There is no way to know whether the Pueblo war captains on Domínguez's campaign of 1678 had any idea of plans already underway for a massive revolt.

Po'pay, unlike Clemente, appears to have been more than a paramount war captain, most likely a major religious leader of the Tewa summer people.[31] Through skillful negotiations and, according to Naranjo and other witnesses, a campaign of fear and coercion, he gained the temporary allegiance of both spiritual and military leaders across a broad sector of the northern and western Pueblo world. As the time drew near, Po'pay and his chief lieutenants—several of whom had dangerous kinship ties to Spaniards—would use knotted yucca-fiber cords and smoke signals to spread the word.

* * * *

The bloody Pueblo Revolt of August 1680—the first and swiftest act of the Pueblo-Spanish War—caught the Spaniards notoriously off guard. That

Saturday, 10 August, feast day of San Lorenzo, veteran Capt. Francisco de Anaya Almazán and eight herders had drawn routine duty guarding horses near the Tewa pueblo of Santa Clara. Attacked without warning, two of the herders fell dead as Anaya and the others spurred hell-bent for Santa Fe. After a terrifying, ten-day Pueblo siege of their capital, Spanish survivors broke out, and their besiegers let them go. Six weeks later, just northwest of El Paso, Governor Otermín's aides counted 1,946 refugees. Upriver, some four hundred of their neighbors lay dead. The Pueblos had taken back their world.[32]

None of the twenty-one friars slain in their missions had died farther south than San Marcos in the Galisteo Basin or Santo Domingo on the Rio Grande.[33] The epicenter of revolt was in the north (as it would be again in 1696, 1805, 1837, and 1847). The Southern Tiwas, Piros, and Tompiros had either abandoned their pueblos earlier or gone south with the Spaniards. Not surprisingly, when Otermín mounted an abortive reconquista in the winter of 1681, he had with him not only twenty-one Manso Indian auxiliaries from El Paso, but also fifty-six Piros, thirty-one Southern Tiwas, and nine renegades from Jemez.[34]

The decade-long second act of the Pueblo-Spanish War played itself out between 1681 and 1691, severely punishing both sets of widely separated former combatants. Exiled Spaniards and contingent Pueblo Indians endured misery in refugee camps around El Paso. And, up the Rio Grande, independent Pueblo Indians, rid of their colonial overlords for the time being, fell back into disunion.

Keresan war captain Bartolomé de Ojeda watched it happen. Raised in the missions, Ojeda, like Clemente, spoke and wrote Spanish. Evidently he had taken an active part in the Pueblo Revolt. Later, when Gov. Domingo Jironza and southern Pueblo fighters marched upriver to sack Zia in 1689, Ojeda fought them like a wounded mountain lion. Captured and taken to El Paso, Ojeda experienced a change of heart and quit the revolt.

Testifying before Governor Jironza, the rehabilitated Ojeda not only related in graphic detail how Jemez, Acomas, Zunis, and Hopis had put to death seven Franciscans in 1680, but also the subsequent discord he had observed among the Pueblos. The Keres of Zia, Santa Ana, San Felipe, and Cochiti, along with the Jemez, Taos, and Pecos Pueblos, warred incessantly against the Tewas and Picuris. The Acomas had split; one faction abandoning their stronghold to join other disenchanted Keres at Laguna. Zunis and Hopis were also at war. Apaches traded with some pueblos and committed hostilities against others, while Utes raided wherever they could.[35]

Whether Ojeda had the alliances and misalliances straight, his testimony implied severe disharmony in the Pueblo world. Moreover, endemic Pueblo factionalism tore apart certain Pueblo communities, notably Acoma and Pecos. Taken together, such disintegration invited the Pueblo-Spanish War's third and final act: Spanish restoration of the kingdom in the 1690s.

Capable, lisping, forty-seven-year-old Diego José de Vargas Zapata Luján Ponce de León y Contreras acceded to the governorship of New Mexico in exile at El Paso in February 1691. Vargas would use Pueblo Indian auxiliaries against other Pueblos more often and more effectively than any governor before or after him. A significant number of Pueblo leaders now recognized that rule by one of their own offered less security and fewer benefits than the colonial regime. To rally such "pro-Spanish" headmen, Vargas relied on Ojeda, who became the governor's chief advance man, recruiter, and adviser on Indian affairs. Other Pueblo leaders, who vowed to die rather than allow the Spaniards' return, led their people to mesa-top fortifications and dared Vargas to come get them.

Vargas's strategy of restraint during his ritual reconquest in 1692 won the Spanish governor steadfast Pueblo allies in future battles. He had refused to loot abandoned Pecos Pueblo. Hence, in the last days of 1693, as Spaniards stormed the many-tiered citadel Tewas and Tanos had built right over the top of the old governor's palace, one hundred and forty Pecos fighters joined Vargas's command. Indian-occupied Santa Fe fell. Precarious as their hold proved to be, the Spaniards were back.[36]

In 1694, Vargas, relying consistently on more Pueblo Indian auxiliaries than Spanish men-at-arms, assaulted and eventually carried the three high places fortified by breakaway Keres warriors from Santo Domingo and Cochiti on the Mesa of la Cieneguilla de Cochiti, defiant Jemez on San Diego Mesa, and Tewas and Tanos atop Black Mesa.[37] The Keres had splintered, yet Ojeda kept the majority of his kin from Zia, Santa Ana, and San Felipe solidly in the Spanish camp.

We may never sort out the hatreds and loyalties that drove Vargas's Pueblo Indian allies. Were their ambivalent passions born during the Pueblo-Spanish War or summoned from obscure memories that long antedated that conflict? What possessed Ojeda's Keresan auxiliaries to battle other Keres fortified on Cieneguilla Mesa? When he led these same Keresan fighters up San Diego Mesa against Jemez defenders, did their motivation harken back to the fourteenth century when belligerent ancestors of these Jemez pushed roughly into Keresan territory? Whatever impelled them, Pueblo Indians had fought other Pueblo Indians during the Spanish conquest just as they did again during the Spanish restoration.

When open revolt flared once more in June 1696, ending the lives of five more Franciscans and some twenty Spanish colonists, Vargas scrapped diplomacy and campaigned hard, always with Pecos and other Pueblo fighting men at his side.[38] After 1696 Pueblo warriors never again fought against other Pueblos on a large scale. By year's end, the Pueblo-Spanish War was over.

Instinctively, the kingdom's old defensive codependence between Pueblos and Spaniards fell back into place.[39] Vargas, in fact (imprisoned by his successor in Santa Fe, acquitted in Mexico City, and reappointed to the governorship of New Mexico in 1703), led a campaign against Faraón Apaches in the early spring of 1704. His forty-some presidial soldiers and armed colonists were outnumbered typically three-to-one by Pueblo Indian auxiliaries from at least a dozen villages, but most from Pecos. Abruptly, operations ceased. Don Diego de Vargas, recolonizer and twice governor of New Mexico, had fallen ill evidently with dysentery, and died a few days later.[40]

* * * *

By the time Fray Nicolás Hidalgo allegedly grabbed Pedro Acomilla's penis in 1638, Spaniards had occupied New Mexico for forty years. Another forty-two years passed before the revolt of 1680. During those eighty-two years, the Pueblo Indians' population shriveled by two-thirds, from some sixty thousand to twenty thousand. Similarly, the number of Pueblo communities fell from around ninety to fewer than forty.[41] Did Po'pay feel the urgency to act knowing that Pueblo war societies had shrunk notably since the days of his father, further still since those of his grandfather? Like sand in an hour glass, the Pueblos' numerical superiority was slipping away.

And all the while, time ripened. Experiences were stored up. Some Pueblo Indians resisted, failed, and died; Spanish governors gouged the colony and left; colonists' children played with Pueblo children. On campaign after campaign, Pueblo Indian war captains, serving alongside Spaniards, grew in confidence and in acceptance of each other. Then, in the 1660s and 1670s as the forces of nature bore down on the kingdom, certain Franciscans saw the devil leering from every shadow, and more and more Pueblo Indians turned again to the kachinas. Finally, the sons of August showed the way. It may be that the stunning success of the Pueblo Revolt in 1680 owed most to the singular and undeniable fact that it was such a long time coming.

Notes

1. Ramón A. Gutiérrez, When Jesus Came, the Corn Mothers Went Away: Marriage, Sexuality, and Power in New Mexico, 1500–1846 (Stanford, Calif.: Stanford University Press, 1991), 75–76, 114, 123, 127–28, 209–10.
2. Stephen Plog, Ancient Peoples of the American Southwest, Ancient Peoples and Places series (New York: Thames and Hudson, 1997), 146–51, 158–60, 167–69; Steven A.

297

LeBlanc, *Prehistoric Warfare in the American Southwest* (Salt Lake City: University of Utah Press, 1999); and James F. Brooks, "Violence, Exchange, and Renewal in the American Southwest," *Ethnohistory* 49 (winter 2002): 205–18.

3. See, for example, Philip Wayne Powell, *Soldiers, Indians, and Silver: The Northward Advance of New Spain, 1550–1600* (Berkeley: University of California Press, 1952), 158–71.

4. "The Relación de la Jornada de Cíbola, Pedro de Castañeda de Nájera's Narrative, 1560s (copy, 1596)," in *Documents of the Coronado Expedition, 1539–1542: "They Were Not Familiar with His Majesty, nor Did They Wish to Be His Subjects,"* ed. and trans. Richard Flint and Shirley Cushing Flint (Dallas, Tex: Southern Methodist University Press, 2005), 420.

5. "La Relación Postrera de Cíbola (Fray Toribio de Benavente's Narrative), 1540s," in *Documents of the Coronado Expedition*, Flint and Flint, 299.

6. Richard Flint, *Great Cruelties Have Been Reported: The 1544 Investigation of the Coronado Expedition* (Dallas, Tex: Southern Methodist University Press, 2002), 286.

7. Castañeda, "The Relación de la Jornada de Cíbola," in *Documents of the Coronado Expedition*, Flint and Flint, 398.

8. Diego Pérez de Luxán in George P. Hammond and Agapito Rey, *The Rediscovery of New Mexico, 1580–1594: The Explorations of Chamuscado, Espejo, Castaño de Sosa, Morlete, and Leyva de Bonilla and Humaña*, Coronado Cuarto Centenial Publications, 1540–1940 (Albuquerque: University of New Mexico Press, 1966), 187–88. Thanks to David Snow for the reference.

9. George P. Hammond and Agapito Rey, eds., *Don Juan de Oñate, Colonizer of New Mexico, 1595–1628*, 2 vols., Coronado Cuarto Centennial Publications, 1540–1940 (Albuquerque: University of New Mexico Press, 1953); and Marc Simmons, *The Last Conquistador: Juan de Oñate and the Settling of the Far Southwest*, Oklahoma Western Biographies series (Norman: University of Oklahoma Press, 1991).

10. Gaspar Pérez de Villagrá, *Historia de la Nueva México, 1610*, ed. Miguel Encinias, Alfred Rodríguez, and Joseph P. Sánchez (Albuquerque: University of New Mexico Press, 1992).

11. "Spaniards who left written records of the [Coronado] expedition generally ignored the roles, and even the very presence, of the *indios amigos*." Richard Flint, "Without Them, Nothing Was Possible: The Coronado Expedition's Indian Allies," *New Mexico Historical Review* 84 (winter 2009): 65.

12. Hammond and Rey, *Don Juan de Oñate*, 1:470.

13. Frederick Webb Hodge, George P. Hammond, and Agapito Rey, eds., *Fray Alonso de Benavides' Revised Memorial of 1634*, Coronado Cuarto Centennial Publications, 1540–1940 (Albuquerque: University of New Mexico Press, 1945), 68–69, 70.

14. Hodge, Hammond, and Rey, *Benavides' Revised Memorial*, 77–78, 301 n. 107.

15. A number of historians, including Carroll L. Riley, have noted the potential danger to Spaniards of reliance on armed Pueblo fighting men. Yet no one has focused specifically on Pueblo auxiliaries in the seventeenth century. Oakah L. Jones Jr. began his coverage in the 1690s, writing mistakenly, "Pueblo Indians were not used extensively by the Spaniards for early campaigns against the raiding tribes." While France V. Scholes acknowledged that the alcaldes mayores oversaw "the employ-ment of Indians as house servants, farm laborers, and herdsmen," he said nothing

about their recruitment of Pueblo auxiliaries. Carroll L. Riley, *The Kachina and the Cross: Indians and Spaniards in the Early Southwest* (Salt Lake City: University of Utah Press, 1999), 156, 197, 204–6; Oakah L. Jones Jr., *Pueblo Warriors and Spanish Conquest* (Norman: University of Oklahoma Press, 1966), 36; and France V. Scholes, "Civil Government and Society in New Mexico in the Seventeenth Century," *New Mexico Historical Review* 10 (April 1935): 91–93.

16. "The Franciscans of New Mexico to the Viceroy, Santo Domingo, September 8, 1659," in *Historical Documents Relating to New Mexico, Nueva Vizcaya, and Approaches Thereto, to 1773*, ed. Charles Wilson Hackett, vol. 3 (Washington, D.C.: Carnegie Institution, 1937), 187.

17. For more than a century, Spaniards had been using Native auxiliaries and commissioning their leaders. Powell, *Soldiers, Indians, and Silver*, 158–71.

18. Rick Hendricks, "Pueblo-Spanish Warfare in Seventeenth-Century New Mexico: The Battles of Black Mesa, Kotyiti, and Astialakwa," in *Archaeologies of the Pueblo Revolt: Identity, Meaning, and Renewal in the Pueblo World*, ed. Robert W. Preucel (Albuquerque: University of New Mexico Press, 2002), 183.

19. John L. Kessell, "Esteban Clemente, Precursor of the Pueblo Revolt," *El Palacio* 86 (winter 1980–81): 17.

20. John L. Kessell, *Kiva, Cross, and Crown: The Pecos Indians and New Mexico, 1540–1840* (Washington, D.C.: National Park Service, 1979), 212, 217–20. See also James E. Ivey, "'The Greatest Misfortune of All': Famine in the Province of New Mexico, 1667–1672," *Journal of the Southwest* 36 (spring 1994): 76–100.

21. Juan Rodríguez de Medrano y Mesía, Appointment of Juan Domínguez de Mendoza, 11 September 1670, Santa Fe, document no. 22, in Marc Simmons and José Antonio Esquibel, *Juan Domínguez de Mendoza* (forthcoming).

22. Fray Angélico Chávez, *Origins of New Mexico Families: A Genealogy of the Spanish Colonial Period*, rev. ed. (Santa Fe: Museum of New Mexico Press, 1992), 58.

23. Diego López Sambrano quoted in Kessell, "Esteban Clemente," 16.

24. 2 Samuel 11:1 (New Revised Standard Version).

25. Riley, *The Kachina and the Cross*, 197, 296.

26. "Diego López Sambrano, Declaration, Hacienda of Luis de Carbajal, December 22, 1681," in *Revolt of the Pueblo Indians of New Mexico and Otermín's Attempted Reconquest, 1680–1682*, ed. Charles Wilson Hackett and Charmion Clair Shelby, 2 vols., Coronado Cuarto Centennial Publications, 1540–1940 (Albuquerque: University of New Mexico Press, 1940), 2:292–303.

27. "Fray Francisco de Ayeta, Opinion, Hacienda of Luis de Carbajal, December 23, 1681," in *Revolt*, Hackett and Shelby, 2:305–18, especially 309.

28. "López Sambrano, Declaration," in *Revolt*, Hackett and Shelby, 2:301.

29. Riley, *The Kachina and the Cross*, 197, 296.

30. "Pedro Naranjo, Declaration, Río del Norte, December 19, 1681," in *Revolt*, Hackett and Shelby, 2:245–49. Historian Barbara De Marco provides comments and a full Spanish transcription of Naranjo's testimony. Barbara De Marco, "Voices from the Archives I: Testimony of the Pueblo Indians on the 1680 Revolt," *Romance Philology* 53 (spring 2000): 415–26.

31. Alfonso Ortiz, "Popay's Leadership: A Pueblo Perspective," *El Palacio* 86 (winter 1980–81): 18–22.

32. John L. Kessell, *Pueblos, Spaniards, and the Kingdom of New Mexico* (Norman: University of Oklahoma Press, 2008), 120–28.

33. For the list of Franciscans killed, see Hackett, *Historical Documents*, 335–39.

34. "Muster, Ancón de Fray García, November 7–10, 1681," in *Revolt*, Hackett and Shelby, 2:200–1; and John L. Kessell and Rick Hendricks, eds., *By Force of Arms: The Journals of don Diego de Vargas, New Mexico, 1691–93* (Albuquerque: University of New Mexico Press, 1992), 12–20.

35. Silvestre Vélez de Escalante, "Extracto de Noticias," ca. 1778, trans. Eleanor B. Adams, pp. 156–61, Eleanor B. Adams Collection, Center for Southwest Research, University of New Mexico, Albuquerque; and Kessell, *Pueblos, Spaniards, and the Kingdom of New Mexico*, 131, 137–40, 148.

36. Kessell and Hendricks, *By Force of Arms*; and John L. Kessell, Rick Hendricks, and Meredith D. Dodge, eds., *To the Royal Crown Restored: The Journals of don Diego de Vargas, New Mexico, 1692–94* (Albuquerque: University of New Mexico Press, 1995).

37. Hendricks, "Pueblo-Spanish Warfare in Seventeenth-Century New Mexico."

38. John L. Kessell, Rick Hendricks, and Meredith D. Dodge, eds., *Blood on the Boulders: The Journals of don Diego de Vargas, New Mexico, 1694–97* (Albuquerque: University of New Mexico Press, 1998), 723–1065.

39. See Jones, *Pueblo Warriors*.

40. John L. Kessell, Rick Hendricks, Meredith D. Dodge, and Larry D. Miller, eds., *A Settling of Accounts: The Journals of don Diego de Vargas, New Mexico, 1700–1704* (Albuquerque: University of New Mexico Press, 2002), 219–26.

41. Excluding the Zuni and Hopi pueblos, Elinore M. Barrett calculated that between 1600 and 1680 the Pueblo people had abandoned fifty of some eighty-one communities and that their population fell from about sixty thousand to an estimated fifteen thousand. Elinore M. Barrett, *Conquest and Catastrophe: Changing Rio Grande Pueblo Settlement Patterns in the Sixteenth and Seventeenth Centuries* (Albuquerque: University of New Mexico Press, 2002), 115–16.

So What's Truth Got to Do with It?

REFLECTIONS ON OÑATE AND THE BLACK LEGEND

John L. Kessell

Near the end of volume one in the series, Harry Potter pleads with Prof. Albus Dumbledore, headmaster of Hogwarts School of Witchcraft and Wizardry, for the truth about his life. "'The truth.' Dumbledore sighed. 'It is a beautiful and terrible thing, and should therefore be treated with great caution.'"[1]

At the foundation, somewhere, lies absolute truth—wars take place, Miguel de Cervantes lived, planet earth revolves around the sun. On top of such unassailable facts, however, as time passes, we slather layer upon layer of interpretation, opinion, and emotion. Then we dig back down to pry out "the truth." We want to know who to blame for a war, how did Cervantes survive captivity by Barbary pirates, what is causing global warming?

First off let us ignore the postmodernists' claim that none of us can possibly know objectively what actually happened, only subjectively what is said to have happened. As historians, that is our business—to say what happened, to pursue historical truth as objectively as possible. Historians Jacques Barzun and Henry F. Graff suggest in *The Modern Researcher* (1992) that practitioners of the craft apply six rules: accuracy, orderliness, logic, honesty, self-awareness, and imagination (I might add calmness). Evidence gathered in this way,, one

---

Professor Emeritus and founding editor of the Vargas Project at the University of New Mexico, John L. Kessell is the author of *Pueblos, Spaniards, and the Kingdom of New Mexico* (University of Oklahoma Press, 2008). "So What's Truth Got To Do with It" is a revised version of a talk presented on 25 April 2009, at the annual Thanksgiving and Awards Banquet of the New Mexico Hispanic Culture Preservation League, Albuquerque.

bit reinforcing or challenging another, provides us with the probability upon which to base our "truth," that is, the probability that something actually happened pretty much the way we say it did.[2]

So what about the Black Legend? Finally, the twenty-third edition of the *Diccionario de la lengua española*, first published by the Real Academia Española in 1780, has defined the term "black legend (*leyenda negra*): 1. Anti-Spanish opinion spread since the 16th century. 2. Unfavorable and generalized opinion about anyone or anything, generally unfounded."[3]

In a way, it is a shame that in 1914 Spanish historian Julián Juderías suggestively titled his book *La leyenda negra* (*The Black Legend*), and not more literally "*La denigración de España* (The Blackening of Spain)," surely more fact than legend.[4] Juderías was referring of course to the exaggerated anti-Spanish propaganda of other nations, which he showed convincingly was mostly a hateful legend. Spaniards were simply not *that* bad, especially when compared with other imperialists.

Black Legends are as natural and visceral as human hatred. With what other color might we expect Spain's jealous sixteenth- and seventeenth-century international rivals to have painted the western world's overbearing Roman Catholic superpower? What other way to stereotype Spaniards than as monstrously bigoted, crafty, cruel, and greedy? And surely nowhere did the propaganda mills grind more noisily than in Protestant England or more persistently than in English North America. Documenting the process, historian Phillip Wayne Powell chose an unequivocal synonym for the Black Legend, *Tree of Hate*, subtitling his classic work *Propaganda and Prejudices Affecting United States Relations with the Hispanic World*.[5]

Black legends are easily born. Yet they are harder to kill than a snake. A recent and venomous example is the blatant anti-Hispanic tone of the television production "The Last Conquistador," which, in 2008, set out to chronicle the production of John Sherrill Houser's monumental statue of Juan de Oñate. Through clever editing, innuendo, and untruth, the documentary's producers cast New Mexico's founder as an archvillain.[6]

Obvious as such prejudice is, hunters of the snake beware. Our understandable tendency is to jab at its writhing body, driving untruth too far in the other direction, exchanging its black skin for an equally flawed whitened version. Today, some descendants of New Mexico's Hispanic colonists go too far in their efforts to counter the Black Legend, excusing the transgressions of their ancestors too readily. It is a sensitive matter of degrees: yes, like most of humanity, they may have acted badly, but not *that* badly.[7]

With historical truth, not legend, as our goal, how then do we approach New Mexico's Juan de Oñate? Despite the Ordinances for New Discoveries, promulgated in 1573, which substituted the term pacification for conquest, Oñate was in every way a conqueror.[8] In 1598 with six or seven hundred culturally Hispanic but racially mixed *primeros pobladores*—children, women, and men, hardly any of them soldiers—Oñate broke into an interlocking Pueblo Indian world of perhaps eighty towns and sixty thousand people.

Nine frustrating years later, his funding exhausted and his dreams sunk in empty assay reports, New Mexico's founding proprietor and first governor resigned. In our day, however, certain events of Oñate's administration have taken on a new and contentious life. Reviewing these occurrences fairly demands of us the above-mentioned accuracy, orderliness, logic, honesty, self-awareness, and imagination (as well as calmness) if we are to arrive at the probability that such events actually happened pretty much the way we say they did.

These lightning-rod events include the death of Maese de campo Juan de Zaldívar late in 1598, the battle at Acoma Pueblo in January 1599, and the subsequent trial of Acoma prisoners. Oñate's colony had arrived uninvited in a marginal land of little rainfall, just as other groups had for centuries. The great difference was that the Spaniards' sudden migration came from so far away in distance and in culture. In their persons and in their baggage came much that was new, both attractive and frightening to the Pueblo Indians. Some of these aliens were likely nasty individuals who considered themselves superior in every way to Native peoples, but the majority, we can fairly assume, were ordinary folk who, like colonists and migrants everywhere, sought a new and better life elsewhere. Still, their goal was to impose a foreign sovereignty over the Pueblos' homeland.

The acts of obedience dutifully documented by legalistic Spaniards at Pueblo Indian gatherings were in no sense "treaties" between consenting nations.[9] Despite the efforts of designated Indian interpreters, it was impossible to convey European concepts of law and sovereignty to New Mexico's Native inhabitants. Nevertheless, at the base of their imposing rock on 27 October 1598, a concourse of the Acoma people looked on as Governor Oñate administered the ritual of vassalage to both majesties, God and king. Spiritual salvation, peace, and justice were to be the Acomas' rewards. "The governor reminded them," reads an English translation of the act, "that they should realize that by rendering obedience and vassalage to the king our lord they would become subject to his will and laws, and that if they failed to observe them they would be punished as transgressors of the orders of their king and natural master."[10]

Evidently other Pueblo Indians considered the Acomas overbearing, which stands to reason, given the apparent invulnerability of their mesa-top stronghold. We cannot know for certain whether a faction of Acomas began to plot against the Spanish invaders right away, as poet-captain Gaspar Pérez de Villagrá wants us to believe. Riding past Acoma alone, Villagrá fell into a horse trap but survived. Then, in mid-November, Juan de Zaldívar, Oñate's nephew and second-in-command, with a contingent of men-at-arms pressed westward to overtake the governor, who had set out in the hope of reaching the Gulf of California. The circumstances under which Zaldívar and a dozen of his men died at Acoma are also uncertain, since only Spanish testimony survives.[11] Was their intent to trade peaceably for needed supplies, or did their unreasonable demands provoke the Acomas to violence? Was the killing premeditated or self-defense? On the basis of existing documentation, we simply cannot know.

Following the death of Juan de Zaldívar, Oñate was left with only two choices: withdraw his vulnerable colony—probably outnumbered in the Pueblo world a hundred to one—or attempt to bring the Acoma perpetrators to European justice, while the rest of the Pueblo world looked on. He chose the latter. Adhering to his culture's legal and ecclesiastical requirements, Governor Oñate consulted the Franciscans of the colony who declared the campaign a just war by a Christian prince "to attain and preserve peace . . . not for mere craving for power, revenge, or greed." And the friars' opinion referred more than once to Oñate as conqueror.[12]

Considering available living space atop the mesa, probably not many more than a thousand Acomas dwelled there. According to eyewitness Villagrá, the three-day battle, fought between 22 and 25 January 1599, was a bloody affair. Treasurer Alonso Sánchez, also present, reckoned "that more than eight hundred persons died, and the prisoners taken numbered five hundred women and children, and eighty men."[13]

The notorious trial of the Acoma captives, staged at centrally located Santo Domingo Pueblo, followed European precedents for dealing swiftly with rebellion. Oñate's brutal sentence aimed to dissuade further violence. He condemned male prisoners who appeared to be at least twenty-five, the full legal age under Spanish law, "to have one foot cut off", then, counter-productively, to "twenty years of personal servitude." Males twelve through twenty-four and females over twelve would serve without mutilation for twenty years. The governor declared Acoma children under twelve innocent of their parents' crimes, yet he orphaned them. He entrusted the girls to fray Alonso Martínez, the Franciscan superior, who escorted them to Mexico City to be distributed among convents. The boys remained in New Mexico to either escape or be raised among colonist families.[14]

While the abduction of Acoma children probably caused the deepest immediate grief, the image of dismemberment is what most offends today's

304

sensibilities. This practice was, however, standard penal procedure among Europeans of Oñate's day. To excuse in part the severing of a foot by alleging, on the basis of a supposedly missing document, that Oñate's sentence applied only to the toes is an example of beating the Black Legend snake with a white stick.[15]

The sentence, dated 12 February 1599, and preserved today in the Archivo General de Indias, Sevilla, Spain, reads unequivocally "*a los yndios de beynte y cinco años para arriba a que se le corte un pie y en beynte años de serbicio// personal*" ("Indian men twenty-five years of age and older are to have one foot cut off and to render twenty years of personal servitude"). At least three other contemporary documents proclaim "*se les cortaron los pies.*"[16]

Yet, just ten days before the battle at Acoma began, Governor Oñate instructed commander Vicente de Zaldívar, surviving brother of the slain Juan, to recognize the uncivilized nature and incapacity of the Indians and therefore "to make more use of royal clemency than of the severity that the case demands." Zaldívar had full authority, in the event of a Spanish victory, to execute publically captive males of fighting age or to show mercy. In the case of mercy, Oñate demanded: "you should seek all possible means to make the Indians believe that you are doing so at the request of the friar with your forces. In this manner they will recognize the friars as their benefactors and protectors and come to love and esteem them, and fear us."[17]

Would the granting of such mercy not have served Oñate's purposes after the well-publicized trial? A methodical note in the proceedings does say, however, that the sentence was executed in Santo Domingo and other pueblos, "where the Indians whose hands and feet were to be cut off were punished on different days."[18] But just how, we should ask, was this intentionally brutal sentence actually carried out? In what way were the prisoners punished? Did armed Spaniards repeatedly gather the onlookers, raise high the sword or axe, then on cue have a Franciscan intercede? Here was a theatrical act scripted by Oñate himself in his instructions to Zaldívar. What better method to reinstall the friars in Pueblo communities after the Acoma war?

Two further witnesses for the prosecution, seeking to discredit Oñate, gave ambiguous second-hand testimonies that imply the foot chopping. Yet, the historical record makes no mention of a one-footed Acoma slave. Cutting off a foot, after all, rendered a potential worker all but useless. The second witness concluded that within a year "most of the slaves had run away, that they had tried to reestablish the pueblo," a remarkable project for one-footed men.[19] Oñate's Spaniards may indeed have performed the mutilations, but a close reading of the documents raises reasonable doubt.

305

To the suggestion of reasonable doubt, author David Roberts registered immediate offense, branding the idea "not only sophistry at its feeblest, but a deep insult to the Acomans themselves."[20] By all means let us condemn past brutality, but why is it insulting to the descendants of alleged victims to learn that perhaps the particulars were not as bad as they thought?

Elsewhere, I have been accused of *perpetuating* the Black Legend. One Amazon.com reviewer of *Spain in the Southwest: A Narrative History of Colonial New Mexico, Arizona, Texas, and California* (2002) bristled at my statement that Oñate's colonists "willed to dominate," signing her review, "One very disgusted Spanish girl."[21] Let us face it, colonization is domination. And as noted before, this is a sensitive matter of degrees: bad but not *that* bad. Like it or not, conquest would seem to be the innate human behavior of those of us who enjoy greater numbers and superior technology.

No matter how Oñate's brutal sentence played out, is it not time, four hundred years later, to forgive? Put bluntly to get over it? Unforgiveness—enshrining one's victimhood—does provide a satisfying power over the accused. By claiming moral high ground, unforgivers also grab attention. But they do so at a price. Not to forgive demands that one remains mired in negativity. A few vocal Acomas and their sympathizers attempted to halt the production of John Houser's huge equestrian statue of Oñate , but despite considerable press coverage they failed. Earlier, New Mexico Hispanics and their sympathizers tried to usurp the placement of a statue of Po'pay, leader of the Pueblo Revolt of 1680, in the National Statuary Hall of the U.S. Capitol, but their efforts also proved futile. And those two failures greatly enhanced the historical landscape of New Mexico.

So, what has truth got to do with it? Obviously not as much as forgiveness. But who goes first? Those Acoma descendants who charge Oñate with racist genocide, or the descendants of Oñate's colonists who would change the name of the Pueblo Revolt to the St. Lawrence Day Massacre? Just get over it! But who goes first?[22]

Notes

1. J. K. Rowling, *Harry Potter and the Sorcerer's Stone* (New York: Scholastic Press, 1998), 298.

2. Jacques Barzun and Henry F. Graff, *The Modern Researcher*, 5th ed. (New York: Harcourt Brace Jovanovich, 1992).

3. *Diccionario de la lengua española*, 23d ed., s.v. "leyenda negra," www.rae.es. As for the word "legend" alone, the *Oxford English Dictionary* considers it "an unauthentic or non-historical story, esp. one handed down by tradition from early times and popularly regarded as historical," and *Webster's Third New International* adds, "although not

entirely verifiable." *The Compact Edition of the Oxford English Dictionary*, (1971) s.v. "legend"; and *Webster's Third New International*, (1986) s.v. "legend." Still, most legends endure precisely because they interweave strands of truth or half-truth.

4. Julián Juderías, *La leyenda negra: Estudios acerca del concepto de España en el extranjero*, 13th ed. (1914; repr., Madrid: Editora Nacional, 1954).

5. Philip Wayne Powell, *Tree of Hate: Propaganda and Prejudices Affecting United States Relations with the Hispanic World*, rev. ed., introd. by Robert Himmerich y Valencia (1971; repr., Albuquerque: University of New Mexico Press, 2008).

6. "The Last Conquistador," Point of View, produced by John J. Valadez and Cristina Ibarra (PBS, 2008).

7. A notable black-legend/white-legend debate took place between Lewis Hanke and Benjamin Keen, two eminent historians of Spanish America, in the pages of *The American Historical Review* between 1969 and 1971.

8. John L. Kessell, *Spain in the Southwest: A Narrative History of Colonial New Mexico, Arizona, Texas, and California* (Norman: University of Oklahoma Press, 2002), 73. The belief that conquests had ended in 1573 and "there had not been a conquistador in the New World for over 50 years" appears in New Mexico Hispanic Culture Preservation League, "Excerpts from the NMHCPL Newsletters," www.nmhcpl.org/News_Letter.html.

9. The assertion that the Oñate acts of obedience were treaties "drawn up and affirmed to by both parties guaranteeing the rights and responsibilities of the Indians and Spanish" appears to be another article of faith of the New Mexico Hispanic Culture Preservation League. "Excerpts from the NMHCPL Newsletters."

10. George P. Hammond and Agapito Rey, eds., *Don Juan de Oñate, Colonizer of New Mexico, 1595–1628*, 2 vols., Coronado Cuarto Centennial Publications, 1540–1940 (Albuquerque: University of New Mexico Press, 1953), 1:355. For context, see Marc Simmons, *The Last Conquistador: Juan de Oñate and the Settling of the Far Southwest*, Oklahoma Western Biographies series (Norman: University of Oklahoma Press, 1991), 132–48; and John L. Kessell, *Pueblos, Spaniards, and the Kingdom of New Mexico* (Norman: University of Oklahoma Press, 2008), 25–50.

11. Gaspar Pérez de Villagrá, *Historia de la Nueva México*, 1610, ed. Miguel Encinias, Alfred Rodríguez, and Joseph P. Sánchez, Pasó por aquí series (Albuquerque: University of New Mexico Press, 1992), 175–82, 193–208; and Rubén Sálaz Márquez, *The Pueblo Revolt Massacre* (Albuquerque, N.Mex.: Cosmic House, 2008), 18–19.

12. Hammond and Rey, *Don Juan de Oñate*, 1:452.

13. Ibid., 1:427.

14. For the trial of the Acomas, see Hammond and Rey, *Don Juan de Oñate*, 1:428–79.

15. "According to Dr. Eloy Gallegos, some twenty-four warriors were ordered to have *puntas de pies*, toes (not feet) cut off as punishment for murdering members of the original trading party and then plunging their people into war. According to Dr. Gallegos, who actually inspected the original document in the archives in Guadalajara, Mexico, this was the least severe punishment that could be effected under the law of that time." Rubén Sálaz Márquez, "Oñate and the Acoma War," History Not Hype, www.historynothype.com/Onate_AcomaWar.html. See also Rubén Sálaz Márquez, *Pueblo Revolt Massacre* (Albuquerque, N.Mex..: Cosmic House, 2008), 23. When Gallegos returned to the archive, the document was missing. "La Polémica de Acoma," *NMHCPL Newsletter* 10 (September 2008).

16. Archivo General de Indias, [hereafter AGI], Patronato, 22, Sevilla, Spain; and AGI, Audiencia de México, 26. For the translation, see Hammond and Rey, *Don Juan de Oñate*, 1:477, 478; 2:615, 649–50.

17. Hammond and Rey, *Don Juan de Oñate*, 1:457, 459.

18. Ibid., 1:478.

19. Ibid., 2:649–50. In 1606 a certification of Juan Martínez de Montoya's services states that he and a party of friars visited a functioning Acoma Pueblo in late 1603 or early 1604. France V. Scholes, "Juan Martínez de Montoya, Settler and Conquistador of New Mexico," *New Mexico Historical Review* 19 (October 1944), 338–39.

20. David Roberts, *The Pueblo Revolt: The Secret Rebellion that Drove the Spaniards out of the Southwest* (New York: Simon and Schuster, 2004), 92.

21. Rozana al Jinan, "Same Old Black Legend Rhetoric," review of *Spain in the Southwest*, by John L. Kessell, Amazon.com Customer Reviews, May 2002.

22. A heartening act of reconciliation occurred at Acoma Pueblo in May 2009, when thanks to the good offices of Albert J. Gallegos, Honorary Consul of Spain in Santa Fe, Spain's ambassador to the United States, Jorge Dezcallar de Mazarredo, presented to the Acoma Tribal Council and the people of the pueblo a symbolic silver-headed cane of authority in the name of King Juan Carlos I. Previously, the king himself, during a visit to New Mexico in 1987, had presented similar canes to other pueblos.

Mas Allá

BERNARDO DE MIERA Y PACHECO AND THE EIGHTEENTH-CENTURY KINGDOM OF NEW MEXICO

John L. Kessell

M *as allá* . . . on beyond, over yonder, farther on, always farther on.
        One early fall night, an ailing scout, eighty-six days on the trail and uncertain of where he was, lay moaning in the darkness of an Indian hut while an old Paiute shaman chanted and performed curing rites over him. This small and weathered white man had been suffering stomach cramps throughout most of the journey. Pain showed in his tired blue eyes. He trusted the genius of the Native peoples to cure him. His mixed-blood trail mates, most of them traders with the Utes of the southern Rockies, squatted around him.

They had been exploring some of the most challenging mountain and high desert country in the American West, landscapes mas allá and previously unseen by any but their Native inhabitants. Often these aliens relied on Indian guides. Before the uninvited guests found their way back, they would kill and eat some of their horses, just to stay alive.

The sick man, a seasoned frontier veteran, was not Kit Carson, but Bernardo de Miera y Pacheco, a Spaniard. And this rough, dry landscape was not yet Mexican or U.S. territory, but part of Spain's boundless Kingdom and Provinces of New Mexico. The year was 1776.

Professor Emeritus and founding editor of the Vargas Project at the University of New Mexico, John L. Kessell is the author of *Pueblos, Spaniards, and the Kingdom of New Mexico* (University of Oklahoma Press, 2008). The present article is based on a lecture at the Albuquerque Public Library on 21 July 2012. A longer study by the author, *Miera y Pacheco: A Renaissance Spaniard in Eighteenth-Century New Mexico*, is scheduled for publication by the University of Oklahoma Press on 4 August 2013, the 300th anniversary of Miera's birth.

Miera was one of the most versatile and fascinating historical figures of the eighteenth-century colony. Not a braggart, he did not bother on many occasions to sign his works, a frustration to us today. Ambidextrous in the broadest sense, his varied endeavors included "engineer and captain of militia" on Indian campaigns; explorer and cartographer of lands never before mapped; merchant; luckless silver miner; debtor and debt collector; district officer; rancher; craftsman in metal, stone, and wood; and prolific religious artist. For the last seven years of his life, don Bernardo served as a *soldado distinguido* (distinguished soldier) at the Santa Fe presidio. He was also a devoted Roman Catholic, husband, and the father of two sons and a daughter.

Never one to idle at home by the hearth, Miera always seemed to be planning something. He tried to restore old cannons in 1756, but failed and had to let the local blacksmith finish the job. In 1777 he advised King Carlos III of Spain about how to better defend the northern frontier of New Spain. Two years later, he supervised construction of a dam that washed out almost overnight. Some of his New Mexican neighbors claimed that Miera's projects were dangerous and wanted him exiled from the kingdom. They also resented his influence, calling him Gov. Juan Bautista de Anza's pet. As an artist, however, people recognized Miera's talents. He produced the iconic carved and painted stone altar screen that still graces Cristo Rey Church in Santa Fe today.

Miera lived a life bigger than any bronze statue. He deserves to have his name enshrined on a mountain somewhere in the Four Corners, or a new wilderness area, or a gorge, or a towering monolithic pinnacle. On his surprisingly detailed map of the Domínguez-Escalante Expedition in 1776, Miera himself wrote in block letters "LAGUNA DE MIERA" across a mirage bordering "tierra incógnita," but the name did not stick (ill. 1). On that same painstaking chart, Miera marked with a circle and cross every campsite on their five-month odyssey, including San Juan Capistrano, where the queasy Spanish explorer put himself in the care of a Paiute medicine man on the night of 22 October 1776 (ill. 2).

Why not rename Utah Lake or a boulevard in Provo? The first non-Indian booster to marvel at the scene in 1776, Miera enthusiastically promoted the lake's potential to the king of Spain. We have Escalante this and Escalante that, and of course Carson National Forest. So why not Lake Miera?

* * * *

Biographers of Miera begin at a notable disadvantage. Virtually nothing is known about his first twenty-eight years from the day of his birth in 1713 in the verdant Montañas de Burgos of northern Spain until his marriage in 1741 in the dry desert of Chihuahua at the presidio of Janos. We have his birth and marriage certificates, but almost nothing in between. Hence, the first chapter is rather lean.[1]

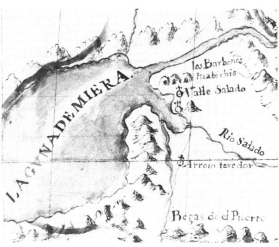

ILL. 1. LAGUNA DE MIERA
(Detail from Miera, "Plano Geographico," 1778; courtesy Eleanor B. Adams Papers, MSS 826 bc, Center for Southwest Research, University Libraries, University of New Mexico)

ILL. 2. SAN JUAN CAPISTRANO
(Detail from Miera, "Plano Geographico," 1778; courtesy Eleanor B. Adams Papers, MSS 826 bc, Center for Southwest Research, University Libraries, University of New Mexico)

What was his youth like? Where did he go to school? How did he get his training in math and geometry, drawing, painting, sculpture, and map making? When and for what reasons did he emigrate? Was it the pull of an offer from New Spain he simply could not refuse? Or the push of an unspeakable family tragedy, a failed first marriage, a scandal? If young Miera had committed a heinous crime and fled, he would surely have used an alias at Janos. On what ship and with whom did he take passage to the Spanish Indies? Where did he disembark? And why did he end up in this arid corner of the Spanish Empire? Fertile ground for the novelist!

As historians, we can pick up the strands of Miera's life story at his marriage to María Estefanía de los Dolores Domínguez de Mendoza, descended from a proud New Mexican family that had fled for their lives two generations earlier before the calamitous Pueblo Indian Revolt of 1680 and never looked back. Miera, twenty-seven, and Estefanía, eighteen, vowed to have and to hold. Their first child, Anacleto (Cleto) Bernardo de Miera y Pacheco, made his appearance in San Felipe el Real de Chihuahua, a discreet eleven months after the wedding. By the time Cleto's little brother Manuel came along in 1743, Miera had moved the family to primitive but thriving El Paso del Norte, gateway to upriver New Mexico.[2]

Without knowing it, the Mieras' move to El Paso in the early 1740s coincided with a local economic upturn, and their departure for Santa Fe in the mid-1750s got them out just as it receded. During their dozen years' residence, El Paso del Norte (ill. 3), according to historian Rick Hendricks, "was demonstrably more important economically than the colonial capital, Santa Fe."[3]

Still, Miera struggled at odd jobs to support his family. Without rank in the regular military, Miera rode on five Indian campaigns while at El Paso. As engineer and captain of militia on the vain offensive against Gila Apaches in 1747, he supposedly drew a map, now missing. He also surveyed the Camino Real from El Paso to Chihuahua, refusing an eight-peso-a-day government expense account as a favor to the crown. That map, too, is missing.[4]

While in El Paso, Miera bought farmland and registered an unproductive silver mine in the Organ Mountains. He rented mules and hauled twenty arrobas of copper from Sonora. Even then, he was not making enough to pay his bills. Estefanía bore him a daughter, María, and the couple grieved the death of little Juan, a newborn third son.[5]

In February 1751, Miera stood in front of El Paso's government house. For the third day in a row, the town crier announced the auction of damaged dry goods confiscated from four French contraband traders who had shown up illegally in New Mexico the previous fall. Miera was the only bidder, and he offered for the lot its full appraised value — 420 pesos, 6 reales, a considerable sum. (The annual salary for a soldier at El Paso's presidio was 350 pesos.) We suspect that Miera was acting as agent for a Chihuahua merchant.[6]

Early in 1755, confronted by a demand that he pay an overdue debt of 407 pesos, 5 reales for goods he had purchased in Chihuahua, Miera declared bankruptcy and found himself in jail. How, he protested from his cell, was he ever to recover and pay his debts, "under arrest in this jail, suffering the foul weather of the present season, the loss of my health, and the notorious misery of my poor wife and children?"[7]

His plea was heard. Within a year, resettled in Santa Fe, Miera had found

ILL. 3. EL PASO DISTRICT
(Detail from Miera map, 1758; courtesy John L. Kessell, Kiva, Cross, and Crown: The Pecos Indians and New Mexico, 1540–1840 [Washington, D.C.: National Park Service, 1979], 510–11)

312

a patron. Gov. Francisco Antonio Marín del Valle (1754–1761) needed a cartographer. And, thanks to the governor's very rich wife, he could pay for whatever he wanted. Moreover, Marín del Valle named Miera alcalde mayor of Pecos and Galisteo. The Mieras' economic rehabilitation had begun.[8]

Having accompanied the governor on his inspection of the kingdom, Miera drew in 1758 a detailed map of New Mexico—from El Paso's far flung settlements in the south to the northern mountains beyond Taos and from the eastern buffalo plains to the Hopi mesas in the west. The map delighted the viceroy in Mexico City, which made Marín del Valle happy.[9]

New Mexico's first couple wanted to be remembered as patrons of the arts. That suited Miera, the artist. All his maps for Marín del Valle featured vignettes: leaping buffalos, Hopi girls, armed Comanches, a battle between Faraón Apaches and Spaniards, and even the pope in his chariot hitched to the lions of Castile, a not-so-subtle reminder of the Vatican's utter dependence on Spain (ills. 4 and 5). With their minds set on a lasting monument

Right: ILL. 4. LEAPING BUFFALO
(Detail from Miera map, 1758; courtesy John L. Kessell, Kiva, Cross, and Crown: The Pecos Indians and New Mexico, 1540–1840 *[Washington, D.C.: National Park Service, 1979], 510–11)*

Bottom: ILL. 5. DANCE AND DRESS OF THE INDIANS OF NEW MEXICO
(Detail from Miera map, c. 1760; courtesy John L. Kessell, Kiva, Cross, and Crown: The Pecos Indians and New Mexico, 1540–1840 *[Washington, D.C.: National Park Service, 1979], fol. 166)*

313

to themselves, the governor and his wife bought a lot across the plaza from the governor's palace in Santa Fe. Here would rise, with the help of Miera, engineer and mathematician, the handsome *Castrense*, or military chapel.[10]

Visitors to humble Santa Fe in 1761, standing in the doorway of this newly built structure, might have rubbed their eyes. At the far end of its dim one-hundred-foot-long nave stood an unexpected three-tiered gallery of saints in bas relief. Roughly nineteen feet wide and twenty-five feet tall, built of fitted, carved, and brightly painted white stone blocks, it was the unsigned work of Miera, sculptor and painter. Only recently have art historians Felipe R. Mirabal and Donna Pierce attributed to Miera this singular piece, the only carved-stone altar screen in the colony.[11]

When his patron left New Mexico, Miera adapted. Commissions from the colony's Franciscan missionaries and from pious civilians kept him carving and painting. Evidently he drew no maps for the next decade and a half. He had begun a small cattle herd on his Pueblo Quemado rancho outside Santa Fe, but the property was too cramped. Hence in 1768, he petitioned for a *sitio* (parcel of land) of one-square league, some 4,428 acres, in broken scrub-covered hills, mesas, and gullies on the Río Puerco at a place called the Cañada de los Álamos. The land was free, but the risk evident. Spanish officials, by granting lands in the Río Puerco Valley, hoped to form an unofficial buffer between Hispanos on the east and Navajos to the west. Miera got the grant and overnight became a sizable landholder.[12]

That same spring, the Mieras' elder son Cleto, who had abandoned his studies for the priesthood and become a soldier, married the Santa Fe alcalde's daughter. That day Miera and doña Estefanía danced with New Mexico's best. If not among the intermarried upper crust, they had joined the capital's elite. Memory of his few nights in the El Paso jail had faded. Now fifty-four years old and rightly acknowledged as map maker, artist, and landowner, Miera might have considered slowing down.[13]

* * * *

Yet, during the eight eventful years that followed, Miera showed no signs of letting up. He served a term as alcalde mayor of the Keres district. Then in 1776, at the age of sixty-two, he set out on a vision quest with two Franciscans that would have killed many a younger man. Renowned Borderlands historian Herbert Eugene Bolton called their trek a "pageant in the wilderness." A puny dozen men in all, they were hardly fleas on an elk's back. Miera and the younger friar, Silvestre Vélez de Escalante, a *paisano* (countryman) from the same region in Spain, were well acquainted. Miera had carved and painted a fine wooden altar screen for fray Silvestre's mission church at Zuni (ill. 6). Pieces of it, collected in the nineteenth century (read stolen) for eastern museums, have in recent years been repatriated to the pueblo.[14]

Father Vélez de Escalante, junior partner on their vision quest, kept the diary. He had convinced his superior, fray Francisco Atanasio Domínguez, that the seasoned Miera would be worth bringing along, if for nothing more than to make a map. And that turned out well. Otherwise, during their crazy, four-month pack trip—a wobbly, 1,500-mile oval around the Four Corners of New Mexico, Colorado, Utah, and Arizona—Miera showed signs of insubordination. After all, his stomach hurt. When it finally dawned on the friars early in October that they would never make it to Monterey in Alta California before winter, Miera caused a near mutiny, urging his trail mates to keep going. If they had, all would have frozen to death like the Donner party in 1846.[15]

All his life in New Mexico, Miera maintained close ties to Chihuahua. Doña Estefanía had family there, and there exists the remote possibility that Chihuahua businessman Luis Francisco de Miera was Miera's illegitimate cousin Luis from Spain, which would explain why he gravitated to the area in the first place. In Chihuahua in 1777, Miera drafted his job application to the king, a document now at the Newberry Library

ILL. 6. SAN MIGUEL, ZUNI, 1775–1776
(Sculpture by Miera; courtesy E. Boyd, Popular Arts of Spanish New Mexico [Santa Fe: Museum of New Mexico Press, 1974], 100)

in Chicago. A year later, he dated in Chihuahua the best-known version of his map of the Domínguez-Escalante Expedition, held today by the British Library in London.[16]

And it was in Chihuahua in 1778 that Miera met the famed Lt. Col. Juan Bautista de Anza, newly appointed governor of New Mexico (1778–1788). The two men hit it off from the start. Anza was doña Estefanía's second cousin. More significant, Miera shared with Anza a grand vision of westward expansion: connecting New Mexico, Sonora, and the Californias.[17]

Only days after Anza took over as governor, he enlisted don Bernardo as a soldado distinguido, a designation reflecting Miera's Spanish birth and his previous service. He was finally in the army, along with his two sons. According to Miera's enlistment papers, "He is 5′ tall, sixty-five years old, his faith Apostolic Roman Catholic, and his features as follows: gray hair and eyebrows, blue eyes, rosy fair complexion, straight nose, with full gray beard." Anza promoted Cleto to squad leader. He stood 5′ 1″ with light chestnut hair and eyebrows, fair skin, and handsome face. Younger son Manuel, who gave his occupation as painter, had "chestnut hair and eyebrows, dark gray eyes, rosy fair complexion, straight nose, with full beard, and two scars: by the right side of his temple and on the calf of his left leg." All three Mieras were married; all three were literate.[18]

As a dutiful agent of Spain's reforming Bourbon king Carlos III, Anza was expected to play God, to turn this churlish, ingrown colony of cousins into a bastion of empire. The result, using historian Carlos R. Herrera's term, was Anza's "social-militarization program." And most New Mexicans hated him for it. To be fair, it was not all Anza's fault. He did not invent his king's reforms; he merely imposed them with an iron hand. Any poor householder who could not muster a firearm, for example, had two months to equip himself with a bow and twenty-five arrows or face, in the words of Anza's stern edict, "the penalty for non-compliance of imprisonment for two months in the jail of this villa."[19]

For generations, nuevomexicanos had dispersed throughout the kingdom, ignoring the heightened threat of Comanches, Apaches, Navajos, and Utes. The colonists' indefensible ranchos dotted the hills and mountain valleys. Anza's response, a strict new building code, called for the construction of defensible settlements, each consisting of thirty-five to fifty armed families. Saw, adze, and axe in hand, New Mexicans were not to rest, even on religious holidays, until the settlements were finished.[20]

At the same time, the governor commissioned Miera to draw him a detailed administrative map of the colony, showing its current indulgent

disarray. Ready by the end of 1779, this map was all business: no papal chariots, Hopi hairstyles, or leaping buffalos. Miera delineated clearly within colored lines the sprawling districts of New Mexico's eight alcaldías mayores, dotting them with countless hamlets (ill. 7).[21]

As much as they cursed his reforms—always more bullying on paper than in practice—New Mexicans had to hail their new chief for his military prowess. Anza's campaign into the southern Rockies late in the summer of 1779 was brilliant. With

ILL. 7. LEGEND ON MAP OF NEW MEXICO
(Detail from Miera map, 1779; courtesy Real Academia de Historia, Madrid, Spain)

reliable intelligence that Comanches, led by their formidable war chief Cuerno Verde, were massing to attack New Mexico at harvest time, Anza resolved to beat them to the punch.

In command of some six hundred presidial soldiers, armed civilians, and Pueblo Indian auxiliaries, plus a couple hundred allied Utes and Jicarilla Apaches, the Spanish governor skillfully outmaneuvered the Comanches to score a resounding victory. The campaign map, today in Spain's Archivo General de Indias, reveals Anza's strategy. The document is unsigned, but indubitably the work of Miera, seemingly his last as cartographer. The real trophy that memorable day was Cuerno Verde's distinctive green-horn head-dress, which, according to one version of the story, may have ended up in the Vatican Museum.[22]

The glow of Anza's victory did not last. Instead, he set Santa Fe on a howl. Just who first suggested relocating the plaza we really do not know. But since Anza actually decreed it, he took the blame. The existing "palace" of the governors and churches were to be torn down and rebuilt south of the Santa Fe River on higher, drier ground (where state government buildings stand today). Not only would this radical urban renewal have utterly disrupted the lives of the 1,915 souls who lived across the river, but it would also have required the demolition or rebuilding to code of 274 homes. No one recorded what Miera thought of deconstructing the Castrense, a building he had designed to house his master work.[23]

He need not have worried. The gutsy delegation of Santa Fe citizens, who left the colony by stealth, succeeded in laying their protests before the commandant general of the northern frontier at his headquarters in Arizpe, Sonora. Of course they exaggerated. Among a host of ills, they accused a tight little cabal of ruling the kingdom: Governor Anza and his wife, the corrupt presidial paymaster, and don Bernardo de Miera y Pacheco. Rewarding their bravado, the commandant general listened. He ordered Anza to postpone indefinitely moving New Mexico's seat of government and to pardon these protesters. Charges against Miera evaporated.[24]

Through it all, Miera kept carving and painting, rarely taking liberties with the saints, but faithfully striking their poses from the printed engravings he copied. Yet all through his career, Miera tended to bestow upon his holy subjects long fingers and unusually big ears (the better to hear our earthly intercessions?). Right into the 1780s, Miera, likely assisted by younger son Manuel, accepted commissions for religious art (ill. 8). Pious or penitent patrons often donated payment for a certain panel, statue, or an entire altar screen, a welcome supplement to the Mieras' family income. Besides, religious art was not as stressful as civic affairs.

For the aging Miera and Estefanía, life was becoming a blur of
toasts and tears, births and deaths.
Grandchildren kept coming. Both
sons lost their young first wives and
remarried. More grandchildren.
Then, in December 1783, one of
the shortest days of the year became
for the Miera clan the darkest. That
day Doña Estefanía died.

We know so very little about her. Her marriage to Miera had lasted forty-
two years, with no hint of scandal in the public record. She had given birth,
nurtured, and reared the couple's two sons and a daughter. She had lost at
least one infant son. Through hard times and not so hard, she had tended the
home fires during the long absences while her restless husband tried his hand
at varied pursuits and scouted the West. How often did he ask her counsel
or her pardon? And how often did he listen? We can only ponder what such
a life on the frontier had done to her beauty. Evident to all, however, was
doña Estefanía's foundational strength as Catholic wife and mother. They
laid her to rest in the Castrense, a sacred space dominated by her husband's
majestic stone altar screen, with room for him beside her.[25]

But he was not ready to join her yet. Despite the void in his life, the seventy-
year-old Miera neither lost interest in the affairs of the colony nor quit carving
and painting. His thirty years' experience with the colony's Native peoples had
earned Miera a privileged seat at Governor Anza's strategy sessions.

When delegations of Comanches who still revered Anza's victory over
Cuerno Verde began turning up in Santa Fe to drink chocolate at the palace
and talk peace, Miera stood by to counsel the governor. Such negotiations
finally culminated on a cold day in February 1786 when all of Santa Fe turned
out to gawk at the western Comanches' paramount chief, Ecueracapa, and
his staff, who had come to ratify a treaty of peace and alliance (ill. 9). But
sadly, Miera, who had gone to bed every night for decades sensing a fearsome
Comanche moon rising in the east, did not live to see it set in 1786.[26]

He died on 11 April 1785 and was buried the next day in the Castrense
beside doña Estefanía. Governor Anza noted in his elegant penmanship at

ILL. 9. COMANCHE LEADER
(Detail from Miera map, c. 1760;
courtesy John L. Kessell, Kiva, Cross,
and Crown: The Pecos Indians
and New Mexico, 1540–1840
[Washington, D.C.: National Park
Service, 1979], fol. 166)

the foot of Miera's enlistment papers the subject's "natural death," indicating that he did not die on active duty or otherwise violently, or as the victim of a recognizable disease, like smallpox or measles. We do not know if the stomach malady Miera suffered on his exploration with the friars in 1776 contributed to his eventual death. Santa Fe santero and archaeologist Charles M. Carrillo suspects that the earlier condition might have been Crohn's disease. Regardless, the cause of death was considered natural.[27]

As he sought preferment in 1777, Miera had pronounced a self-fulfilling prophesy, expressing to Carlos III his desire "to die in your royal service." The Santa Fe presidial roster for 1 May 1785 reported that two soldiers had died, Miera and another man, and that two recruits had enlisted. One of the latter, twenty-three-year-old Luis Manuel Rivera, a farmer, 5'3", of "ruddy skin, black hair and eyebrows, dark eyes, aquiline nose, scars on left hand and on thigh of left leg," was to take the place of the deceased Miera.[28]

Take the place of Miera? Such a premise almost certainly would have given Anza pause. The Spaniard from Cantabria was after all related to the governor by marriage. More important, as a member of Anza's inner circle, Miera for the past seven years had placed at the governor's disposal his unrivaled knowledge of the kingdom's human and physical geography. All over New Mexico as well, in churches and in private homes, the artist had left his mark.

Although little is known of his early life in Spain, the man and his accomplishments mas allá in New Mexico still inspire. Had someone asked Anza to characterize the deceased Miera in a word, the governor might have chosen *universal*—"knowledgeable and accomplished in many and varied fields."[29] Nothing was truer.

Descanse en Paz
Don Bernardo Pascual Joaquín de Miera y Pacheco
Distinguido y Universal
(August 4, 1713–April 11, 1785)

ILL. 10. MIERA'S SIGNATURE
(Courtesy John L. Kessell, Kiva,
Cross, and Crown: The Pecos
Indians and New Mexico, 1540–1840
*[Washington, D.C.: National Park
Service, 1979], 387)*

Notes

1. Bernardo Pascual Joaquín de Miera y Pacheco, Baptism, 13 August 1713, Santibáñez (Santander), Spain, r. 1297485, microfilm, Church of Jesus Christ of Latter-day Saints Family History Library, Salt Lake City, Utah [hereafter FHL]; and Marriage of Don Bernardo de Miera y Pacheco and Estephanía Domínguez, 20 May 1741, Janos (Chihuahua), Mexico, Mission 2000 database, National Park Service, www.nps.gov/applications/tuma/detail2.cfm?Event_ID=7442.

2. María Estefanía de los Dolores Domínguez de Mendoza, Baptism, 7 January 1723, Janos, Mexico, r. 1156625, microfilm, FHL; Anacleto Bernardo de Miera y Pacheco, Baptism, 30 April 1742, Chihuahua, Mexico, r. 162661, microfilm, FHL; and Cañada de los Álamos Grant, 1768, no. 585, subser. 5.2, Surveyor General/Court of Private Land Claims Records, Spanish Archives of New Mexico I, New Mexico State Records Center and Archives, Santa Fe [hereafter SANM I, NMSRCA].

3. Rick Hendricks, "The Camino Real at the Pass: The Economy and Political Structure of the Paso del Norte Area in the Eighteenth Century," *Password* 44 (spring 1999): 13–27 (quotation, 14).

4. Miera y Pacheco to Carlos III, Memorial, 26 October 1777, Chihuahua, Mexico, MS 1165, Ayer Manuscript Collection, Newberry Library, Chicago; and John L. Kessell, "Campaigning on the Upper Gila, 1756," *New Mexico Historical Review* 46 (April 1971): 133–60.

5. Pedro Joaquín Díaz Veanes, 16 January 1745, El Paso, tomo 3, no. 38, Registro y Posesión de don Bernardo de Miera y Pacheco, Archivo Histórico del Supremo Tribunal de Justicia del Estado de Chihuahua. Thanks to Rick Hendricks for photocopies of these documents. Rick Hendricks, "Searching for the Lost Padre: Eighteenth-Century Mining Claims in the Organ Mountains and Greater El Paso del Norte Area," *Password* 46 (summer 2001): 55–78; and Felipe R. Mirabal, "Defining the Colonial World: The Explorations of don Bernardo de Miera y Pacheco," lecture, 14 August 2011, New Mexico History Museum, Santa Fe.

6. Vélez Cachupín, Santa Fe, proceedings against four Frenchmen; goods confiscated and sent to Chihuahua under guard, 1751, no. 514, Spanish Archives of New Mexico II, New Mexico State Records Center and Archives, Santa Fe [hereafter SANM II, NMSRCA].

7. Demand for payment, Francisco Joaquín Sánchez de Tagle, 8–20 January 1755, El Paso, ff. 181–201, r. 3, bk. 2, microfilm, 1750 (cont.), Juárez Municipal Archive, University of Texas at El Paso. Thanks to Rick Hendricks for this reference.

8. John L. Kessell, *Kiva, Cross, and Crown: The Pecos Indians and New Mexico, 1540–1840* (Washington, D.C.: National Park Service, 1979), 385–86.

9. Ibid., 507–12. See also Chantal Cramaussel, "El mapa de Miera y Pacheco de 1758 y la cartografía temprana del sur del Nuevo México," *Estudios de Historia Novohispana* 13 (1993): 75–92; and Danna A. Levín Rojo, "Representación del espacio y política imperial. El mapa de Nuevo México de Bernardo de Miera y Pacheco que preserva el Museo Nacional del Virreinato," *Septentrión* 2 (July–December 2007): 6–43, www. scribd.com/doc/66288477/Mapa-de-Nuevo-Mexico-Miera-y-Pacecho.

10. Eleanor B. Adams and Fray Angélico Chávez, eds., *The Missions of New Mexico, 1776: A Description by Fray Francisco Atanasio Domínguez with Other Contemporary Documents* (Albuquerque: University of New Mexico Press, 1956), 32–39.

11. E. Boyd, *Popular Arts of Spanish New Mexico* (Santa Fe: Museum of New Mexico Press, 1974), 109–10; and Donna Pierce and Felipe Mirabal, "Tale of an Anonymous Altar Screen," *Spanish Market Magazine* 12, no. 1 (1999): 60–67. Miera's authorship is now widely accepted. See Robin Farwell Gavin, "New Mexico's Indo-Hispano Altar Screens," *El Palacio* 116 (winter 2011): 42–48.

12. Cañada de los Álamos Grant, 1768, no. 585, SANM I, NMSRCA.

13. Marriage of Anacleto de Miera y Pacheco and María Felipa Tafoya, 29 May 1768, Santa Fe, r. 31, M-50, box 26, microfilm, 1728–1783, Archives of the Archdiocese of Santa Fe [hereafter AASF].

14. Herbert E. Bolton, *Pageant in the Wilderness: The Story of the Escalante Expedition to the Interior Basin, 1776* (Salt Lake City: Utah Historical Society, 1950); Mirabal, "Defining the Colonial World"; and Boyd, *Popular Arts*, 98–115.

15. Fray Angélico Chávez and Ted J. Warner, eds., *The Domínguez-Escalante Journal: Their Expedition through Colorado, Utah, Arizona, and New Mexico in 1776* (Provo, Utah: Brigham Young University Press, 1976). See also Greg MacGregor and Siegfried Halus, *In Search of Domínguez and Escalante: Photographing the 1776 Spanish Expedition through the Southwest* (Santa Fe: Museum of New Mexico Press, 2011).

16. Miera y Pacheco to Carlos III, 26 October 1777, Chihuahua, Mexico, MS 1165, Ayer Manuscript Collection, Newberry Library, Chicago. A translation appears in Bolton, *Pageant in the Wilderness*, 243–50. See also Marilyn Britton, "Correspondence of Bernardo de Miera y Pacheco," *Herencia* 14 (January 2006): 2–16; Don Bernardo de Miera y Pacheco, "Plano geografico de la tierra descubierta y demarcada por Don Bernardo de Miera y Pacheco al rumbo del Noroeste y Oeste del Nuevo Mexico," 1778, Chihuahua, Mexico, Add. MS 17661.D, Archives and Manuscripts, British Library, London; and Demand for payment, Francisco Joaquín Sánchez de Tagle, 8–20 January 1755.

17. Mirabal, "Defining the Colonial World"; and Alfred Barnaby Thomas, ed., *Forgotten Frontiers: A Study of the Spanish Indian Policy of Don Juan Bautista de Anza, Governor of New Mexico, 1777–1787* (Norman: University of Oklahoma Press, 1932).

18. Bernardo de Miera y Pacheco, Anacleto de Miera y Pacheco, Manuel de Miera y Pacheco, Filiaciones, 1779, ff. 770, 831, 836, r. 21, Miscellaneous Documents, Spanish Archives of New Mexico, New Mexico State Records Center and Archives, Santa Fe.

19. Carlos R. Herrera, "The King's Governor: Juan Bautista de Anza and Bourbon New Mexico in the Era of Imperial Reform, 1778–1788" (PhD diss., University of New Mexico, 2000); and Juan Bautista de Anza, 27 August 1782, Santa Fe, no. 843, SANM II, NMSRCA.

20. Herrera, "The King's Governor," 264–74.

21. Bernardo de Miera y Pacheco, "Plano de la Provincia interna de el Nuebo Mexico . . . ," 1779, Real Academia de Historia, Madrid, Spain, Colección Boturini.

22. Thomas, *Forgotten Frontiers*, 66–71, 121–42; Bernardo de Miera y Pacheco, "Plano de la Tierra que se andubo y descubrio en la Campaña . . . ," 1779, Archivo General de Indias, Sevilla, Spain, Colección Torres Lanzas, México, no. 577; and Phil Carson, "In Search of Cuerno Verde's Headdress," *Pueblo (Colo.) Chieftain*, 3 October 1993.

23. Fray Juan Agustín de Morfi in Thomas, *Forgotten Frontiers*, 91–92.

24. Complaint of New Mexico citizens, 21 June 1780, Arizpe, Sonora, Mexico, Biblioteca Nacional de México, México, D.F., Archivo Franciscano, doc. no. 1926.

25. Burial of Estefanía Domíngues, 13 December 1783, ff. 643, r. 40, Bur-51, Castrense box 28, microfilm, 1779–1833, AASF.

26. Thomas, *Forgotten Frontiers*, 292–345.

27. Burial of Bernardo de Miera y Pacheco, ff. 651, r. 40, Bur-51, Castrense box 28, microfilm, 1779–1833, AASF; Bernardo de Miera y Pacheco, Filiación, 1779; and Charles M. Carrillo, personal communication, 17 June 2012, Santa Fe.

28. Miera y Pacheco to Carlos III, 26 October 1777, Chihuahua, Mexico, MS 1165, Ayer Manuscript Collection, Newberry Library, Chicago; and Santa Fe presidial roster, 1 May 1785, no. 927a, SANM II, NMSRCA.

29. *Diccionario de autoridades*, 3 vols. (1726–1737; fac. ed., Madrid: Editorial Gredos, 1979) 3:392. The final four lines in italics are my imagined epitaph, not Governor Anza's.

A Bicentennial Tribute in Stained Glass

Historias Pequeñas Series

JOHN L. KESSELL

Among the most versatile citizens of Spanish colonial New Mexico, Bernardo de Miera y Pacheco, who died in Santa Fe in 1785, even today leads a parade of heroes portrayed in stained glass at the Colorado State Capitol in Denver. But what, one may ask, is he doing there? Having just written a preliminary biography of don Bernardo, *Miera y Pacheco: A Renaissance Spaniard in Eighteenth-Century New Mexico* (Norman: University of Oklahoma Press, 2013), I wanted to find out. I wondered too if the artist of the piece might still reside in Denver.

In 1976 the state of Colorado, unique among the fifty, commemorated two centennials: one hundred years since statehood in 1876 and two hundred years since independence in 1776. Thus the Colorado Centennial-Bicentennial Commission (CCBC), created in 1971 well in advance of this double milestone, went all out. Projects and events numbered "over 3,000." These included the Southern Ute Inter-Tribal Powwow at Ignacio, "Un Día con la Raza" in Denver, and a revival of "The Ballad of Baby Doe" at the Central City Opera House. Most members of the CCBC had some idea of what was happening when the territory became a state in 1876, but few could tell you anything about the region in 1776.[1]

Professor Emeritus of History at the University of New Mexico, John L. Kessell was founding editor of the Vargas Project, which, with the collaboration of Rick Hendricks, Meredith D. Dodge, and Larry D. Miller, resulted in the six-volume *Journals of don Diego de Vargas, 1691–1704* (Albuquerque: University of New Mexico Press, 1989–2002). Kessell's latest book, *Miera y Pacheco: A Renaissance Spaniard in Eighteenth-Century New Mexico* (Norman: University of Oklahoma Press, 2013) won the Weber-Clements Prize for 2014 of the Western History Association. He is retired just east of Durango, Colorado, in country mapped by Miera in 1776.

Back in the eighteenth century, Spain claimed all of what would become Colorado. Still mostly unknown to any but its Native American inhabitants, this region of the Rockies and Plains lay within Spain's ill-defined Kingdom and Provinces of New Mexico. Hispano traders had long ventured north into Ute country, but left scant impressions. Then in 1765, two little-known exploratory probes led by Capt. Juan Antonio María de Rivera searched in vain for silver as far as the Gunnison.[2]

Not, however, until the banner year 1776, when another Spanish "expedition" cut across western Colorado (northbound between today's Durango and Rangely), carefully recording their progress, did the future state have a hook to hang its bicentennial hat on. But who, the CCBC wanted to know, were these guys, and what were they doing out there?

New Mexico's colonial governor, hard pressed in the 1770s to defend the kingdom against Comanche raiders, had given these '76ers his blessing, along with a copy of Rivera's diary, but little else. If, with no military escort, these amateur adventurers thought they could open a path from Santa Fe to Monterey in Alta California, a goal of the central government in Mexico City, they were welcome to try. Scheduled to depart from Santa Fe on 4 July 1776, they did not set out until the 29th, however, because of a Comanche attack just south of the capital.

Hardly "a pageant in the wilderness," they numbered only twelve. Their inexperienced leaders, two visionary Franciscans, fray Francisco Atanasio Domínguez and diarist fray Silvestre Vélez de Escalante, were relying on an veteran, Spanish-born civilian explorer and mapmaker, don Bernardo de Miera y Pacheco. They never made it to California. An early winter and dwindling provisions turned them back. Nonetheless, they were the earliest Europeans to explore the Colorado Plateau and eastern Great Basin, circumscribing an immense, wobbly, 1,700-mile oval around the present-day Four Corners of New Mexico, Colorado, Utah, and Arizona.[3]

Two hundred years later, in the 1970s, Escalante's diary and Miera's map provided bicentennial planners with a heroic journey to commemorate. The Four Corners Regional Commission, with federal help, launched a ballyhooed re-enactment, wayside exhibits, and diverse publications. Meanwhile, each state funded its own projects.[4]

In Colorado the CCBC vowed not to slight the state's multiethnic heritage. The contemporary Chicano movement headed by Rodolfo "Corky" Gonzales frequently made headlines. A violent confrontation with Denver police in March 1973 at Crusade for Justice headquarters was still fresh in the public's mind.[5] Hence the CCBC's Ethnic Minority Council, among numerous other projects, resolved to honor outstanding individuals from the state's four largest minorities, "Black, Chicano, Native America and Oriental." Each would be portrayed in a stained-glass

Bernardo de Miera y Pacheco by Carlota D. Espinoza, stained glass, 1976. Colorado State Capitol, Denver. Photograph by Jim Steinhart, 2012. Photograph courtesy Jim Steinhart.

window installed at the State Capitol in Denver, a Colorado tradition. Subcommittees comprised of people from the four groups would "select both the subject of the window and the artists involved."[6]

Seemingly an afterthought, the project was rushed to completion. The CCBC did not announce it until June of 1976, yet by mid-September not only had the subjects been chosen but also the artists. Denver santero and folklorist Carlos Santistevan recalls that the Chicano Subcommittee discussed several centennial subjects, among them longtime legislator Casimiro Barela (who already had a stained-glass portrait at the Capitol), as well as various members of the prominent Baca clan. Harkening back to the lone documented bicentennial presence in Colorado, the Domínguez-Escalante "expedition" of 1776, the subcommittee rallied around mapmaker Bernardo de Miera y Pacheco.[7]

Selection of an artist proved more contentious. Eight artists competed for the honor. Given only weeks to prepare her entry, Chicana muralist Carlota D. Espinoza of Denver even today remembers the stress. She had been working at the time on dioramas for the Denver Museum of Natural History and Science. Briefed along with the other project artists about the subject and expedition, Espinoza traveled to the Palace of the Governors in Santa Fe, where she saw one of Miera's maps. An individual who could have provided more details about Miera was out of town, and she had to get back to work in Denver.

Visualizing her subject as, in her words, "kind of a Spanish mountain man," Espinoza submitted a small mock-up of her concept, a standing portrait of Miera with busts of Fathers Domínguez and Escalante on either side. Members of the Chicano Subcommittee liked it and voted to award her the commission. They asked her to prepare a paper version as large as the window, some five by eight feet, but she did them one better, producing a colorful, full-sized oil painting. Despite the rush, the Chicano Subcommittee of the Ethnic Minority Council of the CCBC had chosen well on both counts, subject and artist.[8]

Bernardo de Miera y Pacheco, born in the hill country of far northern Spain in 1713, had emigrated to New Mexico by the early 1740s. Although little is known of his youth and early training, over the next forty years he embraced his new life with unusual gusto. He married the daughter of an old-line New Mexico clan and raised a family. Like his neighbors, he farmed, ranched, and took part in military campaigns. But unlike most of them, he administered two of New Mexico's eight districts. He also painted and sculpted the people's favored saints while creating for New Mexico's governors by far the most accurate maps of the colony to date. In short the resourceful Spanish immigrant reinvented himself as the quintessential Hispanic colonist of New Mexico and what later became Colorado.[9]

Carlota Espinoza had never heard of Miera before she entered the competition in 1976. When we met in Denver in April 2015, I was eager to learn who or

Carlota D. Espinoza and John L. Kessell, Denver, 28 April 2015. Photograph courtesy John L. Kessell.

what had suggested to her Miera's handsome, determined face. Was it a living person, her father or an uncle perhaps, or the portrait of a particular Spaniard? Neither, she assured me: it was pure inspiration.

Neither did Espinoza know of the one documented physical description of her subject. Modestly describing himself as a farmer, don Bernardo de Miera y Pacheco was in 1779, according to his enlistment in the Santa Fe presidial garrison, "five feet tall, sixty-five years old, his faith Apostolic Roman Catholic, his features as follows: gray hair and eyebrows, blue eyes, rosy fair complexion, straight nose, with full gray beard." Save for his blue eyes, Espinoza had envisioned her subject with uncanny precision.[10]

When the Elysian Stained Glass Company of Denver rendered her oil painting, however, she was not pleased. The glass colors were not what she had chosen. Mostly they were too dark, especially Miera's face. She asked the workers in the shop to take out that piece and give her a clear glass. Never having done so before, Espinoza "learned glass painting on the spot." Although she wanted to correct other features, there was no time. The CCBC insisted on unveiling and dedicating at least two of the windows before the next legislative session convened in early 1977. The ceremony for the Chicano and Black American windows took place in the Colorado State Capitol at noon on 7 January 1977, and Espinoza attended. Gov. Richard D. Lamm gratefully accepted the windows in the name of the people of Colorado.[11]

Almost forty years later, she explained to me some of the symbolism of her art. The dark blue area behind Miera's neck and shoulders represents the ocean he crossed. The four dots on his collar and cuffs symbolize the Four Corners. He holds in his right hand a small statue of the Virgin Mary and a paint brush, iden-

Carlota D. Espinoza and stained glass
image of Bernardo de Miera y Pacheco.
Colorado State Capitol, Denver, 28 April
2015. Photograph courtesy John L. Kessell.

tifying him as a sculptor and painter of religious subjects. In his left hand, Miera
grips a mostly unrolled map and a cartographer's wheel.

On either side of Miera's central standing figure, somewhat below his waist,
appear busts of his two Franciscan trail mates, both in the characteristic blue
habits of New Mexico's friars. Father Domínguez looks straight ahead from
Miera's left side (observer's right). Knowing that Domínguez was born in Mexico City, but not that he was as "Spanish" as Escalante, the artist gave him certain Mexican features. Father Escalante, a compatriot of Miera from the same
region in Spain, looks very European. Below him is Spanish imagery framed by
"the cord of travel." Below Domínguez is Mexican imagery inside "the cord of
time."

Two profiles peek out from behind the fathers. Behind Escalante is a self-por-
trait of artist Espinoza in her early thirties, representing a Hispanic woman. An
Indian looks out from behind Domínguez. Had the artist known more about her
subject, Espinoza says she would have made the feminine profile Miera's daughter María, and the Indian the Paiute medicine man who tried to cure Miera's
stomach ailment during the expedition.

Because Espinoza's ancestors came from northern New Mexico and the lower
San Luis Valley, she graciously donated her preliminary, full-sized oil painting of
Miera to the Cultural Center in San Luis, Colorado. It is currently displayed in a
stairwell during the remodeling of the center.[12]

Bernardo de Miera y Pacheco by Carlota D. Espinoza, oil on canvas. San Luis Cultural Center, San Luis, Colo. Photograph courtesy John L. Kessell.

Carlos Santistevan of the Chicano Subcommittee, who favored both subject and artist, commented in the CCBC's final report that the stained-glass window of Bernardo de Miera y Pacheco "will long remain as a source of pride to all Chicano and Hispano people. It will serve as a constant reminder to all that Chicanos built this land, not as subjects but as fellow citizens."[13]

And so it serves today.

Notes

1. G. D. Barrante, comp., *"Once in a Hundred:" Final Report of the Colorado Centennial-Bicentennial Commission* (Denver: A. B. Hirschfeld Press, 1977), 5.

2. A major study of Rivera and his two expeditions by Stephen G. Baker and Rick Hendricks is forthcoming from by Western Reflections Press in late 2015.

3. See Herbert E. Bolton, *Pageant in the Wilderness: The Story of the Escalante Expedition to the Interior Basin, 1776* (Salt Lake City: Utah State Historical Society, 1950). The book was reprinted several times leading up to and during the Bicentennial.

4. Two outstanding Bicentennial-inspired publications are Fray Angélico Chávez, trans., and Ted J. Warner, ed., *The Domínguez-Escalante Journal: Their Expedition through Colorado, Utah, Arizona, and New Mexico in 1776* (Provo, Utah: Brigham Young University Press, 1976); and Walter Briggs, *Without Noise of Arms: The 1776 Domínquez-Escalante Search for a Route from Santa Fe to Monterey* (Flagstaff, Ariz.: Northland Press, 1976).

5. "Chicano Shot, Killed, Police Wounded in Denver," *Albuquerque (N.Mex.) Journal*, 18 March 1973, A-2; and Neil Foley, *Mexicans in the Making of America* (Cambridge, Mass.: Harvard University Press, 2014), 168–70.

6. Barrante, *"Once in a Hundred,"* 39, 88–91.

7. Carlos Santistevan, interview with author, Denver Public Library, 29 April 2015; and Barrante, *"Once in a Hundred,"* 88–91. The subjects and artists chosen by the other three ethnic subcommittees were: Aunt Clara Brown, a former African American slave who became a beloved member of the community in Central City (artist Vernon Rowlette); Southern Ute Chief Buckskin Charlie (artist Eugene Naranjo) and Ute Mountain Ute Chief Jack House (artist Norman Dale Lansing, who shared the Native American window); Chin Lin Sou, Chinese entrepreneur (artist Chen Ting-Shih), and Naoichi Hokazono, Japanese entrepreneur (artist Yuriko Noda, who shared the Asian American window).

8. Carlota D. Espinoza, interview with author, Denver Public Library, 28 April 2015; and Espinoza, email to author, Denver, 8 May 2015.

9. John L. Kessell, *Miera y Pacheco: A Renaissance Spaniard in Eighteenth-Century New Mexico* (Norman: University of Oklahoma Press, 2013).

10. Quoted in Kessell, *Miera y Pacheco*, 138.

11. Barrante, *"Once in a Hundred,"* 42, 88; Espinoza, email to author, 8 May 2015; "The Presentation of Stained Glass Windows to the Citizens of Colorado," Denver, 7 January 1977, Carlos Santistevan, private collection; and Kessell, *Miera y Pacheco*, 60, 113.

12. Espinoza, interview with author, 28 April 2015; and Espinoza, email to author, 8 May 2015.

13. Barrante, *"Once in a Hundred,"* 111.

The Pueblo-Spanish War, 1680–1696
Neither Black nor White

John L. Kessell

Readers of the *New Mexico Historical Review* will know of the so-called Black Legend, the notion that since the beginning of time, of all history's colonizers, Spaniards were the worst! Englishmen in the sixteenth century dove with relish into translating Spanish atrocities, then projecting them as gruesome copper-plate engravings. Shakespeare meanwhile brought Spanish villains to the stage. Even in our day, Henry Higgins still wails, "I'd prefer a new edition of the Spanish Inquisition than to ever let a woman in my life!"[1]

And of course, there is also the White Legend, whereby Spaniards were the great civilizers, purveyors of Christianity, horses, wheat, and peach trees—and not a whisper of smallpox, measles, and flu. But neither black nor white lenses will permit us to see far into the dense, roiling cloud of the Pueblo Revolt, act one of the Pueblo-Spanish War.[2]

Most today will agree that colonization, the subjection of one people by another, is mostly bad, and that sooner or later, the subjugated are likely to react. In 1680, after generations of living together yet apart, two thousand colonists and ten times as many Pueblo Indians met on the killing fields, driven by both acts of high humanity and acts of senseless cruelty.

After the bloody, hand-to-hand combat atop Acoma mesa in 1599, periodic unrest troubled the colonial Kingdom and Provinces of New Mexico.

Long retired from the University of New Mexico Department of History, John L. Kessell has kept an oar in with *Whither the Waters: Mapping the Great Basin from Bernardo de Miera to John C. Fremont* (University of New Mexico Press, 2017), revealing how Miera beckoned Western cartographers down faulty waterways for two generations.

Sporadically, Pueblos rose and murdered isolated Franciscan missionaries. And occasionally, Spaniards uncovered wider conspiracies, enabled in part by the Pueblos' faulty use of Spanish as a common language. Then, about 1670, unnamed informers betrayed the alleged mastermind of a general revolt.

Thoroughly Hispanicized, Esteban Clemente of Abo was the most trusted Indian in the colony. As native governor of the eastern frontier, and of commanding presence, Spaniards addressed him as don Esteban. In 1660, at the urging of Franciscan missionaries, Clemente formally denounced Pueblo kachina religion. Later that decade however, as drought and famine fastened especially upon the Salinas pueblos, don Esteban experienced a change of heart that cost him his life.[3]

His trial is missing. Only the single statement of a colonist ten years after the fact survives. When Clemente, "whom the whole kingdom secretly obeyed," was found out, Spaniards:

> hanged the said Indian, don Esteban, and quieted the rest, and when the property of the said Indian was sequestered there was found in his house a large number of idols and entire kettles full of idolatrous powdered herbs, feathers, and other trifles.[4]

Drought, Apache raiding, and Pueblo unrest continued. A new governor, eager to make a name for himself, arrived in 1675. Informed by colonists that the Tewa-speakers northwest of Santa Fe were growing ever more insolent toward their missionaries, Juan Francisco Treviño ordered a vigilante sweep through their *pueblos* (towns). Spaniards rounded up suspected native sacred leaders—they called them sorcerers—confiscated "many idols, powders, and other things," and helped themselves to Tewa horses. Again the trial record is gone. What remains is Treviño's sentence: four of the forty-seven prisoners to be hanged as deterrent examples; for the other forty-three, whipping and servitude.

But Tewas were tough, among the most effective auxiliary fighters recruited by the Spaniards, mostly against Apaches and Navajos. Now they staged a near coup. More than seventy Tewa men, armed with war clubs and shields, pushed their way into Treviño's quarters and demanded the release of the prisoners. "Wait a while, children," stammered the governor, "I will give them to you and pardon them on condition that you forsake idolatry and iniquity."[5]

Not likely. Although Spaniards never learned his baptismal name, one of the released prisoners with stripes across his back now assumed Clemente's mantle. In fear-based (and possibly peyote-laced) secrecy over a five-year span, he wove together across the half-dozen Pueblo languages a coalition of native religious leaders and war captains. The coalition members, thanks to the Spaniards unwitting recruitment and training, already knew each other. Only in retrospect, after the stunning outbreak of the Pueblo Revolt, did informants reveal this arch-conspirator's native name—Po'pay.[6]

For as long as they lived, surviving colonists remembered the feast of San Lorenzo, 10 August 1680, as their day of infamy. That day, veteran Capt. Francisco de Anaya Almazán and a small detachment were guarding a presidial horse herd near the Tewa pueblo of Santa Clara. Suddenly, and without apparent provocation, these formerly peaceful Pueblo neighbors, painted for war, rushed Anaya and his herders, killing two. As the dazed Spaniard spurred hell-bent for Santa Fe, other Pueblo rebels overran his ranch and murdered his entire family. An Indian witness later identified the nude body of Anaya's wife "out on a field, her head bashed in, and a very small infant dead at her feet."[7]

Miles away, drifting gray smoke signaled the Pueblo Indians' supreme act of defiance. Later, Pecos Pueblo blamed the Tewas. After first torching the roof, vengeful teams of wreckers, whoever they were, tore down adobe by adobe the massive church at Pecos Pueblo, grandest Spanish structure in all the colony. Although Pecos Indians warned their elderly missionary to flee to Santa Fe, other rebellious Indians killed him en route.[8]

Overnight, the *casas reales*, the Spanish government complex in Santa Fe, became the survivors' prison, as more and more Spanish colonists straggled in with their grisly stories, and more and more Pueblo fighters gathered outside the walls. When the besiegers cut off the water supply to the casas reales, Governor Antonio de Otermín and perhaps a thousand others finally broke out amid heavy casualties. The rebels watched from the mesa tops and let them go. Weeks later, the pathetic remnant, a reported 1,946 Spanish refugees, reached El Paso, which for the next dozen years would host the New Mexico colony-in-exile. Some four hundred of their kin lay dead upriver, along with twenty-one Franciscan friars.[9]

So fell a gray curtain on the Pueblo Revolt of 1680, the first act of the Pueblo-Spanish War—a war in three acts. The long-drawn-out second act, a decade-long impasse between 1681 and 1691, saw both Pueblo and Hispano combatants widely separated and deeply fractured. Upriver, Po'pay could not hold together the war coalition once their common Spanish oppressors were gone. At the same time, privation and desertion wracked the Spanish colony-in-exile at El Paso, as disillusioned nuevomexicano deserters streamed south to Chihuahua.

A single Pueblo Indian personified this decade of mixed loyalties, motives, and emotions. Born in the Keres pueblo of Zia or Santa Ana, Bartolomé de Ojeda, like don Esteban Clemente, learned from the Franciscans how to be a Spaniard. Such literate Indians were known as *indios ladinos* (latinized Indians).

A mixed-blood Keres war captain, Ojeda must have joined the rebels during the war's first act in 1680. During the second act nine years later, when a probe of Spaniards and Indian allies stormed the heavily defended Zia Pueblo, Ojeda, twice-wounded, fell into Spanish hands. According to Spanish sources, near death and impelled by fear of hell, he begged for confession. Carried south to El Paso, Ojeda not only recovered, but also lived to play a pivotal role in act three, the Spanish restoration, from 1692 to 1696.

We cannot know what caused Bartolomé de Ojeda's conversion from Pueblo independence fighter to Spanish ally, the reverse of Esteban Clemente. Ojeda, however, emerged as war captain of Pueblo Indians in the service of the Spanish Reconquest. He also mentored the Spaniards' new governor, don Diego de Vargas. Briefing Vargas about the jealous dissensions that had torn apart the Pueblo union, Ojeda may have believed he could lessen his people's suffering by smoothing the Spaniards' inevitable reentry.[10]

On Governor Vargas's reconnaissance in 1692, Ojeda proved indispensable as advance man, interpreter, and negotiator of a peaceable Spanish restoration. On this occasion, having secured no more than symbolic oaths of renewed allegiance by Pueblo headmen, the Spaniards withdrew to El Paso. By Vargas's count, the Spaniards had baptized 2,214 people of all ages and recovered seventy-four ransomed captives.[11]

Mostly women and children, these ransomed Hispano captives had lived a dozen years among Pueblo Indians. Whatever their treatment, they had learned the languages and ways of their captors. Their subsequent role as cultural brokers we can only imagine, since their stories are lost in the gray mists of time. We can assume, nonetheless, that not every captive wanted to be ransomed. An intriguing Zuni oral tradition tells of fray Juan Greyrobe, a Franciscan who went native and ducked when Governor Vargas passed through Zuni in 1692 (an ironic twist since the friars in New Mexico wore blue not gray).[12]

If Vargas counted on a peaceful reentry in 1693, he was a fool. Encumbered by a thousand colonists, he reached Pueblo-occupied Santa Fe amid the swirling snow of an early winter. The rebel occupiers had constructed an Indian pueblo over the Spanish town. Sadly, no one sketched this unique, perennially rebuilt adobe pile, once-Spanish, then-Pueblo, and again-Spanish. Negotiations failed. The Tano and Tewa occupiers refused to move out, so Vargas stormed the town.

The Spaniards might not have succeeded had 140 Pecos fighting men not put themselves under the Spanish governor's banner. Instead, relying on these Pueblo Indian allies, the Spaniards violently retook their capital during the last days of 1693. Vargas straightaway had seventy male prisoners shot.[13]

As the battle raged, Ojeda neutralized the Keres people of Zia, Santa Ana, and San Felipe. Other Pueblo fighters rumored to be rallying never showed. Observing his Pecos allies in combat against other Pueblo Indians, Vargas foresaw the way forward—divide and conquer. Meanwhile, however, his miserable colonists huddled in Santa Fe's fouled casas reales. Worse, its newest occupants had no food. These restored colonists had either to bargain for maize with willing Indians or to loot it from abandoned pueblos. They did both.

Ojeda informed Vargas that Pueblo resisters were fortified atop three prominent mesas, daring the Spaniards to come get them. Tewas and Tanos occupied steep-sided, brooding Black Mesa, twenty-some miles northwest of Santa Fe. Again summoning his Pecos allies, the Spanish governor tried to besiege Black Mesa during stormy February and March but fell short.

Not all the Keres had joined Ojeda. Resisters from Cochiti had migrated to Kotyiti on Horn Mesa. Here in April, Vargas's presidial soldiers, civilian militia, and a hundred Zia, Santa Ana, and San Felipe fighters led by Ojeda successfully overran the stronghold. Most of the defenders fled, only to regroup and attack four days later, freeing half their captive women and children.

Forty-five miles west of Santa Fe, defiant Jemez rebels looked down from towering upper Guadalupe Mesa. In July 1694, a similar, multiethnic Spanish force attacked the mesa stronghold using two trails, the second revealed by Ojeda's men. The sound and fury lasted all morning. Seven of the defenders reportedly jumped off the mesa to their deaths (or to a miraculous salvation). 361 Jemez noncombatants fell into Spanish hands to be used by Vargas as bargaining chips in a high-stakes gamble. He would release their women and children if the Jemez men, whom Vargas had just defeated, would join his force in a renewed siege of Black Mesa. That September, when the Tewa defenders of Black Mesa peered over the edge to see Spaniards and other Pueblo Indians harvesting their maize, they finally chose to come down and be pardoned.[14]

The fall of the three mesa-top strongholds emboldened Vargas to reinstall Franciscan missionaries and Native officials, first at Pecos, and by the end of 1694, at a number of other pueblos. The following year, however, fortunes shifted and everyone suffered. A deadly epidemic, unspecified in the documents, and food shortages—worsened by the arrival of two further cohorts of colonists— set nerves on edge. Then Vargas's project to ease crowding in Santa Fe backfired.

Founding a second municipality, Santa Cruz de la Cañada, upriver in today's Española Valley made sense. Unfortunately, this area, farmed by Spaniards before the Revolt, had been recently occupied by Tano refugees expelled from Santa Fe in 1693. Forced to move again, these Tanos and the still-smoldering Tewas now rose in a second Pueblo Revolt.

Despite reports of growing Tewa impertinence, Vargas was caught off guard. This second revolt erupted in June 1696. It proved neither as widespread nor as lethal as the first, but that was of little comfort to the five murdered Franciscans and the families of twenty-one dead colonists. Vargas took the field with his usual command of presidial soldiers, armed civilians, and Pueblo auxiliaries, mostly from Pecos. The scene at San Ildefonso, a Tewa pueblo northwest of Santa Fe, sickened him. Hastily, he ordered Pecos Indians and soldiers to push over a wall of the gutted church and bury the two Franciscans and several colonists whom the rebels had locked inside to roast or suffocate.

Defeating the Pueblo insurgents in a series of bloody skirmishes, Vargas had restored order by the year's end. While the Spanish nobleman usually kept his composure, when at last his men killed rebel leader Lucas Naranjo, whom Vargas had installed two years earlier as war captain at Santa Clara, Vargas lost it. "I was very pleased," he dictated, "to see that apostate rebel dog in that state: a pistol shot through the right temple had caused his brains to spill out, leaving the head hollow. What little remained was scooped out to take to his pueblo."[15]

A few debts remained to settle with the western pueblos. The isolated Hopis broke away permanently, but never again after 1696 would New Mexico's Pueblo Indians and Hispanos resort to war. At last, the curtain had fallen on the third and final act of the Pueblo-Spanish War.[16]

But peace had come at a terrible price. Pecos Pueblo tore itself apart. Pecos fighters who joined Vargas must have thought Spaniards were good for something, surely spoils, trade, defense, and often a good laugh. At the same time, within the pueblo's confining walls, other Pecos families hardened their hearts toward Spaniards.

Such internal dissension characterized the closed Pueblo world. The archaeological record is replete with Pueblo communities breaking apart. And nowhere in the historical record is this drama played out more passionately than at Pecos Pueblo during the 1696 revolt. For ages, the walls of Pecos had contained two peoples in taut symbiosis: the more conservative farming summer people who looked westward toward the Rio Grande Pueblos and the more liberal hunting and trading winter people, who looked toward the Great Plains and the rising sun. Hence, outsiders' welcome depended on the season in which they approached the pueblo.[17]

Don Juan de Ye, the Native governor who led the Pecos auxiliaries in storming Santa Fe, later had gone among the Taos people as Governor Vargas's emissary and was never seen again. In June 1696, Ye's heavy-handed successor, indio ladino don Felipe Chistoe, responded to the Spanish governor's urgent call with a hundred Pecos fighting men. He also confided to Vargas that a disloyal faction among the Pecos people was treating with the rebels, at the same time proposing a lethal remedy. He would lure the dissenting leaders to a meeting and murder them. Vargas approved.

Days later, Chistoe invited the anti-Spanish headmen to a parley in the gray dimness of a Pecos kiva, the most sacred built space in the Pueblo world. Old Diego Umbiro, their spokesman, urged that all Spaniards die since they were "of a different flesh." Offended, Chistoe leapt up brandishing his governor's staff while his men overpowered Umbiro and three others, and hanged them. A Pueblo version of death in the cathedral, Chistoe's purge set the pueblo on a downward spiral as aggrieved relatives repeatedly sought revenge then fled to asylum elsewhere.

A fifth member of the alleged anti-Spanish cabal, who escaped death in the kiva, Chistoe shot later and delivered the rebel's head, hand, and foot to Governor Vargas in Santa Fe. "When all the citizens of this villa saw them," Vargas reported, "they were surprised at this Indian's loyalty. I thanked him and gave him and the others gifts."[18]

The Pueblo-Spanish War, like so many human confrontations, tempts us to choose either soulful, noble-hearted Pueblo Indians or callous, cruel-hearted Spaniards. Neither distortion, however, "neither black nor white," offers a realistic view of this momentous turning point in the history of colonial New Mexico.

Notes

1. Bartolomé de las Casas, *A Brief Account of the Destruction of the Indies Or, a faithful NARRATIVE OF THE Horrid and Unexampled Massacres, Butcheries, and all manner of Cruelties, that Hell and Malice could invent, committed by the Popish Spanish Party on the inhabitants of West-India, TOGETHER With the Devastations of several Kingdoms in America by Fire and Sword, for the space of Forty and Two Years, from the time of its first Discovery by them* (1552; repr., London: Oxford University Press, 2011); Paula Blank, *Shakespeare and the Mismeasure of Renaissance Man*, (Ithaca, N.Y.: Cornell University Press, 2006), 100–105; and Rex Harrison, vocalist, "I'm an Ordinary Man," *My Fair Lady*, directed by George Cukor (Burbank, Calif.: Warner Bros. Pictures, 1964).

2. Regarding the Black Legend, Ricardo García Cárcel argues, "It is neither a legend, insofar as the negative opinions of Spain have genuine historical foundations, nor is it black, as the tone was never consistent nor uniform. Grays abound, but the color of these opinions was always viewed in contrast [to what] we have called the white legend." Ricardo García Cárcel and Lourdes Mateo Bretos, *La leyenda negra* (Madrid, Spain: Grupo Anya, S.A., 1990), 84. Passage translated to English from Spanish by the author. The White Legend, in opposition to the perceived Black Legend, is the theme of typical essays in the newsletter of the New Mexican Hispanic Culture Preservation League. For example, see Rubén M. Sálaz, "Native Survival Part of Legacy," New Mexican Hispanic Culture Preservation League, accessed 11 March 2019, http://www.nmhcpl.org/uploads/Native_Survival_Part_of_Legacy.pdf. This article was also published in the *Albuquerque (N. Mex) Journal*, 19 December 1998; Doña Conchita Lucero, "Santiago Our Protector," New Mexico Culture Preservation League, accessed 11 March 2019, http://www.nmhcpl.org/uploads/Santiago_Our_Protector.pdf; and Eugene Hill, "Ordinance '99,'" New Mexico Culture Preservation League, accessed 11 March 2019, http://www.nmhcpl.org/uploads/ORDINANCE_99.pdf.

3. John L. Kessell, "Esteban Clemente: Precursor of the Pueblo Revolt," *El Palacio* 86, no. 4 (Winter 1980–81): 16–17.

4. Charles Wilson Hackett and Charmion Clair Shelby, eds., *Revolt of the Pueblo Indians of New Mexico and Otermín's Attempted Reconquest, 1680–1682*, 2 vols. (Albuquerque: University of New Mexico Press, 1942), 2: 299–300.

5. Ibid., 300–301.

6. John L. Kessell, *Pueblos, Spaniards, and the Kingdom of New Mexico* (Norman: University of Oklahoma Press, 2008), 106, 126–27. For Po'pay's possible use of peyote, see David H. Snow, "Whole Pots Full of Idolatrous Powdered Herbs," *The Kiva: Journal of Southwestern Anthropology and History* 82, no. 2 (2016): 117–36.

7. John L. Kessell, *Pueblos, Spaniards, and the Kingdom of New Mexico*, 121; and Fray Angélico Chávez, *Origins of New Mexico Families* (Santa Fe: Museum of New Mexico Press, 1992), 4.

8. John L. Kessell, *Kiva, Cross, and Crown: The Pecos Indians and New Mexico, 1540–1840* (Washington, D.C.: National Park Service, U.S. Department of the Interior, 1979), 227–28, 239.

9. Hackett and Shelby, *Revolt of the Pueblo Indians*, 1: 3–162.

10. Kessell, *Pueblos, Spaniards, and the Kingdom of New Mexico*, 131–32, 137–40, 138.

11. *The Journals of Don Diego de Vargas*, ed. John L. Kessell, Rick Hendricks, Meredith D. Dodge, vol. 2, *By Force of Arms: The Journals of don Diego de Vargas, New Mexico, 1691–93* (Albuquerque: University of New Mexico Press, 1992), 607.

12. On the legend of fray Juan Greyrobe, see T. J. Ferguson, "Dowa Yalanne: The Architecture of Zuni Resistance and Social Change during the Pueblo Revolt," in Robert W. Preucel, ed., *Archaeologies of the Pueblo Revolt: Identity, Meaning, and Renewal in the Pueblo World* (Albuquerque: University of New Mexico Press, 2002), 41.

13. *The Journals of Don Diego de Vargas*, ed. John L. Kessell, Rick Hendricks, and Meredith D. Dodge, vol. 3, *To the Royal Crown Restored: The Journals of don Diego de Vargas 1692–1694* (Albuquerque: University of New Mexico Press, 1995), 373–542.

14. Rick Hendricks, "Pueblo-Spanish Warfare in Seventeenth-Century New Mexico: The Battles of Black Mesa, Kotyiti, and Astialakwa," in Robert W. Preucel, ed., *Archaeologies of the Pueblo Revolt* (Albuquerque: University of New Mexico Press, 2002) 180–97.

15. *The Journals of Don Diego de Vargas*, ed. John L. Kessell, Rick Hendricks, and Meredith D. Dodge, vol. 4, *Blood on the Boulders: The Journals of don Diego de Vargas, New Mexico, 1694–97* (Albuquerque: University of New Mexico Press, 1998), 888.

16. A recent study of Indian slavery, privileging material over religious causes, attempts to portray the Pueblo Revolt as a slave rebellion. Certainly Indian slavery existed in the Pueblo-Spanish world, but the Pueblos, while oppressed, were certainly not slaves in the traditional sense. Andrés Reséndez, *The Other Slavery: The Uncovered Story of Indian Enslavement in America* (New York: Houghton Mifflins Harcourt, 2016), 167–71.

17. For more on the Pueblos' endemic internal dissension, see Kessell's *Kiva, Cross, and Crown*.

18. Kessell, Hendricks, and Dodge, eds., *Blood on the Boulders*, 1008; and Kessell, *Kiva, Cross, and Crown*, 229–30, 288–89.

Not So Fast, Mr. Jefferson
How a Mexican Priest and the Ghost of Bernardo de Miera Saved Texas and New Mexico for Spain

JOHN L. KESSELL

Whether Bernardo de Miera smiled from the grave in 1811, twenty-six years after his death, we will never know. But in that year, firsthand data from his most original map, revised by his hand in Chihuahua in 1778, surely helped postpone the United States' annexation of Texas and New Mexico. And hardly anyone knew.

After a notably full career as a cartographer, religious artist, and colonial administrator, Bernardo de Miera y Pacheco died in Santa Fe in 1785. Miera's iconic map, the "Plano Geographico" (1778), resulted from a four-month vision quest in 1776 with Franciscan friars Francisco Atanasio Domínguez and Silvestre Vélez de Escalante. While their "expedition" fell short of opening a northern trail between Santa Fe, New Mexico, and Monterey, California, they were the first recorded Europeans to probe the Colorado Plateau and the eastern Great Basin.[1] This vast interior region of canyons, plateaus, and ever-distant purple mountains would remain Spanish territory well into the nineteenth century, despite an eager challenge from the young United States. By the time diplomats from the two countries finally cleaved the continent in 1819 by the Adams-Onís Treaty, that challenge was at least sixteen years old.

Long retired from the University of New Mexico Department of History, John L. Kessell has kept an oar in with *Whither the Waters: Mapping the Great Basin from Bernardo de Miera to John C. Frémont* (University of New Mexico Press, 2017), revealing how Miera beckoned Western cartographers down faulty waterways for two generation

President Thomas Jefferson reckoned his plum Louisiana Purchase of 1803 included a bloated Texas. Outlined for the first time with shading on John Melish's "Map of the United States with the contiguous British & Spanish Possessions" (1816), Texas, as Jefferson envisioned it, stretched west and north up the Rio Grande (Río del Norte) to its junction with the Pecos (Puerco). From there it ran north through present-day New Mexico to a latitude above Taos (Tous), then west and north up the Rio Grande to that river's headwaters in present-day Colorado. While Jefferson's reckoning left Santa Fe, ancient capital of the Kingdom and Provinces of New Mexico, and its *camino real* lifeline just barely within Spanish territory, much of what Spaniards had long explored and considered theirs to the east and north would have ended up in the United States.[2]

Louisiana, colonized by France, later occupied by Spain, and illegally sold to the United States by Napoleon Bonaparte, never included Texas. The two Spanish provinces, in fact, each answered administratively to a different general command: Louisiana to Havana, Cuba, and Texas to Chihuahua. It was imperative then for His Catholic Majesty to set the U.S. president straight.[3]

Carlos IV's royal order of 20 May 1805 instructed Viceroy José de Iturrigaray of New Spain to compile a rigorous documentary defense of Louisiana's western boundary and of Texas as a separate Spanish province. The viceroy appointed a scholarly priest, Father Melchor de Talamantes, to do just that. Veteran naval officer and cartographer Gonzalo López de Haro, best known for his part in Spain's occupation of Nootka Sound, would serve as Talamantes' assistant "for making the proper drawings and charts."[4]

When the liberal Talamantes fell from grace in 1808, authorities appointed another scholar-cleric to carry on in his stead. For the next four years—right on through the vicious first phase of Mexican independence and Napoleon's disruption in Europe—sixty-year-old Father José Antonio Pichardo of the Oratory of San Felipe de Neri dedicated the remainder of his life to the project, amassing a huge, argumentative treatise of 5,127 *fojas* (pages), and dying soon thereafter.[5] Throughout the process, Father Pichardo consulted and tediously reconciled thousands of primary and secondary sources bearing on the history of northern New Spain, among them Bernardo de Miera's "Plano Geographico" (1778). Although Pichardo considered Miera an amateur and his map "very badly done" and "a mere rough draft," he simply had nothing else like it. Despite allegedly irregular latitudes and longitudes, seeming disagreements with the diary of Domínguez and Escalante, and Pichardo's belief "that only some places on the whole map are properly located," he finally resolved to use it anyway. In his own words, Pichardo confessed:

At the beginning, I doubted whether I would take a copy of it to add to the rest of the maps which go in document 74, but finally I decided to

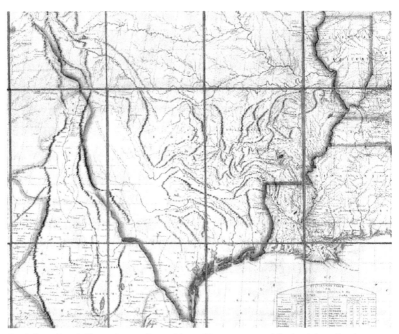

Fig. 1. President Jefferson's grandiose vision of Texas as part of the Louisiana Purchase. John Melish, "Map of the United States with contiguous British & Spanish Possessions, 1816" (detail). David Rumsey Historical Map Collection, no.5168001.

make it, because it gives a good idea of the lands of New Mexico, and of those which surround it in the four cardinal directions, and because it is the only one so complete. . . . I have also copied it on map 19, document 74, fitting it in as best I could, and correcting it in some particulars from information taken from other writers, and from my own conjectures.[6]

Sparing further barbs, Pichardo now annexed Miera's map of the Rio Grande corridor from south of El Paso to north of San Pasqual. "It is attached," he explained, "to the first map, in document 74, under the same number 15 [*sic*], in as much as the two form one."[7] Recognizing the importance of the Sierra de las Grullas (Rocky Mountains) and the Continental Divide, Pichardo incorporated in his text the Santa Fe cartographer's note: "This range is the backbone of this North America, for the waters of many rivers which rise there empty into the two seas, that of the South [the Pacific] and the Gulf of Mexico. In it cranes (*grullas*) breed."[8]

At some point, the pragmatic Pichardo ordered cartographer López de Haro, now his assistant, to roll out the "Plano Geographico" and copy verbatim, but

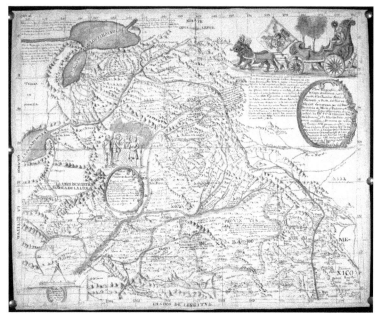

Fig. 2. The Miera map roundly criticized by Father Pichardo, then copied by his Order. Bernardo de Miera y Pacheco, "Plano Geographico de la tierra descubierta, nuevamente," Chihuahua, 1778, The British Library, Add. Ms. 17.661.D.

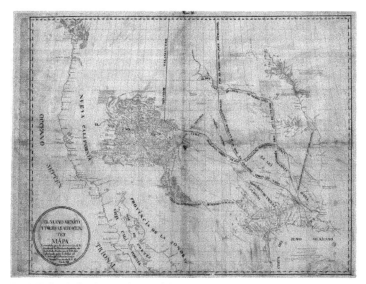

Fig. 3. Father Pichardo's rendering of the entire Trans-Mississippi West, 1811. "El Nuevo Mexico y Tierras Adyacentes," Mapoteca Manuel Orozco y Berra, Mexico City, 1134-7278-A.

without attribution, most of Miera's data. López was not, however, to copy the illuminations, not the allegorical blindfolded pope nor the bearded Paiutes. He was to omit, moreover, the two ornate ovals, the first containing the map's title and authorship and the second Miera's symbols. As a result, on López de Haro's copy, the symbol (usually a tiny circle surmounted by a cross) marking Domínguez and Escalante's ninety-odd, long-cold campsites appear as inhabited places. (The same symbol marks New Mexico's three upriver population centers: Albuquerque, Santa Fe, and Santa Cruz de la Cañada.) López sought with considerable success to duplicate Miera's busy topography. There are mountains and flat-topped mesas everywhere, and even some of the geological features Miera drew representationally, like Navajo Mountain and El Cabezon. Adding to the busyness, López also copied word-for-word all of Miera's annotations, with two conspicuous exceptions. Miera's lengthy ethnographic testimony that Comanches, not Spaniards, were lords of the southern plains, did not serve Spanish interests. Nor did the note telling of Domínguez and Escalante's decision to turn back far short of Monterey.

One Miera note that López retained would set westering North Americans on a merry chase. The note described a fictitious but possibly navigable river flowing out of the Great Salt Lake toward the setting sun. Although the western border of Miera's map chopped this imaginary River of the West off short, subsequent cartographers soon projected it all the way to San Francisco Bay. After all, that's what rivers did, flow to the sea, right?

Although Pichardo's map would lay out the entire Trans-Mississippi West, the density of greater New Mexico—from the Great Salt Lake (Laguna de los Timpanogos) to the presidio of El Paso (Paso del Norte)—drew the observer's eye. Miera's thick-spread data made it appear that all of New Mexico was populated. Perhaps this explains the map's curiously modest title: "*El Nuevo Mexico y Tierras Adyacentes*" ("New Mexico and Adjacent Lands"). This sprawling chart, after all, was meant to illuminate Pichardo's epic "Treatise on the Limits of Louisiana and Texas," and not simply New Mexico.

The second most detailed region depicted is the Pacific Northwest, reflecting López de Haro's previous experience as explorer and cartographer. And the third, the area of well-watered east Texas and lower Louisiana from where the eventual dividing line would likely commence. To reflect Spain's far-flung and long-standing influence west of the Mississippi, Pichardo had López de Haro loosely trace several Spaniards' routes well into or beyond Texas: explorer Francisco Vázquez de Coronado (1540–1542); Hernando de Soto's second-in-command, Luis de Moscoso (1542); Texas developer marqués de San Miguel de Aguayo (1720–1721); military inspector Pedro de Rivera (1727–1728); and New Mexico renegade Juan Domínguez de Mendoza (1683–1684).

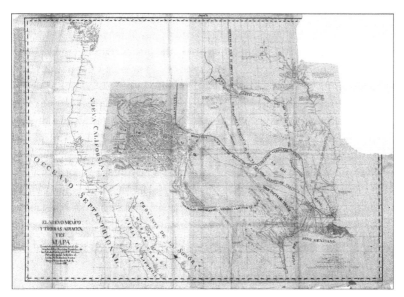

Fig. 4. Another version of Pichardo's Map, with Miera's data crudely pasted in place. "El Nuevo Mexico y Tierras Adyacentes," 1811, Barry Lawrence Ruderman Antique Maps, no. 433050pdc.

Pichardo further instructed López to lay down on the map four proposed boundaries between Spanish and U.S. territory, those of his disgraced predecessor Father Melchor de Talamantes, Texas missionary fray José María Puelles, Texas governor Ángel de Martos Navarrete, and finally that "PROPOSED BY M.R. D'ANVILLE AND CONFIRMED BY FATHER D.N JOSE PICHARDO." Frenchman Jean Baptiste Bourguignon d'Anville was Pichardo's favorite cartographer; López de Haro's name appeared nowhere on the map. Pichardo dedicated the chart in 1811 to then-viceroy Francisco Javier Venegas. It was large—some 35" by 46½".[9] Until recently, scholars believed that only one copy existed, the finished version that resides today at the Mapoteca Manuel Orozco y Berra in Mexico City. Of late, however, a somewhat mysterious second copy has turned up. Purchased at auction in France (no longer under Spanish patrimony) by cartographic scholar Barry Lawrence Ruderman, this cruder version was sold recently to the Library of Congress. Several overlays of Miera's material have been pasted hastily in place and the blank northeast corner of the map is torn away. Despite its crudeness, this version appears not to be a preliminary dummy but instead a later revision.[10]

A notable achievement, the original map was inked and dated 1811. Yet Father Pichardo's bulky treatise, called for by royal order in 1805, still had not

Fig. 5. Félix María Calleja, Viceroy of
New Spain (1813-1816). From México
a través de los siglos, vol. 3.

been forwarded to Spain. Had the overworked scholar-priest not died in 1812, the bureaucrats' delays would have killed him. Not until May 1813, six months after Pichardo's death, did Viceroy Félix María Calleja explain to authorities in Spain the reason for the holdup—only 1,969 of its 5,127 fojas had been copied so far. Years dragged by. Finally, on 30 September 1816, Calleja announced to the Spanish secretary of state that the job was done. He was sending the treatise in "two large boxes containing thirty-one small folio volumes, bound in red sheep-skin." Although "well advanced," the maps meant to accompany it were not yet ready because copyist López de Haro, "the only person qualified for the task in this realm," had been taken ill. Still, López had "been strictly charged to complete them very soon."[11]

The lead draftsman's sickness may explain why the hand that transcribed Miera's data on the revision does not match that which is on the clean copy. The material is virtually the same. But did either version ever arrive in Spain? The treatise did, we know.[12] Pichardo's map might have been sent, or not. Historian Philip Coolidge Brooks presumed that "López de Haro had completed the copying of the accompanying map, upon which he had been working when the documents were forwarded." Still, we do not know that either version of the map ever caught up with the treatise. No copy is known today to exist in any Spanish or U.S. archive.[13]

Diplomat Narciso de Heredia, the key Spanish official in negotiations with the United States, definitely had access in Spain to Pichardo's massive and unwieldy treatise. He failed consistently, however, to mention the Mexican priest or a map. It pained Heredia that final treaty negotiations would take place in Washington, D.C., and not in Madrid. Referring to the thirty-one volumes compiled in Mexico in response to the royal order of 1805, Heredia complained in 1817 that "it is not possible to ship them [to Washington], even less to copy them, which would be a very long process." Instead, Heredia and his assistants culled Pichardo's work and forwarded material they considered pertinent to Luis de Onís, Spanish minister to the United States. On 19 July 1817, special envoy Francisco Martínez Pizarro wrote to Onís advising him that he was sending in advance an extract from volume 29 containing references to territorial limits dating between 1678 and 1790. "I shall do the same," Martínez Pizarro continued, "with the remaining volumes, as rapidly as the laborious task proceeds of selecting the useful statements which are mixed therein with many inconsequential ones; which is the more troublesome because of the fact that none of the thirty-one volumes in the collection has an index."[14]

Martínez Pizarro, who acquired for his own use a copy of John Melish's map (1816), delivered the resulting collection to Onís in the United States on 3 October 1818, too late to have made much difference in final negotiations of the Adams-Onís Treaty. Nonetheless, the material Father Pichardo so meticulously compiled surely steeled Onís to insist on the pre-existing Sabine River boundary between U.S. lower Louisiana and Spanish Texas.

By the terms of the Adams-Onís Treaty, signed on George Washington's birthday, 22 February 1819, Spain ceded east and west Florida to the United States and its claim to the Oregon country, while the United States abandoned its claim to Texas. In great detail, the treaty resolved numerous financial claims and counterclaims, including a U.S. agreement to pay its own citizens for their verifiable claims against Spain. Last to be agreed upon, but set forth as Article Three, was the international boundary between the two countries:

> The Boundary Line . . . shall begin on the Gulph of Mexico [sic], at the
> mouth of the River Sabine in the Sea, continuing North, along the West-
> ern Bank of that River, to the 32d degree of Latitude; thence by a Line
> due North to the degree of Latitude, where it strikes the Río Roxo of
> Nachitoches, or Red-River, then following the course of the Río-Roxo
> Westward to the degree of Longitude, 100 West from London and 23
> from Washington, then crossing the said Red-River, and running thence
> by a Line due North to the River Arkansas, thence, following the Course
> of the Southern bank of the Arkansas to its source in Latitude, 42. North,
> and thence by that parallel of Latitude to the South-Sea [the Pacific]. The
> whole being as laid down in Melishe's Map [sic] of the United-States,
> published at Philadelphia, improved to the first of January 1818.[15]

Such islands as there might be in those three rivers would belong to the United States, but their waters and navigation would be common to both nations.

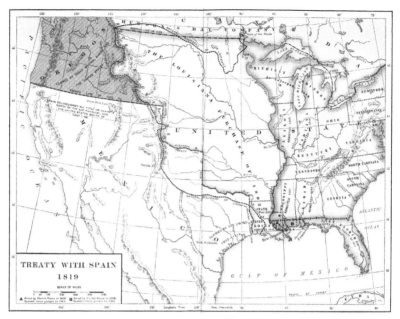

Fig. 6. The Adams-Onís Treaty Line, 1819. Map Credit: Courtesy the private collection of Roy Winkelman.

Reckoning now by the Adams-Onís line, Santa Fe found itself safely buffered for the time being, 360 miles inside Spanish and (after 1821) Mexican territory to the east and 450 miles to the north. For a shorter time, Texas remained Spanish/Mexican as well.[16] Jefferson had been thwarted. Louisiana included neither Texas nor any part of New Mexico. In whatever ways Spanish negotiators may have used it, the sheer bulk of supporting material that Father Pichardo amassed, with or without his map of 1811, lent weight to their arguments.

And so, for the entire coming generation, thousands of motley travelers on the Camino Real de Tierra Adentro crowding the animated plazas of San Antonio and Santa Fe would be spared the *zozobra* (the foreboding, gut-wrenching uncertainty) of the Stars and Stripes waving from the presidial flag pole.

¡Bravo, padre Pichardo! ¡Bravo, ghost of don Bernardo!

NOTES

1. For a preliminary biography of Miera, see John L. Kessell, *Miera y Pacheco: A Renaissance Spaniard in Eighteenth-Century New Mexico* (Norman: University of

347

Oklahoma Press, 2013). Bernardo de Miera y Pacheco, cartographer, *Plano Geographico de la tierra descubierta, nuevamente,* 1778, 81 x 69 cm, British Library, Map Collections, Additional MS. 17,661.d.

2. Philip Coolidge Brooks, *Diplomacy and the Borderlands: The Adams-Onís Treaty of 1819,* University of California Publications in History, vol. 24 (Berkeley: University of California Press, 1939), 6, 39–42; and John Melish, cartographer, *Map of the United States with the Contiguous British & Spanish Possessions,* 1816, 89 x 145 cm, David Rumsey Historical Map Collection, Image 5168.001, 1:3,9000,000 scale.

3. Brooks, *Diplomacy and the Borderlands,* 30.

4. José Antonio Pichardo, *Pichardo's Treatise of the Limits of Louisiana and Texas,* 4 vols., ed. Charles Wilson Hackett, trans. Charmion Clair Shelby and Mary Ruth Splawn, 4 vols. (Austin: University of Texas Press, 1931–1946), 4:42.

5. During his inventory of Mexican archives, Herbert Eugene Bolton rediscovered Pichardo's lengthy documentary treatise at the Secretaría de Relaciones Exteriores. Herbert E. Bolton, *Guide to Materials for the History of the United States in the Principal Archives of Mexico* (Washington, D.C.: Carnegie Institution, 1913; Kraus repr.: New York, 1963), 234–35; and Hackett, *Pichardo's Treatise of the Limits of Louisiana and Texas,* 4 (1946): 470. See also Felix Calleja and Philip Coolidge Brooks, "Pichardo's Treatise and the Adams-Onís Treaty," *Hispanic American Historical Review* 15 no. 1 (February 1935): 94–99.

6. *Pichardo's Treatise of the Limits of Louisiana and Texas,* 2 (1934): 40–41.

7. Ibid. The number at the top of the map is unequivocally 19.

8. Ibid., 42–44, 84, 88, 268.

9. Bolton (*Guide to Materials for the History of the United States in the Principal Archives of Mexico,* 366) found the Pichardo map in the cartographic section of the Secretaría de Fomento, Colonización, e Industria in Mexico City. José Antonio Pichardo, *El Nuevo Mexico y Tierras Adyacentes. Mapa Levantado para la demarcacion de los Limites de los Dominios Españoles y de los Estados Unidos por el P. D. Jose Pichardo quien lo dedica al Ex.mo S.or D. Francisco Xavier Venegas Virrey de esta N.E., etc. Año de 1811,* 95 x 127 cm, Mexico City, Mapoteca Manuel Orozco y Berra, 1134-7278-A. Carl I. Wheat merely lists the Pichardo map in his monumental *Mapping the Transmississippi West, 1540–1861,* 5 vols. (San Francisco, Calif.: Institute of Historic Cartography, 1957–1963), 1:253–54; 2:214. Wheat's measurements are 36" x 45", the Mapoteca's are 95 x 127 cm. See also John L. Kessell, *Whither the Waters: Mapping the Great Basin from Bernardo de Miera to John C. Frémont* (Albuquerque: University of New Mexico Press, 2017), 62–63, wherein I assumed incorrectly that the Library of Congress "dummy" version came first.

10. José Antonio Pichardo, *El Nuevo Mexico y Tierras Adyacentes. Mapa Levantado para la demarcacion de los Limites de los Dominios Españoles y de los Estados Unidos por el P. D. Jose Pichardo quien lo dedica al Ex.mo S.or D. Francisco Xavier Venegas Virrey de esta N.E., etc. Año de 1811,* Mexico City, manuscript maps, 91 x 126 cm, Library of Congress, https://www.loc.gov/item/2016588016/. The accompanying narrative implies that Pichardo's map was used in negotiating the Adams-Onís Treaty but offers no conclusive evidence that it was actually present. On his "Plano Geographico" (1778), Miera described the ruins preserved today in Aztec National Monument as follows: "Aqui se manifiestan las Ruinas de grandes Poblaciones de Yndios antiguas." The copyist(s) of both Pichardo versions placed the modifier with the noun: "Aqui se manifiestan las

ruinas de grandes poblaciones antiguas de Yndios." Because of the sloppy pasting job, the following place names are partially obliterated on the revision: Río Sulfureo de las Piramides, Llano de St. a Gertrudis, Paganpachi, Chegui (totally obliterated), and Ojo de N.a Sra. And there are two St. Claras. The Miera data on one were obviously copied from the other, not separately from Miera's original. The fact that one section of the revision is pasted over several place names that show fully on the clean version indicates that the former was copied from the latter. Additional details—a more finished version of the Mississippi Delta and Gulf Coast, and a few new or variant names—also confirm that the cruder map was a revision.

11. Viceroy Félix María Calleja quoted in Calleja and Brooks, "Pichardo's Treatise," 95–96. It is not unreasonable to imagine López de Haro, ailing and pressured by his superiors, delegating to an intern the job of copying every word of Miera's data (between 37 and 44 degrees of latitude and 91 and 102 degrees of longitude) on a separate sheet to be pasted in place later. Another sheet was required for the south and for many place names along the east side. The intern formed his "g" differently.

12. By order of the Spanish secretary of state, receipt of the treatise was to be acknowledged to the viceroy in Mexico City, along with the admonition "that we await the maps. [*In another hand:*] Done. 24 May [1817]." Anonymous quoted in Calleja and Brooks, "Pichardo's Treatise," 96.

13. Brooks, *Diplomacy and the Borderlands*, 81. The author also mentions the presentation of "certain documents, and a [n unspecified] map" at a meeting of the Spanish Council of State during the summer of 1817. He referred specifically to the Pichardo map in a discussion of confusion over the Red and Colorado Rivers, but did not say that it was actually present at the negotiations (p. 98). A recent preliminary search of the most logical archives in Spain failed to turn up a copy of the Pichardo map. Luis Laorden, personal correspondence to author, 30 September 2017.

14. Francisco Martínez Pizarro quoted in Calleja and Brooks, "Pichardo's Treatise," 97–98.

15. Article Three of the Adams-Onís Treaty quoted in Brooks, *Diplomacy and the Borderlands*, 206.

16. Ibid., 161–65.

Bibliography

MANUSCRIPTS: *Principal Archives, Libraries, and Collections Cited*

Archives of the Archdiocese of Santa Fe, New Mexico (AASF)
Archives of the Archdiocese of Tucson, Arizona (AAT)
Archivo de Hidalgo del Parral, Chihuahua, México
Archivo de Parish, Granados, Sonora, México
Archivo de Protocolos Notariales, Cádiz, Spain (APNC)
Archivo del Colegio de la Santa Cruz Querétaro, México

> Convento Franciscano, Celaya, México

Archivo del Gobierno de la Mitra de Hermosillo, Sonora, México (AGMS)
Archivo del marqués de la Nava de Barcinas, Madrid, Spain (AMNB)
Archivo General de Indias Sevilla, Spain (AGI)

> Audiencia de Guadalajara
> Audiencia de México
> Contratación
> Indiferente
> Juzgado de Arribadas
> Patronato

Archivo General de la Nación, México (AGN)

> Californias
> Historia
> Indios
> Misiones
> Provincias Internas, tomos
> Reales Cedulas

Archivo General de Notarias del Distrito Federal, México
Archivo Histórico Nacional, Madrid, Spain (AHN)

> Indiferente
> Protocolos

Archivo Histórico de Hacienda, México (AHH)

> Temporalidades

Archivo Histórico del Supremo Tribunal de Justicia del Estado de Chihuahua, México
Archivo Parrochial de Morata del Conde, Zaragoza, Spain
Archivo Parrochial de Morata del Jalón, Zaragoza, Spain

Archivo de Rafael Gasset Dorado, Madrid, Spain
Biblioteca Nacional Madrid, Spain
Biblioteca Nacional, México

Archivo Franciscano,

Bancroft Library, University of California, Berkeley (TBL)

Bolton Research Papers (BRP)
A.L. Pinart Coleccion de Pimería Alta

Center for Southwest Research, University of New Mexico (CSWR)
Church of Latter Day Saints

Family History Library

Eleanor B. Adams Papers, Center for Southwest Research, University of New
Mexico (EBAP)
Mexican Archives of New Mexico, New Mexico State Records Center and
Archives, Santa Fe (MANM)
Museo Naval, Madrid, Spain
National Park Service (NPS), Mission 2000 Data Base
Newberry Library, Chicago, Illinois

Ayer Collection

Parroquia de la Asunción, Sagario, México
Parroquia de Santa María, Torrelaguna, Madrid, Spain
Pontificio Ateneo Antoniano, Franciscan General Library, Rome

Fr. Marcellino de Civezza Collection

Spanish Archives of New Mexico, New Mexico State Records Center and
Archives, Santa Fe

SANM I
SANM II

OTHER WORKS:

Adams, Eleanor B. "The Historical Society of New Mexico Honors France
Vinton Scholes," *Americas 27* (January, 1959).
————. "Two Colonial New Mexico Libraries 1704, 1776," *NMHR 19*
(April, 1944).
————., ed. Bishop Tamarón's Visitation of New Mexico, 1760. Albuquerque: University of New Mexico Press, 1954.
————. and Chavez, Angelico Fray, eds. *Missions of New Mexico, 1776:
A Description by Fray Francisco Atanasio Domínguez with Other Contemporary Documents*, Albuquerque: University of New Mexico Press,
1956.
Alegre, Francisco Xavier. *Historia de la Provincia de la Compañía de Jesús
de Nueva España*. Ernest J. Burrus and Félix Zubillaga, eds. *4 vols.*
Roma: Institutum Historicum Societatis Jesu, 1956–1960.

Almada, Francisco. *Diccionario de Historia, Geografía y Biografía Sonorenses*. Chihuahua: Ruiz Sandoval, 1952.

———. *Resumen de Historia del Estado de Chihuahua*. Chihuahua: Gobierno de Chihuahua, 1955.

Ambrose, Stephen. *Undaunted Courage: Meriwether Lewis, Thomas Jefferson, and the Opening of the American West*. New York: Simon and Schuster, 1996.

Arricivita, Juan Domingo. *Crónica seráfica y apostólica del Colegio de Propaganda Fide de la Santa Cruz de Querétaro en la Nueva España*. México: Felipe de Zúñiga y Ontiveros, 1792.

Baker, Steven, and Hendricks, Rick. *Juan Rivera's Colorado, 1765: The First Spaniards Among the Ute and Paiute Indians on the Trails to Teguayo: The Comprehensive Illustrated Trail Study and Ethnohistory with the Original Rivera Journals and English Translations*. Lake City: Western Reflections Press, 2015.

Baltasar, Juan. *Apostólicos Afanes de La Compañía de Jesús*. México: Editorial Layac, 1944.

Bancroft, Hubert Howe. *History of Arizona and New Mexico, 1530–1888*. San Francisco: History Company, 1889.

———. *History of Mexico, vol. 3*. San Francisco: History Company, 1883–1888.

———. *History of the North Mexican States and Texas, 1531–1800, vol. 1*. San Francisco: History Company, 1886–1889.

Bandelier, Adolph. *Final Report of Investigations Among the Indians of the Southwestern United States, Part 2*. Cambridge: John Wilson and Son, 1892.

Barbastro, Francisco. *Compendio de lo más Notable que han Trabajado en Sonora los Hijos del Colegio de Santa Cruz, 1768–1783*. Baviácora: Colegio de Santa Cruz, 1788.

Barrante, G. D., comp. *"Once in a Hundred", Final Report of the Colorado Centennial-Bicentennial Commission*. Denver: A.B. Hirschfield Press, 1977.

Barrett, Elinore. *Conquest and Catastrophe: Changing Rio Grande Pueblo Settlement Patterns in the Sixteenth and Seventeenth Centuries*. Albuquerque: University of New Mexico Press, 2002.

Bartlett, John. *Personal Narrative of the Explorations and Incidents in Texas, New Mexico, California, Sonora, and Chihuahua*. New York: D. Appleton & Company, 1854.

Barzun, Jacques and Graff, Henry. *The Modern Researcher*. New York: Harcourt Brace Jovanovic, 1992.

Benavante, Toribio de. "La Relación Postera de *Cíbola*," *Documents of the Coronado Expedition, 1539–1542*. Richard and Shirley Cushing Flint, eds. Dallas: Southern Methodist University Press, 2005.

Benavides, Alonso de. *Memorial of Fray Alonso de Benavides, 1630*. Emma Burbank Ayer, trans. Albuquerque: Calvin Horn Publishers, 1965.

353

Blanco, Ramón. *Apuntes Históricos Sobre el Colegio de Misioneros de Herbon.* Lugo: Artes Gráficas de Gerardo Castro, 1925.

Blank, Paula. *Shakespeare and the Mismeasure of Renaissance Man.* Ithaca: Cornell University Press, 2006.

Bloom, Lansing. "The Vargas Encomienda," *NMHR 14* (October, 1939).

Bolton, Herbert Eugene. *Anza's California Expeditions, 5 vols.* Berkeley: University of California Press, 1930.

————. *Guide to Materials for the History of the United States in the Principal Archives of Mexico.* Washington DC: Carnegie Institution, 1913.

————. *Kino's Historical Memoir of Pimería Alta: A Contemporary Account of the Beginnings of California, Sonora, and Arizona, vol. 1.* Berkeley: University of California Press, 1948.

————. *Outpost of Empire: The Story of the Founding of San Francisco.* New York: Alfred A. Knopf, 1931.

————. *Pageant in the Wilderness: The Story of the Escalante Expedition to the Interior Basin, 1776.* Salt Lake City: Utah Historical Society, 1950.

————. *Rim of Christendom: A Biography of Eusebio Francisco Kino, Pacific Coast Pioneer.* New York: Macmillan, 1936.

Bonneville, Benjamin L. E. "A Map of the Scout of Lt. Col. Miles's Southern Column Through the Country of the Coyotero Apaches in June, and July 1857," *National Archives, Record Group 77.* Washington DC: National Archives, 1857.

Boyd, E. *Popular Arts of Spanish New Mexico.* Santa Fe: Museum of New Mexico Press, 1974.

Briggs, Walter. *Without Noise of Arms: The 1776 Domínguez-Escalante Search for a Route from Santa Fe to Monterey.* Flagstaff: Northland Press, 1976.

Britton, Marilyn. "Correspondence of Bernardo de Miera y Pacheco," *Herencia 14* (January 2006).

Brooks, James. *Captives and Cousins: Slavery, Kinship, and Community in the Southwest Borderlands.* Chapel Hill: University of North Carolina Press, 2002.

————. "Violence, Exchange, and Renewal in the American Southwest," *Ethnohistory 49* (Winter, 2002).

Brooks, Philip. *Diplomacy and the Borderlands: The Adams-Onis Treaty of 1819.* Berkeley: University of California Press, 1939.

Brown, Jonathan. "Herrera the Younger: Baroque Artist and Personality," *Apollo LXXXIV* (London, 1966).

Burrus, Ernest. *Misiones Norteñas Mexicanas de la Compañía de Jesús, 1751–1757.* México: Biblioteca Histórica Mexicana, 1963.

Calleja, Félix and Brooks, Philip. "Pichardo's Treatise and the Adam-Onis Treaty," *Hispanic American Historical Review 15, no. 1* (February 1935).

Canto Tellez, Antonio. *Guía de la Provincia de Madrid*. Madrid: Diputación Provincial de Madrid, 1958.

Carson, Phil. "In Search of Cuerno Verde's Headress," *Pueblo Chieftain 3* (October 1993).

Castañeda de Nájera, Pedro de. "Relación de la Jornada de Cíbola," *Documents of the Coronado Expedition, 1539–1542*. Richard and Shirley Cushing Flint, eds. Dallas: Southern Methodist University Press, 2005.

Chavez, Fray Angelico. *Origins of New Mexico Families in the Spanish Colonial Period*. Santa Fe: Museum of New Mexico Press, 1954.

———, and Warner, Ted. *The Domínguez-Escalante Journal: Their Expedition through Colorado, Utah, Arizona, and New Mexico in 1776*. Provo: Brigham Young University Press, 1976.

Colligan, John. *Juan Páez Hurtado Expedition of 1695: Fraud in Recruiting Colonists for New Mexico*. Albuquerque: University of New Mexico Press, 1995.

Cook, Warren. *Flood Tide of Empire: Spain and the Pacific Northwest, 1543–1819*. New Haven: Yale University Press, 1973.

Coues, Elliot. *On the Trail of a Spanish Pioneer, the Diary and Itinerary of Francisco Garces, 2 vols.* New York: Francis Harper, 1900.

Cramaussel, Chantal. "El Mapa de Miera y Pacheco de 1758 y la Cartografía Temprana del Sur Nuevo México," *Estudios de Historia Novohispana 13* (1993).

Cutter, Charles. *The Legal Culture of Northern New Spain, 1700–1810*. Albuquerque: University of New Mexico Press, 1995.

———. *The Protector de Indios in Colonial New Mexico, 1659–1821*. Albuquerque: University of New Mexico Press, 1986.

De Marco, Barbara. "Voices from the Archives I: Testimony of the Pueblo Indians on the 1680 Revolt," *Romance Philology 53* (Spring 2000).

Decorme, Gerard. La Obra be los Jesuitas Mexicanos. México: Antigua Librería Robredo de José Porrúa e Hijo, 1941.

Di Peso, Charles. *The Sobaipuri Indians of the Upper San Pedro River Valley, Southeastern Arizona*. Dragoon: Amerind Foundation, 1953.

———, and Matson, Daniel, trans. "The Seri Indians in 1692 as Described by Adamo Gilg," *Arizona & the West VII* (Spring 1965).

Días Veanes, Pedro Joaquín. "Registro y Posession de don Bernardo de Miera y Pacheco," *Archivo Histórico del Supremo Tribunal de Justicia del Estado de Chihuahua, tomo 3, no. 38*. El Paso (Jan. 19, 1745).

Dobyns, Henry. *Hepah California! Journal of Cave Johnson Couts from Monterey, Nueva Leon, Mexico to Los Angeles,1848–49*. Tucson: University of Arizona Press, 1961.

Domínguez Ortiz, Antonio. *La Sociedad Española en el Siglo XVII, 2 vols.* Madrid: Consejo Superior de Investigaciones Científicas, 1964.

———. *Las Clases Privilegiadas en la España del Antiguo Regimen*. Madrid: Ediciones ISTMO, 1973.

Donahue, John. *Jesuit Missions in Northern New Spain, 1711-1767.* Berkeley: University of California, 1957.

Dunne, Peter. "Captain Anza and the Case of Father Campos," *Mid-America, 23* (1941).

———. *Juan Antonio Balthasar, Padre Visitador to the Sonora Frontier 1744-1745.* Tucson: University of Arizona Press, 1957.

Ebright, Malcolm and Hendricks, Rick. *Witches of Abiquiu: The Governor, the Priest, the Genízaro Indians and the Devil.* Albuquerque: University of New Mexico Press, 2006.

———, Hendricks, Rick, and Hughes, Richard. *Four Square Leagues: Pueblo Indian Land in New Mexico.* Albuquerque: University of New Mexico Press, 2014.

Echarri Ibarra, Francisco. *Directorio Moral.* Madrid: Imprenta Real, 1780.

Elliott, J.H. "Barbarians at the Gates: Bárbaros: Spaniards and Their Savages in the Age of Enlightenment," *New York Review of Books 23* (February, 2006).

Emory, W.H. *Notes of a Military Reconnaissance, from Fort Leavenworth, in Missouri to San Diego, in California Including Parts of the Arkansas, Del Norte, and Gila Rivers.* Washington DC: Wendell and Benthuysen, 1848.

Escriche, Joaquín, *Diccionario Razonado de Legislación y Jurisprudencia, 4 vols.* Bogotá: Editorial Temis, 1997.

Escudero, José Agustín de. *Noticias Estadísticas de Sonora y Sinaloa.* México: R. Rafael, 1848.

Espinosa, Manuel. *Crusaders of the Rio Grande: The Story of Don Diego de Vargas and the Reconquest and Refounding of New Mexico.* Chicago: Institute of Jesuit History, 1942.

———. *First Expedition of Vargas into New Mexico, 1692.* Albuquerque: University of New Mexico Press, 1940.

Espinoza, Carlota, interview with John Kessell, Denver Public Library, May 8, 2015.

Esquibel, José and Colligan, John. *Spanish Recolonization of New Mexico: An Account of the Families Recruited at Mexico City in 1693.* Albuquerque: Hispanic Genealogy Research Center, 1999.

Ferguson, T.J. "Dowa Yahlanne: The Architecture of Zuni Resistance and Social Change During the Pueblo Revolt," Robert Preucel, ed. *Archaeologies of the Pueblo Revolt: Identity, Meaning, and Renewal in the Pueblo World.* Albuquerque: University of New Mexico Press, 2002.

Fernández Duro, Cesareo. *Armado Española Desde la Unión de los Reinos de Castilla y de Aragón, 9 vols.* Madrid: Sucesores de Rivadeneyra, 1895-1903.

Figueroa García, Francisco, ed. *Documentos para la Historia de México, cuarta serie, tomo 1.* México: Imprenta de Vicente García Torres, 1856.

Flint, Richard. *Great Cruelties Have Been Reported: The 1544 Investigation of the Coronado Expedition.* Dallas: Southern Methodist University Press, 2002.

————. "Without Them Nothing Was Possible: The Coronado Expedition's Indian Allies". *NMHR 84* (Winter, 2009).

————, and Shirley Cushing Flint, eds. *Documents of the Coronado Expedition, 1539–1542: They Were Not Familiar with His Majesty, nor Did They Wish to Be His Subjects.* Dallas: Southern Methodist University Press, 2005.

Flint, Timothy. *The Personal Narrative of James O. Pattie of Kentucky.* Chicago: Lakeside Press /R. R. Donnelley & Sons Co., 1930.

Foley, Neil. *Mexicans in the Making of America.* Cambridge: Harvard University Press, 2014.

Garate, Donald. "Basque Ethnic Connections and the Expedition of Juan Bautista de Anza," *Colonial Latin America Historical Review 4* (Winter, 1995).

————. *Juan Bautista de Anza: Basque Explorer in the New World.* Reno: University of Nevada Press, 2003.

————. "Who Named Arizona? The Basque Connection," *Journal of Arizona History 42* (Spring, 1999).

García Cárcel, Ricardo and Bretos, Lourdes Mateo. *La Leyenda Negra.* Madrid: Grupo Anya. SA, 1990.

Gardiner, Arthur. "Letter of Father Middendorff, S.J., Dated from Tucson, 3 March 1757," *The Kiva 22* (1957).

Gavin, Robin. "New Mexico Indo-Hispano Altar Screens," *El Palacio 116* (Winter 2011).

Geiger, Maynard. "A Voice from San Xavier del Boc," *Provincial Annals of Santa Barbara Mission,* Santa Barbara, 1953.

Gerhard, Peter. *A Guide to the Historical Geography of New Spain.* Cambridge: Cambridge University Press, 1972.

Gómez, Arthur. "Royalist in Transition: Facundo Melgares, the Last Spanish Governor of New Mexico, 1818–1822," *NMHR 68* (October, 1993).

Greenleaf, Richard. "Eleanor Burnham Adams: Historian and Editor," *NMHR 60* (January 1985).

Griffen, William. "Notes on the Seri Indian Culture, Sonora, Mexico," *Latin American Monographs 10.* Gainesville: University of Florida Press, 1959.

Gutierrez, Ramon. *When Jesus Came the Corn Mothers Went Away: Marriage, Sexuality, and Power in New Mexico, 1500–1846.* Stanford: Stanford University Press, 1991.

Hackett, Charles *Wilson,* ed. *Historical Documents Relating to New Mexico, Nueva Vizcaya and Approaches Thereto, to 1774.* Washington, DC: Carnegie Institution of Washington, 1937.

————, ed. *Pichardo's Treatise of the Limits of Louisiana and Texas, 4 vols.* Austin: University of Texas Press, 1931–1946.

————, ed. *Revolt of the Pueblo Indians of New Mexico and Otermín's*

Attempted Reconquest, 1680–1682, 2 vols. Albuquerque: University of New Mexico Press, 1942.

Hammond, George P. *Noticia de California: First Report of the Occupation of California By the Portolá Expedition, 1770.* San Francisco: Book Club of California, 1958.

———. "Pimería Alta After Kino's Time," *NMHR 4* (1929).

———. "The Zúñiga Journal: Tucson to Santa Fe: The Opening of the Spanish Trade Route, 1788–1795," *NMHR, 6* (1931).

———, and Rey, Agapito, eds. *Don Juan de Oñate, Colonizer of New Mexico, 1525–1628, 2* vols. Albuquerque: University of New Mexico Press, 1953.

———, eds. *The Rediscovery of New Mexico: The Expeditions of Chamuscado, Espejo, Castaño de Sosa, Morlete, and Leyva de Bonilla and Humana.* Albuquerque: University of New Mexico Press, 1966.

Hendricks, Rick. "Antonio de Valverde Cosío," *American National Biography.* John Garraty and Mark Carnes, eds. New York: Oxford University Press, 1999.

———. "The Camino Real at the Pass: The Economy and Political Structure of the Paso del North Area in the Eighteenth Century," *Password 44* (Spring 1999).

———. "The Church in El Paso del Norte in the Eighteenth Century," *Seeds of Struggle, Harvest of Faith.* Thomas Steele, Paul Rhetts, and Barb Awalt, eds. Albuquerque: LPD Press, 1996.

———. "Church-State Relations in Anza's New Mexico, 1777–1787," *Catholic Southwest 9,* 1998.

———. "Pedro Rodríguez Cubero: New Mexico's Reluctant Governor," *NMHR 68* (January 1993).

———. "La Presencia de Tlapujahuenses en la Reconquista de Nuevo México," *Relaciones Estudios de Historia y Sociedad, Michoacán Colegio, 70.* Primavera, 1997.

———. "Pueblo-Spanish Warfare in Seventeenth Century New Mexico," *Archaeologies of the Pueblo Revolt: Identity, Meaning, and Renewal in the Pueblo World.* Robert Preucel, ed. Albuquerque: University of New Mexico Press, 2002.

———. "Searching for the Lost Padre: Eighteenth-Century Mining Claims in the Organ Mountains and Greater El Paso del Norte Area," *Password 46* (Summer 2001).

———. "Spanish-Indian Relations in El Paso del Norte in the Early Eighteenth Century the Rebellion of 1711," *Proceedings of the Ninth Jornada-Mogollon Conference.* Raymond, Maudlin et al., eds. El Paso: Publications in Archaeology 12 (1997).

———, and Wilson, John, eds. *The Navajos in 1705: Roque Madrid's Campaign Journal.* Albuquerque: University of New Mexico Press, 1996.

Hernández, Fortunato. *Las Razas Indígenas de Sonora y la Guerra del Yaqui*. México: Talleres de la Casa Editorial, 1902.

Herrera, Carlos. "The King's Governor: Juan Bautista de Anza and Bourbon New Mexico in the Era of Imperial Reform". Ph.D. dissertation, University of New Mexico, 2000.

Hill, Eugene. "Ordinance 99," *NMHCPL Newsletter*. Albuquerque: NMHCPL.org, accessed March 11, 2019.

Hodge, Frederick Webb, Hammond, George P., and Rey, Agapito, eds. *Fray Alonso Benavides' Revised Memorial of 1634*. Albuquerque: University of New Mexico Press, 1945.

Hough, Walter. *Antiquities of the Upper Rio Gila and Salt River Valleys in Arizona and New Mexico*. Washington DC: Bureau of American Ethnology, *Bulletin 35*, 1907.

————. *Culture of the Ancient Pueblos of the Upper Gila River Region, New Mexico and Arizona*. Washington DC: United States National Museum, *Bulletin 87*, 1914.

Ivey, James. "The Greatest Misfortune of All: Famine in the Province of New Mexico, 1667–1672," *Journal of the Southwest 36* (Spring 1994).

Jackson, Donald, ed. *The Journey of Zebulon Pike with Letters and Related Documents, 2 vols.* Norman: University of Oklahoma Press, 1966.

————, ed. *Letters of the Lewis and Clark Expedition with Related Documents 1783–1854, 3 vols.* Urbana: University of Illinois Press, 1978.

James, Thomas. *Three Years Among the Indians and Mexicans*. Philadelphia: J. B. Lippincott, 1962.

Jinian, Rozana, et al. "Same Old Black Legend Rhetoric," *Amazon.com Customer Reviews (Spain in the Southwes* by John L. Kessell), May, 2006.

Jones, Grant. *The Conquest of the Last Mayan Kingdom*. Stanford: Stanford University Press, 1998.

Jones, Oakah. *Pueblo Warriors and Spanish Conquest*. Norman: University of Oklahoma Press, 1966.

Juderías, Julián. *La Leynda Negra: Estudios Acera del Concepto de España en el Extranjero*. Madrid: Editora Nacional, 1954.

Kamen, Henry. *Spain in the Later Seventeenth Century, 1665–1700*. London: Longmans, 1980.

Kelly, Henry. "Franciscan Missions of New Mexico 1740–1760," *NMHR 16* (1941).

Kessell, John L. "Anza Damns the Missions: A Spanish Soldier's Criticism of Indian Policy, 1772," *Journal of Arizona History 13* (Spring, 1972).

————. "A Bolton for the Nineties: The Spanish Frontier in North America: A Review Essay," *NMHR 68* (October, 1993).

————. "Campaigning on the Upper Gila, 1756," *NMHR 46* (April, 1971).

————. "Esteban Clemente: Precursor of the Pueblo Revolt," *El Palacio 86* (Winter 1980–1981).

————. "The Making of a Martyr: The Young Francisco Garcés," *NMHR* *45* (1970).

————. "A Personal Note from Tumacácori, 1825," *Journal of Arizona History 6* (1965).

————. "The Puzzling Presidio: San Phelipe de Guevavi, Alias Terrenate," *NMHR* (July, 1989).

————. "Spaniards and Pueblos: From Crusading Intolerance to Pragmatic Accommodation," *Columbian Consequences, Vol. 1 Archaeological and Historical Perspectives on the Spanish Borderlands West*, David Hurst Thomas, ed. Washington, DC: Smithsonian, 1989.

————. *Friars, Soldiers, and Reformers: Hispanic Arizona and the Sonora Mission Frontier, 1767–1856.* Tucson: University of Arizona Press, 1976.

————. *Kiva, Cross, and Crown: The Pecos Indians and New Mexico, 1540–1840.* Washington DC: National Parks Service, 1979.

————. *Miera y Pacheco: A Renaissance Spaniard in Eighteenth-Century New Mexico.* Norman: University of Oklahoma Press, 2013.

————. *Mission of Sorrows: Jesuit Guevavi and the Pimas, 1691–1767.* Tucson: University of Arizona Press, 1970.

————. *Pueblos, Spaniards, and the Kingdom of New Mexico.* Norman: University of Oklahoma Press, 2008.

————. *Spain in the Southwest: A Narrative History of Colonial New Mexico, Arizona, Texas, and California.* Norman: University of Oklahoma Press, 2002.

————. *Whither the Waters: Mapping the Great Basin from Bernardo de Miera to John C. Frémont.* Albuquerque: University of New Mexico Press, 2017.

————., et al. *Remote Beyond Compare: Letters of Don Diego de Vargas to His Family from New Spain and New Mexico, 1675–1706.* Albuquerque: University of New Mexico Press, 1989.

————., and Hendricks, Rick, eds. *By Force of Arms: The Journals of Don Diego de Vargas, New Mexico, 1691–1693.* Albuquerque: University of New Mexico Press, 1992.

————, Hendricks, Rick, and Dodge, Meredith D., eds. *Blood on the Boulders: The Journals of Don Diego de Vargas, New Mexico, 1694–1697.* Albuquerque: University of New Mexico Press, 1998.

————, Hendricks, Rick, and Dodge, Meredith D., eds. *To the Royal Crown Restored: The Journals of Don Diego de Vargas, New Mexico, 1692–1694.* Albuquerque: University of New Mexico Press, 1995.

————, Hendricks, Rick, Dodge, Meredith D., Miller, Larry D., eds. *A Settling of Accounts: The Journals of Don Diego de Vargas, New Mexico, 1700–1704.* Albuquerque: University of New Mexico Press, 2002.

————, Hendricks, Rick, Dodge, Meredith D., Miller, Larry D., eds. *That Disturbances Cease: The Journals of Don Diego de Vargas, New Mexico, 1697–1700.* Albuquerque: University of New Mexico Press, 2000.

Kinnaird, Lawrence, ed. *Frontiers of New Spain: Nicolás de Lafora's Description, 1766–1768.* Berkeley: University of California Press, 1958.

Kroeber, Albert. "The Seri Indians," *Southwest Museum Papers 6,* Los Angeles, 1931.

LaFora, Nicolás. *Relación del Viaje que Hizo a los Presidios Internos.* ed. Vito Alessio Robles. México: Editorial Pedro Robredo, 1939.

Lange, Charles. *Cochiti: A New Mexico Pueblo Past and Present.* Carbondale: Southern Illinois University Press, 1959.

Las Casas, Bartolomé de. *A Brief Account of the Destruction of the Indies.* London: Oxford University Press, 2013.

Lavender, David. *The Southwest.* New York: Harper and Row, 1980.

LeBlanc, Steven. *Prehistoric Warfare in the American Southwest.* Salt Lake City: University of Utah Press, 1999.

Lerner, Alan Jay, lyricist, and Loewe, Frederick, music. "I'm an Ordinary Man," *My Fair Lady.* Burbank: Warner Brothers Pictures, 1964.

Levin Rojo, Danna. "Representación del Espacio y Política Imperial. El Mapa de Nuevo México de Bernardo de Miera y Pacheco que Preserva el Museo Nacional del Virreinato," *Septenrión 2* (July-December 2007).

Loomis, Noel, and Nasatir, Abraham. *Pedro Vial and the Roads to Santa Fe.* Norman: University of Oklahoma Press, 1967.

López de Zárate Vargas, José. *Breve Descripción Genealógica de la Ilustre, Quanto Antiquíssima Casa de los Vargas de Madrid.* Madrid: Privately Printed, 1740.

Lucero, Conchita. "Santiago Our Protector," N*MHCPL Newsletter.* Albuquerque: NMHCPL.org, accessed March 11, 2019.

Lynch, John. *Spain Under the Habsburgs.* 2 vols. Oxford: Basil Blackwell, 1981.

MacGregor, Greg and Halus, Siegfried. *In Search of Domínguez and Escalante: Photographing the 1776 Spanish Expedition through the Southwest.* Santa Fe: Museum of New Mexico Press, 2011.

Matson, Daniel, and Schroeder, Albert, eds. "Cordero's Description of the Apache, 1796," *NMHR 32* (1957).

Mattison, Ray. "Early Spanish and Mexican Settlements in Arizona,*" NMHR 21* (1946).

————. "The Tangled Web: The Controversy over the Tumacacori and Baca Land Grants," *Journal of Arizona History 8* (1967).

McGee, W.J. "The Seri Indians," *Annual Report, Bureau of American Ethnology, no. 17,* Washington, DC, 1898.

Melish, John, cartographer. *Map of the United States with the Contiguous British and Spanish Possessions, 1816.* David Ramsey Historical Map Collection, Image 5168.001.

Mesonero Romanos, Ramón de. *El Antiguo Madrid.* 2 vols. Madrid: La Ilustración Española y Americana, 1881.

Miera y Pacheco, Bernardo de, cartographer. *Plano Geographico de la Tierra*

Descubierta Nuevamente, 1779. London: British Library Map Collection, Additional MS 17,661d.

Miribal, Felipe. "Defining the Colonial World: The Explorations of Bernardo de Miera y Pacheco", lecture, Aug. 14, 2011, New Mexico History Museum, Santa Fe.

Molina Campuzano, Miguel. *Planos de Madrid de los Siglos XVII y XVIII.* Madrid: Instituto de Estudios de Adminstración Local, Seminario de Urbanismo, 1960.

Moorhead, Max. *The Apache Frontier: Jacobo Ugarte and Spanish-Indian Relations in Northern New Spain, 1769–1791.* Norman: University of Oklahoma Press, 1968.

——. "Soldado de Cuera: Stalwart of the Spanish Borderlands," *Journal of the West 8* (1969).

Moulton, Gary, ed. *The Journals of the Lewis and Clark Expedition*, 13 vols. Lincoln: University of Nebraska Press, 1983–2001.

Myers, Lee. "Military Establishments in Southwestern New Mexico: Stepping Stones to Settlement," *NMHR 43* (1968).

Nasatir, Abraham, ed. *Before Lewis and Clark: Documents Illustrating the History of the Missouri, 1785–1804*, 2 vols. St. Louis: St. Louis Historical Documents Foundation, 1952.

Navarro García, Luis. *Don José de Gálvez y la Comandancia General de las Provincias Internas del Norte de Nueva España.* Sevilla: Consejo Superior de Investigaciones Científicas, 1964.

Obrador Sintes, Francisco. *Guía de los Archivos de Madrid.* Madrid: Dirección General Archivos y Bibliotecas, 1952.

Ogle, Ralph. *Federal Control of the Western Apaches, 1848–1886.* Albuquerque: University of New Mexico Press, 1970.

Opler, Morris. *An Apache Life-Way: The Economic, Social, and Religious Institutions of the Chiricahua Indians.* Chicago: University of Chicago Press, 1941.

Ortiz, Alfonso. "Popay's Leadership: A Pueblo Perspective," *El Palacio 86* (Winter, 1980–1981).

Padilla, Matías de la Mota. *Historia de la Conquista de la Provincia de la Nueva-Galicia.* México, 1870.

Pearce, T.M. *Place Names of New Mexico: A Geographical Dictionary.* Albuquerque: University of New Mexico Press, 1975.

Pérez Balsera, José. *Laudemus Viros Gloriosos et Parentes Nostros in Generatione Sua.* Madrid: Tipografía Católica, 1931.

Pichardo, José Antonio, cartographer. *El Nuevo México y Tierras Adyacentes, Mapa Levantado para la Demarcación de los Límites de los Dominios Españoles y los Estados Unidos.* México: Mapoteca Manuel Orozco.

——. *Pichardo's Treatise of the Limits of Louisiana and Texas*, 4 vols. Charles Wilson Hackett, ed. Austin: University of Texas Press, 1931–1946.

Pierce, Donna and Mirabal, Felipe. "Tales of an Anonymous Altar Screen," *Spanish Market Magazine 12, no. 1* (1999).

Plog, Stephen. *Ancient People of the American Southwest.* New York: Thames and Hudson, 1997.

Polzer, Charles, and Sheridan, Thomas, eds. *The Presidio and Militia on the Northern Frontier of New Spain: A Documentary History,* Vol.2, Part 2: *Californias and Sinaloa-Sonora, 1700–1765.* Tucson: University of Arizona Press, 1997.

Powell, Philip Wayne. *Soldiers, Indians, and Silver: The Northward Advance of New Spain, 1550–1600.* Berkeley: University of California Press, 1952.

————. *Tree of Hate: Propaganda and Prejudices Affecting United States Relations with the Hispanic World.* Albuquerque: University of New Mexico Press, 2008.

Pradeau, Alberto. *La Expulsión de los Jesuitas de las Provincias de Sonora, Ostimuri, y Sinaloa en 1767.* México: Antigua Librería Robredo de José Porrúa e Hijos, 1959.

Priestly, Herbert. *José de Gálvez, Visitor-General of New Spain (1765–1771).* Berkeley: University of California Press, 1916.

Real Academia Española. *Diccionario de Autoridades* (facsimile), 3 vols. Madrid: Editorial Gredos, 1979.

Resendes, Andres. *The Other Slavery: The Uncovered Story of Indian Enslavement in America.* New York: Houghtom Mifflin Harcourt, 2016.

Riley, Carroll. *The Kachina and the Cross: Indians and Spaniards in the Early Southwest.* Salt Lake City: University of Utah Press, 1999.

Rivera, Pedro de. *Diario y Derroteo de lo Caminado Visto y Observado en la Visita que Hiso a los Presidios de la Nueva España.* Vito Alessio Robles, ed. México: Secretaría de la Defensa Nacional, 1946.

Roberts, David. *The Pueblo Revolt: The Secret Rebellion that Drove the Spanish Out of the Southwest.* New York: Simon and Schuster, 2004.

Roca, Paul. *Paths of the Padres Through Sonora.* Tucson: University of Arizona Press, 1967.

Rowland, Donald. *The Elizondo Expedition Against the Indian Rebels of Sonora, 1765–1771.* Unpublished dissertation, Berkeley: University of California, 1930.

————. "The Sonora Frontier of New Spain, 1735–1745," *New Spain and the Anglo-American West,* vol. 1. Los Angles: Privately Printed, 1932.

Rowling, J.K. *Harry Potter and the Sorcerer's Stone.* New York: Scholastic Press, 1998.

Salaz-Márquez, Rubén. "Native Survival Part of Legacy," *New Mexican Hispanic Culture Preservation League Newsletter.* Albuquerque: NMHCPL .org, accessed March 11, 2019.

————. *The Pueblo Revolt Massacre.* Albuquerque: Cosmic House, 2008.

Sambrano, Diego López. "Declaration of Luis de Carbajal, December 22, 1681," Charles Wilson Hackett, ed, *Revolt of the Pueblo Indians of*

New Mexico and Otermín's Attempted Reconquest, 1680–1682, 2 vols. Albuquerque: University of New Mexico Press, 1942.

Santistevan, Carlos, interview with John Kessell, Denver Public Library, April 29, 2015.

Sauer, Carl and Brand, Donald. "Pueblo Sites in Southeastern Arizona," *University of California Publications in Geography*, vol. 3. Berkeley: University of California, 1930.

Scholes, France V. Annual Report of Carnegie Institution of Washington: Yearbook, vols. 30-48. Washington DC: Carnegie Institution of Washington, 1938–1939.

————. "Civil Government and Society in New Mexco during the Seventeenth Century," *NMHR 10* (April, 1935).

————. "Juan Martínez de Montoya, Settler and Conquistador of New Mexico," *NMHR 19* (October, 1944).

————. "Manuscripts for the History of New Mexico in the National Library in Mexico City," *NMHR* (July 1928).

————. "Royal Treasury Records Relating to the Province of New Mexico, 1596–1683," *NMHR 50* (January and April, 1975).

————, Simmons, Marc, and Esquibel, José, eds. *Juan Domínguez de Mendoza: Soldier and Frontiersman of the Spanish Southwest, 1627–1693.* Albuquerque: University of New Mexico Press, 2012.

Simmons, Marc. *The Last Conquistador: Juan de Oñate and the Settling of the Far Southwest.* Norman: University of Oklahoma Press, 1991.

————. *Spanish Government in New Mexico.* Albuquerque: University of New Mexico Press, 1968.

Smith, William. "The Seri Indians and the Sea Turtles," *The Journal of Arizona History 15* (1974).

Snow, David. "Whole Pots Full of Idolatrous Powdered Herbs," *The Kiva 82* (2016).

Spicer, Edward. *Cycles of Conquest: The Impact of Spain, Mexico, and the United States on the Indians of the Southwest.* Tucson; University of Arizona Press, 1962.

Texeria, Pedro. *Topographía de la Villa de Madrid en 1656.* Madrid: Ayuntamiento de Madrid, 1980.

Thomas, Alfred Barnaby, ed. *After Coronado: Spanish Exploration Northeast of New Mexico, 1696–1727.* Norman: University of Oklahoma Press, 1935.

Thomas, Alfred Barnaby, E. *Forgotten Frontiers–a Study of the Spanish Indian Policy of Don Juan Bautista de Anza.* Norman: University of Oklahoma Press, 1932.

————, ed. *Teodoro de Croix and the Northern Frontier of New Spain, 1776–1783.* Norman: University of Oklahoma Press, 1941.

Thrapp, Dan. *The Conquest of Apachería.* Norman: University of Oklahoma Press, 1967.

Torrez, Robert. *UFOs Over Galisteo and Other Stories of New Mexico's History.* Albuquerque: University of New Mexico Press, 2004.

Treutlein, Theodore. *Sonora: A Description of the Province by Ignaz Pfefferkorn.* Albuquerque: University of New Mexico Press, 1949.

Valdez, John, and Ibarra, Christine, producers. "The Last Conquistador," *Point of View.* PBS, 2008.

Vásquez de Prada, V. *Historia Económica y Social de España*, Vol. 3. Madrid: Confederación Española de Cajas de Ahorros, 1978.

Venegas, Miguel. *Noticia de la California y su Conquista Temporal y Espiritual.* Andrés Marcus Burriel, ed. 3 vols. Madrid: Viuda de Manuel Fernández, 1757.

Villagrá, Gaspar Pérez de. *Historia de la Nueva México, 1610.* Miguel Espinosa, et al., eds. Albuquerque: University of New Mexico Press, 1991.

Villa-Señor, José Antonio de. *Teatro Americano: Descripción General de los Reynos, y Provincias, de la Nueva España, y sus Jurisdicciones.* Vol. 2. México, 1746-48.

Weber, David J. *Barbaros: Spaniards and Their Savages in the Age of Enlightenment.* New Haven: Yale University Press, 2005.

———. "*Curriculum Vitae Academicae,*" http://faculty.smu.edu/ dweber/CV.htm.

———. *The Spanish Frontier in North America.* New Haven: Yale University Press, 1992.

———. "Turner, the Boltonians, and the Borderlands," *The American Historical Review 91* (February, 1986).

Wheat, Carl. *Mapping the Transmississippi West, 1540–1861*, 5 vols. San Francisco: Institute of Historic Geography, 1957–1963.

Will de Chaparro, Martina. *Death and Dying in New Mexico.* Albuquerque: University of New Mexico Press, 2007.

Wood, Raymund. "Francisco Garcés, Explorer of Southern California," *Southern California Quarterly 51* (1969).

Index

Milton Keynes UK
Ingram Content Group UK Ltd.
UKHW050955140624
443818UK00020B/56